BUSINESS HISTORY IN LATIN AMERICA

Liverpool Latin American Studies, New Series 1

Business History
in Latin America:
The Experience of Seven Countries

edited by Carlos Dávila and Rory Miller

translated by Garry Mills and Rory Miller

LIVERPOOL UNIVERSITY PRESS

First published 1999 by
LIVERPOOL UNIVERSITY PRESS
Senate House, Abercromby Square
Liverpool, L69 3BX

British Library Cataloguing-in-Publication Data
A British Library CIP record is available

ISBN 0-85323-723-9 *paper*

Typeset by Carnegie Publishing, Chatsworth Rd, Lancaster
Printed and bound in the European Union by
Bell and Bain Ltd, Glasgow

Contents

Preface

This volume of essays has its roots in an invitation from Carlos Dávila to various colleagues elsewhere to participate in a panel at the annual conference of CLADEA (Consejo Latinoamericano de Escuelas de Administración) in Bogotá in November 1992. The idea was simply to bring together specialists working on business history in different countries of the region in order to compare the state of the subject and trends in research. In fact a lively panel resulted, with much discussion both within the formal sessions and in numerous conversations once the formal proceedings were over. The extent of common ground amongst the contributors and the seriousness with which they had undertaken the task of reviewing and explaining the literature on individual countries was sufficient for us to decide that it would be worth publishing revised versions of the papers in order to provide others with a sense of how the subject was developing in Latin America. To this end two more chapters, on Argentina and Chile, were commissioned, and the original essays were published in Spanish in 1996 as *Empresa e historia en América Latina: un balance historiográfico* (Bogotá: Tercer Mundo/Colciencias).

The purpose of this English-language edition is to bring these essays to the attention of other readers. It is intended for a number of different groups: specialists in business history elsewhere who do not possess a detailed knowledge of Latin American business or a knowledge of Spanish but who may be interested in the way the subject has developed in a region which has attracted much attention since the debt crisis of the 1980s; students who are beginning work on the subject and are looking for guidance in the form both of a historiographical commentary and a detailed bibliography; and Latin American specialists in other branches of history and the social sciences who have little acquaintance with the history of business in the region. In comparison with the Spanish-language edition, this one has a totally new introduction, the chapters have been updated in order to encompass items published to the end of 1997, and the bibliography has been expanded.

This English-language edition would not have been possible without either the earlier editorial work undertaken in Bogotá or the support offered by the Institute of Latin American Studies (ILAS), University of Liverpool, and in particular its director, Professor John Fisher. ILAS subsidised the translation costs and Garry Mills, then a postgraduate student in the Institute, undertook the task of creating a first draft from the Spanish in which all the chapters other than the Brazil chapter were originally written. The editors are extremely grateful to both John Fisher and Garry Mills for their support and hard work in bringing this book to the point of completion. John Fisher, in particular, showed enormous patience when delays in finalising the chapters intervened and held up other projects. We would also like to thank all the other contributors who responded promptly, efficiently and with good humour to the suggestions that we made for changes and additions to their chapters. One of the dangers of editing a volume of essays is causing offence to the other contributors; we hope that we have built upon, rather than undermined, the spirit of participation in a joint enterprise which was so evident in the original meeting in Bogotá.

We hope too that this volume may provide some basis for further research and exploration in business history, especially as it is published at a crucial conjuncture in Latin American business as the public sector loses the economic dominance it has enjoyed in almost every country since the 1940s. The contributions and failures of the state, foreign investment, and the domestic private sector in the development of business and the economy in Latin America have been the subject of much controversy for a generation of historians and social scientists since the 1960s. It is our hope that by aiding understanding both of these debates and the empirical research they have generated we may contribute towards the further development of the subject.

Carlos Dávila   Rory Miller
Bogotá, Colombia   *Chester, Great Britain*

Notes on Contributors

Ruth Capriles is professor in the Faculty of Economics and Social Sciences and researcher in the Faculty of Law in the Universidad Católica Andrés Bello in Caracas in Venezuela. She has a doctorate in Political Sciences from the Universidad Central de Venezuela, and possesses a particular interest in the intricate relationship between economic influence and political power, on which many of her publications have focused. In particular she is the author of *Los negocios de Román Delgado Chalbaud* (Caracas, 1991); a three-volume work, *Diccionario de la corrupción en Venezuela* (Caracas, 1989–1992); *La Cultura del Trabajo en Venezuela* (Caracas, 1996); and a work on ethics, *Elementos de un individualismo no posesivo* (Caracas, 1995).

Mario Cerutti obtained his PhD from the University of Utrecht in the Netherlands and is now Professor of American History in the Facultad de Filosofía y Letras in the Univeridad Autónoma de Nuevo León in Monterrey in Mexico. He was the founding editor of *Siglo XIX: Revista de Historia* and edited the journal until 1990. He is also director of the series *Historia económica del norte de México (siglos XIX y XX)*. His most recent books are *Historia de las grandes empresas en México* (with Carlos Marichal, Mexico City, 1997), *Empresarios españoles y sociedad capitalista en México, 1840–1920* (Colombres, 1995), *Frontera e historia económica* (with Miguel Gonzalez, Monterrey, 1994), *Burguesía, capitales e industria en el norte de México* (Mexico City, 1992), and *Burguesía e industria en América Latina e Europa meridional* (edited with Menno Vellinga, Madrid, 1989).

Carlos Dávila obtained his PhD from Northwestern University with a thesis on contemporary economic and political elites in urban Colombia. He has taught for over twenty years at the Universidad de los Andes in Bogotá, where he is now Professor, and has also been Latin American Visiting Fellow at St Antony's College, Oxford and Visiting Research Scholar in the Business History Unit at the London School of Economics. He is the author of *El empresariado colombiano: una perspectiva histórica* (Bogotá, 1986), and *Historia empresarial de Colombia: estudios, problemas, y perspectivas* (Bogotá, 1991). Currently he is working on the indexed housing credit system in Colombia and the history of one of the banks in this sector.

Raúl García Heras earned his PhD from the University of La Plata in Argentina. He teaches economic history at the University of Buenos Aires and is researcher at CONICET, the National Scientific Research Institute in Argentina. He is the author of *Automotores norteamericanos: caminos y modernización urbana en la Argentina, 1918–1939* (Buenos Aires, 1985), and *Transportes, negocios y política: la Compañia Anglo Argentina de Tranvías, 1876–1981* (Buenos Aires, 1994). Currently he is working on the role of the International Monetary Fund, the World Bank, the 'Paris Club', and other international financial institutions in economic policy-making in Argentina between 1955 and 1966.

Marisol Rodríguez de Gonzalo is the deputy director of the Instituto de Altos Estudios Diplomáticos of the Venezuelan Ministry of Foreign Relations, and also Professor of Political Sciences in the Universidad Central de Venezuela. She has a degree in History, and a particular interest in the relations between Venezuela and the United States within a broader American context. She is the author of various articles on both international relations and business history which have been published in various books and journals in Venezuela. In particular she wrote on the development of industry in Venezuela for the *Diccionario de historia de Venezuela* published by the Fundación Polar.

Colin M. Lewis is Senior Lecturer in Latin American Economic History at the London School of Economics and Political Science and an Associate Fellow at the Institute of Latin American Studies at the University of London. He has taught at the Federal University of Pernambuco in Brazil, and at the University of Augsburg in Germany. He has written about foreign investment in railways in Argentina and Brazil and about early industrial growth in Latin America. His recent publications include *The Argentine: from economic growth to economic retardation* (Augsburg, 1996), *The New Institutional Economics and Third World Development* (ed. with John Harriss and Janet Hunter, London, 1995), and *Welfare, Poverty, and Development in Latin America* (ed. with Christopher Abel, London, 1993). He is now undertaking a study of social policy in Argentina and Brazil.

Rory Miller gained his PhD from Cambridge with a thesis on the development of British business in Peru between 1883 and 1930. Since 1973 he has taught the economic history of Latin America at the University of Liverpool, and is now a Senior Lecturer jointly in the School of History and the Institute of Latin American Studies. He has published widely on the modern economic and social history of Peru, particularly on the development of the railways and oil industry, and also has interests in the history of British business in Bolivia. In 1993 he published *Britain and Latin America in the Nineteenth and Twentieth Centuries* (London). Since then he has been working, with support from the Nuffield Foundation, on the evolution of British manufacturing companies in Latin America and on the broader issues of British business decline in the region.

Luis Ortega obtained his PhD from London in 1979 with a thesis on the first stages of economic modernisation in Chile between 1850 and 1879. From 1979 to 1985 he taught in London; in the latter year he returned to Chile and joined the Department of History at the Universidad de Santiago de Chile where he is now Profesor Titular. He has published extensively on the modern economic history of Chile, especially on industrialisation, economic policy, and mining. In 1989 he published *Cincuenta años de realizaciones: Corfo, 1939–1989* (Santiago), and in 1991, as co-author with Julio Pinto, *Expansión minera y desarrollo industrial: un caso de crecimiento asociado, Chile, 1850–1914* (Santiago). Currently he is working, in collaboration with financial support both from the Universidad de Santiago de Chile and the National Fund for Scientific and Technological Research, on company formation in Chile between 1850 and 1914.

Glossary

CEPAL   see ECLA

dependency theories   interpretations of Latin America's underdevelopment which concentrated on the consequences of its economic relationship with the developed world; these ideas were developed by writers such as Fernando Henrique Cardoso, Theotonio dos Santos, Osvaldo Sunkel, and André Gunder Frank during the 1960s

desarrollista   developmentalist

desarrollo hacia adentro   inward-directed development; the policies current in Latin America after the depression of the 1930s

desarrollo hacia afuera   outward-directed development; used to refer to the period before the Great Depression when Latin American economies were stimulated by the growth of foreign trade and investment

developmentalism   theories current in the 1950s and 1960s that emphasised policies designed to overcome the perceived structural obstacles to development

ECLA   the United Nations' Economic Commission for Latin America, founded in 1948; has now become the Economic Commission for Latin America and the Caribbean (ECLAC); the Spanish and Portuguese acronyms have not changed and remain CEPAL

estanciero   Argentine term used to denote the owner of a large livestock ranch *(estancia)*

fazendeiro   Brazilian term used to denote the owner of a large estate *(fazenda)*

hacendado   Spanish-language term used in Latin America to denote the owner of a large estate *(hacienda)*

import-substitution industrialisation (ISI)	the period after the Second World War when Latin American economic policies were designed to stimulate the growth of industries producing for the internal market and thus substituting for imported goods
Izquierda Nacional	the National Left
mestizo	person of mixed race (European and American Indian)
paulista	resident of São Paulo
planalto	the São Paulo plateau
Porfiriato	the period when President Porfirio Díaz ruled Mexico (1876–80, 1884–1911)
rentista	a rentier, someone who lives off rental income or interest; often used in the nineteenth century as a term of abuse for capitalists in general
Sociedad Anónima	Spanish-language term for a limited company
stagflation	the combination of economic stagnation and inflation
structuralism	economic ideas dominant in Latin America in the 1950s and 1960s, particularly associated with the economists based at ECLA; structuralist thinking stressed policies designed to remove the structural impediments to development and the encouragement of industry
turcos	Spanish-language term used to refer to immigrants of Syrian-Lebanese origin

CHAPTER ONE

Business History in Latin America: an introduction

Rory Miller

Enormous changes have taken place in the business environment in Latin America during the last quarter of the twentieth century, making the production of a volume of historiographical essays on the state of business history in seven major countries of the region a particularly timely event.[1] The process of transformation began in the mid-1970s following the installation of the Pinochet regime in Chile and the introduction of economic policies there which were designed to reduce the role of the state and ameliorate the conditions both for Chilean private business and for foreign direct investment. Elsewhere in Latin America at the same time the pronounced economic role of the state began to come into question, in Argentina, for example, under both the Peronists and the military regime that succeeded them.

Since then a major shift in assumptions has occurred throughout Latin America, stimulated by a number of different factors: the macroeconomic success of Chile in controlling inflation and maintaining strong rates of growth after the 1982/83 crisis when other Latin American economies floundered; the failure of alternative state-led attempts to resolve Latin America's economic problems following the debt crisis of the early 1980s; and the ideological bias against the public sector which became apparent in Great Britain under the Thatcher administration and helped to reinforce the predilections of the United States government and international institutions such as the International Monetary Fund and the World Bank. The result has been what seems at times like a total reversal of the assumptions prevalent when 'dependency' theories were at their peak in Latin America during the early 1970s. Policies which stress the removal of barriers to private business and foreign investment are in the ascendant throughout Latin America, while the state is assumed by many to have been a poor manager both of the economy overall and of the thousands of public-sector enterprises which formerly existed but which are now severely diminished in number and significance.

[1] My thanks are due to Carlos Dávila and Colin Lewis for their comments on an earlier draft of this introduction. They are not, of course, responsible for the shortcomings of the final product.

The study of business history in Latin America has developed alongside these changes in attitudes, but also in an environment where for thirty years economic and social history have been seen as central to the understanding of present-day problems. Within the subject there has been a growing emphasis on the period from the mid-nineteenth century onwards and, after a time when research on foreign companies predominated, on the growth of domestic business. Very early in the evolution of the subject, in 1965, the leading North American journal in the field, *Business History Review*, published a special issue devoted to Latin America. What is noticeable about that issue is the prevalence of articles devoted to the colonial period, the major item of interest on post-independence developments being a seminal article by Frank Safford on foreign and national enterprise in nineteenth-century Colombia.[2] Twenty years later a second special issue of the same journal on Latin American business history showed how far and in what directions the subject had developed. All the articles now concentrated on the nineteenth and twentieth centuries (though one overlapped into the colonial era), and much greater attention was paid to the range of archival material now available to the business historian. It is noticeable, however, that over half the issue was concerned with the history of foreign business in Latin America. Moreover, the introduction by the Canadian historian, H. V. Nelles, concentrated almost wholly on work in the English language.[3] In part this reflected the way the research had developed in the 1970s under the influence of debates over imperialism and dependency, but it also indicated a gulf that was beginning to appear between business historians in the North Atlantic world and those working in Latin America itself.

Fortunately for the subject the gap then began to narrow, and this volume is evidence of the rapprochement. Although there are obvious variations from one country to another, dependent in part upon the local business and intellectual environment of each, the authors here concentrate very largely on business history which utilises sources available in Latin America, considers the evolution of locally owned firms and local entrepreneurs alongside their foreign counterparts, and pays attention to enterprises focused on the internal market as well as those in the export sectors, which formerly dominated the economic historiography of Latin America. As these essays illustrate, since the mid-1980s a much greater consciousness of business history as a specific research area of great interest and relevance has developed in Latin America, initially in Mexico, slightly later in Brazil, Colombia, and Argentina, and most recently in the other three countries considered here. This growth in the subject has been underpinned by panels

[2] Frank Safford, 'Foreign and National Enterprise in Nineteenth-Century Colombia', *Business History Review* 39 (1965), 503–26.

[3] H. V. Nelles, 'Latin American Business History since 1965: a view from north of the border', *Business History Review* 59 (1985), 543–62.

at international conferences and by other attempts, besides those here, to evaluate the state of research in individual countries.[4]

The development of business history in Latin America

The economic and social history of Latin America since the middle of the nineteenth century provides the essential background to the evolution of business in the region, and the outlines are well-known.[5] While debate about the state of the Latin American economies after independence and the potential for autonomous growth has been intense, it is clear that the expansion of exports and foreign investment from the middle of the nineteenth century provoked a wide-ranging transformation of the economic orientation, business institutions, and social structures of the region.[6] The growth of demand in Europe and North America for Latin America's exports of foodstuffs and industrial raw materials offered enormous opportunities to those entrepreneurs who controlled vital resources of land and labour. At the same time it highlighted a number of problems: the deficiencies of capital and credit markets in the region; delays in acquiring the information and developing the skills which might have allowed Latin Americans to exert greater influence in markets overseas; difficulties in obtaining and assimilating modern technology; and the incapacity of government at different levels to maximise the advantages that might be gained from access to foreign markets and capital.[7] In socio-political terms the

[4] See, for example, María Inés Barbero, 'Treinta años de estudios sobre la historia de empresas en la Argentina', *Ciclos* 5 (1995), 179–200.

[5] See, for example, Victor Bulmer-Thomas, *The Economic History of Latin America since Independence* (Cambridge, 1994); probably the best economic history of Latin America in Spanish is Ciro F. S. Cardoso and Héctor Pérez Brignoli, *Historia económica de América Latina* (2 vols, Barcelona, 1979). For economic histories of individual countries, see the bibliography at the end of this volume.

[6] The classic exchange over the early nineteenth century was between D. C. M. Platt and Stanley and Barbara Stein: see D. C. M. Platt, 'Dependency in Nineteenth-Century Latin America: an historian objects', *Latin American Research Review* 15: 1 (1980), 113–30; Stanley J. and Barbara H. Stein, 'D. C. M. Platt: the anatomy of autonomy', *Latin American Research Review* 15:1 (1980), 131–46.

[7] In an important and neglected comment on the Platt-Stein debate James Street drew attention to some of these issues, contrasting Argentina and Japan's attitudes towards foreign business and techniques in the late nineteenth century: see James H. Street, 'The Platt-Stein Controversy over Dependency: another view', *Latin American Research Review* 16: 3 (1981), 173–80. One important contrast which has been the subject of much comparative research has been the differing paths of development followed by Argentina and the white dominions of the British empire: see, for example, John Fogarty, Ezequiel Gallo, and Hector Diéguez (eds), *Argentina y Australia* (Buenos Aires, 1979); David Denoon, *Settler Capitalism: the dynamics of dependent development in the southern hemisphere* (Oxford, 1983); D. C. M. Platt and Guido di Tella (eds), *Argentina, Australia, and Canada: studies in comparative development, 1870–1965* (London, 1985); and Jeremy Adelman, *Frontier Development: land, labour, and capital on the wheatlands of Argentina and Canada* (Oxford, 1994).

period around the turn of the century is seen by historians as one of oligarchic domination. In many countries, especially the minor ones, a small group of families with business interests in the export sector, or spheres closely associated with it like banking, gained control of the national state. Elsewhere, as in Colombia or Brazil, national governments were controlled by a shifting alliance of regional oligarchies in which those controlling the areas with greatest access to foreign markets or capital tended to be dominant. Control of the state provided business elites with the means to benefit their personal interests. Their access to tax revenues and foreign loans and their influence over the courts and the forces of order gave them the power to have vital infrastructure built at public expense and to exert greater control over land and labour. Yet the changes induced by the export boom also promoted the rise of elements which would eventually challenge the domination of these elites, in particular the growth of militant labour movements in the cities, export sectors, and transport industries of Latin America, and the development of a strengthening nationalist current which dissident intellectuals transmitted to the middle and working classes in the rapidly expanding urban centres.

Historians see the depression of the 1930s as a central watershed in both the political and economic history of Latin America, although the precursors of the changes which occurred in the decade before the Second World War can be detected much earlier. In almost every major country of Latin America recovery from the crisis depended upon the growth of the internal market and the expansion of manufacturing industry. For a long time little attention was given to the promotion of new export sectors, and foreign direct investment now became dominated by an influx of multinational firms seeking to side-step tariff barriers and other import restrictions in order to maintain their access to growing domestic markets. The state began to play a hugely expanded role, not only with the foundation of central banks and the introduction of a much greater range of policy instruments to manage the economy, but also as an entrepreneur in its own right. Mexico, perhaps, had taken the most significant step in this direction with the expropriation of the foreign-owned oil companies in 1938, although by then there were already public-sector oil companies in several other Latin American countries, most notably Argentina. From the 1940s the expropriation of foreign-owned railways and public utilities as well as the development of basic industries like steel in many countries brought a further enhancement to the business activities of the state; mining, oil, and telecommunications firms were absorbed into the public sector later. This process reached a peak in the early 1970s with wide-ranging programmes of nationalisation in Peru and Chile and a negotiated transfer of foreign-owned oil concessions in Venezuela. Although nationalists of the left and the right had led the public attacks on the foreign companies, there was widespread acceptance, whatever the regime, of the general principles of an interventionist state and a large public sector, particularly in basic industries deemed essential to the process of development. By this point, with radical governments in power in Peru and Chile and physical attacks on leading businessmen in countries like Argentina and Uruguay, the prospects for private business, whether national or foreign, appeared distinctly gloomy.

These developments in the political and economic spheres had a major effect on the growth of economic and business history as disciplines distinct from mainstream history. As several authors in this volume indicate, two waves of theoretical work in particular had an enormous influence on historians. The first was the development of structuralist ideas associated with the United Nations Economic Commission for Latin America (ECLA in English, CEPAL in Spanish) from the 1950s.[8] The second was the growth of more radical dependency theories as structuralism and the model of state-led import-substitution industrialisation ran out of steam in the 1960s.[9] By now, it seemed, both foreign investment and the deficiencies of the private sector had led Latin American countries into a worse position than ever. Many scholars came to the view that, even when provided with substantial aid by the state, local business elites had proved incapable of developing an autonomous growth process. It was easy therefore to argue either that they lacked basic entrepreneurial and managerial qualities or else that they had simply betrayed national interests and sold out to foreign investors. As for the latter, they were often considered simply to have exploited and drained Latin America of resources through their control of technology, capital, and markets, and their greater bargaining power vis-à-vis weak Latin American governments (which for much of the first half of the century, of course, had been controlled by the elites whose inadequacy, disloyalty and incompetence seemed all too evident). This dismissal of the private sector reached its apogee perhaps in the work of André Gunder Frank and his disciples.[10]

---

[8] There is an enormous amount of literature on this. Useful introductions can be found in Cristóbal Kay, *Latin American Theories of Development and Underdevelopment* (London, 1989), chapter 2; Joseph L. Love, 'Raúl Prebisch and the Origins of the Doctrine of Unequal Exchange', *Latin American Research Review* 15:3 (1980), 45–72; E. V. K. Fitzgerald. 'ECLA and the Formation of Latin American Economic Doctrine', in David Rock (ed.), *Latin America in the 1940s: war and postwar transitions* (Berkeley, 1994), pp. 89–108.

[9] See Kay, *Latin American Theories*, chapters 5 and 6; Joseph L. Love, 'The Origins of Dependency Theory', *Journal of Latin American Studies* 22 (1990), 143–68.

[10] André Gunder Frank, *Capitalism and Underdevelopment in Latin America* (Harmondsworth, 1971). Frank's ideas had particular resonance amongst Latin American scholars in the United States and Western Europe, and this was helped by the fact that his work appeared in English long before the other classic 'dependency' text, Fernando Henrique Cardoso & Enzo Faletto, *Dependency and Development in Latin America* (Berkeley, 1979); this was first published in Spanish in 1969. For critiques of the way in which dependency theory was adopted by historians and social scientists see articles by two leading Latin American intellectuals, Fernando Henrique Cardoso, 'The Consumption of Dependency Theory in the United States', *Latin American Research Review* 12: 3 (1977), 7–24; and Tulio Halperín

In some respects this might not have seemed a particularly optimistic scenario for business historians, since there was little reason why anybody should be interested in the evolution of the private sector if it could not contribute to the process of development, yet the amount of research in business history was now expanding rapidly.[11] The explanations for this lie in the rapid growth of higher education evident in the numbers of students, universities, and research institutes, the dominant controversies within Latin American history, and the increasing quantity of source material concerning Latin American business which was becoming available both in the developed world and in Latin America itself. As the contents of the 1985 special issue of *Business History Review* suggest, much of the initial impetus came from the growing quantity of research on foreign firms in Latin America. This in turn was related to the debates over the nature of foreign, especially British, imperialism in Latin America, which intensified in the 1970s as historians found more and more empirical evidence which conflicted with the assumptions of those who advocated theories of informal imperialism and dependency. One of the key figures in stimulating this research, as many have noted, was D. C. M. Platt, Professor of Latin American History at Oxford from 1972. Platt was significant in three ways: first, because in the mid-1960s he identified many business archives in Latin America and in Britain which subsequently proved a fruitful source of primary material; second, because he threw the emphasis on to the analysis of foreign business – host government relations as a key arena for the study of imperialistic behaviour; and third, because of his encouragement of a number of British research students and visiting foreign scholars who began to publish widely from the 1970s.[12] However, it was not just Platt who was responsible for the growth in research on foreign business. In the United States a long tradition of research on British and US firms in Latin America already existed, associated particularly with historians like J. Fred Rippy of the University of Chicago. Some of the key North American scholars whose contribution is recognised in the chapters in this volume, such as Frank Safford and Richard Graham, had commenced their research and published articles of significance before Platt's key contributions began to appear.[13]

Donghi, '"Dependency Theory" and Latin American Historiography', *Latin American Research Review* 17: 1 (1982), 115–30.

[11] This dismissal of the domestic private sector was probably most marked in Chile and Venezuela where, due to the nature and history of the export sectors, the state became the principal actor in the economy: see chapters 4 and 8 of this book.

[12] D. C. M. Platt, 'Business Archives', in Peter Walne (ed.), *A Guide to Manuscript Sources for the History of Latin America and the Caribbean in the British Isles* (London, 1973), pp. 442–513; D. C. M. Platt (ed.), *Business Imperialism, 1840–1930: an inquiry based on British experience in Latin America* (Oxford, 1977); for a brief review of Platt's overall contribution, see Rory Miller, 'Christopher Platt (1934–1989): an appreciation', *Bulletin of Latin American Research* 9 (1990), 117–21.

[13] Safford, 'Foreign and National Enterprise'; Richard Graham, 'A British Industry in Brazil: Rio Flour Mills, 1886–1920', *Business History* 8 (1966), 13–38.

Another important factor behind the expansion of foreign research on business in Latin America was the growth of travel grants and postgraduate studentships for area studies in both Britain and the United States during the 1960s. In Simon Collier's words, 'the great American PhD industry', funded in the case of area studies by federal government grants, was the reason for much of the research undertaken on the economic and business history of Latin America by foreigners.[14] In Britain the introduction of 'Parry' research studentships following a government report into Latin American studies in the mid-1960s had a parallel, if smaller, impact.

What this volume shows, however, in contrast to the earlier collections of papers on Latin America in *Business History Review*, is that, while it was undoubtedly important, the contribution of foreigners to the development of business history in Latin America should not be overestimated. One reason for this is the relative narrowness of focus which many of the foreign scholars working on Latin America displayed. They were concerned primarily either with the dominant controversies over imperialism and dependency or with writing company history of a rather traditional kind, rather than with transferring to the study of Latin America some of the major changes which were taking place in business history in the developed world under the influence of historians like Alfred Chandler or Mira Wilkins.[15] As a result, it is still not easy for historians to envisage and explain just how the development of business in Latin America was different, in spheres like entrepreneurship, structure and organisation, or innovation, from the parallel processes which were occurring in the United States, Europe, or Japan. Foreign research on business history in Latin America has thus developed largely in isolation from the main currents of the discipline. It is rare, for example, for foreign historians of Latin America to employ terminology like 'managerial capitalism', to consider the internal structures and management of firms, or to address some of the major developments in business history such as the concept of the 'free-standing firm' or the use of transaction costs theory to explain strategic decision-making and institutional change.[16]

[14] Simon Collier, 'The Historiography of the "Portalian" Period in Chile', *Hispanic American Historical Review* 57 (1977), 680.

[15] The influence of Alfred Chandler on Latin American historians is mentioned in two essays in this volume, those on Colombia and Brazil, but only as a very recent influence. The key works in this context are probably Alfred Chandler, *Strategy and Structure: chapters in the history of the industrial enterprise* (Cambridge, 1962), and *The Visible Hand: the managerial revolution in American business* (Cambridge, 1977). One important contribution by Mira Wilkins with clear implications for Latin America is 'Comparative Hosts', *Business History* 36: 1 (1994), 18–50. Wilkins' important earlier books, *The Emergence of Multinational Enteprise: American business abroad from the colonial era to 1914* (Harvard, 1970), and *The Maturing of Multinational Enterprise: American business abroad from 1914 to 1970* (Harvard, 1974), are rarely mentioned by historians of Latin America.

[16] See, however, Charles Jones, 'Institutional Forms of British Foreign Direct Investment in South America', *Business History* 39: 2 (1997), 21–41, which relates the evolution of British companies to the concepts of investment groups and free-standing companies.

Central theories about entrepreneurship dating from the early twentieth century such as those of Joseph Schumpeter, Max Weber, or Werner Sombart have also largely been absent from the bibliographies of the foreign scholars.

The other reason not to overestimate the foreign contribution to research is the amount of work that was being undertaken within Latin America, even in the 1960s and early 1970s. In many ways this resembled the early stages of business history in the developed world. There were several company histories, some of which, commissioned by the firms involved and undertaken by both amateur and professional historians, illustrate all the pitfalls of this approach.[17] As in the early stages in Britain and the United States, too, eulogistic accounts of 'pioneering entrepreneurs' were not unknown in Latin America in the 1960s. However, in many countries there was a rather different dimension to the growth of business history compared with Britain or the United States, namely the substantial contribution that was made by sociologists and economists concerned with development problems. For Latin American scholars in both these disciplines the formation, behaviour, and ethos of national elites in the nineteenth and twentieth centuries were a central issue, in line with the preoccupations of both the ECLA and the dependency schools. While very few of these writers carried out archival research, their theoretical contributions did provide a framework within which more empirically minded business historians could operate. Research by Latin American scholars was also stimulated in the 1970s as national and regional archives in many countries became much better organised, employment opportunities in universities and research institutes expanded, and grants became available for research overseas, permitting historians to use the wide range of material available on business in Latin America in the libraries and archives of Europe and the United States. An extremely tragic but ultimately stimulating twist to these developments came with the exile of many Latin American scholars, especially from the Southern Cone countries, as a consequence of the military coups of the 1970s. This was most marked in the case of Chile, where a comparison of the contents of *Historia*, the leading professional journal in the country itself, and *Nueva Historia*, a new journal published by a group of exiles in London in the early 1980s, shows how under the dictatorship those historians who remained in Chile turned their attention to uncontroversial themes in colonial history while those in exile concerned themselves with key issues in the country's development, producing several significant contributions to economic and business history.

[17] For differing British views on the value of company history or the case-study approach to business history see Leslie Hannah, 'New Issues in British Business History', *Business History Review* 57 (1983), 165–74; Donald Coleman, 'The Uses and Abuses of Business History', *Business History* 29: 2 (1987), 141–56; Terry Gourvish., 'Business History: in defence of the empirical approach?', *Accounting Business and Financial History* 5 (1995), 3–16.

Problems, achievements and prospects

Taken together, the essays in this volume illustrate some of the problems which research in Latin American business history has revealed, but they also show how several important themes are emerging in the literature, and suggest some gaps to which greater attention might be paid in the future. One obvious point, which the number of publications cited in different sections of the bibliography at the end of this book makes clear, is that research has advanced much faster in some countries than others, for institutional, economic and academic reasons. Institutionally, higher education developed in rather different directions in the 1970s in individual Latin American countries, depending on the degree of political freedom that existed and the availability of funds. Not surprisingly perhaps, universities and research institutes in Mexico and Brazil, the two largest economies in the region, had greater financial support from the state and from the private sector, offering therefore, an environment within which a subject which was often considered marginal to history and mainstream social science disciplines could advance more strongly. Of the countries studied here the volume of locally researched studies on Mexican business and the growing sophistication of the literature on Brazil are impressive, in contrast to the occasionally more downhearted tone apparent in some of the other chapters.

The economic environment in Latin America also influenced the development of business history as a result of the role played by the state in different countries. As the essays on Chile and Venezuela show, during the twentieth century the state became the most important business actor in both these economies, first because of its use and allocation of the tax revenues generated by nitrate and copper mining in Chile and oil in Venezuela, and then due to the nationalisation of these key resources. Disdain for the contribution that the private sector might make to the development process in Chile and Venezuela was evident in the lack of attention which historians and social scientists paid to business history and the assumptions of failure on the part of national business elites that prevailed in both. Yet very few historians or economists in these countries turned to studying the evolution, management, and performance of public-sector enterprise as opposed to the macroeconomic aspects of the state's role, and the empirical study of the activities of the foreign multinationals which dominated the export sectors before nationalisation remained largely in the hands of scholars overseas who had greater access to the archives.

A further problem evident in these chapters concerns the definition of the field and the identification of the prime themes within it. The common Spanish-language term *historia empresarial*, which is normally used to define it, in fact encompasses three different, if overlapping, spheres: business history in a comparative sense; company history in terms of the empirical case-study; and entrepreneurial history, in the sense of the study of individual pioneers. The authors in this volume take rather different perspectives on this. Their differing interpretations of the term, and hence their expectations, fundamentally affect their evaluation of the state of business history in the countries they are studying. Some are searching for a broad comparative business history which goes beyond the accumulation of case studies of individual companies in order to address both the themes which have been uppermost in the expansion of the subject in the developed world and to isolate the distinctive features of the evolution of business in Latin America. For others, the accumulation of empirical case studies on individual companies and entrepreneurs and written with a certain degree of professionalism is an achievement in itself. As noted already, this divergence of approaches and expectations is a critical and hotly debated issue amongst business historians elsewhere in the world. The problem in Latin America is that it has enormous implications for the future development of the subject insofar as the technically well-informed case study or comparative work may be much more likely to attract the interest of far-sighted managers, academics in business schools, and the remainder of the historical profession than the narrowly focused narrative, descriptive, and uncontroversial case study which many companies prefer for reasons of public relations. What business historians prefer to do, and what they may be financed to do, in Latin America as in Britain, may be two very different things.

The conceptualisation and definition of the subject is part of a broader problem, namely how the business historian working in Latin America adjusts to the neoliberal world, and the extent to which s/he should shake off the ECLA / dependency heritage that has contributed much to the development of the field but which has also distorted it. Striking the right balance between commitment, theory, and empirical data, and making appropriate use of foreign ideas, has been a difficult problem for thirty years. It is not one confined to business history. Historians of Latin America, whether foreigners or natives of the region, have always had to tread a fine line over the adoption of conceptual advances derived from research in the United States and Europe. While they have undoubtedly enriched the subject, they can also imply the imposition of an agenda which is not always attuned to Latin American realities.[18] As Luis Ortega notes towards the end of his chapter on Chile, historians have perhaps been incorrect to expect industry, business, and entrepreneurship to develop in nineteenth-century Chile in the same way as they did in contemporary Europe.[19] Greater advances in understanding the distinctive

---

[18] One can see this in many other areas of Latin American history: examples of relevance to the business historian are the way in which the US concept of 'the melting pot' has often been applied to studies of European immigration, or the way in which US labour historians of the Left searched for a heroic, militant and organised working class in early twentieth-century Latin America, ignoring other significant aspects of labour history.

[19] See especially Ortega's comments on work by Arnold Bauer and Mario Góngora on pp. 69 and 72.

features of business culture in Latin America might come from historians who can shake themselves free of some of their preconceptions about the 'normal' path of development or about 'normal' entrepreneurial and managerial behaviour.

Dwelling on definitional and epistemological problems, however, is almost certainly not the best way to recognise either the achievements of scholars in the past or the possible direction of business history in Latin America in the future. One major advance that does need to be recognised is the discovery and use of a much wider range of source material than might have been expected when research in this area commenced. In the special Latin American issue of *Business History Review* in 1985, Vera Blinn Reber offered a short but useful analysis of the sources available to business historians, commencing with the type of material to be found in national archives and then going on to discuss provincial and municipal archives, bank archives, notarial registers, private business papers, and repositories for printed sources.[20] Looking at the work discussed in the chapters here, there seem to be five principal sources of information which business historians have used.

First, a source which always amazes the foreign newcomer in Latin America is the size and variety of the notarial registers which exist in national and provincial archives. Signing a document before a notary public, a contract for a loan or for the renting, sale, or mortgage of land or property, or else the making of a will, was fundamental to the legal system in all Latin American countries. As a consequence the notarial archives, most of which are in the public domain, contain a vast amount of business information, for example on the formation of partnerships and companies and their financing. The problems in using them lie in their scale and the sheer variety of material they contain. Perhaps for this reason their greatest value in business history has so far probably been most evident at the regional level, where the quantity of registers is much smaller and thus easier to handle than in the national capital.[21] However, the use of personal computers and free-text database software ought now to make the days or months spent reading them more productive, making it possible, for example, to track an individual's business transactions more easily over time. Second, the taxation, company registration, and probate records available in national and regional archives have also been a fruitful source of data on the size, income, and operations of firms and individuals. These sources, of course, also lend themselves to computerised analysis using relational database and spreadsheet software. Third, a whole range of business archives have been discovered, belonging to both defunct and

[20] Vera Blinn Reber, 'Archival Sources for Latin American Business History', *Business History Review* 59 (1985), 670–79.

[21] There are, for example, almost 800 large bound volumes of notarial archives covering Lima, a city of little more than 100,000 people, between 1840 and 1900. Transactions of interest to business historians are scattered throughout them.

living companies, not just overseas, where one might expect them to be better preserved, but also in Latin America itself. It is often stated, and such an assertion appears several times in this book, that businessmen in Latin America have no tradition or desire to retain documents from the distant past. That may be true, but it does not mean that nothing has survived. Several of the most important studies reviewed here have utilised long-forgotten archives which were only discovered once the historian began to ask around within a company or governmental office. Often the problems lie in the need for persistence and the disorganisation of the material, rather than its destruction or inaccessibility. Fourth, since the early nineteenth century there has been a flourishing daily and weekly press in Latin America, and in the capital cities specialised business publications, sometimes in English or German, sometimes in Spanish or Portuguese, began to make an appearance in the late nineteenth and early twentieth centuries. In addition to the independent press the commercial and professional organisations that began to appear at the same time also produced their own journals, with the result that the printed material published by Chambers of Commerce, societies representing landowners or industrialists, and associations of engineers and other professionals has become a fundamental source for many business historians. Fifth, a vital source for the more modern period, not mentioned by Reber (whose interests lay primarily in the nineteenth century) but referred to on some occasions in this book, is oral history. At least in some instances, businessmen have been willing to talk to researchers, if not to open their archives, and some important oral history work has also been conducted amongst managers and workers. This is, of course, a fundamental tool for academics in business schools as well as for sociologists and political scientists contributing to the field, but one much less used by historians, who perhaps prefer the impersonality of archives and libraries, than it should be.

It is evident from some of the chapters here, most obviously those on Mexico, Brazil, and Colombia, that some of the most important advances in understanding the evolution of business in Latin America have taken place through research at the regional level. This has depended on the organisation of provincial archives, which has been a significant development for historians of all kinds in many Latin American countries since the 1970s. One important result, evident in all three chapters, has been to dispel the myth that Latin Americans lacked entrepreneurial capacities, an idea that was quite common in the 1970s when it became clear to radical and nationalist historians that 'national bourgeoisies' had somehow failed. If one looks for entrepreneurship in the sense of identifying and grasping business opportunities and taking risks, then one can find evidence of it throughout Latin America. Research both on foreign firms and local businessmen and governments has also dispelled another myth of the early 1970s, namely that powerful foreign companies were always able to get their way in Latin America in the way in which Frank and others believed.

Rather, the relationship between foreign capital and national interests was, in true post-modernist fashion, a complex one subject to continual contestation and renegotiation, with several cards in the hands of the local players. However, the dispelling of the myths of the early 1970s does not imply that there were no differences between business structures and culture in Latin America and the wealthier nations of the North Atlantic.

For much of Latin America's history after independence both the political and economic environment were uncertain. In economic terms local political disruption and the transmission of commercial and financial crises from Europe as Latin America became more involved in world markets made the nineteenth century a difficult era in which to do business. There were several aspects of political instability which affected business apart from the simple disruption of commerce: the risk of violence and confiscation of property, frequent changes of government policies regarding key sectors of the economy, and later the threat to companies posed, at certain times, by widespread labour unrest. Landowners, of course, always faced the problems of the weather, pests, and diseases, and mine-owners the threat of geological difficulties and flooding as well, while both these groups faced continual uncertainties about prices. In the twentieth century, especially after the 1930s, the problems of inflation, exchange controls, and import restrictions all made life uncertain for the industrialist, even if they provided opportunities for other sectors such as the banks. This seems to have made businessmen in Latin America much more short-term in their strategic thinking than many of their counterparts in more stable economies. Many attempted to preserve a very high degree of liquidity rather than committing themselves to long-term fixed assets in one particular sector. Entrepreneurship had a rather different meaning in Latin America, in the sense that businessmen were often willing to take risks but they generally aimed to preserve a large amount of flexibility so that they could extract themselves easily rather than concentrating their investment in one particular activity. Several of the chapters in this book highlight these issues.

However, it was not only in terms of attitudes that Latin American businessmen differed. There were major contrasts in business institutions between Latin America and the North Atlantic world. Capital markets and managerial capitalism developed much more slowly than in Europe or North America. Founders and owners tried to control their enterprises in person or through a handful of trusted aides. The need for trust also meant that the dominant form of business organisation was not the impersonal limited liability company, but rather the family group. At their peak the most important families in the business elite controlled a whole raft of enterprises in different sectors of the economy. Land or property ownership was vital for status and for access to credit, but the control of local financial institutions, a political role, and a range of interests in commerce, mining, and even industry were also characteristic of the leading groups. Extensive interests in commerce and finance were frequently a means of resourcing other ventures. The organisation was linked together not by a formalised management structure but by networks of family and quasi-kin relationships. It is relatively easy for historians to identify the key family groups in individual countries and regions from the mid-nineteenth century to the late twentieth; the much more difficult task has been to explain the nature of decision-making and strategic thinking within them and the reasons for their rise and decline.

Nevertheless, research in business history has uncovered one common feature of the formation of these groups, one which particularly runs through the chapter on Mexico by Mario Cerutti, and that is the importance of commerce as a means both to accumulate the finance and contacts for diversification into other activities and as a way of gaining business experience. Coupled with this was the fact that commerce was one of the easiest areas for the young male immigrant to enter, as it had been in Latin America since the sixteenth century, and in retrospect immigrant communities appear to have been a fundamental source of entrepreneurship. Europeans, particularly German, Italian, Spanish, and Portuguese immigrants, founded many of the most important business groups in Latin America after 1850. However, although they were undoubtedly significant throughout the region, it would be incorrect to argue that European immigrants were the only source of dynamism. Within Latin America itself there was a fair degree of migration from one country to another, and a common language facilitated the entry of the immigrant entrepreneur into business circles in other countries. It is noticeable, for example, that Carlos Dávila's chapter here on Colombia picks out the railway engineer, Francisco Cisneros, and that on Peru the financier, José Payán: both were Cuban by birth. Chinese and Japanese immigrants from Asia and their descendants have also generated important businesses in several Latin American countries where they were taken as indentured workers in the nineteenth and early twentieth centuries. More recently, the descendants of Arab migrants from the Near East, often referred to generically as *turcos*, have been an important source of new entrants to the business (and indeed political) elites. Detailed research on the business actitivies and networks of many of these communities, however, is often just commencing. Social historians concerned with questions of assimilation have paid much more attention to immigrants than business historians. And, as Colin Lewis makes clear when referring to Minas Gerais in his chapter on Brazil, it may be easy to overestimate the role of immigrants and underestimate sources of entrepreneurship amongst local families, especially away from the coast and the ports. Was it the frequent involvement in commerce or the fact of being a migrant that made such newcomers such an obvious source of business dynamism in Latin America?

For immigrants who accumulated capital through trading activities but who were unable to participate in the formal political system unless naturalised, chambers of commerce, established in many Latin American ports and cities from the middle of the nineteenth century, were one important means of influencing government decisions regarding business. In many countries such institutions came to play a semi-official role, being commissioned by the state to conduct investigations and reviews of economic policy. Later in the nineteenth century other interest group associations, representing landowners, miners, or industrialists, were also founded. As the chapters in this volume indicate, there have been several histories of associations like these, many of which remain in existence, and while some are narrative and largely uncritical others provide important insights into the relationship between business and the state. Such institutional associations reinforced extended kinship networks as a means of gaining access to those holding power at times of political uncertainty, and their significance within the Latin American political environment has remained marked, under both the military regimes of the 1970s and 1980s and the civilian, often neo-populist, governments which replaced them. Historians have also studied other important institutions which were vital to the training of technical experts and managers, such as schools of engineering, and professional associations of groups like engineers or accountants. As business groups in Latin America become larger, more international in focus, and more accustomed to the absorption and development of new technologies and techniques in order to remain competitive, the formation of cadres of professional managers is of crucial importance, but this process has long historical roots.

Research considering questions such as these is really only just beginning to appear, and there are several other issues which require more consideration by specialised historians of business. Examples that come to mind, at the risk of advancing the agenda based on developments in Europe, include the following. First, the question of the legal environment and the enforcement of contracts is of obvious interest to business historians, especially in view of the growing appeal of the 'new institutional economics' associated with scholars such as Douglass North.[22] Issues raised by business historians such as Alfred Chandler and Mira Wilkins concerning the structure and organisation of firms might also be addressed, both by historians of foreign business in Latin America, who have only rarely considered explicitly the problems of managing at a distance, but also by historians of local business who have, on the whole, said little about how control and management evolved as family-based enterprises grew in size and function. How many locally owned businesses in Latin America failed adequately to cope with the transition from family management to managerial capitalism? This raises further questions about the characteristic

[22] Douglass C. North, *Institutions, Institutional Change, and Economic Performance* (Cambridge, 1990); North also contributed a short essay to a useful collection which contains other papers of relevance: John Harriss, Janet Hunter and Colin M. Lewis (eds), *The New Institutional Economics and Third World Development* (London, 1995).

life-cycles of family groups and firms in the Latin American environment.[23] Questions about the value of information, personal networks, and other intangibles in developing or reorientating business enterprise are also relevant here. Once one begins to think along these lines one confronts a further issue, namely the inter-relationships among firms in Latin America and particularly the connections between banks and other firms. Partly because of the secrecy of bankers, partly because of the technical capabilities the historian needs to acquire, the business history of financial institutions has not been anything like as well-developed in Latin America as that of agricultural, commercial or mining enterprise. There is also a glaring gap in the business history literature regarding the organisation, management and performance of the public-sector companies which have begun to disappear as Latin America has been swept by a wave of privatisation. Many such firms became exceedingly large companies which required professional organisation and management. The formation of this cadre of managers in mid-twentieth century Latin America, however, remains largely unknown, except perhaps for Colombia. Judging from the literature reviewed in the chapters which follow, a further issue which has not received the attention it deserves, whether in the public or private sectors, is industrial relations at the level of the plant or the enterprise, a rather different issue from the institutional histories of trade unions and political action which dominate labour history in Latin America.

At the conclusion of his chapter on Chile Luis Ortega comments that 'there is a whole history yet to be written'. Even in those countries in Latin America where research in business history has advanced at a greater speed than in Chile, there is no difficulty in finding questions to ask, topics to research, and the printed sources and archives to investigate them. Our hope is that the reviews of the literature and the insights offered here by the authors of the individual chapters may help to stimulate further research, especially at a time when the burden of Latin America's future development has been placed on the competence and competitiveness of private-sector business and the ability of the state to promote and regulate it.

---

[23] Diana Balmori and Robert Oppenheimer, 'Family Clusters: generational nucleation in nineteenth-century Argentina and Chile', *Comparative Studies in Society and History* 21 (1979), 231–61, make some generalisations about the growth of family groups over three generations, but very few historians have examined the process of decline.

CHAPTER TWO

Business History in Argentina

Raúl García Heras

The aim of this chapter is to review the literature on the history of business in Argentina. It will include texts which may rightly be considered as 'business history', and others which have made significant contributions to this field of knowledge, even though they do not fit into this category exactly. The studies reviewed in this chapter fall into four sections: foreign companies; state enterprises; local private firms; and interest groups and professional associations. In order to understand why certain subjects have received more attention than others in the work undertaken thus far, each section will identify the ideological and intellectual trends that have influenced academic research. The epilogue at the end of the chapter, besides summarising the specific conclusions reached in each section, aims also to outline the most important academic tasks still outstanding in the historiography of business in Argentina and to make some comparisons with the state of the discipline in other Latin American countries.

Foreign companies

The majority of the rail network affected by the programme of nationalisation of public utilities which characterised Argentine economic policy in the period immediately following the Second World War belonged to companies registered in Great Britain. These were the most important foreign investments in the country up to that date. They had played a decisive role in the spectacular growth experienced by the Argentine agro-export economy before 1914, and had remained crucial in the maintenance of close economic links with Great Britain. They symbolised the role Britain played as Argentina's principal trading and financial partner once the country became fully integrated into the international economy during the second half of the nineteenth century. This meant that even though the state also nationalised some smaller French railway companies, the British firms, due to their magnitude, role, and strategic location, became the subject of the first and most important studies undertaken on foreign companies in the country.[1]

---

[1] The French companies which were nationalised were the Ferrocarril Provincial de Santa

These initial academic contributions coincided with the fact that, following the Great Depression and the political and institutional crisis of 1930, a whole range of intellectuals and politicians had begun to re-examine national culture, the bases of economic growth, and the role of foreign investment in Argentina since the nineteenth century.[2] As a result, the work of the popular nationalist, Raúl Scalabrini Ortíz, was instrumental in the anti-imperialist battle designed to denounce the negative influence of the British rail companies in Argentine regional development and the central role they played in the 'colonial' relationship with Great Britain, and thus to contribute to the formation of 'national consciousness'.[3] Moreover, once economic nationalism became consolidated within Argentine politics and a new international economic order began to appear in the post-war period, both Scalabrini and Ricardo Ortiz, a highly educated engineer and member of the Communist Party, reiterated these nationalist charges, asserting the right of the state to control all public utilities as the mainstay of a truly national economic policy in the future. They began to demand the nationalisation of the British-owned railways, and this took place at the beginning of 1948.[4]

Due to the political and economic situation of Latin America during the 1960s and 1970s theories of imperialism and dependency became the pre-eminent paradigms for analysis in the social sciences.[5] This gave rise to a series of important critical studies by Pedro Skupch, Jorge Fodor and Arturo O'Connell on the economic and financial links which had existed between Argentina and Great Britain. These writers naturally alluded to

Fé (1885), the Compañía General de Ferrocarriles de la Provincia de Buenos Aires (1905), and the Ferrocarril de Rosario a Puerto Belgrano (1906).

[2] For a more detailed treatment of these themes, see Mark Falcoff, 'Intellectual Currents', in Mark Falcoff and Ronald Dolkart (eds), *Prologue to Perón: Argentina in depression and war* (Berkeley, 1975), pp. 110–35; Mark Falcoff, 'Raúl Scalabrini Ortiz: the making of an Argentine nationalist', *Hispanic American Historical Review* 52 (1972), 74–101; Marysa Navarro Gerassi, *Los nacionalistas* (Buenos Aires, 1968); and Juan José Hernández Arregui, *La formación de la conciencia nacional, 1930–1960* (Buenos Aires, 1973).

[3] See Raúl Scalabrini Ortíz, *Historia de los ferrocarriles argentinos* (Buenos Aires, 1940).

[4] On the rise of economic nationalism in Argentina and the way in which nationalist attitudes took root at the beginning of the 1940s, see Carlos Waisman, *Reversal of Development in Argentina: postwar counter-revolutionary policies and their structural consequences* (Princeton, 1987); Teodoro Sánchez de Bustamante, '¿Estatización o industria privada en materia de servicios públicos de transportes y comunicaciones?', *Revista de Ciencias Económicas* (October 1943), 963–73; and Salvador Oría, *El estado argentino y la nueva economía: intervencionismo defensivo* (Buenos Aires, 1945). For the arguments in favour of nationalisation of the railways, see Raúl Scalabrini Ortiz, *Los ferrocarriles deben ser del pueblo argentino* (Buenos Aires, 1946); and Ricardo M. Ortiz, *El ferrocarril en la economía argentina* (Buenos Aires, 1946).

[5] For recent analyses of these influences see Robert A. Packenham, *The Dependency Movement: scholarship and politics in development studies* (Cambridge, 1992), and Joseph L. Love, 'The Origins of Dependency Analysis', *Journal of Latin American Studies* 22 (1990), 143–68. An excellent introduction to the evolution of theoretical work within Latin America is Cristóbal Kay, *Latin American Theories of Development and Underdevelopment* (London, 1989).

the role of the railway companies in this relationship. Their work reflected the influence of the nationalist and Marxist tendencies which had been predominant in the 1930s and 1940s, as well as the two intellectual schools prevailing at the time they were writing. Skupch's study in particular was published just at the moment when Peronism, the populist movement which had emerged towards the end of the Second World War, was beginning to regain its political legitimacy after the prolonged exile of its leader. His study formed part of a collaborative project motivated by contemporary academic and intellectual interest in the political, economic and social conjuncture in which Peronism had first emerged as a political alternative.[6] During this period there was no work published on specific British companies from the standpoint of historians influenced by theories of imperialism or dependency. Nonetheless, both these schools were to have a strong influence on the future historiography of these companies by adding a more academic tone to the literature. Moreover, some of these authors implicitly questioned, from a macroeconomic perspective, the implications which these global theories suggested for those studying individual cases.

   Eduardo Zalduendo compared the role of British investment in railway development in Argentina, Brazil, Canada and India during the second half of the nineteenth century. Winthrop R. Wright studied the influence these companies had on the emergence of economic nationalism in Argentina. Although Wright was unable to consult certain invaluable British and Argentine diplomatic sources, he proved that many of the arguments which had been used to criticise the role of the railway companies in politics and the local economy in the 1930s and 1940s and subsequently employed in order to justify nationalisation were in fact unfounded. Relying heavily upon British and North American diplomatic correspondence and a range of sources found in Argentine railway archives, Paul Goodwin showed how local politics conditioned company behaviour and questioned, with considerable justification, the so-called 'economic nationalism' of the populist governments led by Hipólito Yrigoyen between 1916 and 1930. Finally, Colin Lewis, a student of D. C. M. Platt, analysed the links between the railways and Argentine governments up to the 1930s. His study highlights the regulatory role of the state in relation to company activity, and argues that, despite arguments to the contrary, a unified

---

   [6] For work on Anglo-Argentine relations during these years see Jorge Fodor and Arturo A. O'Connell, 'La Argentina y la economía atlántica en la primera mitad del siglo XX', *Desarrollo Económico* 13:49 (1973), 3–65; Pedro Skupch, 'El deterioro y fin de la hegemonía británica sobre la economía argentina, 1914–1947', in Pedro Skupch *et al.*, *Estudios sobre los orígenes del peronismo* (2 vols, Buenos Aires, 1975), II, 5–79. For examples of the nationalist and Marxist historiographical traditions, see Julio and Rodolfo Irazusta, *La Argentina y el imperialismo británico* (Buenos Aires, 1934); Raúl Scalabrini Ortiz, *Política británica en el Río de la Plata* (Buenos Aires, 1940); Ernesto Giúdici, *Imperialismo inglés y liberación nacional* (Buenos Aires, 1940).

'railway lobby' able to defend their interests with total success never existed in Argentina.[7]

During the 1980s the majority of academic analysis continued the efforts at interpretation which, since the early 1970s, had attempted to respond to questions on the role of British companies that the dependency and 'imperialism' schools had failed to clarify. Others, meanwhile, examined the relevance of the concept of 'informal empire' developed by Robinson and Gallagher in the 1950s for the evolution of these companies. The first studies on the small French railway companies mentioned earlier were also published.[8]

Using both British and Argentine sources, and with a somewhat idiosyncratic approach, Lewis analysed the origin, consolidation, and profitability of these companies during the 'golden age' which ended with the First World War. Although his book left significant questions, such as the companies' labour policies, the links which these firms possessed with powerful groups in Argentina and Britain, and their global impact on Argentina's economic development, on one side, it remained the most thorough research produced during this period. A few years later Raúl García Heras highlighted the limited significance of the British railway companies in the development of Anglo-Argentine relations and economic policy in Argentina between 1930 and the 1940s.[9] Andrés Regalsky, who took no part in the debate over business imperialism and dependency, studied French investment in the railway sector up until 1914. The central

[7] Eduardo Zalduendo, *Libras y rieles: las inversiones británicas para el desarrollo de los ferrocarriles en Argentina, Brasil, Canada e India durante el siglo XIX* (Buenos Aires, 1975); Winthrop R. Wright, *British-Owned Railways in Argentina: their effect on the growth of economic nationalism* (Austin, 1974); Paul B. Goodwin, 'The Politics of Rate-Making: British-owned railways and the Unión Cívica Radical, 1921–1928', *Journal of Latin American Studies* 6 (1974), 257–87; Paul B. Goodwin, *Los ferrocarriles británicos y la U.C.R., 1916–1930* (Buenos Aires, 1974); Colin M. Lewis, 'British Railway Companies and the Argentine Government', in D. C. M. Platt (ed.), *Business Imperialism, 1840–1930: an inquiry based on British experience in Latin America* (Oxford, 1977), pp. 395–427. The archives of the railway companies were either destroyed or transferred to different ministries or similar entities after nationalisation. Hence most recent scholars, except for Goodwin and Lewis, have been unable to locate or to consult the papers relevant to the subject in which they were interested.

[8] For the most recent evaluations of the concepts put forward by Robinson and Gallagher and the debate to which they gave rise, see Rory Miller, *Britain and Latin America in the Nineteenth and Twentieth Centuries* (London, 1993), and 'British Investment in Latin America, 1850–1950: a reappraisal', *Itinerario* 19: 3 (1995), 21–52.

[9] Colin M. Lewis, *British Railways in Argentina, 1857–1914: a case study of foreign investment* (London, 1983); Raúl García Heras, 'World War II and the Frustrated Nationalization of the Argentine British-Owned Railways, 1939–1943', *Journal of Latin American Studies* 17 (1985), 135–55; Raúl García Heras, 'Hostage Private Companies under Restraint: British railways and transport coordination during the 1930s', *Journal of Latin American Studies* 19 (1987), 41–67; Raúl García Heras, 'Las compañías ferroviarias británicas y el control de cambios en la Argentina durante la Gran Depresión', *Desarrollo Económico* 29:116 (1990), 477–505.

themes of his valuable articles were the origin and form of such investments, their profitability, the influence of the French companies in the economic development of the province of Santa Fé, and the reasons why these companies could not compete with the more established British network.[10]

Finally, William Fleming, clearly questioning the theories of Robinson and Gallagher, concluded that the building of railways did not help towards the construction of an informal British empire in Argentina. Moreover, even though he recognised that many British companies did concentrate their services in the pampas in order to serve the agro-export economy, he argued that others such as the Gran Oeste Argentino contributed towards the development of regional economies.[11]

Other British companies in the fields of manufacturing, shipping, farming, commerce, banking, finance, and public services also contributed to the close economic relations between Argentina and Great Britain. However, only a handful of studies have documented the evolution and development of such companies. Most of these deal with the activities of commercial banks and 'merchant banks' after the second half of the nineteenth century. The pioneering work appeared in the early 1960s when David Joslin, a leading British economic historian, completed the official history of the Bank of London and South America (BOLSA), taking it up to the merger of BOLSA and the Anglo-South American Bank in 1936.[12]

Twenty years later British and Latin American academics published three groups of closely related scholarly work. First, a well-known Argentine historian, Samuel Amaral, published the definitive work on the controversial loan which Baring Brothers of London had provided to the provincial government of Buenos Aires in 1824. Amaral questioned whether the concept of 'imperialism' was in fact appropriate to the analysis of such a transaction.[13] Second, researchers began to analyse Argentina's public debt

[10] Andrés M. Regalsky, 'Las inversiones francesas en los ferrocarriles argentinos, 1887–1900', *Siglo XIX: revista de historia* 3:5 (1988), 125–66, and 'Foreign Capital, Local Interests, and Railway Development in Argentina: French investments in railways, 1900–1914', *Journal of Latin American Studies* 21 (1989), 425–52.

[11] William Fleming, *Regional Development and Transportation in Argentina: Mendoza and the Gran Oeste Argentino, 1885–1914* (New York, 1987), and 'Profits and Visions: British Capital and Railway Construction in Argentina, 1854–1886', in Clarence B. Davis and Kenneth E. Wilburn (eds), *Railway Imperialism* (New York, 1991), pp. 71–84.

[12] David Joslin, *A Century of Banking in Latin America: to commemorate the centenary in 1962 of the Bank of London and South America Limited* (London, 1963). For a more recent work, putting the British banks in South America in the context of British overseas banking more generally, see Geoffrey Jones, *British Multinational Banking, 1830–1990* (Oxford, 1993). For a recent study of Argentine banking in the 'Golden Age', see Andrés Regalsky, 'La evolución de la banca privada nacional en Argentina, 1860–1914: una introducción a su estudio', in Pedro Tedde and Carlos Marichal (eds), *La formación de los bancos centrales en España y Amércia Latina* (2 vols, Madrid, 1994), II, 35–59.

[13] Samuel Amaral, 'El empréstito de Londres de 1824', *Desarrollo Económico* 23:92 (1984), 559–87.

before the Great Depression, in some cases within a broader Latin American context. Carlos Marichal, a historian from the Colegio de Mexico, initially examined the complex financial relations between Argentina and bankers in Paris, London and Berlin during the feverish decade of the 1880s. He also provided a lucid explanation of the role and strategies of the different banking houses in the issue of Argentine public loans. Years later he extended his balanced but critical approach to a full-scale study of the public debt of the different nations of Latin America between the wars of Independence and the Great Depression. Frank Griffith Dawson placed the 1824 loan in the context of the first Latin American foreign debt crisis. Although he refrained from entering into the major controversies on the subject, his examination of the London press did offer considerable insights into the views of British investors.[14] Third, the first official historical accounts of the prestigious London financial houses based on their own archives and other primary and secondary sources were published in Britain. All these monographs examined, rather tangentially but still with a certain amount of depth, the role of Baring Brothers, Cazenove & Co., Morgan Grenfell, and Schroders in the financing of Argentina's public debt, especially between 1880 and 1914.[15]

The role of commercial houses has provoked less interest. Roger Gravil studied the development of Harrods and Gath & Chaves, two modern retail stores established at the turn of the century. His examination of business archives tended to concentrate above all on the impact that the Great Depression had on their activities, but he did not address either the question of their profitability or the ways in which these retailers were able to meet the needs of the consumer market. The organisation and operations of the principal British commercial houses located in Buenos Aires before 1880 is the subject of Vera Blinn Reber's study, based on their own archives, together with those of Barings, the Foreign Office papers, and public and private archives in Argentina. Finally, after consulting the Gibson family papers and the publications and archives of the British Chamber of Commerce in Argentina, Paul Goodwin shed light on the variety of interests represented in the Chamber, and demonstrated how the evolution of Argentine industry, economic nationalism, and Anglo-Argentine relations caused internal differences within the British business comunity.[16]

---

[14] Carlos Marichal, 'Los banqueros europeos y los empréstitos argentinos: rivalidad y colaboración, 1880–1890', *Revista de Historia Económica* 2:1 (1984), 47–82, and *A Century of Debt Crises in Latin America: from Independence to the Great Depression* (Princeton, 1989); Frank Griffith Dawson, *The First Latin American Debt Crisis: the City of London and the Loan Bubble, 1822–1825* (New Haven, 1990).

[15] See Philip Ziegler, *The Sixth Great Power: Barings, 1762–1929* (London, 1988); Kathleen Burk, *Morgan Grenfell, 1838–1989: the biography of a merchant bank* (Oxford, 1989); David Kynaston, *Cazenove & Co., a history* (London, 1991); and Richard Roberts, *Schroders: merchants and bankers* (London, 1992).

[16] Roger Gravil, 'British Retail Trade in Argentina, 1900–1940', *Inter-American Economic Affairs* 29:2 (1970), 3–26; Vera Blinn Reber, *British Mercantile Houses in Buenos Aires, 1810–1880*

Various British tramway companies also contributed to the development of urban passenger transport in Argentina. There are, however, only two studies of the most important firm, the Anglo-Argentine Tramways Co. Ltd. of Buenos Aires. Luis Sommi, a Communist intellectual renowned for his political and trade union militancy, published the first of these works at the beginning of the 1940s with the aim of combating the company's monopolistic aspirations, exposing the retarding impact of British capital in the national economy, and calling upon the working class to unite in the struggle for national liberation. In contrast to this, the more recent study by Raúl García Heras is the first detailed academic analysis and demonstrates the limited extent of the company's influence in Britain and Argentina during the 1930s and early 1940s.[17]

Other studies examine the role of various landowning companies. For example, Gastón Gori, a reformist socialist concerned with the negative economic and social effects of *latifundismo*, was severely critical of the Forestal Land, Timber and Railway Company, the most important firm exploiting resources of *quebracho colorado* in Santa Fé, Chaco and Formosa before the mid-1960s. His study, based on local primary and secondary sources, highlighted their coercive labour policy and the rapacious effects of their activities both on the development and on the environment of the region. Michael Cowen, in a collection of essays inspired by the 'New Business History' influenced by the work of Alfred Chandler, published a rather sketchy paper investigating the origin and development of Forestal Land before 1945, but based it almost entirely on secondary sources. Nonetheless, his analysis complements Gori's in that it pays particular attention to the company's profitability and the reasons why it transferred its operations from Argentina to Africa.[18] Eduardo Míguez, finally,

(Cambridge, Mass., 1979); Paul B. Goodwin, 'Anglo-Argentine Commercial Relations: a private sector view, 1922–1943', *Hispanic American Historical Review* 61 (1981), 29–51. The Gibsons were a family of Scottish origin who settled in the River Plate at the beginning of the nineteenth century. They were merchants and also pioneered the breeding of sheep in Argentina. The best-known member of the family was possibly Sir Herbert Gibson, who had a lengthy business career as a director of several British firms and also chaired the British Chamber of Commerce until the mid-1930s.

[17] Luis V. Sommi, *El monopolio inglés del transporte en Buenos Aires* (Buenos Aires, 1940); Raúl García Heras, 'Capitales extranjeros, poder político y transporte urbano de pasajeros: la Compañía de Tranvías Anglo-Argentina Ltda de Buenos Aires, Argentina, 1930–1943', *Desarrollo Económico* 32:125 (1992), 35–56; *Transportes, Negocios y Política: la Compañía Anglo-Argentina de Tranvías, 1876–1981* (Buenos Aires, 1994); and 'Foreign Business – Host Government Relations: the Anglo-Argentine Tramways Co. Ltd. of Buenos Aires, 1930–1966', *Itinerario* 19: 1 (1995), 85–96.

[18] Gastón Gori, *La Forestal: la tragedia del quebracho colorado* (Buenos Aires, 1965); Michael Cowen, 'Capital, Nation, and Commodities: the case of Forestal Land, Timber and Railway Company in Argentina and Africa, 1900–1945', in J. J. van Helten and Y. Cassis (eds), *Capitalism in a Mature Economy* (Aldershot, 1990), pp. 186–215. The *quebracho* was an indigenous tree which was valuable both for its bark, a source of tannin, and its timber, which was often used for products like railway sleepers on account of its durability.

examined the labour system, business dynamism, and finances of the principal *estancias* belonging to British families and colonisation companies before 1914.[19] Moreover, he also touched upon the current debate about the benefits and limitations of the Argentine agro-export model. Indeed, although he acknowledged that the Argentine agrarian structure of the time resulted in a series of negative political, economic, and social consequences, to a large extent he aligned himself with those who appear not to have recognised the limitations of this model and its contribution to the country's stagnation after 1930.[20]

After the 1880s British, and later North American, capital also played a crucial pioneering role in the meat-packing industry, a sector closely linked to the prevailing primary-export economy, the modernisation of farming, and the export of meat and related products. However, the history of the principal firms involved in this sector has yet to be written.

The pioneering study of Simon Hanson, a North American economist, examined the position of Argentine meat in the British market, and provided some information on the profits of the leading US and British companies in the trade before the early 1930s. In the 1950s Rodolfo Puiggrós, a sophisticated Communist intellectual, analysed the history of this industry and the contributions made by British companies, though he claimed that he had no 'anti-English' prejudice.[21] He did, however, call for the nationalisation of the sector and the development of 'the economic independence of our homeland', demanding state intervention in the economy just at the point when various aspects of Peronist economic policy were the subject of deep debate throughout the country.[22] This work is of added interest as its author was one of the pioneers of a nascent 'National Left' which, unlike the Trotskyists and the Socialist and Communist Parties which opposed it, had begun to support Peronism as a 'national political alternative' for autonomous political and economic development, albeit from a critical perspective.

During the 1960s research on this industry was once again taken up by the academic world. Peter Smith, a well-known historian from the United States, relied upon British and US primary and secondary sources in order to examine the problems caused by the meat packing industry up to the mid-1940s. Nevertheless, the only detailed study of any specific firm in the industry concentrates on the activities of Leibig's Extract of

[19] *Estancia* is the Argentine term for a large cattle ranch.

[20] Eduardo Míguez, *Las tierras de los ingleses en la Argentina* (Buenos Aires, 1985). See above all, his comments on pp. 321–330. For a summary of the historiographical debate over the agro-export model followed by Argentina and the problem of landownership, see Hilda Sábato, *Capitalismo y ganadería en la provincia de Buenos Aires* (Buenos Aires, 1989), pp. 13–20.

[21] Simon G. Hanson, *Argentine Meat and the British Market* (Stanford, 1938); Rodolfo Puiggrós, *Libre empresa o nacionalización en la industria del carne* (Buenos Aires, 1957).

[22] See pp. 26 and 33.

Meat Company, the main producer of meat extract and corned beef, before 1930.[23]

Argentina represented a promising Latin American market in which several North American companies attempted to displace the British from their dominant role in industry, commerce, shipping, banking, and finance, especially after the First World War.[24] Despite the significant role played by these companies in the later evolution of the Argentine economy, the relevant historiography has treated this phenomenon and its well-known repercussions in a rather disparate manner. The expansion of US companies overseas in the 1930s provoked widespread interest among academics and influenced the classic work by Phelps on the activities of their subsidiaries in the major countries of the Southern Cone.[25] The first two general studies of this theme published in Argentina, in contrast, reflected the political and economic situation through which the country was passing at the time they were written as well as the ideology of their authors.

At the end of the 1940s Luis Sommi, the well-known Communist militant who has already been mentioned, documented the growth of the principal North American corporations, especially in the electricity industry. His analysis was greatly influenced by his own personal position and the boycott through which the government of the United States was attempting to isolate and strangle Argentina economically as a reprisal against the economic nationalism, state intervention, and independent foreign policy which marked the early stages of Perón's first administration. Despite his ideological differences with the Peronist regime, therefore, Sommi does recognise some of its 'national achievements'.[26]

A decade later, the governments that succeeded Peronism tried to solve the complex problems which they had inherited by means of foreign investment, a progressive deregulation of the national economy, improved relations with the world powers, and the incorporation of Argentina into the global system of multilateral trade and international payments. In this light Jaime Fuchs, a well-known Communist Party intellectual of that period, carried out a broader sectoral analysis than that of Sommi. He

[23] Peter H. Smith, *Politics and Beef in Argentina: patterns of conflict and change* (New York, 1969); on Liebig's, see J. Colin Crossley and Robert Greenhill, 'The River Plate Beef Trade', in Platt (ed.), *Business Imperialism*, pp. 284–334. Vesteys, the major British packing-house in the trade after the 1920s, came to the attention of the British press in the late 1970s over charges of prolonged tax evasion: see Philip Knightley, *The Rise and Fall of the Vestey Family: the true story of how Britain's richest family beat the taxman and came to grief* (London, 1993); this had first been published under the title *The Vestey Affair* in 1981.

[24] It should be noted that the earliest antecedents of this process occurred at the beginning of the twentieth century, when powerful North American meat-packing firms began to dispute control of Argentine exports and the British market with the British themselves.

[25] See Dudley Maynard Phelps, *The Migration of Industry to South America* (New York, 1936). The author was a well-known specialist in marketing and international economics at the University of Michigan, and also an official of the State Department.

[26] Luis V. Sommi, *Los capitales yanquis en la Argentina* (Buenos Aires, 1949).

thus employed a style of language reminiscent of the calls to form popular fronts in the 1930s in order to denounce the lack of an 'authentically national, progressive and democratic' alternative to combat the 'continued capitulation to the interests of the oligarchy and imperialism'.[27]

On the other hand, there are only a few specific studies which have analysed the petroleum and the automobile industries in any depth and then they have been undertaken from a predominantly macroeconomic perspective. The first important works to be relatively well documented examined the general history of the petroleum industry in the midst of the political battles of the 1950s.

These controversies emerged when, after initially adopting nationalistic and statist economic policies, the Peronist government attempted to solve the country's energy deficit by encouraging new foreign investment. Arturo Frondizi and José Liceaga formulated the main arguments which their party, the Unión Cívica Radical, used in order to denounce these new policies as an unforgivable abandonment of Argentina's principles in favour of imperialism, and they praised the pioneering role that the Argentine state oil company, Yacimientos Petrolíferos Fiscales (YPF), had played both in national oil production and as a model for Latin America.[28] Marcos Kaplan, at that time a young Trotskyist political scientist, was more influenced by the debate provoked by the subsequent collapse of Peronist populism, the failings of state capitalism, and the importance of the oil problem for Argentina, issues to which Fuchs had already alluded. It was for this very reason that he questioned the revolutionary stance attributed to Peronism and its petroleum policy. Much later, now distanced from the political and ideological battles in Argentina but still maintaining a critical perspective, Kaplan concentrated his attention on the historical sociopolitical framework and the rivalry between British and US private companies in the early stages of the petroleum industry.[29]

Studies of a much more academic nature were published in the 1970s. Fernando García Molina, Osvaldo Andino, and Carlos Mayo, all declared advocates of state monopolies, examined in great detail but with a high degree of objectivity the US reaction to the emergence of YPF and the nationalisation of petroleum favoured by the Radicalism of the late 1920s. In contrast, Carl Solberg, although looking at Anglo-American competition during the same period, put the emphasis on their role in the creation of YPF and Argentine petroleum policy before 1930.[30]

---

[27] Jaime Fuchs, *La penetración de los trusts yanquis en la Argentina* (Buenos Aires, 1959).

[28] Arturo Frondizi, *Petróleo y política* (Buenos Aires, 1954); José Liceaga, *Reflexiones sobre el problema petrolero argentino* (Buenos Aires, 1955).

[29] Marcos Kaplan, *Economía y política del petroleo argentino, 1939–1956* (Buenos Aires, 1957), and *Petróleo, estado y empresas en la Argentina* (Caracas, 1972).

[30] Carlos Mayo, Osvaldo Andino, and Fernando García Molina, *Diplomacia, política, y petroleo en la Argentina, 1927–1930* (Buenos Aires, 1976); Carl Solberg, *Oil and Nationalism in Argentina: a history* (Stanford, 1979).

The historiography of the motor industry is much more comprehensive and relatively untainted by such diverse ideological influences. Skupch analysed the consequences of its emergence for British economic hegemony in Argentina. A short monograph by García Heras improved understanding of the business strategies and expansion of Ford, General Motors, and Chrysler in relation to highway development, the urban modernisation of Buenos Aires, the emergence of road transport, and new patterns of consumption in Argentina. Norbert Macdonald studied the growth of Kaiser in the 1950s. A comparison of his case study with the model which Mira Wilkins had suggested in order to examine the history of transnational companies led him to emphasise the Kaiser company's lack of competitiveness in its own homeland and the way in which this affected its business strategy and development within Argentina.[31]

More recently María Beatriz Nofal, an academic and a former official in the Alfonsín government (1983–1989), traced the evolution of the major European and North American motor companies to the 1980s. After examining their economic and technological evolution, their regional location, and their contribution to Argentine economic development, Nofal observed that these companies failed to provide Argentina with the stimulus to create prosperity and industrial development on a level similar to that of the industrialised countries upon which those who had promoted the investment had based their model. James Brennan, a North American historian, studied the political economy of the motor industry in Córdoba, one of the major industrial cities in Argentina during the period from 1955 to 1976. His work concentrates on the business strategies and the labour policies of two firms, Renault and Fiat, as well as their relations with the Argentine state. It is based on sources such as company and trade union archives as well as State Department and Military Intelligence reports found in archives in the United States.[32]

Some Italian and German firms also played a significant role in Argentina's economic development after the late nineteenth century. This subject has, however, aroused much less academic interest. With regard to Italian companies, two works by María Inés Barbero, whose contributions to the analysis of business history as a branch of Argentine economic history will

[31] Pedro Skupch, 'Las consecuencias de la competencia de transportes sobre la hegemonía británica en la Argentina, 1919–1939', *Económica* (La Plata) 17: 1 (1971), 119–41; Raúl García Heras, *Automotores norteamericanos, caminos, y modernización urbana en la Argentina, 1918–1939* (Buenos Aires, 1985); Norbert MacDonald, 'Henry J. Kaiser and the Establishment of the Automobile Industry in Argentina', *Business History* 20 (1988), 329–45.

[32] María Beatriz Nofal, *Absentee Entrepreneurship and the Dynamics of the Motor Vehicle Industry in Argentina* (New York, 1989); James P. Brennan, 'El clasismo y los obreros: el contexto fabril del "Sindicalismo de Liberación" en la industria automotriz cordobesa, 1970–1975', *Desarrollo Económico* 32: 125 (1992), 3–22, and *The Labor Wars in Córdoba, 1955–1976: ideology, work, and labor politics in an Argentina industrial city* (Cambridge, 1994).

be discussed below, are worthy of mention.[33] The first analyses some of the principal characteristics of Italian industrialists in Argentina during the period from 1900 to 1930, noting their heterogeneity and assessing their relationship with the political elite and prominent members of local society. The second examines the case of Pirelli, the first Italian transnational company to be located in Argentina, and which with Dunlop (British), Goodyear and Firestone (North American), and Michelin (French), contributed to the development of the rubber industry.[34]

The history of German companies in Argentina is even more sparsely developed. Luis Sommi's work was the first systematic and global study available. By denouncing the Nazi imperial presence in Argentina in the middle of the Second World War, he wished to contribute to the 'Allied Cause'. Some decades later, Ronald Newton, in his socio-cultural analysis of the German community in Argentina up to 1933, touched lightly on the origins of the German Chamber of Commerce, and the expansion of large companies such as Siemens, AEG, Merck, and Bayer during the 1920s.[35]

Argentine businesses and businessmen

Progress in the historiography of local companies and businessmen has been modest in comparison with that relating to foreign companies. For the most part the literature is confined to studies of the evolution of trading firms in Buenos Aires towards the end of the colonial period and of a famous ranching family from Buenos Aires in the nineteenth century, work on two important regional industries during the period when the agro-export model dominated in Argentina, and research on a few industrial companies of the modern and contemporary period.

At the end of the 1970s Susan Socolow, a distinguished US historian, published an important prosopographical study of traders in Buenos Aires in the era of the Viceroyalty of the River Plate. This is, above all, a work of social history which also examines the commercial activities of this particular group, in particular the case of Gaspar de Santa Coloma, a typical local merchant of the period, and compares the results of this research with the conclusions of David Brading, James Lockhart, and Ruth Pike on the

---

[33] See below, pp. 36 and 38.

[34] María Inés Barbero, 'Empresas y empresarios italianos en la Argentina, 1900–1930', in Congreso Histórico Internacional sobre Emigración, *Studi sull'emigrazione: un analisi comparata* (Biella, 1989), pp. 303–13, and 'Grupos empresarios, intercambio comercial e inversiones italianas en la Argentina: el caso de Pirelli, 1910–1920', *Estudios Migratorios Latinoamericanos* 5 (1990), 311–40.

[35] Luis V. Sommi, *Los capitales alemanes en la Argentina* (Buenos Aires, 1945); Ronald C. Newton, *German Buenos Aires, 1900–1933* (Austin, 1977), and The 'Nazi Menace' in Argentina, 1931–1947 (Stanford, 1992).

merchants of Mexico, Lima and Seville in the eighteenth and sixteenth centuries respectively.[36]

As a consequence of the early primacy of livestock production, the ranchers inevitably became the most powerful group in Argentina. However, until now only the Anchorena family has been subjected to academic analysis. This prominent family of Spanish descent arrived in the River Plate area at the end of the eighteenth century, and became distinguished for its commercial, political, and ranching activities. At the beginning of the 1970s Andrés Carretero was the first to utilise the archives of the family, which are conserved in the Archivo General de la Nación, in order to study its political and business evolution up to 1830. Towards the end of the same decade Jonathan Brown, a North American historian, used the example of this family in order to determine the extent to which the production of dry hides, salted meat, and tallow offered commercial opportunities to ranchers in Buenos Aires province during the first half of the nineteenth century. After a detailed analysis of the administration of their *estancias* and the commercialisation of their products, Brown was able to demonstrate, without losing sight of the fact that their example was unique, how both greater managerial talent and access to commercial capital enabled the Anchorenas to become the most prosperous and efficient *estancieros* of their era in Buenos Aires.[37] More recently a controversial essayist and sociologist, Juan José Sebreli, has carried out the most definitive study of this family, tracing their evolution from the colonial period to the present day.[38] Unlike Brown, in describing the historical and social evolution of the Anchorenas as that of a typical oligarchic family of Buenos Aires, Sebreli's work aimed to analyse the Argentine ruling class from an unashamedly critical perspective. Even so, the inclusion of his study in this review is justified due to his sociological and historical contribution to the evolution of the Argentine livestock entrepreneurs.[39]

The sugar and wine industries contributed to the integration of the Argentine North West and Cuyo into the national economy between the

[36] Susan Migden Socolow, *The Merchants of Buenos Aires, 1778–1810: family and commerce* (Cambridge, 1978). For the cases with which Socolow compares her results, see D. A. Brading, *Miners and Merchants in Bourbon Mexico, 1763–1818* (Cambridge, 1971); James Lockhart, *Spanish Peru, 1531–1560: a colonial society* (Madison, 1968); and Ruth Pike, *Aristocrats and Traders: Sevillian society in the sixteenth century* (Ithaca, 1972), and *Enterprise and Adventure: the Genoese in Seville and the opening of the New World* (Ithaca, 1966).

[37] Andrés Carretero, *Los Anchorena: política y negocios en el siglo XIX* (Buenos Aires, 1970); Jonathan C. Brown, 'A Nineteenth-Century Argentine Cattle Empire', *Agricultural History* 52 (1978), 160–78.

[38] Sebreli collaborated on *Contorno*, a literary review published during the 1950s which grouped together distinguished intellectuals including the Viñas brothers, Adolfo Prieto, Noé Nitrick, and Tulio Halperín Donghi.

[39] Juan José Sebreli, *La saga de los Anchorena* (Buenos Aires, 1985).

second half of the nineteenth century and 1914.[40] Towards the end of the 1970s the valuable global studies by Jorge Balán and Nancy López brought academic attention to these industries for the first time.[41] However, although subsequent studies examined both these industries separately, and with a similarly professional approach, they did not track the history of any individual company.

At the beginning of the 1980s Donna Guy examined the evolution of the sugar industry in the province of Tucumán during the Golden Age of the agro-export model in Argentina. She employed a thematic and chronological approach in order to study the industry's productive mechanisms, its banking and credit arrangements, its transformation under old and new business groups, and its relations with local and national governments. The main concern of the research of Noemí Girbal de Blacha and Daniel Santamaría some years later was the evolution and subsequent crisis of the industry over a longer period. They considered the process of modernisation, production costs, cyclical crises, the action taken by the state to promote the industry, and the behaviour of businessmen who controlled the sector.[42]

There are only two studies on the wine industry before 1914. In the late 1970s Fleming took the case of the province of Mendoza as an example in order to question sociological theories which attributed the backwardness of traditional regions to a supposed latent hostility in such areas towards the emergence of a powerful business class and sustained economic growth. Here, Fleming was able to demonstrate how immigrant pioneers and local entrepreneurs had collaborated in the development of Mendoza's economy at the beginning of the twentieth century. His work also referred to the role played by certain prominent immigrants in the early stages of the wine industry.[43] Employing a more empirical approach than Fleming, Girbal de Blacha assessed the political, economic, and social factors that influenced the development of this industry in the Cuyo. In this way she analysed the business and corporate structure of the industry, highlighting the role

---

[40] Cuyo is the Argentine term for the region around Mendoza and San Juan in the west of the country.

[41] See Jorge Balán and Nancy López, 'Burguesía y gobiernos provinciales en la Argentina: la política impositiva de Tucumán y Mendoza entre 1873 y 1914', *Desarrollo Económico* 17: 67 (1977), 391–435; Jorge Balán, 'La cuestión regional en la Argentina: burguesías provinciales y el mercado nacional en el desarrollo agroexportador', *Desarrollo Económico* 18: 69 (1976), 49–87.

[42] Donna Guy, *Argentine Sugar politics: Tucumán and the Generation of Eighty* (Tempe, 1980); Daniel Santamaría, *Azúcar y sociedad en el noroeste argentino* (Buenos Aires, 1986); Noemí Girbal de Blacha, 'Estado, modernización azucarera y comportamiento empresarial en la Argentina, 1876–1914: expansión y concentración de una economía regional', *Anuario de Estudios Americanos* 66 (1988), 383–417, and 'Azúcar, cambio político y acción empresarial en la Argentina, 1916–1930', *Investigaciones y Ensayos* 41 (1991), 269–314.

[43] In particular he cited the cases of Domingo Tomba, Juan Giol, Miguel Escorihuela, and Balbino Arizu.

played by immigrants whom Fleming had neglected in these processes. She also examined the initial incentives and subsequent protection offered by the state and the periodic crises suffered by the sector.[44]

The final advances in the literature on Argentine business are concerned with a handful of more contemporary industrial companies. By far the most elaborate was the work by Thomas Cochran and Rubén Reina, who in the early 1960s carried out a socio-cultural study of the successful career of Torcuato di Tella, a pioneer of Argentina's metallurgical and electricity industries, and the evolution of SIAM, one of his main companies. Their analysis was based upon interviews with former colleagues and collaborators of Di Tella, his personal and company archives, and secondary sources. However, this study emphasised the individual enterprise of Di Tella himself much more than the commercial evolution of SIAM or the limitations of the European and North American theoretical models used to study businesses and businessmen in Latin America.[45]

There is little other work on manufacturing industry from a business history perspective. In a short introductory book Jorge Schvarzer put together the publicly available information on the origins, evolution, and consolidation of Bunge y Born, a company founded in 1884. Initially based on the cereal trade, its later diversification enabled it to become one of the most important companies in the country. Juan Carlos Korol and Leandro Gutiérrez examined the history of Alpargatas, an Argentine company dedicated especially to the production of mass consumer goods for the internal market. The authors studied the company's archives in order to assess its profitability and the process of capital formation. Finally, Donna Guy was able to use internal documents to analyse the evolution and business dynamics of Refinería Argentina, a sugar refining company in a peripheral market where labour problems, political instability, and periodic crises in the sugar industry eventually resulted in its collapse.[46]

[44] William J. Fleming, 'The Cultural Determinants of Entrepreneurship and Economic Development: a case study of Mendoza Province, Argentina, 1861–1914', *Journal of Economic History* 39 (1979), 211–24; Noemí Girbal de Blacha, 'Ajustes de una economía regional: inserción de la vitivinicultura cuyana en la Argentina agroexportadora, 1885–1914', *Investigaciones y Ensayos* 35 (1987), 409–42.

[45] Thomas C. Cochran and Rubén Reina, *Entrepreneurship in Argentine Culture: Torcuato di Tella and S. I. A. M.* (Philadelphia, 1962). On the archives of this firm see, Silvia Schelenkolewski-Kroll, 'Los archivos de S. I. A. M. Di Tella S. A.: primera organización de fuentes en la historia de las empresas argentinas', *Estudios Interdisciplinarios de América Latina y el Caribe* 3: 2 (1992), 105–22.

[46] Jorge Schvarzer, *Bunge & Born: crecimiento y diversificación de un grupo económico* (Buenos Aires, 1988); Juan Carlos Korol and Leandro Gutiérrez, 'Historia de empresa y crecimiento industrial en la Argentina: el caso de la Fábrica Argentina de Alpargatas', *Desarrollo Económico* 28: 111 (1988), 401–24; Donna Guy, 'Refinería Argentina, 1880–1930: límites de la tecnología azucarera en una economía periférica', *Desarrollo Económico* 28: 111 (1988), 353–71.

State companies

Until the Peronist government which came to power in 1989 commenced the process of privatising public-sector companies and limiting the government to regulatory functions only, the state had played a visible and controversial role as manager of business enterprises within the Argentine economy. This reversal of policy was implemented in response to a profound economic crisis which forced the abandonment of the interventionist paradigm. The state companies were inefficient and no longer filled a dynamic role within the national economy. Instead they seemed to have contributed to corruption, financial disaster, and the stagnation of government.[47]

Two general works successfully provided a historical account of the long history of business activities on the part of the Argentine state. In the late 1960s Marcos Kaplan, employing a sociological approach, was the first to trace in any critical sense the origins and development of the public-sector companies. A decade later, Jorge Schvarzer, an economist, examined the stages of the evolution of the state's business role in Argentina, the causes for such a development, and the contribution made by state companies to the national economy. At that time the military regime that governed Argentina until late 1983 was attempting to dismantle the public-sector companies in order to clean up government finance and return the state to its traditional subsidiary role in the economy. In this light Schvarzer questioned the ideological basis for such a policy and the distorted view of the real role of the state which seemed to be prevalent throughout the country, claiming that these companies could not be blamed for Argentina's backwardness since the state had provided a successful stimulus for economic development in other countries.[48]

Three factors influenced both the orientation and the content of the first two studies which had been published specifically on the Argentine state companies: the debate provoked by the failure of Peronist economic policy; the characteristics of the governments that succeeded the Peronist administration in the late 1950s; and the insights offered by the growing 'National Left', the characteristics of which have already been discussed.[49]

---

[47] This policy commenced with the privatisation of the state airline, Aerolíneas Argentinas, and the telephone monopoly of Entel Argentina SA. For studies of the privatisation process in Argentina, see Peter Calvert, 'Privatisation in Argentina', *Bulletin of Latin American Research* 15 (1996), 145–56; Felipe de la Balze, *Remaking the Argentine Economy* (New York, 1991); Arnaldo Bocco and Naun Minsberg (eds), *Privatizaciones, reestructuración del estado, y la sociedad* (Buenos Aires, 1991); Luis Eduardo Alonso, *Privatización del transporte y modelos sociales futuros* (Buenos Aires, 1992).

[48] Marcos Kaplan, 'El estado empresario en la Argentina', *Aportes* 10 (1968), 33–69; Jorge Schvarzer, 'Empresas públicas y desarrollo industrial en Argentina', *Economía de América Latina* 3 (1979), 45–68.

[49] See p. 24 of this chapter.

In 1958, in a revised edition of the work in which he had argued for the nationalisation of the English railways in the 1940s, Ricardo M. Ortiz recognised, from the perspective of an orthodox Marxist, the failings of state capitalism under Perón's first government. However, in an implicit attack on those who sought to deny the legitimacy of state enterprise, Ortiz stressed that only under state control could these companies serve as a tool for the transformation of the national economy.[50] At much the same time, two pioneers of the 'National Left', Juan Carlos Esteban and Luis Ernesto Tassara, analysed the evolution of the Dirección Nacional de Industrias del Estado (DINIE), an industrial complex that grouped together the German companies confiscated when Argentina declared war on the Axis powers in the final stages of the Second World War. Apart from asserting the rightful role of the state as an active participant in business, they were highly critical of the Argentine government's decision to return these companies to their owners in an attempt to secure foreign investment, improve relations with the major world powers, and facilitate Argentina's incorporation into the multilateral system of trade and payments.[51]

The 1970s produced two other important contributions to the literature on the history of state companies. In a rather polemical book Jorge Sábato examined the development of Servicios Eléctricos del Gran Buenos Aires (SEGBA), the country's principal electricity company, and he recounted his experiences as the president of its board of directors. Sábato had collaborated with the short-lived government that in 1970–71 challenged certain powerful economic groups which had sought to manipulate official decisions for their own benefit. This administration challenged the activities of transnational capital and the influence of international financial organisations on economic policy, and wished to reassert the role of the state in Argentina's economic development.[52] In this work, therefore, Sábato criticised the agreements signed with the World Bank for the re-equipment of SEGBA, vindicated the role of public companies, and attempted to explain a situation which, in his opinion, had to be changed for the benefit of the country. Ricardo Lesser and Marta Panaia, meanwhile, collaborated

[50] Ricardo M. Ortíz, *El ferrocarril en la economía argentina* (2nd edition, Buenos Aires, 1958). For a similar vindication of the role of the state as entrepreneur, see Aldo Ferrer, *El estado y el desarrollo económico* (Buenos Aires, 1956). Ferrer was an economist closely connected with the Unión Cívica Radical and Arturo Frondizi, the president of Argentina from 1958 to 1962.

[51] Juan Carlos Esteban and Luis Ernesto Tassara, *Valor industrial y enajenación de DINIE* (Buenos Aires, 1958). The decision to incorporate Argentina into the multilateral system of trade and payments was linked to the solution of land-standing conflicts with foreign companies. The aim was to make the country attractive again for foreign investors and solve some serious trade and balance of payments problems. See Raúl García Heras, 'La Argentina y el Club de París: comercio y pagos multilaterales con la Europa Occidental, 1955–1958', *El Trimestre Económico* 63 (1996), 1277–1308.

[52] For an analysis of the nationalist outlook of these policies, see William C. Smith, *Authoritarianism and the Crisis of the Argentine Political Economy* (Stanford, 1991), pp. 165–79.

with Skupch in the study, cited earlier in relation to research on the foreign-owned railways, of the circumstances under which Peronism had emerged. Their contribution contained an analysis of the role played by the military during Argentina's industrialisation in the 1930s and 1940s. Amongst other subjects they concentrated on the origin of Fabricaciones Militares and the role of well-known military industrialists such as General Manuel Savio.[53]

During the 1980s the literature on Argentine public companies was more productive. Solberg, whose earlier work was noted above, provided two impressive and useful studies on YPF, the state petroleum company. In the first of these he examined the career, aggressive management strategy, and influence throughout Latin America of another renowned military industrialist who was the first general manager of the business, General Enrique Mosconi. A few years later a posthumous study by Solberg traced the evolution of YPF during its early years.[54]

After the end of 1983 and the restoration of democracy in Argentina a new generation of Argentine historians published their research on other state companies in a popular series published by the Centro Editor de América Latina. Those which deserve a special mention are the works by Susana Novick, María Angueira and Alicia Tonini. Novick examined the Instituto Argentino de Promoción del Intercambio (IAPI), the controversial official body through which the Peronists monopolised foreign trade between 1946 and 1955 in order to finance their policy of a redistribution of national income and the growth of light industry. Her study, based on the limited documentation available, highlights the ambiguities and the contradictions which, in her opinion, prevented Perón from being able successfully to 'nationalise the economy and free it from the control of the international financial institutions'. For their part, Angueira and Tonini studied two state complexes located in the province of Córdoba, the Fábrica Militar de Aviones (military aircraft factory) established in 1927, and Industrias Aeronáuticas y Mecánicas del Estado, founded in 1952.[55]

In the early 1990s two further significant works on Argentine public

[53] Jorge Sábato, SEGBA: cogestión y Banco Mundial (Buenos Aires, 1971); Marta Panaia and Ricardo Lesser, 'Las estrategias militares frente al proceso de industrialización, 1943–1947', in Panaia et al., Estudios sobre los orígenes, II, 83–164. Fabricaciones Militares was a military industrial complex created in February 1941 to advance Argentina's industrialisation in general and to produce weapons and military supplies for the Armed Forces. Its creation reflected growing concern locally, especially amongst the military, about the shortcomings of national development and the widespread shortages due to the Second World War.

[54] Carl Solberg, 'Entrepreneurship in Public Enterprise: General Enrique Mosconi and the Argentine petroleum industry', Business History Review 56 (1982), 380–99, and 'YPF: the formative years of Latin America's pioneer state oil company, 1922–1939', in John Wirth (ed.), Latin American Oil Companies and the Politics of Energy (Lincoln, 1985), pp. 51–102.

[55] Susana Novick, IAPI: auge y decadencia (Buenos Aires, 1986); María del C. Angueira and Alicia del C. Tonimi, Capitalismo del estado, 1927–1956 (Buenos Aires, 1986); see also Orietta Favaro and Marta B. Morinelli, Petróleo, estado, y nación (Buenos Aires, 1991).

companies were published. Both analyse, with different methodologies and results, the Corporación de Transportes, which monopolised public transport in Buenos Aires from the late 1930s until the early 1960s. Marta Páramo's study epitomises the classic scholarly works which characterised the output of Argentine universities, the Consejo Nacional de Investigaciones Científicas y Técnicas (CONICET), and the Academia Nacional de Historia before the fall of the military government in 1983, after which the promotion of economic and social history became more popular. In contrast, García Heras studied the same company using a more sophisticated approach and a wider range of primary and secondary sources in both Argentina and Great Britain.[56]

Interest groups

The first two important studies of business interest groups in Argentina were published in the late 1960s. Oscar Cornblit, a researcher in the Instituto Di Tella in Buenos Aires, and Dardo Cúneo, a former militant socialist and then a government official during Arturo Frondizi's 'developmentalist' administration of 1958–62, were the respective authors. Cornblit examined the absence of any proposals favouring industry amongst nearly all the political parties, and hence the lack of any real industrial protection, in Argentina before 1930. He argued that this was due to the Argentine industrialists' lack of political representation, especially since nearly all were immigrants, as well as the characteristics of the major political parties. Dardo Cúneo systematically examined the behaviour of landowners and industrialists, as channelled through the associations that represented them, up to the early 1960s. He concluded that both sectors had lacked sufficient vision to enable the country to overcome its backwardness and stagnation.[57]

The subtle personal political motivations behind Cúneo's rigorous research made his work even more significant. In fact, although he never stated it explicitly, Cúneo's criticisms of businessmen were not inconsistent with the complex causes behind the failure and subsequent discrediting of 'developmentalism' in Argentina, especially because of the lack of support which the industrialists had expressed in practice for the policies of the Frondizi government. His work thus reflected the spirit of self-criticism and personal frustration prevalent amongst its supporters and former officials.[58]

[56] Marta Susana Páramo, *Un fracaso hecho historia: la Corporación de Transportes de la Ciudad de Buenos Aires* (Mendoza, 1991); Raúl García Heras, 'State Intervention in Urban Passenger Transportation: the Transport Corporation of Buenos Aires, Argentina, 1939–1962', *Hispanic American Historical Review* 74 (1994), 83–110.

[57] Oscar Cornblit, 'Inmigrantes y empresarios en la política argentina', *Desarrollo Económico* 6:24 (1967), 641–91; Dardo Cúneo, *Comportamiento y crisis de la clase empresaria* (Buenos Aires, 1967).

[58] On the failure of 'developmentalism' in Argentina, see Kathryn Sikkink, *Ideas and Institutions: developmentalism in Brazil and Argentina* (Ithaca, 1991), and 'Las capacidades y

In the 1970s three studies of Argentine industrialists were published. John Freels examined both the role played by industrial associations in Argentine politics and the individual attitudes of their members, basing his research on surveys of public opinion. In a detailed study Jorge Niosi examined the relationship between chambers of business and governments in the period between 1955 and 1969, looking at the participation of members of their management committees in official posts. Finally, in the late 1970s Javier Lindenboim carried out research into the extent of heterogeneity amongst industrialists between the Depression and the immediate post-war period. This was in an attempt to identify the origins of the Confederación General Económica (CGE), a body founded in 1953 which incorporated sectors of the small-scale industrial entrepreneurs who were located mainly in the interior of the country and who aligned themselves with Peronism.[59]

In the 1980s several studies returned to the analysis of the relationship between foreign industrialists and both government and business organisations in Argentina. After examining the role of foreign businessmen in manufacturing and their influence on tariff policy between 1922 and 1928, Lewis modified the emphatic conclusions which Cornblit had reached concerning the industrialists' lack of influence over Argentine economic policy. Barbero and Felder analysed the contribution and role of Italian industrialists in the main business association in the manufacturing sector, the Unión Industrial Argentina, before 1930.[60] Argentina's return to democracy late in 1983 then opened up new directions for the historiography of the country's business groups, both in Argentina and abroad. A research team commissioned by the Fundación Banco Patricios studied the new economic power structure which had emerged from the controversial neo-liberal economic policies that the military government had followed between 1976 and 1983.[61] A North American political scientist, Luigi Manzetti, described the political behaviour, ideology and role of the principal rural interest groups in the democratic transition, using the 'rational choice' paradigm which emphasised the rational and selfish attitude of the

autonomía del estado en Brasil y la Argentina: un enfoque neoinstitucionalista', *Desarrollo Económico* 32: 128 (1993), 543–75; Celia Szusterman, *Frondizi and the Politics of Developmentalism in Argentina, 1958–1962* (London, 1993).

[59] John William Freels, *El sector industrial en la política nacional* (Buenos Aires, 1970); Jorge Niosi, *Los empresarios y el estado argentino, 1955–1969* (Buenos Aires, 1974); Javier Lindenboim, 'El empresariado industrial argentino y sus organismos gremiales entre 1930 y 1946', *Desarrollo Económico* 16: 62 (1976), 163–201.

[60] Colin M. Lewis, 'Immigrant Entrepreneurs, Manufacturing, and Industrial Policy in the Argentine, 1922–1928', *Journal of Imperial and Commonwealth History* 16: 1 (1987), 77–108; María Inés Barbero y Susane Felder, 'Industriales italianos y asociaciones empresariales en la Argentina: el caso de UIA, 1887–1930', *Estudios Migratorios Latinoamericanos* 6–7 (1987), 163–77.

[61] Daniel Azpiazu, Miguel Khavisse, and Eduardo M. Basualdo, *El nuevo poder económico* (Buenos Aires, 1986).

individual, and Mancur Olson's theory of collective action.[62] His methodology was consistent with his personal interest in examining such processes using theoretical constructs which were applicable to human behaviour regardless of a country's specific conditions. At the same time, staff at the Centro de Investigaciones sobre la Sociedad, el Estado, y la Administración (CISEA), with the support of the Ford Foundation, commenced a study of business associations and their role in contemporary Argentine society.[63]

These research projects had two main concerns, influenced by the turbulent political changes of the previous decades. First, what was the nature of Argentine business interest groups, and how had they operated before 1983? Second, what should their relationship with the new democratic system be, and what effect would their attitudes have on its consolidation during the critical period of national reconstruction? Although neither used more than a limited number of primary sources, both Mirta Palomino and Jorge Schvarzer produced solid analyses of the composition, leadership, ideology, and behaviour of the main representatives of the landowning and industrial interests. Schvarzer highlighted the political and social presence of the Unión Industrial Argentina, and its lack of any real commitment to industrial development. In her study of the Sociedad Rural Argentina Palomino debated the conclusions reached in the classic sociological studies of the 1960s on the Argentine elite by Niosi and Imaz.[64]

The tense relations between the constitutional government of Raúl Alfonsín (1983–89) and powerful business groups, whose conduct has been blamed for the failure of his economic policy and the controversial end of his mandate in July 1989, six months early, have had a major influence on the thematic content of the most recent contributions to the historiography of business groups in Argentina.[65] A Canadian academic, Pierre Ostiguy, examined the origin, internal alignments, economic interests, and links with the state of a group of big businessmen known as the *capitanes de la industria* during the 1980s. A year later two well-known Argentine researchers from the Centro Latinoamericano para el Análisis de la Democracia (CELADE), José Nun and Mario Lattuada examined the frustrated attempts of the Alfonsín administration to reform agriculture and its

[62] Luigi Manzetti, 'The Evolution of Agricultural Interest Groups in Argentina', *Journal of Latin American Studies* 24 (1992), 585–616.

[63] Several conspicuous members of CISEA exerted major political influence during the Alfonsín administration (1983–1989).

[64] José Luis de Imaz, *Los que mandan* (Buenos Aires, 1964); Mirta L. de Palomino, *Tradición y poder: la Sociedad Rural Argentina, 1955–1983* (Buenos Aires, 1988); Jorge Schvarzer, *Empresarios del pasado: la Unión Industrial Argentina* (Buenos Aires, 1991). See also Schvarzer's *La industria que supimos conseguir* (Buenos Aires, 1996).

[65] The output of journalists in the early 1990s highlighted this interpretation of the failure of the Alfonsín government. For some distinguished examples, see Luis Majul, *¿Porqué cayó Alfonsín? El nuevo terrorismo económico* (Buenos Aires, 1990); Joaquín Morales Solá, *Asalto a la ilusión: historia secreta del poder en la Argentina desde 1983* (Buenos Aires, 1991).

eventual confrontation with the principal interest groups which represented the sector. The main thrust of their research concentrated on two main questions: the reasons for the failure of the Alfonsín government's agricultural policy, and the implications of this for an understanding of the obstacles which had prevented any constitutional government in the previous fifty years being able to implement the thorough agrarian reforms that they had promised.[66]

Conclusion

The historiography of business in Argentina has, for various reasons, advanced at a very slow and variable rate. Consequently, there remains a lengthy agenda for study, and the field is a long way from the levels of thematic and methodological sophistication achieved in the developed world and certain other Latin American countries.

One of the main reasons for this present predicament has been the evolution of the Asociación Argentina de Historia Económica, founded as recently as 1981. Indeed, one could even argue that business history as a specialised subject area did not emerge until the association's thirteenth annual conference in 1992, when the first special panel, coordinated by María Inés Barbero, took place. This experiment was repeated, with greater success, at the fifteenth annual conference in 1994.[67]

The lack of attractive and prestigious publication outlets has also contributed to the relative backwardness of the literature on business history in Argentina. For several decades *Desarrollo Económico*, published by the Instituto de Desarrollo Económico y Social, was the only recognised academic journal in the country that dealt with new themes. The possibilities for publication were broadened when, in 1983, the University of Tandil began to publish the *Anuario del Instituto de Estudios Históricos*, and the University of Buenos Aires resumed publication of the *Boletín del Instituto Emilio Ravignani* and a new journal, *Ciclos en la Historia, la Economía y la Sociedad* was also launched.[68]

[66] Pierre Ostiguy, *Los capitanes de la industria: grandes empresarios, política y economía en la Argentina de los años 80* (Buenos Aires, 1990); José Nun and Mario Lattuada, *El gobierno de Alfonsín y las corporaciones agrarias* (Buenos Aires, 1991). For two later studies which emphasised how the political and economic power of business organisations thwarted the plans of the Alfonsín government, see Marcelo Luis Acuña, *Alfonsín y el poder económico: el fracaso de la concertación y los pactos corporativos entre 1983 y 1989* (Buenos Aires, 1995), and Carlos H. Acuña, 'Business Interests, Dictatorship and Democracy in Argentina', in Leigh A. Payne (ed.), *Business and Democracy in Latin America* (Pittsburgh, 1995), pp. 3–48.

[67] In this panel María Inés Barbero presented the first review of Agentine business history, subsequently published as 'Treinta años de estudios sobre la historia de empresas en Argentina', *Ciclos* 5: 8 (1995), 179–200.

[68] Hopefully, with the creation of the Centro de Estudios Económicos de la Empresa y el Desarrollo, to be directed by Jorge Schvarzer, the School of Economics of the University of Buenos Aires will take the lead in the institutionalisation of business history in Argentina.

The advance of business history has, to a large degree, also depended on the contribution made by Anglo-Saxon academics, some of whom have had only a fleeting interest in the country's history. As a consequence, a marked contrast exists in two principal publishing markets, England and the United States, between the growth in the literature on the economic and social history of foreign companies in Brazil, Chile, Guatemala, and Mexico, and the relative shortage of monographs on Argentina.[69] Similarly, the business activities of the Argentine state have not resulted in the publication of works to compare with those on Venezuela, Mexico, and Brazil in the 1980s.[70] There is also no English-language literature on Argentina comparable to that published during the 1980s on traders and local industrialists and their relationship with the political elite, the state, and foreign capital in Mexico.[71]

What have been the most notable advances and problems in Argentine business history? Without a doubt, although the literature possesses certain characteristics which require more discussion, the historiography of foreign companies has been the focus of the largest number of studies. They have been concerned primarily with British capital and companies, in particular the railways and other transport firms, since these were the activities in which British investment in Argentina was concentrated. Moreover, the evolution of many foreign companies has only ever been examined or mentioned within the framework of Argentina's relations with Great Britain, the United States or Germany. The ideological conflict evident within the literature has also contributed more to the clarification of the relationship between writers, intellectuals and politics than to the history of the companies being studied. Finally, this historiography is the section

---

[69] The relative lack of literature specifically on Argentina contrasts with the publication of major works such as Paul B. Dosal, *Doing Business with the Dictators: a political history of United Fruit in Guatamala, 1899–1944* (New York, 1993); Jonathan Brown, *Oil and Revolution in Mexico* (Berkeley, 1992); Harold Blakemore, *From the Pacific to La Paz: the Antofagasta (Chili) and Bolivia Railway Company, 1888–1988* (London, 1990); Marshall T. Eakin, *British Enterprise in Brazil: the St John d'El Rey Mining Company and the Morro Velho Gold Mine, 1830–1960* (Durham, 1989); Duncan McDowell, *The Light: Brazilian Traction, Light and Power Company Limited, 1899–1945* (Toronto, 1988); Allen Wells, *Yucatán's Gilded Age: haciendas, henequen, and International Harvester, 1860–1915* (Albuquerque, 1985); and W. M. Mathew, *The House of Gibbs and the Peruvian Guano Monopoly* (London, 1981).

[70] See Gene Bigler, *Economía política y capitalismo del estado en Venezuela* (Madrid, 1981); Thomas J. Trebat, *Brazil's State-Owned Enterprises: a case study of the state as entrepreneur* (Cambridge, 1983); Laura Randall, *The Political Economy of Mexican Oil* (New York, 1989), and *The Political Economy of Venezuelan Oil* (New York, 1987).

[71] See, for example, Mark Wasserman, *Capitalists, Caciques, and Revolution: the native elite and foreign enterprise in Chihuahua, Mexico, 1854–1911* (Chapel Hill, 1984); David W. Walker, *Kinship, Business, and Politics: the Martínez del Río family in Mexico, 1823–1867* (Austin, 1987); Alex M. Saragoza, *The Monterrey Elite and the Mexican State, 1880–1940* (Austin, 1988); and Jackie R. Booker, *Veracruz Merchants, 1770–1829: a mercantile elite in late Bourbon and early independent Mexico* (Boulder, 1992).

which has depended most on contributions from foreign academics, principally those from Britain and North America.

The historiography of local business and businessmen, and their interest group associations, is even less developed. For example, there are very few regional studies specifically on sugar, the wine industry, or the *yerba maté* producers.[72] This is due to the shortage of foreign academics who have been willing to follow the route pioneered by Fleming and Guy, and the fact that what will eventually become sound and extremely competent research teams in the country's interior are still in their formative stages. What is perhaps even more surprising is that with the exception of the works discussed earlier and Samuel Amaral's recent book there are also very few specific studies on livestock producers and their main representative association, the Sociedad Rural, which might offer a microeconomic contribution to the present debate over the dynamics of the controversial agro-export model between 1880 and 1930.[73]

Furthermore, as noted already, even though public enterprise played a major role in the Argentine economy until very recently, here too the historiography is also very sparse, for at least three reasons. First, although they made a significant academic contribution, the studies carried out by nationalists, Marxists or members of the Izquierda Nacional, all of whom took the initiative in this field, became trapped in an almost permanent debate over defining key aspects of national economic policy like the role of the state, policies towards foreign investment, and the opening up of the economy. At the same time, secondly, unlike the case of the British-owned railways, there was insufficient academic research that might have reappraised the affirmations of these authors and marked out new directions for the literature to take. Third, in addition to this, the public sector in Argentina never had the type of archival tradition prevalent in the United States, Western Europe or Mexico, and this also discouraged studies of public companies. In order for this situation to be reversed it is essential that the efforts made by officials in the Archivo General de la Nación and the Fundación Antorchas in Buenos Aires to preserve and classify the archives of the recently privatised state companies should come to fruition.[74]

All of this, therefore, gives some indication of the enormous tasks still pending to develop the historiography of business in Argentina. The final paragraphs of this essay outline some suggestions for future research and provide a brief note on some easily accessible sources for researchers who may be interested.

The history of foreign companies in Argentina is noteworthy for the

[72] *Yerba maté* is an indigenous tea widely consumed in the River Plate region.

[73] See pp. 29 and 37; Samuel Amaral, *The Rise of Capitalism on the Pampas: the estancias of Buenos Aires, 1785–1870* (Cambridge, 1998).

[74] For the characteristics of some of these archives and the efforts of the Archivo General de la Nación and the Fundación Antorchas to rescue them, see *La Nación* (Buenos Aires), 19, 20, and 21 July 1993.

shortage of case studies on the petroleum, meat-packing, and public utility companies. There is a need for literature that could fill this academic abyss and thereby deepen understanding of Argentina's economic relations with the world's leading powers. Similarly, whilst keeping away from the political controversies in which some of the earlier historiography became entangled, such research could serve as a timely reminder of the controversial role which foreign companies played in Argentina's history. A good starting point for future researchers in this field might be the history of Liebig's Extract of Meat Company whose extensive archives, scarcely used as yet, are held by Unilever at Port Sunlight, near Liverpool. Then there is the history of the Bank of London and South America, whose archives may also be consulted, albeit with certain restrictions, in the library of University College and, in the case of the recent records, at the headquarters of Lloyds Bank in the City of London.

With regard to Argentine companies and businessmen and their interest group associations, there is an urgent need for three types of research. The first should be a detailed study of the Confederación General Económica (CGE), the body which represented many industrialists, building upon James Brennan's pioneering work.[75] The history of the Sociedad Rural Argentina, the main association of livestock producers, is a subject that also requires scholarly scrutiny, especially from its founding in the mid-nineteenth century to the period following the Second World War. To facilitate such inquiries researchers might take advantage of the CGE's archives, and the excellent library and collection of secondary sources and periodical publications which the Sociedad Rural possesses at its head-quarters in Buenos Aires. Another academic priority might be research on major family companies such as the Terrabusi, a foodstuffs company established in the early 1930s and recently taken over by Nabisco Holding Inc., a North American transnational.[76] The biographies of businessmen like Miguel Miranda, José Ber Gelbard, and Rogelio Frigerio, who along with their industrial activities, participated actively in the business associations and the political affairs of their time would also be important studies of figures about whom current knowledge is fragmentary.[77]

---

[75] See p. 36 of this chapter; James P. Brennan, 'Industrialists and *Bolicheros*: business and the Peronist populist alliance, 1943–1976', in James P. Brennan (ed.), *Peronism and Argentina: essays in interpretation* (Wilmington, 1997).

[76] See *Clarín*, 15 April 1994.

[77] Miranda devoted himself to the food-canning and preserves industry. As president both of the Banco Central and the Consejo Económico y Social he was in charge of the early economic policies of the Peronist administration during the second half of the 1940s. Gelbard, an industrialist from the North West of Argentina, was the first President of the Confederación General Económica and then Minister for the Economy in the Peronist administration of 1973–74. Frigerio, an entrepreneur in textiles, mining, and farming, was a controversial official and ideologue of Argentine *desarrollismo* at the end of the 1950s. On Gelbard, see a rather sensationalist book, María Seoane, *El burgués maldito: la historia secreta de José Ber Gelbard* (Buenos Aires, 1998).

As noted earlier, the state will not play an important role in the Argentine economy for the foreseeable future. However, prominent public companies like YPF, the military armaments firms, and public utility companies stand out as once significant bastions of the Argentine state enterprise which remain neglected by historians.[78] This has occurred at a time when, for various reasons, this subject remains a highly pertinent issue. All the available literature on Argentine economic policies lacks a balanced historical view of these public corporations. Moreover, only a thorough understanding of the past experiences of state companies in Argentina could help the debate over such companies to transcend theory, prejudice and unjustified triumphalism, and thus create an effective role, with concrete objectives, for the state to play in the future.

---

[78] For a pioneering piece on one of the most important of the state development banks, see Marcelo Rougier, 'El financiamiento bancario a las empresas industriales: antecedentes y orígenes del Banco de Crédito Industrial de la Argentina', *Estudios Interdisciplinarios de América Latina y del Caribe*, forthcoming.

CHAPTER THREE

Business History in Brazil
from the mid-nineteenth century to 1945

Colin M. Lewis

The bibliography on Brazilian business history is limited but growing rapidly.[1] In part this is due to the novelty of the subject, which is only now emerging as a distinct discipline or, more accurately, being consolidated as a clearly identifiable branch of economic history in the country. This process is not peculiar to the literature on Brazil. The same phenomenon can be observed elsewhere in the Latin American historiography and in writing about Asia, regions of Africa, and central and southern Europe. As in the case of Colombia, Chile and, possibly, Mexico, the study of Brazilian business history has been enriched by the quality of new research into economic history at national and regional level. Nevertheless, in all of these countries, economic history itself remains a young discipline (or a recently revived subject).

Economic history and business history: schooling the Brazilian literature

Writing on business history is indebted to various intellectual traditions which may be traced directly to distinct approaches in the general social science literature.[2] Analyses of the history of the society and economy of Brazil before the Second World War reflect larger controversies about the nature of contemporary Latin American development which in turn provoked a reappraisal of the recent and the not-so-recent past. Three major schools may be identified. Many texts written during and after the 1950s and 1960s were shaped successively by structuralist and dependency

---

[1] This chapter has benefited from suggestions made by Sergio de Oliveira Birchal, Carlos Dávila, José Gabriel Porcile Meirelles, and Terry Gourvish, as well as from comments made at seminars at the Universidad de los Andes, Bogotá, the Universidade de São Paulo, and the London School of Economics and Political Science. These contributions are gratefully acknowledged.

[2] Terry Gourvish, 'Business History: in defence of the empirical approach?', *Accounting, Business and Financial History* 5 (1995), 3–16; Charles Harvey and Geoffrey Jones, 'Business History in Britain in the 1990s', *Business History* 32:1 (1990), 5–16.

perspectives, while in the last decade or so a recognisable revisionist current, based on new empirical research, has begun to emerge.

As is widely appreciated, structuralist theory took shape under the auspices of ECLA or CEPAL.[3] *Cepalino* analyses were both descriptive and prescriptive and, at the same time, historical and predictive. In the period immediately after the Second World War developmentalists, in their concern to explain and remedy Latin America's perceived sluggish industrial growth, drew upon the ideas of Keynes and economic nationalists to challenge liberal economic orthodoxy, particularly in the areas of trade theory and the functions of the state. Focusing on internal bottlenecks and structural disjunctures in the world economy, *cepalinos* stressed the historic limits, and likely future costs, of export-led growth. They observed that the gains to Latin American countries from economic specialisation and participation in a relatively open world trading system were not as great as predicted by conventional liberal theory, given differing income elasticities of demand for primary and secondary products, the cumulative consequences of cyclical instability in the international system, and imperfect factor markets in the industrialised economies. In sum, these effects resulted in the concentration of productivity gains occasioned by technical innovation in the so-called central, industrialised economies and deteriorating terms of trade for peripheral, primary producing economies.

The analytical and policy content of *cepalismo*, and the criticisms which it attracted, have been well rehearsed elsewhere and are beyond the scope of this chapter.[4] However, two aspects of the debate are of relevance for any discussion of Brazilian business history. These were the general assumptions about Latin American entrepreneurial talent that permeated much of the initial research and reports of the Commission, and the early application of *cepalino* tenets to writing on Brazil. Underpinning both the theoretical discussion and the policy prescription that emanated from Santiago during the formative years of ECLA was the assumption that the

[3] ECLA has now become ECLAC, the Economic Commission for Latin America and the Caribbean.

[4] For a brief review of *cepalismo* and the criticisms that it provoked, see Christoper Abel and Colin M. Lewis (eds), *Latin America: Economic Imperialism and the State* (London, 1991) pp. 3–5, 11–14, 398–400; Cristóbal Kay, *Latin American Theories of Development and Underdevelopment* (London, 1989). Authentic statements and restatements of Latin American developmentalism can, of course, be found in the extensive writing of Raúl Prebisch of which the following is but a small sample: *The Economic Development of Latin America* (New York 1950); *Change and Development: Latin America's great task* (New York 1970); 'A Critique of Peripheral Capitalism', *CEPAL Review* 1 (1976), 9–76; 'A Historic Turning Point for the Latin American Periphery', *CEPAL Review* 18 (1982), 7–24. See also Joseph L. Love, 'Raúl Prebisch and the Origins of the Doctrine of Unequal Exchange', *Latin American Research Review* 15: 3 (1980), 45–72; Virgil Salera, 'Prebisch on "Exchange and Development: Latin America's great task"', *Inter-American Economic Affairs* 24:4 (1971), 67–80; and John Sproas, 'The Statistical Debate on the Net Barter Terms of Trade between Primary Commodities and Manufactures', *Economic Journal* 90 (1980), 107–28.

continent possessed a fund of entrepreneurship. Specifically with regard to the manufacturing sector and particularly both the larger and the medium sized economies, it was argued that there was a national industrial entrepreneurial class lurking in the wings, waiting to seize the initiative. At a given conjuncture such as acute instability in the international trading and financial system, it only required benevolent state action to liberate this initiative from the constraint of unfair foreign competition in order to foster endogenous development driven by rapid industrialisation and headed by national capital. The events first of the First World War and then the 1930s and 1940s appeared to provide some support for this view as the number of 'manufacturing' firms (and occasionally industrial capacity) had grown in such periods. Towards the latter part of the First World War, and again during the second half of the 1930s, there had also been an appreciable increase in intra-regional trade, partly in manufactures.[5]

Of even more direct concern, scholars working on Brazil were amongst the first to pioneer the historical application of developmentalism. The writing of Celso Furtado has made a signal contribution both to the study of the economic history of Brazil and to the *cepalino* school of analysis. Furtado has written extensively on Latin American and Brazilian economics and history and on the political economy of development. Although much of his early work has been refined and revised, his principal texts remain essential reading.[6] In his work on Brazil, Furtado referred to the cyclical pattern of Brazilian growth based upon a succession of export staples. Until coffee emerged as the predominant commodity during the second half of the nineteenth century, there was little to show on the positive side of the balance sheet after several centuries of export activity. Up to this point Furtado found little evidence that a national market was developing. On the contrary, subsistence predominated, and Brazil remained an archipelago of loosely linked export enclaves. Monopoly rent seeking and resource exploitation rather than profit maximisation and productivity-enhancing investment characterised mono-export booms that were often short-lived. Resources were overwhelmingly concentrated in the dominant export activity of the moment, and factor immobility hastened economic

[5] Carlos F. Díaz Alejandro, 'Latin America in the 1930s', in Rosemary Thorp (ed.) *Latin America in the 1930s: the role of the periphery in world crisis* (London, 1984), pp. 17–49; Colin M. Lewis, 'Industry in Latin America before 1930', in Leslie Bethell (ed.) *Cambridge History of Latin America* (Cambridge, 1986), IV, 267–323; Wilson Suzigan, *Industrialização brasileira: origem e desenvolvimento* (São Paulo, 1986).

[6] Celso Furtado first elaborated his thoughts on the nature of Brazilian economic expansion in *A economia brasileira: uma contribução a analise do seu desenvolvimento* (Rio de Janeiro, 1954). A more specifically historical dimension appeared in his later study *Formação econômica do Brasil* (Rio de Janeiro, 1961) subsequently translated into English as *The Economic Growth of Brazil: a survey from colonial to modern times* (Berkeley, 1963). See also his *Economic Development of Latin America: historical background and contemporary problems* (Cambridge, 1970) for a succinct continental statement of the *cepalino* approach.

contraction whenever resource depletion or changes in world market conditions undermined the buoyancy of export production.

Not until the emergence of coffee was there a sustained endogenous multiplier effect, and by then earlier mono-product booms had fostered anti-progressive, seigneurial attitudes amongst the oligarchy and led to the consolidation of a conservative, patrimonial state. Only with great difficulty were these negative traits eroded by new social and economic configurations associated with coffee production, especially in the province of São Paulo after the 1860s. For Furtado, coffee production on the *paulista planalto* was critical for development, in terms of demand expansion, factor supply, and market integration, although he expressed some doubts about the consequences of the coffee policy foisted upon government by planters during the early decades of the twentieth century.[7] Did continuing official support for coffee (often involving deficit funding) induce an over-commitment to the commodity, or serve proto-Keynesian functions? There is now an extensive literature devoted to coffee and development. Much of this literature is of interest to business historians, and the principal texts will be considered in subsequent sections of this essay.

By the later 1960s perceived flaws in the ECLA development model provoked radical criticism of both *cepalino* development policy and the school of historical analysis associated with it. The distorted nature of Latin American industrialisation, particularly the failure to promote domestic capital goods production and the dominant position of foreign corporations as well as stagflation, balance of payments problems and continuing social inequity, were seized upon by opponents of the Commission. After approximately two decades of discussion, policy innovation, and the dissemination of developmentalist propaganda, what had been accomplished? Others have attempted elsewhere to establish the ideological provenance of dependency analysis or the intellectual connection between *dependencia* and *cepalismo*.[8] For this purpose, the content of the dependency

---

[7] Wilson Suzigan provides a concise account of this and other aspects of the debate about industrialisation: see *Indústria brasileira: origem e desenvolvimento* (São Paulo, 1986) pp. 21–44, especially pp. 25–28. See also Carlos M. Peláez, *História da industrialização brasileira* (Rio de Janeiro, 1972); Wilson Cano, *Raizes da concentração industrial em São Paulo* (São Paulo, 1977) pp. 202–24; S. Siber 'Análise da política econômica e do comportamento da economia brasileira, 1929–39', in Flavio Versiani and João R. M. de Barros, *Formação econômica do Brasil: a experiência da industrialização* (São Paulo, 1977). For a discussion of coffee policy and industrialisation see, in addition, Carlos M. Peláez, 'Analise econômica do programa brasileira de sustentação de café, 1906–45', *Revista brasileira de economia* 25:4 (1971), 5–211; Thomas H. Holloway, *The Brazilian Coffee Valorization of 1906: regional politics and economic dependence* (Madison, 1975); Antonio Delfim Netto, *O problema do café no Brasil* (São Paulo, 1959).

[8] Abel and Lewis, *Economic Imperialism*, pp. 10–20, offer an account of the origins and evolution of the dependency debate and the nature of the links between *cepalino* and dependency thought. See also Love, 'Raúl Prebisch and the Origins'; Kay, *Latin American Theories*, pp. 125–96; Lídia Goldenstein, *Repensamos a dependência* (São Paulo, 1994). A review

debate, its focus on the social as well as the economic, and the central contributions made by authors writing on Brazil is the point at issue. The origins of the modern debate about dependency can be dated to the appearance of the seminal works published by André Gunder Frank and Fernando Henrique Cardoso and Enzo Faletto.[9] These texts addressed the problem of Latin American development over the long term and both devoted substantial attention to Brazil.

Frank's analysis, which some critics viewed as over-general and ahistorical, drew upon Marx to explain the underdevelopment of Latin America in terms that in fact proved paradoxical for many traditional marxists. Concentrating upon exchange rather than production, Frank argued that Brazilian development had been frustrated by an early (external) form of capitalist penetration which had sustained pre-modern, anti-developmental social structures with the result that progressive capitalism had been frustrated. These anti-progressive forces inhibited local capital accumulation in Brazil, constrained the growth of the market, and prevented the industrial bourgeoisie and proletariat from performing their historic role. Combining an analysis of the internal and the external dimensions of the problem, though devoting less attention to Brazil than Frank, Cardoso and Faletto offered a more dynamic, differentiated account of Latin American development which derived in part from Cardoso's earlier work on social elites.[10] This text delivers to students of business history a convincing periodisation of the pattern and process of Brazilian development. Although Cardoso had earlier been rather pessimistic about the entrepreneurial capacity of the national bourgeoisie, he now stressed the ability of the nineteenth-century *paulista* elite to retain control of economic resources, and the willingness of planters to divert coffee profits into other sectors, principally social overhead projects and manufacturing. This process was partly explained by the nature of coffee production and the place of Brazil in world commodity markets. The outcome, however, was a pragmatic approach to investment and the inculcation of the ethos of profit maximisation in place of a narrow concentration upon agricultural enterprise and risk aversion said to characterise rural oligarchies elsewhere in Brazil and Latin America.

of the principal 'failures' of ECLA industrial strategy is provided in Colin M. Lewis, 'Industry in Latin America', in Walther L. Bernecker and Hans W. Tobler (eds), *Development and Underdevelopment in America: contrasts of economic growth in North and Latin America in historical perspective* (New York, 1993), pp. 264–302.

[9] André Gunder Frank, *Capitalism and Underdevelopment in Latin America: historical studies of Chile and Brazil* (New York, 1967); Fernando H. Cardoso and Enzo Faletto, *Dependencia y desarrollo en América Latina* (Mexico, 1968). The English translation was not published for ten years, but was much extended: *Dependency and Development in Latin America* (London, 1979)

[10] Fernando H. Cardoso, *Capitalismo e escravidão no Brasil meridional* (São Paulo, 1962); see also his later work, *Ideologias de la burgesía industrial en sociedades dependientes (Argentina y Brasil)* (Mexico, 1971)

Several authors contributing to marxist and nationalist strands of the dependency debate, especially those writing about 'dependent development', provide detail and interpretative comment about official policy, markets, social actors, commercial organisations, and institutional formation which is of direct relevance to any survey of Brazilian business history. The work of Hélio Jaguaribe, Theotonio dos Santos, Octavio Ianni, Nelson Werneck Sodré, and Peter Evans is among the most informative and noteworthy for its historical content.[11] Much of this scholarship, like that of the *cepalino* school, directly addresses issues of industrial expansion and absorbed earlier work on the subject.[12]

Enriched by the mutual antagonism of much dependency and structuralist scholarship, the last decade or so has witnessed the emergence of innovative accounts of the period preceding the Second World War. A significant part of this new research has emanated from economic and social historians associated with the University of Campinas who have contributed the 'late capitalism' (or, rather, 'very late' capitalism) approach to industrial development. Amongst the main exponents of what may properly be described as the 'Campinas School' are Wilson Suzigan, João M. Cardoso de Mello, and Wilson Cano.[13] Although much of this literature is consciously concerned only with the narrow theme of industrialisation and devotes a great deal of attention to policy issues, it has a larger impact. For example, while Suzigan is primarily interested in constructing a proxy for industrial investment from capital goods imports, his monograph is of relevance to business historians as it provides pen pictures of several firms. These point to changes in the pattern of corporate organisation and finance, and chart the origins of entrepreneurship. Cano also supplies biographical information on individual entrepreneurs as well as individual companies. Cardoso de Mello develops Gerschenkron's ideas about institutional substitutability in late industrialising economies and the opportunities or constraints which derive from the international setting. All these studies provide hard evidence for scholars seeking to apply Chandlerian, Weberian

[11] Helio Jaguaribe, *Desenvolvimento econômico e desenvolvimento político* (Rio de Janeiro, 1962); Theotonio dos Santos, *Dependencia y cambio social* (Mexico City, 1970); Octavio Ianni, *Industrialização e desenvolvimento social no Brasil* (Rio de Janeiro, 1963); Nelson Werneck Sodré, *História da burguesia brasileira* (Rio de Janeiro, 1964); Peter Evans, *Dependent Development: the alliance of multinational, state and local capital in Brazil* (Princeton, 1979).

[12] Roberto C. Simonsen, *A indústria em face da economia nacional* (São Paulo, 1937) and *História econômica do Brasil* (São Paulo, 1937). The classic marxist analysis of the colonial period and its legacy remains Caio Prado Jr., *História econômica do Brasil* (São Paulo, 1956). Informative and still highly regarded, Nicia Villela Luz, *A luta pela industrializção do Brasil: 1808 a 1930* (São Paulo, 1961) gives a good account of elite attitudes to manufacturing which complements, for the period 1930–45, Octavio Ianni, *Estado e capitalismo: estructura social e industrialização no Brasil* (Rio de Janeiro, 1965).

[13] Suzigan, *Indústria brasileira*; João M. Cardoso de Mello, *O capitalismo tardio* (São Paulo, 1982); Wilson Cano, *Raizes da concentração industrial em São Paulo* (São Paulo, 1981).

or Schumpeterian concepts to the study of corporations or entrepreneurship in Brazil.

Recent currents in the economic historiography, notwithstanding the paramountcy of themes such as coffee and industrialisation, and a tendency on the part of many scholars to equate industrialisation with development, have resulted in new lines of enquiry of relevance to the business historian.

Business and Brazilian development

Many of the enduring debates in Brazilian economic and political history have obviously shaped directions in the study of business history. As implied above, for the period addressed by this chapter, the principal themes in the Brazilian historiography include the nature of regime change in 1889 and 1930; state policy and ideology; regional and sectoral disparities; coffee and development; industrialisation; the impact of the external environment and exogenous events; social change and societal modernisation. Few themes have had a more productive impact upon business history than controversies about entrepreneurship and the economic consequences of official policy.

The assertion of many structuralists and early dependency writers that 1930 became a point of departure in the modern history of Brazil because the process of industrialisation, or an opportunity for industrialisation, occurred at that point provoked criticism from all sides. If the significance of exogenous shocks is central to the controversy about industrialisation and development, the source of entrepreneurship is central to the debate about industrialisation itself.

The modern origin of the controversy dates from Warren Dean's seminal study of *paulista* industrial expansion.[14] Dean's research, now widely accepted, shows that modern industrial business emerged in the decades following the 1880s. However, his assertion that the majority of industrial entrepreneurs in pre-Second World War Brazil were of foreign origin has been less well received. For Dean, while *paulista* planters were agents of agricultural modernisation and the growth of coffee production, and exports underwrote industrial expansion, industrialists were drawn exclusively from the ranks of overseas merchants, immigrant penny capitalists (or foreigners who made good in the coffee sector), and expatriate managers. This view has been successfully challenged by exponents of the *cepalino* and Campinas schools.[15] As a result there are now several first class studies on entrepreneurial formation, mainly at province/state level. Among the best examples are the works of Zelia M. Cardoso de Mello on

---

[14] Warren Dean, *The Industrialization of São Paulo, 1880–1945* (Austin, 1969).

[15] Albert Fishlow, 'Origins and Consequences of Import Substitution in Brazil', in L. E. Di Marco (ed.), *International Economic Development: essays in honour of Raúl Prebisch* (New York, 1972), pp. 311–65; Suzigan, *Indústria brasileira*, chapter 1.

São Paulo and Domingos A. Giroletti and A. M. Vaz on Minas Gerais.[16] Cardoso de Mello illustrates the growing diversity of investment portfolios held by *paulista* capitalists during the second half of the nineteenth century, while the works on Minas Gerais also chart the flow of finance from agriculture to manufacturing. These micro-studies provide a wealth of qualitative and quantitative data on family firms and limited companies and have superseded earlier accounts by Souza Martins and Faria.[17] This new research, while acknowledging the presence of foreigners, also confirms the domestic origin of much entrepreneurial talent. It demonstrates, too, the importance of family connections. Capital for new ventures in transport and manufacturing was invariably raised from family members or close business associates. Hence, family business networks or groups were rapidly consolidated, and managerial expertise acquired in one area transferred to another.[18] These phenomena were hardly peculiar to Brazil; parallel patterns were observable in many other countries.

Recent work on Minas Gerais, that of Domingos Giroletti, L. A. V. Arantes and J. H. Lima, extends the challenge to Dean initiated by the Campinas school, but cautions against over-generalisation from the case of São Paulo.[19] Following Campinas scholars, these authors acknowledge the contributions of immigrants to regional industrial growth while stressing the significance and quality of native *mineiro* entrepreneurship. However, in emphasising the autonomous nature of early industrial growth in such regions in the interior, they point to a process that was less export-driven than the *paulista* experience. Until the turn of the century manufacturing in Minas Gerais, in terms of market growth, source of capital and entrepreneurship, was largely divorced from the foreign trade sector, which played such an important role in sustaining industry in urban centres in the littoral. As indicated below, most recent scholarship on São Paulo, Minas Gerais and, indeed, other parts of Brazil such as Rio de Janeiro and Pernambuco, considers a common set of questions: the social origin of businessmen; the factors that encouraged transfers of resources from

[16] Zelia M. Cardoso de Mello, *São Paulo, 1845 – 1895: metamórfoses da riqueza* (Sáo Paulo, 1991); A. M. Vaz, *Cia. Cedro e Cachoeira: história de uma empresa familiar, 1883–1987* (Belo Horizonte, 1990); Domingos A. Giroletti, *Industrialização de Juiz de Fora, 1850–1930* (Juiz de Fora, 1988). Of related interest and offering a distinct perspective on São Paulo, Tamás Szmrecsanyi, 'Agrarian bourgeoisie, regional government and the origins of São Paulo's modern sugar industry', paper presented at the Symposium on Elites and Economic Management in Latin America, XIX and XXth Centuries, 47th International Congress of Americanists, Tulane 1990.

[17] José Souza Martins, *Empresário e empresa na biografia do conde Matarazzo* (Rio de Janeiro, 1967); A. Faria, *Mauá* (Rio de Janeiro, 1926).

[18] See, for example, G. M. Mascarenhas, *Centenário da fábrica do Cedro, 1872–1972* (Belo Horizonte, 1972).

[19] Giroletti, *Industrialização de Juiz de Fora*; L. A. V. Arantes, *Os origens da burguesia industrial em Jiuz de Fora, 1858–1912* (Juiz de Fora, 1991); J. H. Lima, *Café e indústria em Minas Gerais, 1870–1920* (Petrôpolis, 1981).

agriculture to manufacturing; the relations amongst firms operating in an industry; and the processes of technical and managerial diffusion.

Though less directly related to business operations at firm level, broader accounts of government macroeconomic policy clearly inform opinion about the general environment within which business operated, and shed light on connections between business and the state. As already indicated, historians of the Campinas school touch upon the theme of state policy and private capital. Peter Evans' major book provides a reference point for this discussion, while Steven Topik, in a revisionist account, examines the regulatory and entrepreneurial role of the state during the Old Republic (1889–1930).[20] Focussing on policy areas such as fiscal and monetary issues, support for the coffee export sector, transport, and the tariff, Topik also offers insights into mechanisms which were partly devised to sustain or foment private business initiatives. Most authors writing on government policy, however, acknowledge the trail-blazing study of Villela and Suzigan, who examine the interaction between economic cycles and policy change and illustrate a process of 'learning-by-doing' amongst policy-makers and lobbyists.[21]

As identified by Villela and Suzigan, the key areas of macroeconomic management were money supply, fiscal policy, the exchange rate, and foreign debt. There is now an extensive bibliography devoted to each of these themes.[22] Nevertheless, further research is required on contacts between business and government. Focussing on two issues during the Vargas period, worker training and social welfare, Barbara Weinstein's excellent study indicates what may be accomplished.[23] She demonstrates that during a period when most authors have argued that business lobbies were weak, and economic and social policy determined by an agenda set by an increasingly authoritarian, autonomous regime, entrepreneurs had a substantial influence on policy. What would research into nineteenth-

[20] Evans, *Dependent Development*; Steven Topik, *The Political Economy of the Brazilian State, 1889–1930* (Austin, 1987).

[21] Anibal Villanova Villela and Wilson Suzigan, *Política do governo e crescimento da economia brasileira, 1889–1945* (Rio de Janeiro, 1973). See also Winston Fritsch, *External Constraints on Economic Policy in Brazil, 1889–1930* (London, 1988).

[22] For a selection of recent work, see Carlos Manuel Pelaez and Wilson Suzigan, *História monetária do Brasil* (Brasília, 1976); Flavio and Teresa Versiani, 'A industrialização brasileira antes de 1930', in Versiani and Barros (eds), *Formação economica*, pp. 121–42; Eliana A. Cardoso, 'Desvalorizações cambiais, indústria e café: Brasil, 1862–1906', *Revista Brasileira de Economia* 35: 2 (1981), 85–106; Maria Barbara Levy, 'The Brazilian Public Debt, 1824–1913', in Reinhard Liehr (ed.), *La deuda pública en América Latina: una perspectiva histórica* (Frankfurt am Main, 1995), pp. 209–54; Gustavo H. B. Franco, *Reforma monetária e inestabilidade durante a transição republicana* (Rio de Janeiro, 1983); R. W. Goldsmith, *Brasil, 1850–1984: desenvolvimento finenciero sob um seculo de inflação* (São Paulo, 1986).

[23] Barbara Weinstein, 'The Industrialists, the State, and the Issues of Worker Training and Social Services in Brazil, 1930–1950', *Hispanic American Historical Review* 70 (1990), 379–404, and *For Social Peace in Brazil: indstrialists and the remaking of the working class in São Paulo* (Chapel Hill, 1997).

century business associations reveal? Eugene Ridings has shown that the sources to sustain such scholarship exist.[24]

Relatively new directions in the historiography have contributed to sectoral and regional studies that make a contribution to Brazilian business history. Arguably, the bibliography on agriculture, railways, manufacturing, commerce, and banking has most to offer the business historian. On agriculture (essentially coffee), Dean's earlier work about *paulista fazendeiros* and land policy has probably been superseded by that of Eisenberg.[25] Essentially a socio-institutional study, Eisenberg's account of the *paulista* coffee lobby in the late 1870s encapsulates the production and other problems experienced by a modernising rural capitalist class at a critical moment in the consolidation of the new coffee economy. His research presents a convincing account of the difficulties confronting a would-be national bourgeoisie in late nineteenth-century Brazil. The contrast that Eisenberg establishes between the São Paulo coffee capitalists and the sugar producers of north-east Brazil who had featured in his earlier volume is startling.[26] Tamás Szmrecsányi, who has also written extensively on aspects of rural economy and society, offers an informative account of entrepreneurship, policy and the consolidation of an early agribusiness complex in a neglected sector of the *paulista* economy, cane sugar production and processing.[27] Much of this scholarship seeks to extend in time and space the earlier pioneering micro studies on rural capitalism by Stanley Stein and Warren Dean who considered the evolution of coffee counties in Rio de Janeiro and São Paulo respectively.[28] Both examine in great detail the mechanics of plantation enterprises from inception to maturity and decline.

While disagreeing about detail and points of interpretation, Almir El-Kareh, Odilon Nogueira da Matos, Robert Mattoon, Colin Lewis and F. A. M. de Saes have all made important contributions to business history in their various books and articles on railways.[29] De Saes, Nogueira de

---

[24] Eugene W. Ridings, *Business Interest Groups in Nineteenth-Century Brazil* (Cambridge, 1994).

[25] Warren Dean, 'Latifundia and Land Policy in Nineteenth Century Brazil', *Hispanic American Historical Review* 51 (1971), 606–625; 'The Planter as Entrepreneur: the case of São Paulo', *Hispanic American Historical Review* 36 (1966), 138–152; Peter L. Eisenberg, 'A mentalidade dos fazendeiros no congreso agrícola de 1878', in José R. Lapa (ed.), *Modos de produção e realidade brasileira* (Petrópolis, 1980).

[26] P. L. Eisenberg, *The Sugar Industry in Pernambuco: modernization without change, 1840–1910* (Berkeley, 1974).

[27] Szmrecsányi, 'Agrarian bourgeoisie' and *Pequena história da agricultura no Brasil* (São Paulo, 1990). See also his work on the later period, *Planejamento da agroindústria canavieira do Brasil, 1930–1975* (São Paulo, 1979).

[28] Stanley J. Stein, *Vassouras: a Brazilian coffee county, 1850–1900* (Cambridge, Mass., 1957); Warren Dean, *Rio Claro: a Brazilian plantation system, 1820–1920* (Stanford, 1976).

[29] Almir C. El Kareh, *Filha branca de mãe preta: a companhia da estrada de ferro D. Pedro II, 1855–1865* (Petrópolis, 1982); Odilon Nogueira da Matos, *Café e ferrovias: a evolução ferroviaria de São Paulo e o desenvolvimento da cultura cafeeira* (São Paulo, 1974); Robert

Matos and Lewis consider inter-corporate rivalries and the strategic planning of individual firms, and the former also gives a great deal of attention to profitability at firm level. Mattoon, Lewis and particularly de Saes identify examples of technology transfer and of conflict amongst state, local private, and foreign-owned companies. They also focus on the extent of state support for private initiative in the sector. Lewis and de Saes place a positive construction on local management and shareholding, presenting railways as a vector for the diffusion of managerial skills and institutional means of finance to other sectors of the economy. Mattoon tends to depict *paulista* investment in railway scrip in less dynamic terms, limited in focus and largely *rentier* in nature. Similar issues are raised by Giroletti and Herminio in their monograph on an earlier form of transport, the União e Industria turnpike between Rio de Janeiro and the interior.[30] Some of this material also addresses issues of finance and explores the hesitant role of local actors in emergent regional capital markets. Not surprisingly, this literature is richest for São Paulo and Rio de Janeiro.[31]

As will already be obvious, there is an extensive bibliography, old and new, on manufacturing. Stein's magisterial study of the cotton textile industry at a national level remains a standard work of reference, although much new writing, following the Dean thesis on São Paulo, tends towards the regional.[32] Most work also inclines towards the sub-sectoral. There are solidly researched accounts on the textile industry in a number of provinces or states.[33] Several concentrate upon a single company or small group of

H. Mattoon, 'Railroads, Coffee and the Growth of Big Business in São Paulo, Brazil' *Hispanic American Historical Review* 57 (1977), 273–292; Colin M. Lewis, *Public Policy and Private Initiative: railway building in São Paulo, 1860–1889* (London, 1991); Francisco Azevedo Marqués de Saes, *As ferrovias de São Paulo, 1870–1940* (São Paulo, 1981), and *A grande empresa de serviços públicos na economia cafeeira* (São Paulo, 1986).

30 Domingos A. Giroletti and Antonio Herminio, *A companhia e a rodovia União e Industrial e o desenvolvimento de Juiz de Fora, 1850–1900* (Belo Horizonte, 1980).

31 In recent years, María Barbara Levy has made several contributions to the study of the emergence and growth of the Rio de Janeiro capital market. See her monograph, *História da Bolsa de Valores do Rio de Janeiro* (Rio de Janeiro, 1977) and paper on 'The Brazilian Public Debt', already cited. See also Stephen Haber, *The Efficiency Consequences of Institutional Change: financial market regulation and industrial productivity growth in Brazil, 1866–1934* (Cambridge, 1996); Gail Triner, 'The Formation of Modern Brazilian Banking, 1906–1930: opportunities and constraints presented by the public and private sectors', *Journal of Latin American Studies* 28 (1996), 49–74. For additional information on traders and the beginnings of a local capital market see Joseph E. Sweigart, *Coffee Factorage and the Emergence of a Brazilian Capital Market, 1850–1888* (London, 1987). Also of interest is an earlier regional study, T. de Azevedo and E. Q. Vieira Lins, *História do banco da Bahia* (Rio de Janeiro 1969).

32 Stanley J. Stein, *The Brazilian Cotton Manufacture: textile enterprise in an underdeveloped area, 1850–1950* (Cambridge, Mass., 1957).

33 Vaz, *Cia. Cedro e Cachoeira*; Roberto Borges Martins, 'A indústria textil doméstica de Minas Gerais no século XIX', *Anais do II Seminario sobre a Economia Mineira* (Belo Horizonte, 1983), pp. 77–94; Luis C. Soares, *A manufactura na formação económica e social escravista no sudeste: um estudo das actividades manufactureiras na região fluminense, 1840–1880* (Niteroi, 1980).

closely connected family firms. In addition, there have been a few attempts to emulate Dean and project a larger regional analysis of industry.[34] Finally, the economic and business historian will find much of interest on regional economic and sectoral development, if rather less about individual enterprises, in the excellent set of volumes about regional and federal politics around the turn of the century produced by Joseph Love, Robert Levine, Eul-Soo Pang, and John Wirth.[35]

Towards a new research agenda

Very recent research, mainly undertaken by young Brazilian scholars, has broken new ground. Business records have been identified, and methods and perspectives from the North American and European business history literature have been used in order to interpret this material. There is now a growing body of texts consciously depicted as business history. Recent writing has also given additional focus to the general direction of research, and encourages speculation about future developments in the historiography. Inevitably, several of the themes that command attention are not new, although there are others which are distinctly innovative. However, despite the intrinsic quality of much of the new research output, too many studies continue to be framed within the context of the questions raised by the structuralist and dependency debates. While not entirely pernicious, the tendency to conform with or to seek to rebut precepts established during fruitful exchanges of the 1960s and 1970s may have inhibited the infusion of alternative approaches to the subject. Few studies on Brazil, for example, make adequate use of the insights of Alfred Chandler, though this will undoubtedly change.[36] There is also scope for an absorption by historians of some of the notions current in management science.[37] Knowledge of basic concepts advanced by industrial relations theorists, games

---

[34] J. A. de Paula, 'Dois ensâios sobre a genese da industrialização em Minas Gerais: a siderugia e indústria textil', *Anais do II Seminario sobre a Economia Mineira* (Belo Horizonte, 1983), pp. 19–76; Sergio Silva, *Expansão cafeeira e origems da indústria no Brasil* (São Paulo, 1976); Cano, *Raizes da concentração*; Ana Celia Castro, *As empresas extrangeiras no Brasil, 1860–1913* (Rio de Janeiro, 1979). These works point to dynamic changes in corporate organisation and the general diffusion of a 'business mentality.'

[35] Joseph L. Love, *Rio Grande do Sul and Brazilian Regionalism,1882–1930* (Stanford, 1971); Richard M. Levine, *Pernambuco in the Brazilian Federation, 1889–1937* (Stanford, 1978); Eul-Soo Pang, *Bahia in the First Brazilian Republic: coronelismo and oligarchies, 1889–1934* (Gainesville, 1979); John D. Wirth, *Minas Gerais in the Brazilian Federation, 1889–1937* (Stanford, 1977).

[36] Some very recent studies reflect the influence of Chandler. See Sérgio de Oliveira Birchal, 'Entrepeneurship and the Formation of a Business Environment in Nineteenth-Century Brazil: the case of Minas Gerais' (PhD thesis, University of London, 1994), pp. 107–84; Wilson Suzigan and Tamás Szmrecsányi, 'Os investimentos estrangeiros no início da industrialização do Brasil', in Sérgio S. Silva and Tamás Szmrecsányi (eds), *História econômica da Primeira República* (São Paulo, 1996), pp. 261–83.

[37] See Birchal, 'Entrepreneurship and the Formation', pp. 52, 137–38, 146–59.

theory strategists, new approaches in the economic literature to the theory of the firm (notably the 'old' and 'new' institutionalism), and possibly a greater awareness of systems of modern corporate finance might enable business historians working on Brazil to chart a more secure course through the disparate, fragmented sources of documentation available.[38] The injection of a little more 'business theory' might encourage speculative extrapolations of entrepreneurial behaviour or long-run developments at company or industry level from data sources that are limited or discontinuous.

Novel and continuing areas of dynamic research for the pre-Second World War period can be identified under two interlocking headings: the family background and technical competence of entrepreneurs on the one hand, and the organisation of production on the other. The former covers enduring themes such as the social origin, nationality and intellectual formation of businessmen. In addition, it touches upon their status, political connections, and proficiency in dealing with other domestic and external social actors, or in other words their ability to construct an environment that was conducive to business initiative and/or to influence policy. These are subjects that draw upon Weberian and Schumpeterian ideas of the businessman as aberrant innovator. The latter heading, rooted in the scholarship of Chandler, Schumpeter and perhaps Rostow, embraces more prosaic themes: the generation of capital and the financial structure of the firm; labour supply, recruitment, organisation, and training; technology, technological adaptation, and the mechanics of production; marketing and distribution.

In addition to texts on entrepreneurial formation listed above, there are a limited number of works, mainly produced by sociologists, which specifically address questions of social and political status and technical competence. These identify areas of further exploration for historians.[39] As already indicated, the study of sources of 'corporate' investment has been invigorated by the excellent work of Cano, Cardoso de Mello and Vaz. These authors point to what might be achieved by historians. Mattoon

[38] For examples of what can be achieved, see Stephen Haber, *The Efficiency Consequences*, and also 'Regulatory Regimes, Capital Markets, and Industrial Development: a comparative study of Brazil, Mexico, and the United States of America, 1840–1930', in John Harriss, Janet Hunter, and Colin M. Lewis (eds), *The New Institutional Economics and Third World Development* (London, 1995), pp. 265–82.

[39] Fernando H. Cardoso, *Empresário industrial e desenvolvimento econômico do Brasil* (São Paulo, 1972); F. C. Prestes Motta, *Empresários e hegemonia política* (São Paulo, 1979); Eli Diniz, *Empresário, estado e capitalismo no Brasil, 1930–45* (São Paulo, 1978); V. C. Piccini, 'De-se formar empresários?', *Anais da IX Reunião da ANPAD* (Florianopólis 1985), pp. 5–34; Domingos A. Giroletti, *A formação do empresário industrial* (Belo Horizonte, 1991); see also Martins, *Conde Matarazzo*, and other works by Cardoso listed above. One of the few historians to inject elements of modern 'business science' into the study of businessmen is Luis C. Bresser Pereira, *Empresários e administradores no Brasil* (São Paulo, 1974); more diffuse is the compilation of C. Aquino (ed.), *História empresarial vivida* (São Paulo, 1987).

also provides a more restrained account of risk-taking portfolio diversification. Collectively, this scholarship substantially extends the discussion initiated by Dean and taken up by the Campinas school and scholars writing on other regions. Much more research, however, is required on the subject of finance and management in terms of the transition from family firm or private business to public limited company and (possibly) multidivisional corporation. For much of the period studied, the Brazilian commercial code identified three types of firms which were subject to distinct regulatory regimes: partnerships, involving a few individuals, which did not enjoy limited liability; small private firms benefiting from partial limited liability; fully limited companies which were subject to rigorous registration and disclosure requirements. These distinctions are of interest to the historian not only because status carried financial and administrative implications, but also because the form of organisation directly influences the nature and availability of the surviving archives. Juridical status and security of property rights were also of paramount concern to businessmen and shareholders of the period.

As students of business history appreciate, the 'labour question' was of over-riding importance. Slavery in Brazil was not abolished until 1888. This fact, coupled with the size of the country, the weight of the subsistence sector, slow population growth, regionally specific flows of foreign immigrants, and the inadequacy of transport facilities meant that the labour market was at best highly stratified and probably functioned only at local level until at least the 1930s. Regional studies confirm this and indicate how 'the labour issue' was perceived and resolved. Eisenberg argues convincingly that labour scarcity was perceived by *paulista* coffee producers as the key problem confronting business around the third quarter of the nineteenth century, while Libby, writing on the relatively isolated interior province of Minas Gerias, shows how the transition from slavery to free labour was handled there.[40] Hence, labour problems were conceived largely in technical terms, those of supply, training, and discipline, in the sense of adaptation to a set rhythm of production. Thomas Skidmore is probably correct in arguing that 'order' was less of a problem. The literature on labour, essentially urban labour, before 1930 points to a weak, divided, vulnerable component of society. In the countryside and in small towns, unemployment, underemployment and a near monopoly of the means of violence enjoyed by employers limited scope for worker solidarity. After the 1930s the state appears to have experienced little difficulty in controlling labour.[41]

---

[40] Eisenberg, *A mentalidade*; Douglas C. Libby, *Transformação e trabalho em uma economia escravista: Minas Gerais no século XIX* (São Paulo, 1988), *Trabalho escravo e capital estrangeiro no Brasil: o caso de Morro Velho* (Belo Horizonte, 1984), and 'Proto-Industrialisation in a Slave Society: the Case of Minas Gerais', *Journal of Latin American Studies* 23 (1991), 1–35. See also Maria L. Lamounier, *Da escravidão ao trabalho livre* (Campinas, 1988).

[41] Thomas E. Skidmore, 'The Historiography of Brazil, 1889–1964, Part II', *Hispanic*

Supply and quality of labour, however, were a problem. By the late 1870s the effective end of the internal slave trade and the rapid westward movement of the coffee frontier triggered by the railway boom earlier in the decade were heightening fears of a general labour crisis on the *planalto*. Similar concerns, possibly a reflection of developments in the new coffee districts, were expressed by businessmen engaged in manufacturing and mining in the interior.[42] Planters and industrialists during the 1870s and beyond were anxious to increase the supply of diligent workers. Solutions were rarely uniform, but the language of the contemporary debate displayed a preference for immigrant labour, which was regarded as vastly superior to the home-grown variety.[43] But access to immigrant labour was almost exclusive to the coffee districts and the cities of the south-centre. Elsewhere employers were forced to draw workers from the subsistence sector or else rely on coerced labour, although the internal slave trade had tended to drain slaves from the towns and non-coffee regions to the state of São Paulo. Consequently, many employers had to confront the problems of training, and the inculcation of 'modern' habits of reliability and regularity and of communal living and collective discipline. Later these themes would be subsumed in the debate about worker education and labour productivity. Giroletti's study of a textile mill in Minas provides an example of how these problems were conceived and resolved, as do the excellent monographs by Libby.[44]

Access to equipment and skilled personnel, including managers, was a

American Historical Review 56 (1976), 85. For an informative collection of edited documents on the history of organised labour and relations between workers and employers, see the two-volume compilation, Paulo Sérgio Pinheiro and Michael H. Hall, *A classe operária no Brasil: documentos (1889–1930). Vol. 1: o movimento operário* (São Paulo, 1979), and *A classe operária no Brasil: documentos (1889–1930): Vol. II: condições de vida e de trabalho, relações com os empresários e o estado* (São Paulo, 1981). For studies on immigration, labour, and class formation, see in particular Michael M. Hall, 'Immigrants and the Early São Paulo Working Class', *Lateinamerikas Jahrbuch für Geschichte von Staat, Wirschaft und Gesellschaft* 12 (1975), 393–405; Paulo Sérgio Pinheiro, 'Classes médias urbanas: formação, natureza, intervenção vida política', in Boris Fausto (ed.), *História Geral da Civilização Brasileira. III: O Brasil Republicano. 2: Sociedade e instituições, 1889–1930* (São Paulo, 1978), IX, 7–37; Sheldon L. Maram, *Anarquistas, imigrantes e movimento operário brasileiro, 1890–1920* (Rio de Janeiro, 1979), and 'The Immigrant in the Brazilian Labor Movement, 1890–1920', in Dauril Alden and Warren Dean (eds), *Essays concerning the Socioeconomic History of Brazil and Portuguese India* (Gainesville, 1977); Ruth Berins Collier and David Collier, *Shaping the Political Arena: critical junctures, the labor movement and regime dynamics in Latin America* (Princeton, 1991).

[42] Eisenberg, *A mentalidade*; Lewis, *Railway Building in São Paulo*; Libby, *Transformação e trabalho*, and *Trabalho escravo*.

[43] Thomas W. Merrick and Douglas H. Graham, *Population and Economic Development in Brazil: 1800 to the present* (Baltimore, 1979); Thomas E. Skidmore, *Black into White: race and nationality in Brazilian thought* (New York, 1974); George R. Andrews, *Blacks and Whites in São Paulo, Brazil, 1888–1988* (Madison, 1991).

[44] Domingos A. Giroletti, *Fábrica: convento e disciplina* (Belo Horizonte, 1991); Libby, *Transformação e trabalho* and *Trabalho escravo*.

further barrier that had to be overcome by pioneer firms. Procurement
overseas and the adaptation of managers and machines to the local environment presented the most feasible short to medium term solution before
the transfer of technology and skills might promote a growth of indigenous
supply. For the nineteenth century Vaz (on the cotton textile industry),
Giroletti (on turnpikes), and Mattoon (on locally financed railways in São
Paulo) all detail the extent of these difficulties. The availability of modern
technology and qualified machinists and middle management was critical.
However, as Eakin and Eisenberg demonstrate, the diffusionist function
of individual enterprises, or foreign capital as a whole could be limited,
even though they might be highly successful companies. Offering evidence
from a British-owned mining company, Eakin shows how even dynamic
firms could adapt to the local political economy, tailoring needs to Brazilian
circumstances rather than serving as a vector for widespread capitalist
modernisation or a model for corporate reorganisation.[45] In the case of
the sugar industry in Pernambuco Eisenberg depicts the problems facing
firms which failed adequately to adapt to local conditions.[46] Clearly the
prospects for technological and administrative transfer were much more
problematic in mining or agriculture than in the transport sector. However,
additional similar studies are required.

Market knowledge and distribution constitute yet another area that
deserves the attention of business historians. Documents from the nineteenth century demonstrate how entrepreneurs were constantly exercised
by sudden changes in demand and the threat of competition. Exchange
rate fluctuations, whether driven by the volume or price of exports or
occasioned by monetary policy, could influence the availability of imports;
cycles of railway building might open up new domestic markets or introduce
the threat of competition from overseas or from neighbouring towns or
provinces; the state of the harvest directly affected local purchases. For
much of the nineteenth century, businesses complained of inadequate
means of transport. This implied considerable barriers to entry into industry
and possibly fostered oligopoly. However, most firms tended to complain
about the need to hold large stocks (of raw materials or finished items)
and of imperfect systems of distribution. Producers were often prey to
middlemen who supplied essential inputs or handled onward sales to
retailers. In a capital hungry environment, few enterprises possessed sufficient funds to integrate backwards or engage in direct trading. And only
coffee planters possessed either sufficient financial resources to invest
substantially beyond central productive activities or the influence to mobil-
ise the state to act to resolve production bottlenecks and construct a more
favourable environment in which to conduct business. How did businesses

45 Marshall C. Eakin, *British Enterprise in Brazil: the St. John d'el Rey Mining Company and
the Morro Velho Gold Mine, 1830–1960* (Durhan, NC., 1989).
46 Eisenberg, *Modernization without change.*

cope with these difficulties? These are also areas, like the debate about technology transfer, that would benefit from research into business associations.

Conclusion

Clearly particular themes in the general economic historiography on Brazil have framed issues of interest to historians of business. Entrepreneurship, the origin and chronology of industrial expansion, the political economy of coffee in São Paulo, and the generally sluggish performance of the Brazilian economy for much of the period have all influenced the discourse. Intellectual currents in the social sciences such as *cepalismo* and dependency have also had an impact. Perhaps the most fruitful consequence of the interaction between business history and broad interpretative trends in other branches of the discipline has been the stimulation of empirical, micro-level research. This process may not be unconnected with the substantial changes that have taken place in Brazil in the last few decades. Rapid growth from the late 1960s to early 1980s profoundly altered the economic configuration of the country. Urbanisation, industrialisation and the transformation of corporate structures were among the most obvious consequences of that growth, along with a substantial expansion in higher education. Several businesses which survive from an earlier period are now anxious to promote the study of their origin. In so doing, Brazilian companies may be following an example set by state institutions or quasi-official and semi-private bodies such as the Instituto de Planejamento Economico e Social, the Fundação Getúlio Vargas, and the Centro Brasileiro de Análise e Planajamento (CEBRAP), which had already began to collate and reconstruct macroeconomic time series and assemble qualitative social data for the nineteenth and early twentieth centuries.

The way forward is clear. Further work is required in areas such as management structures and corporate organisation. For many regions and sectors there is still ample opportunity for research on individual entrepreneurs. Labour and the organisation of production should also continue to command attention. The financial sector and the relationship between business and local sources of finance or world capital markets is virtually an unexplored field. More systematic research is also required on the entrepreneurial role of the Brazilian government, both at a national and a regional level, during the period preceding the Second World War. Existing studies hint at the critical role of the state in promoting individual companies in the textile, mining and transport sectors. Did government aspire to a Gerschenkronian role? Perhaps, with additional case-study research, there will be an opportunity for further generalisation and new contributions to the theoretical literature.

CHAPTER FOUR

Business History in Chile
1850–1945

Luis Ortega

Business history is one of many areas in which Chilean historiography provides evidence of its limited development. In general terms, this situation is explained by two factors. First, this is a relatively new field of research within the discipline. It has evolved in conditions of great difficulty, and is therefore weak in institutional terms. The second factor goes beyond the sphere of historiography, and has more to do with the dominant trends in the economic and social development of the country. From 1927 until 1974 the state was the principal actor in the economic arena. It is only in the last twenty years that the business elite has begun to occupy a central role in Chilean life. Only then did businessmen, as a group, discover the need to become an object of historical study in themselves, and some historians found them to be an attractive topic, even though not an essential one.

A review of the economic historiography of Chile confirms the fact that the history of business has been a marginal component in the development of the subject. However, such an analysis also enables us to gain a better understanding of the vicissitudes and determinants of the historical research which has taken place on the business elite.

The economic historiography of Chile and the history of the business elite

Despite a relative decline in the study of economic history during the last decade, due fundamentally to the immense boom which has occurred in the study of social history, the subject has experienced a significant, if limited, advance since the early 1960s. As a consequence, our knowledge of the process of economic development in Chile is not only much broader, but it has also become firmly established on more solid foundations.

This academic development was made possible by a number of different phenomena. The economic evolution that Chile experienced between 1940 and the mid-1970s stimulated, from the very beginning, a series of questions which were quickly picked up by specialists, not only from the field of history, but from other disciplines too, most notably economics. The complex and controversial process of economic development in Chile during this period provoked authors from varying intellectual backgrounds into attempts to trace its historical roots in order to explain the initial success, stagnation, and final collapse of the growth strategy based on import substitution industrialisation (ISI). Within the literary output produced in these years, studies of Chilean society and the Chilean economy reflected the two principal areas into which the relatively modest developments in business history were incorporated. This was at a time when the country had 'turned inward' after over a century of staking its future on export development.

In this context an abundance of literature seeking to unravel the origins of Chile's relatively low level of economic development began to appear. These years saw the emergence of a group of economists who were to acquire an enormous social and intellectual influence in Chile, and who became the most important contributors to the two great interpretative traditions which arose at this point. The first of these schools comprised the select group of intellectuals connected with ECLA or CEPAL, which was founded in 1948 and established its headquarters in Santiago.[1] Their work introduced a whole new analytical dimension into the debate over development. The second intellectual stream is identified with the work of historians and economists aligned with diverse tendencies within the Chilean Left. This ultimately led to the employment of various analytical categories and tools derived from orthodox Marxist analysis in all its various expressions.[2]

The ideas which became known as the ECLA or *desarrollista* theses were strongly influenced by nationalist critiques of liberalism developed at the beginning of the twentieth century and by Keynesian thought.[3] On that

[1] ECLA and CEPAL are used interchangeably, the latter being the acronym of the Comisión Económica para América Latina, the Spanish-language title of the institution. On ECLA, see E. V. K. Fitzgerald, 'ECLA and the Formation of Latin American Economic Doctrine' in David Rock (ed.), *Latin America in the 1940s: war and postwar traditions* (Berkeley, 1994), pp. 89–108, and for an evaluation of the influence of the CEPAL economists generally, Cristóbal Kay, *Latin American Theories of Development and Underdevelopment* (London, 1989), chapter 2. See also the chapter on Brazil in this volume for an evaluation of the *cepalino* economists' influence on the writing of Brazilian economic and business history (pp. 44–46).

[2] On the Chilean Left in the period after the 1930s, see Paul W. Drake, *Socialism and Populism in Chile, 1932–1952* (Urbana, 1978), and Julio Faúndez, *Marxism and Democracy in Chile: from 1932 to the fall of Allende* (New Haven, 1988). Chile was unique amongst Latin American countries in developing two powerful left-wing political parties, the Communists and the Socialists, as well as many other smaller left-wing groupings, which polled well in successive elections and eventually gained the presidency in 1970 with the electoral victory of Salvador Allende.

[3] Various adjectives have been used to describe this body of thought. In Spanish these economists are normally known as *desarrollistas* or else *cepalinos* or *cepalistas* (the use of one term rather than another is a matter of personal preference). In English they are commonly known as 'the ECLA school' or the 'structuralists'.

foundation *cepalinos* formulated a relentless critique of the orthodox liberalism of the nineteenth century, in particular over its assumptions regarding the external sector and the role of the state. It was within this context that economists close to the ECLA school claimed that from the end of the colonial period until the 1860s, as a result of appropriate economic policies, Chile had experienced a period of marked expansion and maturing of the economy which had put the country on the threshold of the route to development. However, mistaken economic policies, including the 1864 reform of the Customs Tariff, which had lowered import duties, and the 1860 Banking Law, which had relaxed financial disciplines, had then introduced some local ingredients which held back the process of national development in two ways. First, the devaluation of the currency resulting from the new banking arrangements subsequently led to financial corruption. The second problem lay in the gradual but irresistible foreign penetration of the economy. In short, with these two measures the ruling elite had opted for the easiest means to maintain its own levels of consumption, a process which reached its peak in the so-called 'denationalisation' of the nitrate industry.[4] Once this had occurred, the elite could live off the rents generated by the export of this product, but at the cost of maintaining the country in a state of backwardness or underdevelopment. In this context the initial entrepreneurial spirit became exhausted, or, to use the words of the most distinguished exponent of this intellectual tradition, the outcome was 'the decline, not to mention the disappearance, of the pioneering spirit that was so marked during the early years [of the republic]'.[5]

As far as the question of periodisation is concerned, those following this line of argument took the view that the frustration of the 1860s was followed by seven decades of spasmodic growth which were a product of extravagance, inefficiency, the secular backwardness of agriculture, and the elite's acquiescence in permitting asymmetric external economic relationships to continue as the 'motor' of the national economy. Looking backwards through Chilean history, therefore, a double frustration was evident: the first in the middle of the nineteenth century, when the first expansionary

---

[4] In 1880 Chile captured the nitrate fields belonging to Peru and Bolivia and thus acquired a global monopoly of this product. The nitrate plants which had belonged to the Peruvian state since its partial expropriation of the industry in 1875 were returned to the private sector, and in the course of the following decade foreign companies gained a dominant position in the industry. On this period see especially Thomas F. O'Brien, *The Nitrate Industry and Chile's Crucial Transition, 1870–1891* (New York, 1982).

[5] Aníbal Pinto, *Chile: un caso de desarrollo frustrado* (3rd edition, Santiago, 1973), p. 81. This book was first published in 1958; a fourth edition was published by the Universidad de Santiago de Chile in 1996, with a preface by President Eduardo Frei. In Pinto's view the moment at which the 'frustration' of development occurred was the same as that which the nationalist critic, Francisco A. Encina, had originally picked out as crucial in his highly influential essay, *Nuestra inferioridad económica* (Santiago, 1911). The latter book had run through six editions by 1986.

phase of *desarrollo hacia afuera* (outward-directed development) ground to a halt and the second in the middle of the twentieth century, when the growth phase of *desarrollo hacia adentro* (inward-directed development) was coming to an abrupt end.

According to this interpretation, endogenous or national, rather than external, factors produced the first major frustration. This argument fits neatly with the nationalist critique put forward at the turn of the century, which held a section of the elite directly responsible for Chile's difficulties. Rather than blaming a shortage of capital as the principal factor in the country's failure, Aníbal Pinto highlighted the ruling classes' low propensity to save and invest due to their 'preference for refined and sterile greed'. Their high level of consumption, modelled on European norms, had three major consequences: the inappropriate spending of disposable surpluses; the sterile channelling of external and internal credits; and the retarded productive methods of the agrarian sector. The bourgeoisie became consumers rather than businessmen. This propensity lay behind a wholesale and permanent opening of the Chilean market to the world economy, thus creating a conduit through which both external instability and the models of conspicuous consumption could pass. In the end this created an interface between a weak economy in Chile and strong ones in the developed world. There was therefore a structural dimension to Chile's problems: the relationship between unequal economies. It then followed as a logical consequence from this proposition that the elite, which had also demonstrated its incapacity for political leadership during the 'Parliamentary Republic' (1891–1924), was incapable of guiding the country along the path of economic development. Such a task, therefore, became a national concern.

The fulfilment of that mission was the setting for the period of *desarrollo hacia adentro* (inward-directed development) which, roughly from the 1930s until its collapse in the 1960s, constituted the final phase of the *cepalino* model. Internal factors were viewed as fundamental to the problems of this period, whether they were decisions regarding economic policy made in response to sectoral interests, or the disjuncture between economic and socio-political developments. The explanations for the country's inability to establish a coherent policy that might have permitted it to collect the rewards from a more than adequate connection with foreign markets, and thus compensate for the domestic deficits which blocked 'take-off', lay primarily in factors internal to Chile.

The social, intellectual, and political transcendence of the ECLA interpretation was profound. The concepts developed by the *cepalinos* acquired such a significance that they became a part of everyday language. Examples of this were not only the phrase 'frustrated development', but also the idea of a 'spendthrift and greedy oligarchy' which was incapable of leading the country along the path of development, due more than anything to the absence of any entrepreneurial nucleus within the oligarchy which might be capable of dismantling old structures and other obstacles to progress. During the 1950s and the 1960s, therefore, the ECLA school was able to formulate an interpretation of Chile's economic and social history which became, without any doubt, the most popular and politically influential in the country, and endured, regardless of the opinion of professional historians, until the mid-1970s. Even the historical texts published by the so-called 'New Left' and the dependency school were based, at least in part, on the facts and the ideas and concepts which emanated from this source.[6]

At the same time as the *cepalinos* were making their contributions to the discussion, Chilean Marxist historiography also made a vigorous entry into the academic arena. From the very beginning this school demonstrated a strong 'economistic' slant and a rigid inflexibility typical of the mechanical application of the analytical categories developed by the Academy of Sciences of the Soviet Union, as was so often the case at that time. The Marxist tradition was characterised by the publication of works of synthesis which attempted a general interpretation of the economic process, whilst highlighting its fundamental features. Its contribution in terms of detailed monographs, like that of the ECLA school, was consequently somewhat limited.[7]

From the point of view of chronology, the Marxist historians of the 1950s and 1960s preferred to focus their attention on the period between 1830 and 1930. In studying this century they gave priority to the analysis of those themes that contributed to their political 'praxis', the structuring and legitimation of the programmes of the left-wing parties in Chile. Within this context the economic characteristics of the period between 1850 and 1900 came under particular scrutiny. Attempts to characterise and define the prevailing mode of production at this time opened up an intense debate amongst historians of a Marxist persuasion. However, the tyranny of these

[6] Much has been written on the transition from *cepalino* or structuralist ideas to the dependency school. See, in particular, Joseph Love, 'The Origins of Dependency Theory', *Journal of Latin American Studies* 22 (1990), 143–68, and Kay, *Latin American Theories*, pp. 130–62. For parallel developments in other Latin American countries, see the chapters on Brazil and Peru in this volume (pp. 46–47 and 137). André Gunder Frank, one of the most influential 'dependency' writers for English-speaking readers, made extensive use of Pinto's work in the chapters on Chile in his *Capitalism and Underdevelopment in Latin America* (London, 1971).

[7] Julio César Jobet, *Ensayo crítico del desarrollo económico social de Chile* (Santiago, 1955). Hernán Ramírez Necochea analysed the late eighteenth-century economy in his *Antecedentes económicas de la Independencia de Chile* (Santiago, 1969). He also published *Historia del movimiento obrero de Chile: siglo XIX* (Santiago, 1956); *Historia del imperialismo en Chile* (Santiago, 1960), and *Balmaceda y la contrarrevolución de 1891* (Santiago, 1969, with a second edition in 1972). See also Luis Vitale, *Interpretación marxista de la historia de Chile* (5 vols, Santiago, Frankfurt-am-Main, Caracas, 1967–1982), volumes 1 and 2 of which cover the colonial period. Another influential Marxist writer was Marcello Segall, *El desarrollo del capitalismo en Chile: cinco ensayos dialécticos* (Santiago, 1953).

concepts and categories meant that these historians became bogged down in a prolonged and somewhat sterile debate about the 'feudal' or 'capitalist' character of Chile's economic structures in the late nineteenth century. In the end, due to the highly abstract nature of the debate, very little was contributed to historical research overall.

For these historians the first thirty years of the twentieth century marked an important watershed in Chile's history. Having focussed their attention during the period between 1830 and 1900 on such problems as the 'mode and social relations of production' and the 'dominant class' (for which several different terms were used), in the early twentieth century they could transfer their attention to workers' movements, popular parties and movements, and imperialism. From an analytical point of view, the turning point could be pinpointed as the precise moment when, in the view of these historians, the development of national capitalism had been frustrated, namely the civil war of 1891. The Marxist school was unanimous in its praise of President José Manuel Balmaceda (1886–1891). They saw Balmaceda as a moderniser, a progressive, and an enemy of imperialism and the oligarchy. They therefore argued that his defeat in the civil war also represented the end of a unique historic project which would have opened the way for the autonomous development of national capitalism. Once Balmaceda had been defeated the only legacy remaining to Chile consisted of archaic forms of production, foreign penetration, corruption, and decadence.[8]

This analytical approach necessarily meant that the intrinsic importance of the long period between 1891 and 1938 for the history of capitalist development became reduced in significance. After the 1891 civil war, which marked the strategic defeat of Chilean capitalism in the eyes of the Marxist historians, there could no longer be a capitalist or bourgeois history in any 'national' sense; the chief actors in Chile's history were now the victors in the civil war, in other words the imperialists, and the incipient force that was the only one in Chile capable of challenging them with any success, the proletariat.[9] Such academic reasoning by Marxist historians meant that they abandoned a wide range of themes and problems which might have become subjects for research. Topics such as the accumulation of capital, the characteristics and the workings of the external sector, the market and industrialisation, and the business elite remained noticeably

[8] The support of manufacturing business for Balmaceda, both during his government and in the civil war, an idea developed by Ramírez, was convincingly refuted by Henry W. Kirsch: 'Balmaceda y la burguesía nacional: realidad o utopía' (mimeo, Santiago, 1970). On this theme see also the book by Maurice Zeitlin, *The Civil Wars in Chile (or the bourgeois revolutions that never were)* (Princeton, 1984).

[9] Gabriel Salazar, 'El movimiento teórico sobre desarrollo y dependencia en Chile, 1950–1975', *Nueva Historia* 4 (1982), 37. *Nueva Historia* was the periodical publication of a group of Chilean historians exiled in Great Britain. Nineteen issues were published between 1981 and 1986.

absent from their scholarly repertoire. Nor were these subjects developed in the research of economists of the same ideological persuasion who later attempted a global interpretation of the development of the Chilean economy.[10] From this viewpoint, therefore, the bourgeoisie had lost its national character, insofar as it had not completed its historic task, and the state had become the principal instrument for the future development of Chile. The bourgeoisie was thus assigned a marginal role and in the process it was assumed to have lost its business verve.

Despite these limitations one must also highlight the successes of this historiographical current. Appearing like an earth tremor during the 1950s, this approach dramatically changed the way in which historical research was conducted in Chile. In particular, since its emphasis on economic issues gave precedence to this line of analysis, it led historians to ascribe greater importance to certain subjects which had hitherto been under-researched. In addition, a number of these contributions resulted in major controversies, which led in turn to further significant advances in historical research.

However, both these approaches, the *cepalino* and the Marxist, tended to lose validity after the 1973 coup d'état which overthrew the Allende government. The former suffered from the gradual decline in the acceptability of its theories, while the latter became the object of severe repression and then also lost significance due to the global crisis of socialism. Nevertheless, as far as business history was concerned, the legacy of both these approaches was complex, since writers in these traditions had downplayed the idea of an entrepreneurial elite in Chile and laid emphasis upon the paralysis of national capitalist development.

Historians are also absent from the study of the major changes that the entrepreneurial class has experienced over the last thirty years. Again, scholars from other disciplines have enthusiastically, though not in great numbers, taken over the task of analysis. Oscar Muñoz, an economist who for three decades has made important contributions to Chile's economic history, was thus one of the first scholars to take a close look at the emerging entrepreneurial group in the 1980s. Later he broadened the scope and depth of his analysis.[11] Cecilia Montero, a sociologist, has made significant advances in the study of the entrepreneurial class which emerged during the Pinochet dictatorship. Two of her publications suggest that more may be expected on this score.[12]

[10] José Cademártori, *La economía chilena: un enfoque marxista* (Santiago, 1970); Sergio Ramos, *Chile ¿una economía en transición?* (Santiago, 1973).

[11] Oscar Muñoz, *Chile y su industrialización: pasado, crisis y opciones* (Santiago, 1986), especially chapters 2–8. Nine years later Muñoz returned to the subject in his *Los inesperados caminos de la modernizacón económica* (Santiago, 1995), especially pp. 39–65, which looks specifically at businessmen.

[12] Cecilia Montero, 'La evolución del empresariado chileno. ¿Surge un nuevo actor?', *Estudios Cieplan* 30 (1990), 91–122, and *La revolución empresarial chilena* (Santiago, 1997).

Academic research: economic growth and the firm

Just at the time that these changes in Chile's political economy started to occur a group of economists had begun seriously to investigate the periods immediately before and after the Second World War in search of answers to questions to which both the ECLA and the Marxist schools had given priority. However, the *cepalinos* enjoyed undeniable advantages in this effort. First, they were not subject to the demands and pressures of economic and political contingency. Second, they possessed the academic experience which enabled them to observe these problems through a different lens and to work on them employing a methodology and theoretical assumptions which led them to make significant advances.

In 1960 a young lawyer and future economist published a book which, if read with care, should have changed Chileans' perceptions regarding the economic and business evolution of the country. In contrast to the dominant interpretation of a mongrel and unsuccessful ruling elite, with all its seigneurial attitudes, the research of Ricardo Lagos showed that a powerful capitalist bourgeoisie did exist, albeit one which was quite small in size.[13] The results of this study opened up a whole new stage in the subject of economic history. On the one hand, Lagos had used up-to-date research methods, analytical techniques, and economic concepts, giving his work a high degree of respectability. On the other, it forced a reappraisal of the focus and the assumptions which had previously been used to analyse the diverse aspects of economic life during the republican period. In the presence of a vigorous and modern nucleus of businessmen in Chile, it was no longer possible to sustain the old argument of a failed oligarchy. It was now a matter of lifting the veil of mystery which still covered the economic history of the period before the Second World War. Moreover, both the national and the international conjunctures had created an especially favourable moment for this to happen.

Ever since the late 1950s Chilean universities had embarked upon vast training programmes for young academics, which included sending many of them to foreign universities, especially in the United States. In addition, in North America the enormous development of programmes of Latin American Studies during the 1960s had resulted in what Simon Collier some years later termed 'the energetic attentions of the great American Ph.D industry'.[14] Amongst the group of academics working in Chile, economists developed a small but important number of works on economic history, while scholars in the United States produced an impressive flow of research.[15] The combined production of these two groups represented

[13] Ricardo Lagos, *La concentración del poder económico en Chile* (Santiago, 1960). By 1973 this work had gone through five editions.

[14] Simon Collier, 'The Historiography of the "Portalian" Period (1830–1891) in Chile', *Hispanic American Historical Review* 57 (1977), 680.

[15] The quantity of doctoral theses on Chilean history produced in the English-speaking

a major turning point for economic historiography and by implication for business history, even though the latter still remained only a marginal theme to the main thrust of the research.

Industry

In this environment Ricardo Lagos continued his contribution to economic history with his doctoral thesis. This was completed in 1966 and published by the then Instituto de Economía of the University of Chile the same year. The same institution also published two other major works stemming from theses completed by Carlos Hurtado and Oscar Muñoz. The research of these three academics confirmed the need to modify assumptions about the chronological landmarks of industrialisation, which was seen by both the ECLA and Marxist schools as the motor for Chilean economic growth and the key to development, by showing how the beginnings of the process dated as far back as the second half of the nineteenth century. This meant that it was necessary to reconsider the prevailing characteristics of the period between 1850 and 1945 and reassess the role played by the major actors.[16]

The historical analysis of industrialisation by Marcello Carmagnani, who published a carefully researched study of the evolution of the economy between 1860 and 1920, complemented the work by Hurtado, Lagos and Muñoz. Carmagnani, a historian by training, employed more empirical evidence than the others, and demonstrated the need for a reconceptualisation and reappraisal of the entire economic process of this period.[17]

However, the sharpening of social and political conflicts in Chile in the late 1960s and early 1970s was echoed in developments amongst academics, up to the point at which they became fatally enmeshed in the whirlpool of events which culminated in the coup d'état of September 1973. Thereafter, both academic debate and the publication of economic history in Chile sank into a period of long and painful decline which lasted until the mid-1980s.

Nevertheless, it was just at this time that the results of numerous research projects undertaken by PhD students in the United States began to be

countries between 1923 and 1981 is significant: 152, most of which were submitted after 1950. See Baldomero Estrada, 'Tesis sobre historia de Chile realizadas en Gran Bretaña, Estados Unidos, y Francia', *Nueva Historia* 8 (1983), 251–75.

16 Ricardo Lagos, *La industria en Chile: antecedentes estructurales* (Santiago, 1966); Carlos Hurtado, *Concentración de población y desarrollo económico: el caso chileno* (Santiago, 1966); Oscar Muñoz, *Crecimiento industrial de Chile, 1914–1965* (Santiago, 1968). In the following twenty years Muñoz was the only one of these three authors who continued his research on industrialisation: see his *Proceso a la industrialización chilena* (Santiago, 1972); *Estado e industrialización en el ciclo de expansión del salitre* (Santiago, 1977); and *Chile y su industrialización: pasado, crisis y opciones* (Santiago, 1986). Among recent constributions, see the valuable yet debatable book by Patricio Meller, *Un siglo de economía política chilena* (1890–1990) (Santiago, 1996).

17 Marcello Carmagnani, *Sviluppo industriale e sottosviluppo economico: il caso cileno, 1860–1920* (Turin, 1971).

published. At least with respect to economic history, for almost a decade after 1974 the bulk of the new publications about Chile stemmed from the large number of doctoral theses which were subsequently transformed into books. This phenomenon was not just confined to the United States. It also occurred in all the other countries where the academics within the 'Chilean diaspora' which followed the Pinochet coup had managed to find a refuge. This was, as Paul W. Drake has put it, the intellectual outcome of the 'political earthquakes' in Chile.[18]

Amongst the first books to be published was that of Henry W. Kirsch on industrialisation. As well as modifying the chronology, by taking the story back to the beginning of the 1880s, and drawing attention to the marked foreign component in the composition of the Chilean business elite, Kirsch's research initiated a period of important studies on this theme.[19] In the early 1980s, just at the point when industrialisation was ceasing to be regarded as the central axis of development strategy in Chile, two further articles on the subject were published in Great Britain.[20] The latest study on this theme published overseas has established a new conceptual framework for research, influenced by recent debates concerning similar processes in Europe. In an important article Arnold Bauer argues that the traditional attitude of scepticism towards the achievements of the Chilean industrial elite should be abandoned. Instead, the history of this group should be evaluated on its own terms, rather than with respect to the reference point of industrial development in Europe, the criterion which had been employed until then.[21]

In 1983, in the setting of the celebrations to mark the centenary of the Sociedad de Fomento Fabril, the organisation representing industrialists,

[18] Paul W. Drake, 'El impacto académico de los terremotos políticos: investigaciones de historia chilena en inglés, 1977–1983', *Alternativas* 2 (1983), 56–78.

[19] Henry W. Kirsch, *Industrial Development in a Traditional Society: the conflict between entrepreneurship and modernization in Chile* (Gainesville, 1977). By 'foreign' Kirsch was referring to immigrants who settled in Chile rather than expatriate firms.

[20] Luis Ortega, 'Acerca de los orígenes de la industrialización chilena, 1860–1879', *Nueva Historia* 2 (1981), 3–54, and Gabriel Palma, 'Chile, 1914–1935: de economía exportadora a sustitutiva de importaciones', *Nueva Historia* 7 (1983), 165–92. Palma published versions of this paper in English: 'From an Export-Led to an Import-Substituting Economy: Chile, 1914–1939', in Rosemary Thorp (ed.), *Latin America in the 1930s: the role of the periphery in world crisis* (London, 1984), pp. 50–80, and 'External Disequilibrium and Internal Industrialization: Chile, 1914–1935', in Christopher Abel and Colin M. Lewis (eds), *Latin America, Economic Imperialism, and the State: the political economy of the external connexion from independence to the present* (London, 1985), pp. 318–338. Ortega later broadened the scope of his research on this topic: 'El proceso de industrialización en Chile, 1850–1930', *Historia* 26 (1991–92), 213–46. On obstacles to industrialisation, see both Jorge Marshall, *La nueva interpretación de los orígenes de la industrialización chilena* (Santiago, 1988), and Luis Ortega, 'Los límites de la industrialización en Chile, 1850–1880', *Revista de Historia Industrial* (Barcelona) 5 (1995), 73–79.

[21] Arnold J. Bauer, 'Industry and the Missing Bourgeoisie: consumption and development in Chile, 1850–1950', *Hispanic American Historical Review* 70 (1990), 227–53.

a volume was published in Chile which included a section containing much information on businessmen in this sector. Unfortunately this work offered little in the way of analysis. In this text, like those mentioned above, what is noticeable is the marginal treatment given to individual entrepreneurs and firms within the business elite.[22]

Agriculture

Despite the important role that the agricultural sector has played in Chilean life, a mere five works were published on its history during the 1950s and 1960s. Once again the business dimension was marginal, which meant that foreign academic contributions were all the more decisive in the analysis of Chilean agricultural history.[23] The best example is that of Arnold J. Bauer. This author, who managed to isolate the fundamental problems of the rural economy, demonstrated at length that the absence of an entrepreneurial elite in agriculture was due to a number of factors. Those connected to economics, although important, were merely one amongst many. Above all Bauer emphasised the heavy burden of colonial institutions and practices.[24]

Where Bauer adopted a chronological approach to the subject, other authors broached the specific issue of the landowners. All arrived at similar conclusions, namely that the political and social power wielded by this group meant that there was very little need for the development of a nucleus of landowners with modern entrepreneurial capacities in the Chilean countryside.[25] However, this emphasis on the social characteristics of landowners meant that scholars tended to ignore issues like the organisation of labour and practices of land exploitation. Moreover, this slant in

[22] Sergio Ceppi et al., Chile: 100 años de industria (1883–1983) (Santiago, 1983).

[23] These works were: Rafael Baraona et al., Valle de Putaendo: estudio de estructura agraria (Santiago, 1961); Horacio Aránguiz, 'La situación de los trabajadores agrícolas en el siglo XIX', Estudios de las Instituciones Políticas y Sociales 2 (1967), 5–31; Mario Ballesteros, 'Desarrollo agrícola chileno, 1910–1955', Cuadernos de Economía 2 (1965), 153–76; Silvia Hernández, 'Transformaciones tecnológicas en la agricultura de Chile central: siglo XIX', Cuadernos del Centro de Estudios Socioeconómicos 3 (1966), 1–32; Gonzalo Izquierdo, Un estudio de las ideologías chilenas: la Sociedad Nacional de Agricultura en el siglo XIX (Santiago, 1968).

[24] Bauer's most important work is undoubtedly Chilean Rural Society: from the Spanish conquest to 1930 (Cambridge, 1975). Also important are some of his papers: 'Expansión económica en una sociedad tradicional: Chile central en el siglo XIX', Historia 9 (1970), 137–233; 'The Hacienda "El Huique" in the Agrarian Structure of Nineteenth-Century Chile', Agricultural History 46 (1972), 103–39; and (jointly with Anne H. Johnson) 'Land and Labour in Rural Chile, 1850–1935', in Kenneth Duncan and Ian Rutledge, Land and Labour in Latin America: essays on the development of agrarian capitalism in the nineteenth and twentieth centuries (Cambridge, 1977), pp. 83–102.

[25] These works are: Jean Carrière, Landowners and Politics in Chile: a study of the Sociedad Nacional de Agricultura (Amsterdam, 1980); Cristóbal Kay, 'The Development of the Chilean Hacienda System, 1850–1973', in Duncan and Rutledge (eds), Land and Labour, pp. 103–39; Thomas C. Wright, Landowners and Reform in Chile: the Sociedad Nacional de Agricultura, 1919–1940 (Urbana, 1982).

the analysis has continued to have a strong influence on the latest research carried out in Chile. In the most important of these recent publications, rather than factors like competitiveness, organisational training and ability, technical capacity, and innovation, the social and political gravitation of the landowners remains the central theme.[26]

Mining

Mining has been the motor which has driven the Chilean economy from the beginning of the republic until the present day.[27] Nevertheless, the most important analyses of this sector have simply provided evidence of its technical backwardness, especially with regard to extraction, at least before the beginning of the twentieth century when copper companies based in the United States initiated their operations in Chile. Once this happened, two opposing tendencies appeared. One part of the industry enjoyed a high level of capital investment and worked on a large scale, while the other possessed a low, though growing, level of capitalisation, advancing instead through labour-intensive techniques and the efforts of small and medium-sized businessmen.[28]

The latter type of production can be assimilated into the history of traditional copper mining in Chile. This dominated world markets until the 1870s, as a result of the high mineral content of Chilean ores and the persistence of high prices on the international market. Those studies available on this period show that as a result of these advantages the owners of copper mines seldom turned to innovation or investment as a means of increasing productivity.[29] When, from 1870 onwards, new and more

[26] José Bengoa, *El poder y la subordinación: historia social de la agricultura chilena* (Santiago, 1988).

[27] Markos Mamalakis, *The Growth and Structure of the Chilean Economy: from independence to Allende* (New Haven, 1976), p. 105. Mamalakis surveys the period from 1830 to 1930 in just one chapter.

[28] The most recent study of this sector is Julio Pinto and Luis Ortega, *Expansión minera y desarrollo industrial: un caso de desarrollo asociado (Chile, 1850–1914)* (Santiago, 1991). While this covers aspects such as profitability and the use of surpluses, the labour force, demand, and technological development in detail, it scarcely mentions the factor of entrepreneurship. An important study on a major nineteenth-century mining entrepreneur has also been published: Ricardo Nazer, *José Tomás Urmeneta: un empresario del siglo XIX* (Santiago, 1993). This book analyses in some depth the multiple activities of this businessman.

[29] Leland R. Pederson, *The Mining Industry of the Norte Chico, Chile* (Evanston, 1966); Pierre Vayssière, *Un siècle de capitalisme minière au Chili, 1830–1930* (Paris, 1980). See also John Mayo, 'Commerce, Credit, and Control in Chilean Copper Mining before 1880', in Thomas Greaves and William W. Culver (eds), *Miners and Mining in the Americas* (Manchester, 1985), pp. 29–46, and William W. Culver and Cornel J. Reinhart, 'The Decline of a Mining Region and Mining Policy: Chilean copper in the nineteenth century', in Greaves and Culver (eds), *Miners and Mining*, pp. 68–81; Clark W. Reynolds, 'Development Problems of an Export Economy: the case of copper and Chile', in Markos J. Mamalakis and Clark W. Reynolds, *Essays on the Chilean Economy* (Homewood, 1965), pp. 203–398; Joanne Fox

efficient producers began to compete on the global market, the dramatic fall in world copper prices largely eliminated Chile from it. Chile only managed to regain a presence in the international market during the second decade of the twentieth century due to the commencement of large-scale mining and the presence of US capital.

It thus appears something of a paradox that nineteenth-century mining, a decisive sector of the economy, but one so little studied until very recently, should have become the most important and prolific source for the strong views about the prosperity of Chile and its businessmen which entered the social imagery of the country. Mining provides the principal foundation for interpretations which stress the vigorous growth in the Chilean economy up to the 1860s and the presence of so-called 'pioneering entrepreneurs'. This argument still prevails, in spite of the fierce criticism it has received from Mario Góngora, perhaps the most important Chilean historian of the twentieth century.

In fact, according to Góngora, the point of departure in the debate over the problem of entrepreneurship in the nineteenth century was the paradigm of progress selected both by the scholars discussing this problem and by the nineteenth-century actors themselves. However, this did not correspond with the Chilean realities of the period. The social, economic, and historic circumstances of England and the United States at the time represented a totally different situation from that of Chile. At this time there existed in Chile a high level of spontaneity and adventurism, and not only were these traits predominant in the so-called 'entrepreneurial spirit' of the men who symbolised this 'pioneering age', but they also, in Góngora's words, 'lacked the austerity and thrifty mentality of the Manchester manufacturers, and ... resembled much more the Spanish conquistadores of the sixteenth century in what Werner Sombart defined as "adventurous capitalism"'. However, it was not only this that constituted the essence of the entrepreneurial problem in nineteenth-century Chile. In Góngora's view it was also related to the fact that, lacking any real bourgeois consciousness, the mining entrepreneurs 'quickly integrated themselves into the landed aristocracy and political oligarchy after the pioneering stage'. Thus the possible development of another, perhaps the most important, facet of the modern businessman, namely that of acting as an agent of social change, became diluted in Chile.[30]

Przeworski, *The Decline of the Copper Industry in Chile and the Entrance of North American Capital* (New York, 1980); Luis Valenzuela, 'The Copper Smelting Company "Urmaneta y Errázuriz" of Chile: an economic profile', *The Americas* 53 (1996), 235–72; Steven S. Volk, 'Mine Owners, Money Lenders, and the State in Mid-Nineteenth Century Chile', *Hispanic American Historial Review* 73 (1993), 67–98; William W. Culver and Cornel J. Reinhart, 'Capitalist Dreams: Chile's response to nineteenth-century world copper competition', *Comparative Studies in Society and History* 31 (1989), 722–744.

[30] Mario Góngora, *Ensayo crítico sobre la noción de Estado en Chile en los siglos XIX y XX* (Santiago, 1981), p. 38. Sombart noted moreover that those 'entrepreneurs' were in fact too weak 'to divert economic life into new channels': cf. his *El apogeo del capitalismo* (2 vols, Mexico City, 1984), I, 28.

In this context it could be argued that the onus of the Hispanic tradition, from both a cultural and economic viewpoint, was so great that it left its mark on a high proportion of the economic initiatives undertaken by Chileans right up to the start of the twentieth century. Moreover, this burden from the past was reflected in the fact that the English capitalists who first advanced into Chile after independence preferred not to become so enmeshed in traditional production activities that they began to overturn ancestral practices.

The coal mining industry was ignored by historians for decades. However, recent studies now suggest a contrast between the development of this sector and that of the more traditional forms of mining, copper and silver, at least in terms of the extraction of minerals. The period between 1840 and 1900 was in fact characterised by high levels of investment and productivity, and by the development of related activities which became horizontally and vertically integrated with coal mining, a development which reflected the presence of a small but nonetheless significant group of entrepreneurs. These businessmen, however, have not been the subject of specific studies, whether individually or collectively, and there is no literature on their activities after 1900.[31]

A panorama similar to that of coal and copper is to be found in the other crucial area of mining, nitrate. Despite its crucial importance in the economic system for over fifty years and the abundance of literature on the sector, research on the businessmen active in it remains extremely marginal. Only one work, out of a relatively high number on nitrate as a whole, manages to avoid this oversight. This is Thomas F. O'Brien's study, which provides a collection of biographical profiles of Chilean entrepreneurs in the industry, ranging from relatively unknown individuals to figures of major importance. The author uses these to illustrate his arguments on the nitrate regions of greatest significance, showing how some of the most prominent businessmen in the ruling elite became incorporated into the industry, further reinforcing their social and political dominance.[32]

---

[31] Roland E. Duncan, 'Chilean Coal and British Steamers: the origin of a South American industry', *Mariner's Mirror* 61 (1975), 271–281; Luis Ortega, 'The First Four Decades of the Chilean Coal Mining Industry', *Journal of Latin American Studies* 14 (1982), 1–32, and *La industria del carbón de Chile, 1840–1880* (Santiago, 1988).

[32] O'Brien, *The Nitrate Industry*. Work on the nitrate industry generally is abundant; the most significant studies are Oscar Bermúdez, *Historia del salitre desde sus orígenes hasta la Guerra del Pacífico* (Santiago, 1963), and also his *Historia del salitre desde la Guerra del Pacífico a la revolución de 1891* (Santiago, 1984); Michael Monteón, *Chile in the Nitrate Era: the evolution of economic dependence, 1880–1930* (Madison, 1982); Múñoz, *Estado e industrialización*; Carmen Cariola and Osvaldo Sunkel, *Un siglo de historia económica de Chile, 1830–1930* (Santiago, 1990). The latter also appears as 'Chile: ensayo de interpretación', in Roberto Cortés Conde and Stanley J. Stein (eds), *Latin America: a guide to the economic history, 1830–1930* (Berkeley, 1977), pp. 275–97. An important article which reappraises the contribution of nitrate to the Chilean economy in response to the arguments of Cariola and Sunkel is Manuel Fernández, 'El enclave salitrero y la economía chilena, 1880–1914', *Nueva Historia* 3 (1981), 2–42.

However, O'Brien's study stops with the civil war of 1891. Despite the availability of archives, therefore, especially for the foreign firms engaged in the industry, a major business history of nitrate before the foundation of the Compañía Salitrera de Chile (Cosach) in 1930 remains to be written, and there is hardly anything at all on the industry after the early 1930s. The potential of the archives, especially those of Antony Gibbs & Sons and Balfour Williamson, two of the leading British firms in the industry, is shown by a number of partial studies: Robert Greenhill's investigation of the relationship between the merchant houses and the Chilean state before 1914, Juan Ricardo Couyoumdjian's work on the First World War, and Thomas F. O'Brien's later work on the Guggenheims' attempts to modernise the technology of the industry.[33]

The tertiary sector

There have also been relatively few significant advances in the study of the tertiary sector. Although there are an appreciable number of works on trade, transport services, communications, and financial questions, the studies which have addressed these topics have tended to concentrate more on the operational dimension and the evolution of these activities over time rather than those who initiated and developed them.[34] However, as in the case of the economic sectors reviewed above, despite the limited analysis of the entrepreneurial variable, the reader in search of details concerning businessmen will discover important material that may help to elucidate the principal questions and problems about their role. In this context, even though its main focus is on the activity of British merchants in Chile, Eduardo Cavieres' work provides background material and details which are fundamental to an understanding of the successes and failures of Chilean entrepreneurs in an economic activity as vital as the external sector.[35]

---

[33] Robert Greenhill, 'The Nitrate and Iodine Trades, 1880–1914', in D. C. M. Platt (ed.), *Business Imperialism, 1840–1930: an inquiry based on British experience in Latin America* (Oxford, 1977), pp. 231–83; Juan Ricardo Couyoumdjian, 'El mercado de salitre durante la Primera Guerra Mundial y la posguerra, 1914–1921: notas para su estudio', *Historia* 12 (1974/75), 13–55; Thomas F. O'Brien, '"Rich Beyond the Dreams of Avarice": the Guggenheims in Chile', *Business History Review* 63 (1989), 122–59. Apart from the British merchant houses' archives, those of the Anglo-South American Bank and the US house of W. R. Grace & Co., both of which were heavily involved in the development of the nitrate industry after the turn of the century, have also been made accessible to historians.

[34] The most important works concerning communications, services, and maritime transport are J. J. Johnson, *Pioneer Telegraphy in Chile, 1852–1876* (Stanford, 1948); Jay Kinsbruner, 'Water for Valparaiso: a case of entrepreneurial frustration', *Journal of Inter-American Studies and World Affairs* 10 (1968), 635–661; Claudio Véliz, *Historia de la marina mercante* (Santiago, 1961); Roland E. Duncan, 'William Wheelwright and Early Steam Navigation in the Pacific', *The Americas* 32:2 (1975), 257–281.

[35] Eduardo Cavieres, *Comercio chileno y comerciantes ingleses, 1820–1880: un ciclo de historia económica* (Valparaiso, 1988). The author had trailed the publication of the book with a

A new research agenda?

The new economic development model imposed by the military dictatorship after 1974 created conditions in which business history acquired a hitherto unheard of relevance in Chile. The development strategy based on the market and the private sector placed businessmen in the centre of national life, and naturally the historical literature did not remain unaffected by these trends. Undoubtedly, this new situation provided major incentives for the output of historians, but it also opened up numerous pitfalls, especially for those who advocated and endorsed the model. Like its originators and propagandists, the historians who have approached this topic have tended to exhibit a strong ideological and proselytising tendency, which has at times impaired a potentially very important development in economic history.

One example of this was a joint publication of several scholars who turned once again to the cases of the individuals whom different historical traditions had established as 'pioneers' during the nineteenth century. They outlined a story which became a veritable panegyric to private initiative. In the view of the authors concerned, the 'seven figures whose biographies' made up the book demonstrated that 'the spirit of initiative and business sense were the common denominator' amongst them.[36] The proselytising liberal nature of this publication was followed by another study which, though from an academic perspective, also used history as a legitimising factor for the new development project. At some point in the mid-1970s an important collection of essays under the provocative title of *Empresa privada* (Private Business) was published, evaluating the evolution, current situation, and future perspectives of this sector. This was the moment 'at

suggestive study, 'Estructura y funcionamiento de las sociedades comerciales de Valparaíso durante el siglo XIX, 1820–1880', *Cuadernos de Historia* 4 (1984), 61–86. The symbiotic relationship between Chilean and British capitalists, as it would be called many years later, and the dominance of the latter which eventually resulted, had already been the subject of an important study by Thomas O'Brien, 'The Antofagasta Company: a case study of peripheral capitalism', *Hispanic American Historical Review* 60 (1980), 1–31. For internal transport the most suggestive study is Robert B. Oppenheimer, 'National Capital and National Development: financing Chile's Central Valley railroads', *Business History Review* 56 (1982), 54–75, which analyses the financing of railway construction, the role of private shareholders, and that of the public sector. For a more recent commissioned business history of railways in the north of Chile, written in a classically British manner, see Harold Blakemore, *From the Pacific to La Paz: the Antofagasta (Chili) and Bolivia Railway Company, 1888–1988* (London, 1989). On foreign interest in public utilities after the First World War, see Linda Jones *et al.*, 'Public Utility Companies', in D. C. M. Platt (ed.), *Business Imperialism, 1840–1930: an inquiry based on British experience in Latin America* (Oxford, 1977), pp. 94–114.

[36] *Los pioneros* (Santiago, 1974). The team which carried out this work was led by the journalist, Hermógenes Pérez de Arce of the conservative daily, *El Mercurio*. Two of the seven individuals discussed, José Santos Ossa and José Tomás Urmeneta, later had their business abilities questioned by Mario Góngora, *Ensayo crítico*, p. 29.

which Chile was handing over to the private sector the principal responsibility for leading the process of economic development'. In this context
it seemed essential to respond to the main challenge of the period, namely
that 'the new generation should know and possess a full understanding of
the values that private business required'.[37]

Two papers by Fernando Silva stand out from these publications, not
just for their historiographical value, but also for their methodological
rigour and quality, features which, curiously, are not very common amongst
authors who align themselves with these economic policies.[38] In sharp
contrast to the tendency of most right-wing authors to extol individuals,
both before and after the publication of *Empresa privada*, Silva looked for
elements within the structure of the economy that might contribute towards
an explanation of the weakness of the entrepreneurial sector during the
nineteenth century, especially during the first half of it. His brief, but
rigorous, analysis of economic conditions up to the 1840s led him to suggest
that rather than it being a problem of individuals and their cultural and
psychological characteristics, it was more a question of there being no
'opportunity for the classic procedures of the capitalist entrepreneur: both
the rhythms and the scale of Chilean economic life meant that they were
unnecessary'. This provided an explanation for their ignorance of traditional commercial techniques which had been employed and accepted in
Europe for centuries: the bill of exchange, double-entry book-keeping, and
banking operations. All of this was a result of the fundamental characteristics of the economic system, which was marked by 'the lack of far-
reaching economic stimuli which might have been capable of developing
imagination, techniques and capital'.

This argument provides an explanation for the limited number of firms
genuinely worthy of such a title and the reduced number of entrepreneurs
in Chile during this period. However, once the appropriate incentives did
begin to appear, especially at the end of the 1840s, true businessmen did
eventually appear on the scene.[39] In this way Silva's work of entrepreneurial
discovery commenced just at the point at which Encina believed that a
golden age of business enterprise was beginning to close. This opened up
a whole new line of research, with actors, initiatives, and characteristics
which were rather different from those highlighted in the literature until
then.[40] Unfortunately, despite the promise of his work, Silva did not
continue developing this topic in a systematic manner.

[37] Escuela de Negocios de Valparaíso, *Empresa Privada* (Valparaíso, n.d.), p. 12. This
volume was probably published in 1976.

[38] Fernando Silva, 'Comerciantes, habilitadores y mineros: una aproximacón al estudio de
la mentalidad empresarial en los primeros años de Chile republicano, 1817–1840', in *Empresa
privada*, pp. 37–71, and 'Notas sobre la evolución empresarial chilena en el siglo XIX', in
Empresa privada, pp. 73–91.

[39] Silva, 'Comerciantes, habilitadores y mineros', pp. 38–39.

[40] Silva, 'Notas sobre la evolución empresarial chilena'.

The theme was taken up from a similar analytical perspective at the beginning of the 1980s, but the focus again came from a sociological and cultural viewpoint, and with a strongly ideological slant. Within the context of a general history of Chile it was thus claimed that although the Chilean of the nineteenth century was not lacking in 'entrepreneurial spirit', he did not possess it to the extent necessary to create a business ethos which required 'method, steadiness, control of expenditure, technical ability, order, punctuality [and] the patience to await results which would appear only after years of perseverance and effort'. It was therefore impossible in the last twenty-five years of the nineteenth century to construct a type of firm or an individual entrepreneur capable of creating, transmitting, and perpetuating an industrial tradition. In words reminiscent of Encina, Gonzalo Vial, the author of this work and the current doyen of conservative historiography in Chile, attributed all this to the 'disdain for manual labour, contempt for Chilean manufactured products, the influence of *education*, [and] the decline in the vitality and initiative of the ruling class'.[41]

In the midst of a national and international environment which was favourable to a reappraisal of business, three other works on this theme were published during the period of military rule. Two look at a particular Chilean capitalist, while the third analyses the role of the Sociedad de Fomento Fabril, the principal association for the promotion of industry, during the late nineteenth and early twentieth centuries. These were the last of the studies undertaken in this period from a neoliberal perspective.[42] The former, dedicated to the business activities of José Tomás Ramos, studied the behaviour of one of the most important merchants in Valparaíso in the middle of the nineteenth century in a competent and, for the Chilean environment, a novel manner. They highlight his wide ranging initiatives, not only in the field of commerce, but also in production and shipping.[43] However, Juan Vargas, the principal author, immersed himself in the broader debate with less success, though not without also attempting to find an explanation for the so-called decline of entrepreneurial spirit which seemed to be evident in the last quarter of the century. In his view, the generation which controlled the economic activities of commerce and production at that point possessed 'less business enterprise than ... its

---

[41] Gonzalo Vial, *Historia de Chile, 1891–1973* (Santiago, 1981), vol I, tomo II, p. 491. The emphasis in the latter quotation is mine: it emphasises a crucial continuity with the ideas formulated by Encina ... in 1911! Vial continued with this theme and a similar analytical focus in 'Tradición y mentalidad industrial en Chile', in Ceppi *et al.*, *Chile: 100 años de industria*, pp. 357–360.

[42] Juan Vargas and Gerardo Martínez, 'José Tomás Ramos Font: una fortuna chilena del siglo XIX', *Historia* 18 (1982), 355–392; Juan Vargas, *José Tomás Ramos Font: una fortuna chilena del siglo XIX* (Santiago, 1988); Juan Vargas 'La Sociedad de Fomento Fabril, 1883–1920', *Historia* 13 (1976), 5–53.

[43] Vargas and Martínez, 'José Tomás Ramos Font'. The important contribution that economists can make to historical work is quite evident from this article.

predecessors'. This, he argued, quoting Encina, was nothing more or less than the expression of the death of 'that audacious, almost adventurous, initiative' which had become 'the first victim of classical education and its twin sister and successor, scientific education'.[44] Nevertheless, at the end of a complex and abstruse analysis, marked by weaknesses in his handling of concepts, Vargas decided that these factors, although important, were not definitive. He thus arrived at the paradoxical conclusion that Chile had possessed entrepreneurs when the characteristics of the economy were not appropriate for them, and that they had been extinguished just at the time when the conditions necessary for their growth had begun to appear, though not without some complex difficulties.[45]

Business and entrepreneurial history have not been major themes for historians who do not belong to the neoliberal school. Yet while the subject has received limited attention from other perspectives, such studies, though far less numerous than those of the neoliberals, have been much more creative. According to Sergio Villalobos, one important socio-economic phenomenon of the nineteenth century was the transformation of the firm. Villalobos placed his emphasis on the 'social significance' of the firm rather than its economic or business role, since 'this was essential for the shaping of a bourgeoisie and the appearance of a proletariat, with all its political consequences'. Nevertheless, Villalobos did pose some interesting questions for the analysis of business development. He suggested that from the second half of the nineteenth century there was an evolution from 'very primitive forms of organisation ... towards the calculating, rational businessman, who accepted new production techniques and new ways of linking himself with commerce and credit'. The nature of the firm was also transformed, moving away from simple contracts among families and friends, often for just one transaction, towards stable companies with complex contracts, and later to *sociedades anónimas* and *compañías de*

---

[44] Vargas, *José Tomás Ramos*, pp. 259–260.

[45] The conceptual confusion of Vargas is in evidence when he states that the cause for the decline of the entrepreneurial spirit 'should be sought, on the one hand, in the *steadily increasing capital investments that the modern economic world demanded,* and on the other in the *very strong competition* that the Chileans had to face from powerful foreign firms. In contrast, during the first half of the century (approximately), when the revolution in communications was still being felt, *a modest amount of capital was enough* to operate in any business sector, *without there existing the competition which was so characteristic later.* These circumstances appear to be decisive in understanding why so many Chileans took part in that period in mining speculations, commercial flour-milling, shipbuilding, and other activities, and why so few did so afterwards': Vargas, *José Tomás Ramos*, p. 261. The emphasis is mine. To put it simply, the theory Vargas advances is that there were entrepreneurs in Chile when capitalist development was limited, and that they tended to decline in numbers as capitalism expanded. Vargas had already played down the historical existence of the Chilean entrepreneur during the second half of the nineteenth century in his article on 'La Sociedad de Fomento Fabril', published in 1976.

responsabilidad limitada'.[46] Villalobos also made some significant points about the role that foreigners played in economic growth and business in Chile. He ended his excursion into this subject with a book in which he further developed his initial ideas, but now within the framework of a broader discussion of the 'national bourgeoisie', touching in passing upon their business activities.[47]

The most novel contribution to this subject during the last few years has come from Gabriel Salazar who has made noteworthy efforts to write the history of the Chilean lower classes. In this context Salazar suggested that there existed an entrepreneurial phase in the history of this group of the population which, curiously, runs parallel in terms of the period concerned to that of the 'entrepreneurial pioneers' highlighted in the conservative historiography. For Salazar the economic options for the lower classes became progressively more narrow from the end of the eighteenth century as they became tied to the land or as an alternative engaged in 'the parallel system of banditry', which offered a marginal but widespread popular movement in opposition [to the dominance of the oligarchy]'.[48] However, he argues:

> Before 1850, the normal type of occupation for the lower classes was the entrepreneurial (but manual) exploitation of the resources of the earth ... It was this entrepreneurial movement which led to the territorial expansion of wheat cultivation in the Central Valley, the appearance of farmers everywhere, and the occupation of the lands south of the Bío-Bío River for stockraising and timber production. The same process resulted in the development of pre-industrialised mining, the multiple emergence of ore-pickers and placer-miners, and the rise of precapitalist society in the Norte Chico. And it explains the generally unknown efforts of ordinary people to start up "national industry" in the middle of the nineteenth century.[49]

In other words, it was due to these initiatives that a large part of the growth

[46] Sergio Villalobos, 'Sugerencias para un enfoque del siglo XIX', *Estudios Cieplan* 12 (1984), 9–36. The quotation is from p. 23 of this article. In the same year Alvaro Góngora published an article which also marginally touched upon the problem of the business elite at the end of the nineteenth century: 'Políticas económicas, agentes económicos y desarrollo industrial en Chile hacia 1870–1900', *Dimensión Histórica de Chile* 1 (1984), 9–22. The *sociedad anónima* (SA) and the *sociedad de responsabilidad limitada* (SRL) are the basic forms of company organisation in many Latin American countries. The SRL was roughly equivalent to a limited liability company, and for the most part its shares remained in the hands of the founders and their descendants. The SA is roughly equivalent to a public limited company and had a broader scope for expansion, though trading in its shares was often extremely limited.

[47] Sergio Villalobos, *Orígen y ascenso de la burguesía chilena* (Santiago, 1987), especially pp. 38–59.

[48] Gabriel Salazar, 'Empresariado popular e industrialización: la guerrilla de los mercaderes (Chile, 1830–1885)', *Proposiciones* 20 (1991), 180–231.

[49] Salazar, 'Empresariado popular', 182. The Norte Chico comprises the provinces of Coquimbo and Atacama and was the centre of copper and silver mining in Chile during the nineteenth century.

and expansion of the mid-nineteenth century took place, an idea that is, to say the least, novel and stimulating.

However, what was the nature of this industrialisation, the symbol of the entrepreneurial achievements of the mid-nineteenth century for Salazar? His answer is clearly located in a different tradition, one which corresponds much more to proto-industrial activity and which therefore makes claims for initiatives which may seem rather archaic:

> The popular industries of the nineteenth century comprised small rural establishments which were poorly equipped and operated by family groups rather than by contracted operatives. Today the majority of them would not fit the parameters used to define *pequeña industria* (small-scale industry) or a *microempresa* (a small firm). Nevertheless they developed a concentrated social-productive movement which offered serious opposition to the monop-olistic, authoritarian, and international project of the merchants. Popular industries, located in settlements in the countryside but linked to the outside world by the masses of intrusive street vendors, harrassed and hemmed in the 'cultured cities' of the merchants.

The collapse of this experience, of what Salazar terms *la economía bárbara* (the wild economy), 'came after a continuous series of ambushes and subterranean battles in which the popular classes had to fight time and time again against the powerful anti-productive and anti-popular struggle led by the national and foreign merchant elites and their obedient political agents [in the Chilean congress]'.[50] In this analysis the author neglects the changes which were taking place during this period, most obviously in the diffusion of market relations, and consequently the development of a degree of competition against which such weak productive units could do little or nothing.

Why has this historical interpretation been developed? It is linked to a social programme aimed at achieving a greater role and participation for the popular sectors in contemporary Chile in response to the apparently irresistible neoliberal tide. In other words, it is concerned primarily with rescuing from history alternative solutions for current problems, since despite the 'defeat of the popular classes [in the nineteenth century] in the face of merchant strength, their impact has not been totally diluted. Even today, their far-reaching plans remain significant'.[51]

Nevertheless, today, as yesterday, the signs of the times seem to be directing Chileans towards other paths of development, which, though they may perhaps be less rich in terms of the way in which they value humanity, are, without doubt, enormously effective. In such periods it is hardly surprising to find reactions inspired by elements of romanticism and nostalgia.

---

[50] Salazar, 'Empresariado popular', 196–197.
[51] Salazar, 'Empresariado popular', 183.

Conclusion

The new agenda, like the output of the decades from the 1950s to the 1970s, seems to have concentrated attention on the nineteenth century, thus leaving pending the enormous task of research on the period between 1900 and 1945. Whatever the weaknesses of the published literature for the second half of the nineteenth century, for the first part of the twentieth the volume of research is miniscule. The crucial years from 1925 to 1945, the end of the period covered in this essay, have only been touched upon in a superficial way by the studies discussed above. The literature published during the last fifteen years has simply followed this same pattern.[52]

There are, therefore, numerous tasks which historians still have to undertake. One problem that stands out is that of the status of business history as an academic discipline. There are no chairs in the subject in Chilean universities. With regards to the businessmen themselves it is essential to begin to analyse questions such as their socio-political role; their professional training and performance; the tracing of investment and financial and administrative strategies; processes of company formation; the recruitment of the workforce and employer-labour relations; structures of management; the relationship between businessmen and the state; case studies of key firms; and the development of business at a regional level.

The successful completion of research on business history presents a number of difficulties. First, one must emphasise the customary reluctance of businessmen to authorise historians to consult their archives. Second, once they do grant permission for access to the documents in their possession, they have a tendency to demand some form of panegyric rather than an objective history. Even more worrying is the widespread lack of concern for the preservation of business documents when companies cease their activities. The destruction of archives as a result of this has been as lamentable as it has been frequent. However, the business historian in Chile does have at his disposal the notarial archives and commercial registers of the most important cities, alongside wills, company reports,

---

[52] See Kirsch, *Industrial Development*, and Muñoz's works on industrialisation cited above (footnotes 11 and 16). For the period between 1927 and 1945, which marked the initiation and expansion of state activity in the economy, the classic work remains P. T. Ellsworth, *Chile: an economy in transition* (New York, 1945), still, perhaps, the most complete study of the impact of the world depression of 1929–1932 in Chile and the measures implemented in order to combat it. See also the well-known article of Gabriel Palma, 'External Disequilibrium and Internal Industrialization'. One of the key innovations of the late 1930s was the establishment of the Corporación de Fomento (CORFO), the state agency in charge of Chile's industrialisation programmes between 1939 and 1970. CORFO also financed projects in other areas of the economy. There has been some useful work on this key state development agency: see Markos Mamalakis, 'An Analysis of the Financial and Investment Activities of the Chilean Development Corporation, 1939–1974', *Journal of Development Studies* 5:2 (1977), 118–137; Luis Ortega *et al.*, *50 años de realizaciones: Corfo, 1939–1989* (Santiago, 1989), chapters 1–3.

and various private archives belonging either to companies or individuals.[53] With such resources it is possible to tackle the outstanding academic tasks listed above. To put it in a nutshell, there is a whole history yet to be written.

[53] However, there is not much ground for optimism. A review of the grants approved by the National Fund for Scientific and Technological Research in the 1990s shows that only three projects on enterprises and entrepreneurs have been given funding: one by Eduardo Cavieres dealing with the merchants of Valparaíso during the first half of the nineteenth century, a second one under the charge of Luis Ortega and Pamela Araya dealing with company formation between 1880 and 1914, and a third by Leonardo Mazzei on businessmen in the Concepción region in the latter part of the nineteenth century.

CHAPTER FIVE

Business History in Colombia

Carlos Dávila

In Colombia the study of business history is in its early stages. The first works specifically dedicated to this subject, those of the North American historian, Frank Safford, appeared in the middle of the 1960s.[1] However, the last two decades have seen a slow but gradual expansion of this area of research. The literature is somewhat disparate, produced by individual researchers, rather than research teams. They have come from a wide range of social science disciplines, and been located in very different faculties and university departments: management, history, economics, and sociology. Foreign scholars have made a significant contribution. This is not without merit since Colombians have been opening up a field which is quite well developed on an international level, especially in Great Britain and the United States, and which, from the beginning, has been 'something of a no man's land, on the frontiers between economics, history and sociology'.[2] The literature published since 1965 has resulted in new research themes and stimulated important questions, and it has aroused interest in different units of analysis – regional business elites, companies, entrepreneurs, families of businessmen, economic groups, and business associations – all of which had tended to receive very little attention in Colombia.

The number of important reviews of the historical literature undertaken in the last few years is evidence of the marked advance of research overall in Colombia since the mid-1970s. Nevertheless, these surveys consistently display a lack of interest in business issues, and this is evident both in the approaches of the authors and the works which they consider.[3] At best

[1] Frank Safford, 'Commerce and Enterprise in Central Colombia, 1821–1870' (PhD thesis, Columbia University, 1965), and 'Foreign and National Enterprise in Nineteenth-Century Colombia', *Business History Review* 39 (1965), 503–526. This was translated as 'Empresarios nacionales y extranjeros en Colombia durante el siglo XIX', *Anuario Colombiano de Historia Social y de la Cultura* 3 (1965), 49–69.

[2] Thomas Cochran, 'Actividad empresarial', in *Enciclopedia Internacional de las Ciencias Sociales* (Madrid, 1974), IV, 212.

[3] In a review of the historical literature published between 1978 and 1988, one leading commentator suggested that the study of business elites, a type of business history that was on the dividing line between social history and economics, had 'produced some outstanding results': Jorge Orlando Melo, 'La literatura histórica en la última década', *Boletín Cultural y*

business issues are included in the surveys but analysed in a very marginal or incomplete fashion, or else they are treated with indifference and simply as an appendage to the 'economic historiography'.[4] As a consequence they largely fail to analyse the contributions that have been made to the study of business and businessmen. These surveys have thus omitted numerous studies, particularly on the twentieth century.[5]

Rather than quibbling about such omissions, which are probably inevitable in this type of task, or criticising the criteria used in these otherwise valuable surveys of the historiography, it would be more sensible to advance by means of a specialised review of a field which is just taking shape and which might shed some light on its potential, its utility, and its future research agenda. The survey of the literature on Colombian business history presented in this chapter is an updated and more selective version of a lengthier analysis which was published in 1991 and covered 314 studies but dealt with the theme without making any selection on grounds of

Bibliográfico 25: 15 (1988), 65. In 1989 the government-financed Misión de Ciencia y Tecnología sponsored studies on the state of development and social relevance of 23 disciplines, including history. The prominent historian, Germán Colmenares, offered an incisive, if negative, judgement on the field: 'There are attempts at business history and from time to time monographs of industrial and commercial firms are published. These works, commissioned by the institutions themselves, possess an apologetic tone and their results are normally superficial.' See Germán Colmenares, 'Estado de desarrollo e inserción social de la historia en Colombia', in Ministerio de Educación Nacional, *La conformación de comunidades científicas en Colombia* (Bogotá, 1990), II, 1085.

[4] One example is an essay in a two-volume work published in 1994 which incorporates an extensive discussion of work on Colombia produced overseas. Here the business history of the nineteenth century is considered within a general essay on the economic historiography which is organised in terms of agro-export models, agrarian history, and monetary history. See Oscar Rodríguez, 'La historiografía económica colombiana del siglo XIX', in Bernardo Tovar Zembrano (ed.), *La historia al final del milenio: ensayos de historiografía colombiana y latinoamericana* (2 vols, Bogotá, 1994), I, 187–250.

[5] Also published in 1994 was an analysis of the literature published between 1950 and 1988 on the economic history of Colombia in the nineteenth and twentieth centuries: Jesús Antonio Bejarano, *Historia económica y desarrollo: la historiografía económica sobre los siglos XIX y XX en Colombia* (Bogotá, 1994), appendix, pp. 224–28 and 232–38. This volume is much more than a detailed review of the economic historiography of Colombia, which accounts for three of its six chapters. These are preceded by an interesting and erudite 'attempt at definition'; a contrast between the study of economic history in Colombia and the remainder of Latin America; and an analysis of the relationship between models of economic development and the economic historiography of Latin America. However it includes only fifteen titles on businesses and businessmen, two on foreign businessmen, and a few other relevant works in the section on regional studies. In this respect it does not reflect the care taken in the remainder of the work. Amongst the items omitted are the following: an important book on industrial entrepreneurs in two important intermediate cities, the coffee centres of Manizales and Pereira, Manuel Rodríguez, *El empresario industrial del Viejo Caldas* (Bogotá, 1983); and an article by David Johnson, 'Reyes González Hermanos: la formación del capital durante la regeneración en Colombia', *Boletín Cultural y Bibliográfico* 23:9 (1986), 25–43.

quality.[6] The scope of this chapter and the criteria used in selecting items for discussion are as follows. First, it includes work on the Colombian business elite in the nineteenth and twentieth centuries published after 1940. Second, the emphasis is on academic research published as books or articles, or else produced as postgraduate theses. However, it is not confined to the work of historians, since numerous studies have been carried out by scholars from other social science disciplines. Third, although they are not included in the discussion, the existence of non-academic studies must also be recognised. Memoirs, biographies, commemorative works by journalists and writers, and compilations of documents all represent indispensable sources for the researcher in this field.[7] Fourth, this chapter is not confined to those works which concentrate directly and exclusively on the entrepreneurs and business elites, but it also includes broader studies in economic and social history insofar as they contribute useful elements for the understanding of business history. In the case of the latter they are analysed here from the perspective of the business historian, in the sense that they are of interest primarily for their discussion of the evolution of business behaviour (issues such as economic calculation, risk, innovation, diversification, and performance); the origin and social and cultural environment of the businessman; the motivations and other individual determinants of the activities of entrepreneurs; the education and socialisation of the business elite; the evolution of the structure of the firm; strategy and policy at various levels (individual, family, company, and economic group); the relationship between the business elite and the state; and the ideology and ethos of business in Colombia. In contrast, this chapter excludes those studies which analyse economic growth at an aggregate level whilst ignoring the role played by the main actors and those which give exclusive attention to macroeconomic variables and do not engage in discussion of the microeconomic behaviour of units of production, entrepreneurs, and business groups.

The regional business elite and entrepreneurship in Antioquia

Within the limited bibliography on business and entrepreneurship in Colombia, the best known theme is that of the origins and the role of regional

6 Carlos Dávila, *Historia empresarial de Colombia: estudios, problemas y perspectivas* (Bogotá, 1991). This was published as a monograph by the Facultad de Administración of the Universidad de los Andes, and reprinted in 1996.

7 The comments of the British historian, Malcolm Deas, on what should be considered as scholarly political history and the problems of lack of objectivity normally associated with memoirs and autobiographies, are also very pertinent to the study of business history. 'The militant historian', Deas writes, 'although to some extent "academic" insofar as he includes footnotes or works in a university, is not so easily distinguished from the political activist ...': Deas, 'Comentario al estudio de historiografía política del siglo XX', in Tovar Zembrano, *La historia al final del milenio*, II, 535.

businessmen, especially in Antioquia.[8] In Colombia acute regional differences in terms of the economy, society, and culture have been, and still are, marked. Colombia has always been 'a country of regions', and the differences between settlements have been rather more pronounced than those between the mountains and the coast, or the capital and the provinces, which are typical of other countries in Latin America.[9] Indeed, it was not until the first few decades of the twentieth century that Colombians really laid the foundations of political integration in a centralised national state, and developed an internal market capable of overcoming the persistent obstacles to economic growth represented by small regional markets.

The case of Antioquia attracted attention due to the early industrialisation of Medellín at the beginning of the twentieth century and its important economic role within the country. This led to interpretations of the industrial 'take-off' of the region which emphasised the entrepreneurship of its inhabitants. A book by a North American geographer, James Parsons, published in 1949, highlighted a 'form of Latin Puritanism' of these 'South American Yankees' that troubled numerous foreign researchers.[10]

As a result, during the 1960s and 1970s more studies of Antioquia were published, especially with regard to its business activity, than for any other region in the country. From the North American perspective of 'modernisation' theory (which was in the ascendant in the 1960s and which explained underdevelopment, amongst other things, in terms of an inadequate supply of entrepreneurship due to an inappropriate cultural environment), Antioquia was seen as so atypical that it interested many foreign scholars after Parsons. One of the best known works was that of an economist, Everett Hagen, who in 1962 ruled out economic factors as a means of explaining the 'take-off' in Antioquia in the decades around

---

[8] The region of Antioquia is located between the central and western *cordilleras* of the Andes, and lacks navigable rivers and arable land: its geography poses formidable obstacles to transportation and communication. Interestingly enough, during the nineteenth century antioqueños pioneered investment in gold mining, internal and international commerce, tobacco, coffee, colonisation, and banking. Their best known accomplishment, the early industrialisation of the capital, Medellín, during the first decade of the present century, defies conventional explanations of economic development. In some respects this problem is parallel to that facing historians of Mexico and Brazil, who have had to explain the peculiarities of Monterrey and São Paulo: on the latter cases, see pp. 122–24 and 49–54.

[9] This can be explained in terms of geographical factors, enormous difficulties in communications, the existence of a network of several important urban settlements, and unequal distribution of natural resources, and the differentiated effects among regions of the colonial institutions established by the Spaniards.

[10] James Parsons, *Antioqueño Colonization in Western Colombia* (Berkeley, 1949); a translation was published by the Academia Nacional de Historia in Colombia a year later. The same author also studied colonisation in the North West of Colombia, the banana zone around Urabá, after the middle of the twentieth century: James Parsons, *Antioquia's Corridor to the Sea: an historical geography of the settlement of Urabá* (Berkeley, 1967).

the turn of the century and sought an explanation instead in the ethnic and psychological origins of the Puritan ethic in Antioquia.[11]

The analysis of business thought and action, however, could advance only by means of rigorous historical research and more plausible hypotheses, a task which was carried out almost entirely by English and US historians. The first of these, Frank Safford, published a refutation of Hagen's interpretation in 1967.[12] In the same year Luis Fajardo wrote a short book on the formation of a Puritan 'ethos' within a Catholic society.[13] Years later Ann Twinam was to comment that Hagen's status deprivation thesis 'reduced a complex historical reality to an absurd simplification'.[14] On the economic front Alvaro López Toro's valuable 1970 study examined the disequilibrium between the mining and agrarian sectors in Antioquia, and remarked upon the kind of talents and attitudes that were forged in the mining industry.[15] The following year, however, the voluntaristic interpretation of *antioqueño* growth was revived in the work of a US economist.[16]

During the mid-1970s two studies emerged which provided a new direction for research on businessmen in Antioquia. Roger Brew traced the determinants of industrialisation in the region, entrepreneurship included, and argued that coffee did not initiate but rather accelerated processes which had already been generated in the mining industry and which thus provided the stimulus for a local and autonomous industrialisation in Medellín. This gave rise to 'the conditions for the growth of a class of businessmen with the traditional capitalist virtues'.[17] Ann Twinam's 1976 doctoral thesis, together with her later work, covered the period between 1760 and 1810, when high risks, high liquidity, and sporadic

---

[11] Everett Hagen, *On the Theory of Social Change* (Homewood, IL., 1962). The chapter on Antioquia was translated as *El cambio social en Colombia: el factor humano en el desarrollo* (Bogotá, 1963).

[12] Frank Safford, 'Significación de los antioqueños en el desarrollo histórico colombiano: un examen crítico de las tesis de Everett Hagen', *Anuario Colombiano de Historia Social y de la Cultura* 3 (1967), 49–69.

[13] Luis H. Fajardo, ¿*La moralidad protestante de los antioqueños? Estructura social y personalidad* (Cali, 1968)

[14] Ann Twinam, *Miners, Merchants, and Farmers in Colonial Colombia* (Austin, 1982), p. 6.

[15] Alvaro López Toro, *Migración y cambio social en Antioquia durante el siglo XIX* (Bogotá, 1970).

[16] William Paul McGreevey, *An Economic History of Colombia, 1845–1930* (Cambridge, 1970). This was the first quantitative economic history of Colombia and it was subjected to devastating criticism by leading historians during the mid-1970s. The cliometric current in Colombia has never recovered from this uncertain start, which was associated with the inadequacy of the historical statistics, the fundamental raw material for this type of approach. See Instituto de Estudios Colombianos, *Historia económica de Colombia: un debate en marcha* (Bogotá, 1979).

[17] Roger Brew, *El desarrollo económico de Antioquia desde la independencia hasta 1920* (Bogotá, 1977), p. 407. This book was a translation of Brew's doctoral thesis, 'The Economic Development of Antioquia from 1850 to 1920' (DPhil thesis, Oxford, 1973).

returns were characteristic of commercial activity. As far as trade was concerned these factors determined a style of business behaviour which was characterised by continuous reinvestment but a high level of diversification: in mining, commerce, colonisation, banking, tobacco cultivation, railway construction, coffee, and finally industry.[18] The evolution of studies on the *antioqueño* elite before the middle of the 1980s, with an emphasis on the academic debates which the subject aroused, was also the theme of two papers by Carlos Dávila.[19]

Since the end of the 1970s the number of studies concerning specific aspects of the multifaceted business activity of Antioquia has increased. Some of these contributions will be examined in later sections of this paper covering colonisation, coffee, industrialisation, and the biographies of businessmen. Two essays that suggested various hypotheses and questions regarding the highly diversified business activities of the *antioqueño* bourgeoisie should be mentioned.[20] An extensive volume on the history of Antioquia, published in 1988, included a collection of chapters synthesising research which supported their arguments with various references to businessmen, families, and individual firms in different sectors of economic activity in Antioquia.[21] In 1989 there also appeared a collection of articles on the evolution of commerce and merchants in Medellín from the seventeenth century to the present.[22] Prior to these articles an interesting institutional study of the trade of Medellín in the early twentieth century had been published in 1982, together with another paper on the evolution

[18] Twinam, *Miners, Merchants, and Farmers in Colonial Colombia*, was a revision of her 1976 Yale University dissertation, and was also published in Spanish in 1985. See also her 'De judio a vasco: mitos étnicos y espíritu empresarial antioqueño', *Revista de Extensión Cultural* (Medellín) 9/10 (1981), 105–18.

[19] Carlos Dávila, 'Ciencia y ficción sobre el desarrollo de Antioquia: notas extemporáneas sobre el libro de Everett Hagen', *Revista Universidad Eafit : Temas Administrativas* 41 (1981), 47–68; and 'El empresariado antioqueño, 1760–1920: de las interpretaciones psicológicas a los estudios históricos', *Siglo XIX: Revista de Historia* 5:9 (1990), 11–74.

[20] Marco Palacios, 'El café en la vida de Antioquia', and Ann Twinam, 'Comercio y comerciantes en Antioquia', both in Moisés Melo (ed.), *Los estudios regionales en Colombia: el caso de Antioquia* (Medellín, 1982), pp. 85–98 and 115–34 respectively.

[21] Jorge Orlando Melo (ed.), *Historia de Antioquia* (Medellín, 1988). Within this volume see the following chapters: Gabriel Poveda, 'Breve historia de la minería' (pp. 209–24); María Mercedes Botero, 'Comercio y bancos, 1850–1923' (pp. 243–48); Juan Fernando Echevarría, 'Bancos y finanzas en el siglo XX' (pp. 257–66); Roberto Luis Jaramillo, 'La colonización' (pp. 177–208); Manuel Restrepo, 'La historia de la industria antioqueña, 1880–1950' (pp. 257–67); Fabio Botero, 'Las vías de comunicación y el transporte' (pp. 287–98); Luis Alberto Zuleta, 'El comercio en el siglo XX' (pp. 249–56).

[22] These appeared in a special issue of *Revista Antioqueña de Economía y Desarrollo* 30 (1989). See especially the article of A. L. Casas on the 'valley of merchants' that Medellín was in the seventeenth century (pp. 1–5), that of María Teresa Uribe de Hincapié on the influence of the traders of Medellín in the second half of the nineteenth century (pp. 39–50), and that of María Mercedes Botero on the rise of the local banking elite in the period between 1905 and 1923 (pp. 61–71).

of commerce in Antioquia between 1954 and 1980.[23] Then, in 1989 an article appeared which took up the 'dependency' debate in order to argue that the consolidation of an industrial bourgeoisie only lasted until 1930.[24] In 1994 a study based on the archives of the large Medellín merchant houses between 1850 and 1890 shed some light for the first time on the networks involved in the internal and external commercialisation of gold and silver, a crucial aspect in the accumulation of the financial resources which permitted economic diversification.[25] There is also a recent book on mule transport (arriería), which was vital to mining, commerce, and coffee before the early decades of the twentieth century.[26] Finally, the book by a sociologist, Alberto Mayor, offers an important contribution to the understanding of the business elite in Antioquia. This is a detailed study of the School of Mines and Engineering in Medellín and the role played by the business and management elite educated there during the first half of the twentieth century.[27]

The business elite in other regions of Colombia

There was also entrepreneurial activity in other regions of Colombia, mainly in agriculture and commerce and closely linked first to the agro-export sector, and then to the beginnings of industrialisation.[28] The economic

[23] Fenalco-Antioquia, *El comercio en Medellín, 1900–1930* (Medellín, 1982) [Fenalco is the acronym for the Federación Nacional de Comerciantes]; Santiago Londoño, 'Así ha evolucionado el comercio interior en Antioquia, 1954–1980', *Revista Antioqueña de Economía y Desarrollo* 5 (1982), 66–79.

[24] Kees Koonings and Menno Vellinga, 'Orígen y consolidación de la burguesía industrial en Antioquia', in Mario Cerutti and Menno Vellinga (eds), *Burguesía e industria en América Latina y Europa meridional* (Madrid, 1989), pp. 55–104.

[25] María Mercedes Botero, 'Antecedentes del desarrollo de la economía exportadora: Antioquia, 1850–1890' (MA thesis, Universidad Nacional de Colombia, 1994), and 'Comercio, comerciantes y circuitos mercantiles: Antioquia, 1850–1930' (mimeo, Bogotá, 1996).

[26] Germán Ferro Medina, *A lomo de mula* (Bogotá, 1994). This book, by an anthropologist, is based on the oral evidence of the last generation of *arrieros* (mule-drivers), a group who were indispensable to commerce given the enormous difficulties of any other type of communication in Antioquia.

[27] Alberto Mayor, *Etica, trabajo, y productividad en Antioquia: una interpretación sociológica sobre la influencia de le Escuela Nacional de Minas en la vida, costumbres e industrialización regionales* (Bogotá, 1984). This book stands out for its wealth of documentation, the inspiration it draws from Weberian analyses of the capitalist ethos (applied here in a very Catholic environment), and its contribution to the history of management and the development of professions in Colombia. On the professionalisation of management see Alberto Mayor, 'La profesionalización de la administración de empresas en Colombia', in Rubén Darío Echeverry et al. (eds), *En búsqueda de una administración para América Latina* (Bogotá, 1990), pp. 97–109, and also his article, 'Industrialización colombiana y diferenciación de las profesiones liberales', *Sol Naciente* 1 (1990), 12–23.

[28] In Frank Safford's words, 'Colombians from [the] poorer regions were constantly engaging in new endeavors, whether in manufacturing, exporting or transportation ... Within

and social foundations for this were very different in scale to the amount of wealth that businessmen in Antioquia managed to amass. During the last twenty years academic interest in studying the role of the business elite in other regions of Colombia has increased. This has resulted in several studies which make a contribution to the understanding of Colombian business history written from varying perspectives and focuses. The research covers five regions, four in the interior (Viejo Caldas, Santander, Sabana de Bogotá, Valle de Cauca), in addition to the Atlantic Coast.

This section of the chapter considers each in turn, but some background economic history is required since the evolution of these regions was quite different. Viejo Caldas, a mountainous region lying between Antioquia and the Valle del Cauca, was colonised by *antioqueños* in the late nineteenth century and became the major area for coffee production, with a land-ownership structure characterised by small plots. Its two chief urban centres, Manizales and Pereira, diversified into light industry in the 1960s and 1970s. The Upper Cauca Valley, in the Southwest of the country, was a region of large slave-worked haciendas in the colonial period, and fell into a prolonged depression after the mid-nineteenth century as a result of civil war and the fall of prices for its main export products, tobacco and indigo. After the turn of the century, however, the sugar industry entered a phase of marked expansion and other sectors of arable and livestock farming were also modernised. Cali, the principal city of this region, also became the nation's third largest industrial centre. The centre and east of the country forms a quite heterogeneous economic region, comprising areas such as the Sabana de Bogotá, where large latifundia predominated, the artisan textile production of Santander, which fell victim to cheaper imports in the mid-nineteenth century, and lowland regions which became important for export products like tobacco, quinine, and indigo in the second half of the nineteenth century. Coffee also developed here after 1880 on the basis of large haciendas, while modern manufacturing began to expand in Bogotá itself, making it the leading industrial centre in the country by the middle of the twentieth century. On the Caribbean coast the old colonial port of Cartagena fell into decay during the nineteenth century and was replaced by Barranquilla, which later developed an important industrial base in textiles, sawmills and shipyards. Here, too, the immigration of Europeans was also important in the economic process. Stock-raising, bananas, and cotton, were all important in the agriculture of the region. However, the economic dynamism of Barranquilla was dissipated after the end of the 1930s, when Buenaventura, on the Pacific, replaced it as the principal port for the export of coffee.

In the case of Viejo Caldas, many of the contributions to business history

the limits imposed by their capital resources, by the domestic market, and by the political environment, merchant-capitalists in many regions of Colombia gave a good account of themselves.': 'Foreign and National Enterprise', 525–26.

are at the same time studies of the colonisation process undertaken by *antioqueños*. In 1974 a Canadian historian, Keith Christie, demonstrated the role played by capitalist firms organised by the regional oligarchy which were instrumental in the opening up and exploitation of the land.[29] Colonisation activity was directly linked to serious conflicts over land, not confined to Viejo Caldas. The evolution of these struggles between 1850 and 1950 was examined by another foreign historian, Catherine LeGrand, who confirmed how the landowning businessmen had played a central role in agrarian conflicts with the settlers, a typical feature of rural violence in Colombia.[30] In a 1994 book Albeiro Valencia provides new information on two colonisation companies in Gran Caldas, and on some other businessmen who founded settlements.[31] While one can appreciate the extent of innovation, risk taking, and other characteristics of these expansionist, Schumpeterian businessmen, one also has to acknowledge that within the colonisation companies complicity with government authorities, violence, abuses, and illegal practices were also evident.

The power associated with the extremely diversified sources of wealth in Viejo Caldas (colonisation, trade, mule transport, and coffee) stimulated interest amongst several researchers who, from different theoretical perspectives, questioned the thesis of 'coffee democracy' in Colombia.[32] In a book published at the beginning of the 1970s José Fernando Ocampo refers instead to 'class domination' over Manizales, the regional capital of Viejo Caldas.[33] Keith Christie, in the work noted above, also provides a detailed account of the power of the regional oligarchy before the 1950s.[34] Manuel Rodríguez scrutinised in detail the differences between the founders of manufacturing industry in two cities in the coffee region, Manizales and

[29] The main work of Keith Christie is his doctoral thesis, 'Oligarchy and Society in Old Caldas, Colombia' (DPhil thesis, Oxford, 1974). Part of this thesis concentrated on colonisation, a theme which is particularly relevant to this historiographical essay. See also his 'Antioqueño Colonization in Western Colombia: a reappraisal', *Hispanic American Historical Review* 58 (1978), 260–83. There is a Spanish version of his work, not quite a direct translation of his thesis, published under the title, *Oligarcas, campesinos y política en Colombia: aspectos de la historia socio-política de la frontera antioqueña* (Bogotá, 1986).

[30] Catherine LeGrand, *Frontier Expansion and Peasant Protest in Colombia, 1850–1936* (Albuquerque, 1986).

[31] Albeiro Valencia, *Colonización, fundaciones, y conflictos agrarios* (Manizales, 1994).

[32] From 1880 to World War I coffee cultivation was centred on large haciendas in eastern Colombia. In contrast, the ensuing coffee expansion which took place in western Colombia (chiefly Viejo Caldas and Antioquia), was based on smallholdings and created less inequality of wealth and power. The term *democracia cafetera* was coined to refer to this expansion, but the concept was challenged from the 1970s onwards. However, in 1997 the *democracia cafetera* thesis was revived, but with the focus on the contemporary evolution of the sector, on the occasion of the 70th anniversary of the Federación Nacional de Cafeteros (Fedecafé): see Roberto Junguito and Diego Pizano, *Instituciones e instrumentos de poítica cafetera, 1927–1997* (Bogotá, 1997).

[33] José Fernando Ocampo, *Dominio de clase en la ciudad colombiana* (Medellín, 1972).

[34] Christie, 'Oligarchy and Society'.

Pereira, with respect to their social background, the possibilities of social mobility, and the origins of their initial capital.[35] Ogliastri and Dávila included the three most important towns in the region, Manizales, Pereira, and Armenia, in a sociological study of local business and political elites and the concentration of power in intermediate cities in Colombia in the mid-1970s.[36] Albeiro Valencia provides information on the coffee entre-preneurs who pioneered the processing and export stages of the business and made Manizales the centre for the coffee trade.[37] Finally, an insider, Ignacio Restrepo, provides some valuable, yet scattered and unsystematic, data on the leading businessmen of Manizales for the period between 1925 and 1990.[38]

In contrast to the growing amount of work on Viejo Caldas, the business historiography on the 'eastern belt' of the country, which was important during the second half of the nineteenth century for agrarian exports (tobacco, indigo, quinine, and later coffee), is limited to a handful of works, the pioneer of which was Frank Safford's doctoral thesis on central Colombia between 1821 and 1870.[39] Safford looked explicitly at the theme of business style (ability to evaluate the market, individualism, spirit of innovation, and risk management) of these businessmen, who were con-strained by a difficult geographical environment, high transport costs, and expensive capital. Safford concentrated on the business activity which these entrepreneurs undertook in the import–export business and in small manufacturing companies in Bogotá. Some of the themes of his doctoral thesis, such as the comparison between national and foreign businessmen, and between those from Antioquia and Bogotá, were published as articles during the second half of the 1960s.[40] A re-examination of his interpretation of the failures of manufacturing in the capital, published in 1986, high-lighted the naivety of the businessmen concerned.[41] The documentary and interpretative rigour of Safford's work set the professional standard for Colombian historians, even though very few have followed his thematic interests.

---

[35] Manuel Rodríguez, El empresario industrial del Viejo Caldas (Bogotá, 1983). In this work the author combines archival research and secondary sources with interviews of the principal actors (the founders and managers of the 68 most important industrial firms in both cities). The original work on which the book was based was a Master's thesis at Oxford.

[36] Enrique Ogliastri and Carlos Dávila, 'Estructura del poder y desarrollo en once ciudades intermediarias de Colombia', Desarrollo y Sociedad 12 (1983), 149–88; and 'The Articulation of Power and Business Structures: a study of Colombia', in Mark Mizruchi and Michael Schwartz (eds), Intercorporate Relations: the structural analysis of business (Cambridge, 1987), pp. 233–63.

[37] Albeiro Valencia, Manizales en la dinámica colonizadora, 1846–1930 (Manizales, 1990).

[38] Ignacio Restrepo, 50 años del desarrollo económico en Manizales (Manizales, 1995).

[39] Safford, 'Commerce and Enterprise'.

[40] Safford, 'Foreign and National Enterprise', and 'Significación de los antioqueños'.

[41] Frank Safford, 'Empresarios ingenuos: organización, capital, y conocimientos técnicos en las fábricas de Bogotá, 1814–1850', Revista de Investigaciones (Quindío), 1:2 (1986), 17–26.

The inclusion of the doctoral thesis by another North American historian, David Johnson, in this review of the literature is justifiable in that it is useful in understanding the dynamics of commerce and agriculture in relation to the policies of the radical liberals in the east.[42] Johnson later researched the multiple business activities (quinine, coffee, the import trade, mortgages, and real estate) of the most important company in Bucaramanga, the capital of Santander, between 1880 and 1910. The research in notarial archives evident in this work is exemplary.[43] Focussing upon the same period and on a family which was also prominent in several businesses but whose central activity was the buying and selling of land, the book by Emilio Arenas offers a good insight into the community of merchants in Bucaramanga.[44] In the late 1990s Pierre Raymond, a French sociologist, concluded a detailed account of the prolonged decline of the traditional cane sugar haciendas in the Charalá region.[45] Among recent research in regional history carried out at the state university, one collection of articles contains much of interest for the business historian.[46] The role of German immigration in Santander during the second half of the nineteenth century, which involved some conflict between German merchants and local artisans, has been documented in three works, and there is also a case study of yarn and cloth production in the town of El Socorro, an important artisan centre.[47]

Although regional studies of this type are disparate and often unrelated to each other, and do not form part of any identifiable historiographical trend, one common feature evident of many of them is the very high degree of diversification in the investments of these businessmen and their search for short-term profits. This theme of investment diversification, as well as the nature of their relationship with the state, was examined in Dávila's study of eight affluent businessmen from the Sabana de Bogotá and the Cauca Valley in the period between 1886 and 1930, whom he characterised either as *negociantes* (businessmen oriented towards speculation) or modern entrepreneurs who played a key role in local industrialisation.[48] Both groups

---

[42] David Johnson, 'Social and Economic Change in Nineteenth-Century Santander' (PhD thesis, University of California at Berkeley, 1975). This was published in Spanish as *Santander, Siglo XIX: cambios socioeconómicos* (Bogotá, 1984).

[43] Johnson, 'Reyes González Hermanos', 25–43.

[44] Emilio Arenas, *La casa del diablo. Los Puyana: tenencia de tierras y acumulación de capital en Santander* (Bucaramanga, 1982).

[45] Pierre Raymond, *Hacienda tradicional y aparcería* (Bucaramanga, 1997).

[46] Silvano Pabón, Carmen Ferreira et al., *Ensayos de historia regional* (Bucaramanga, 1995).

[47] Horacio Rodríguez, *La inmigración alemana al estado soberano de Santander en el siglo XIX: repercusiones socio-económicas de un proceso de transculturación* (Bogotá, 1968); Manuel Garnica, 'Guarapo, champaña y vino blanco', *Boletín Cultural y Bibliográfico* 29 (1992), 41–59; Thomas Fischer, 'Craftsmen, Merchants, and Violence in Colombia: the *sucesos de Bucaramanga* of 1879', *Itinerario* 20: 1 (1996), 79–99; Ramiro Gómez, 'Primera fábrica de hilados y tejidos del Socorro', *Boletín de Historia y Antigüedades* 68: 733 (1981), 509–17.

[48] Carlos Dávila, *El empresariado colombiano: una perspectiva histórica* (Bogotá, 1986), pp. 1–89.

were major components of a national governing class (a contrast to the fragmented regional ruling classes) which arose in this period. This theme of
the regional fragmentation of the dominant classes in Colombia had been
analysed earlier by Marco Palacios, yet another historian of Colombia who
obtained his doctorate under the supervision of Malcolm Deas in Oxford.[49]

Moving westwards, to the region of Cauca, there are only five studies
related to businessmen in this fertile valley, apart from a handful on regional
industrialisation which are covered later in this chapter. Four of them
examine the business elite in the sugar industry. In contrast to the diversity
of the historiography of other regions in terms of the origins of the scholars
involved, in the case of the Valle del Cauca four of the studies were carried
out by researchers from the local state university, some from the History
department and others from Sociology. The first, by a sociologist, examines
the sugar industry from its inception in 1860 until 1980.[50] Two years later
a British sociologist, Charles Collins, wrote on the formation of the sugar
bourgeoisie between 1930 and 1940.[51] In 1986 Dávila's comparison of large
family business groups in the Valle de Cauca and Bogotá was published,
and in the same year two students completed a case study of the transition
experienced on a sugar estate between 1850 and 1923 when it passed from
being an hacienda to an industrialised agribusiness.[52] This followed a theme
which had begun with Rojas's book.

However, as the recent book by the historian, Alonso Valencia, reminds
us, the Cauca economy was not just about sugar. Valencia examines the
business policies and strategies of six commercial firms during the second
half of the nineteenth century.[53] Thomas Fischer then studied a resounding
conflict which took place in 1885 and in which the owner of one of them,
an Italian immigrant, became involved. For Fischer this incident illustrates
the nationalist sentiment echoed at the time around conflicts like this and
others related to railways and mining contracts with foreign investors.[54] In

[49] Marco Palacios, 'La fragmentación regional en las clases dominantes en Colombia: una
perspetiva histórica', *Revista Mexicana de Sociología* 42 (1980), 1663–89.

[50] José María Rojas, *Sociedad y economía en el Valle de Cauca: empresarios y tecnología en la
formación del sector azucarero en Colombia, 1860–1980* (Bogotá, 1983). Rojas compares the
owners of the principal sugar mills at the same time as examining the concentration and
centralisation of capital in the sugar industry, the role of management, and the organisation
of an employers' association in the sector.

[51] Charles Collins, 'Formación de un sector de clase social: la burguesía en el Valle de
Cauca durante los años treinta y cuarenta', *CIDSE* 14/15 (1985), 35–90.

[52] Eduardo Mejía and Armando Moncaya, 'La transición de hacienda a ingenio azucarero
industrializado en el valle geográfico del río Cauca, 1850–1923' (thesis, Universidad del
Valle, 1986).

[53] Alonso Valencia, *Empresarios y políticos en el estado soberano del Cauca* (Cali, 1993).

[54] Thomas Fischer, 'El caso Cerruti. Eine Fallstudie zum Verhältnis von staatlicher Autorität
und ausländischer Einflussnahme in Kolumbien im ausgehenden 19. Jahrhundert', in Ute
Guthunz and Thomas Fischer (eds), *Lateinamerika zwischen Europa und den USA. Wechsle-
wirkingen und Transformationprozesse in politik, Ökonomie und Kultur* (Frankfurt-am-Main, 1995),
pp. 57–85.

addition, one should also mention the useful information on the history of the businessman which may be found in the more comprehensive regional history texts written by well-known historians, tutors of some of the authors mentioned above, and published in the early 1980s.[55] More recently, an extensive volume on the regional history of Gran Cauca, edited by Alonso Valencia, included short articles that contributed new information on the regional economy, transportation and colonisation during the nineteenth century and the evolution of the economy during the twentieth.[56]

In the mid-1980s the predominance of the 'Andean viewpoint' in Colombian historiography began to wane with the emergence of a body of literature on the extensive region of the Caribbean or Atlantic coast. This new work was led by a small but prolific group of researchers, for the most part educated overseas, whose work began to concentrate directly on the role of the coastal business elite. This was the case with Eduardo Posada's analysis of the consolidation of a business elite in Barranquilla between the late nineteenth century and the 1930s, when the city ceased to be Colombia's principal port.[57] Posada also produced a paper on the six private banks founded in Barranquilla between 1873 and 1925 and their speculative behaviour. Adolfo Meisel, studied the more conservative banks of Cartagena in the same period. These were predominantly family businesses.[58] In 1988 Posada also published a history of ranching on the Atlantic coast during this period.[59] Earlier he had examined the case of a large hacienda which, due to its efforts to diversify into sugar milling, represented an example opposed to the widely accepted thesis that the colonial hacienda

[55] This is the case with books by Colmenares, Escorcia, and Hyland, although the study of business behaviour is not a central theme for them. See Germán Colmenares, *Sociedad y economía en el Valle de Cauca: terratenientes, mineros y comerciantes, siglo XVIII* (Bogotá, 1983). José Escorcia identified the owners of the large haciendas, their connection with local commerce, and the role of the economic elite of the valley in politics during the first half of the nineteenth century in *Sociedad y economía en el Valle de Cauca: desarrollo económico, social y político, 1800–1854* (Bogotá, 1983). Hyland, for his part, studied the role of the families and clans of wealthy landowners and merchants in the secularisation of ecclesiastical property, as well as the foundation of the first bank in the region in 1873, which gave a stimulus to export agriculture and to transport: Richard P. Hyland, *Sociedad y economía en el Valle de Cauca: el crédito y la economía, 1851–1880* (Bogotá, 1983). See also Hyland's article, 'A Fragile Prosperity: credit and agrarian structure in the Cauca Valley, Colombia', *Hispanic American Historical Review* 62 (1982), 369–406.

[56] Alonso Valencia (ed.), *Historia del Gran Cauca: historia regional del Suroccidente colombiano* (Cali, 1994).

[57] Eduardo Posada, *Una invitación a la historia de Barranquilla* (Bogotá, 1987).

[58] Eduardo Posada, 'Bancos y banqueros de Barranquilla, 1873–1925', in Adolfo Meisel and Eduardo Posada (eds), *¿Por qué se disipó el dinamismo industrial de Barranquilla? Y otros ensayos de historia económica de la Costa Caribe* (Barranquilla, 1993), pp. 41–67; Adolfo Meisel, 'Los bancos de Cartagena', *Lecturas de Economía* 32/33 (1990), 69–96.

[59] Eduardo Posada, 'La ganadería en la Costa Atlántica colombiana, 1870–1950', *Coyuntura Económica* 18 (1988), 143–75.

was dedicated to extensive ranching.[60] The vicissitudes which led to the failure of the Packing House of Coveñas (1918–1938), established in order to export meat from the region, were traced in a monograph based mainly on the local press and official documents.[61] There are also two stimulating studies of a large hacienda in Sinú, a product of *antioqueño* colonisation, concentrating on its administration and operations between 1912 and 1956.[62] A very recent general work on Caribbean regional history is another Oxford doctoral thesis covering the first half of the nineteenth century.[63]

Although Colombia, unlike other Latin American countries, received very little in the way of foreign immigration, those that did come tended to settle in the Caribbean ports. Manuel Rodríguez and Jorge Restrepo have examined the role of foreign businessmen in Barranquilla between 1820 and 1900, picking out especially the German and English traders and their role in the development of maritime and fluvial navigation, railways, and the early stages of manufacturing, and comparing them with Colombian businessmen.[64] Commerce, a 'real school for business', was also the central activity of the highly diversified businessmen of Cartagena, who began enterprises in ranching, mining, and manufacturing at the end of the nineteenth century; this has been the subject of a study by the same authors.[65] The economic activities of Syrian-Lebanese and Palestinian immigrants in the coastal region from 1880 until 1930 are analysed in a paper by Louise Fawcett.[66] Here, as in Eduardo Posada's works, the use

[60] Eduardo Posada, 'La Hacienda Berástegui: notas para una historia rural de la Costa Atlántica', *Huellas* 17 (1986), 4–7. The works of Posada mentioned here, as well as others discussed in the later sections on transport and entrepreneurial history, are linked with his Oxford DPhil thesis. This has now been revised and published as *The Colombian Caribbean: a regional history* (Oxford, 1996). Posada's work is a good example of the potentially fruitful interrelationship between economic and social history and business history.

[61] Adalberto Machado, 'La exportación de carnes y el Packing House de Coveñas, 1918–1938' (thesis, Corporación Tecnológica de Bolívar, 1989).

[62] Luz Elena Echeverri, 'Los trabajadores de Marta Magdalena: una hacienda ganadera al suroeste del departamento de Bolívar, 1912–1956' (thesis, Universidad Nacional de Colombia, Medellín, 1993); Gloria Isabel Ocampo, 'Hacienda, parentesco y mentalidad: la colonización antioqueña en el Sinú', *Revista Colombiana de Antropología* 26 (1986–88), 5–42. Both works illustrate the potential of hacienda archives for research in business history.

[63] Gustavo Bell, 'Regional Politics and the Formation of the National State: the Caribbean coast of Colombia in the first years of independence' (mimeo, Oxford, 1997).

[64] Manuel Rodríguez and Jorge Restrepo, 'Los empresarios extranjeros de Barranquilla, 1820–1900', *Desarrollo y Sociedad* 8 (1982), 77–114.

[65] Jorge Restrepo and Manuel Rodríguez, 'La actividad comercial y el grupo de comerciantes de Cartagena a fines del siglo XIX', *Estudios Sociales* 1 (1986), 43–109.

[66] Louise Fawcett de Posada, *Libaneses, palestinos, y sirios en Colombia* (Barranquilla, 1991). A source book on *turco* immigrants (those from Syria, Lebanon and Palestine) is Eduardo Hakim Murad, *El murmullo de los cedros* (Bogotá, 1993). On a failed attempt by a French immigrant to establish a mining company on the River Sinú in the middle of the nineteenth century see Luis Striffler, *El Alto Sinú* (Cartagena, 1875), and Amparo Lotero, 'Franceses en el Sinú: un *affaire* olvidado', *Boletín Cultural y Bibliográfico* 29 (1992), 60–72.

of the correspondence of foreign consuls, especially the British, is note-worthy. However, one cannot fully understand the coastal economy without making specific references to business activity in other areas such as banana and cotton cultivation, the industrialisation of Barranquilla, and, more recently, coal mining, and these will be discussed in the later sections of this paper.

The businessman in foreign trade, agriculture, and mining

Unlike the studies at a regional level which have been discussed in the previous sections, it is not very common to find books and articles on the different sectors of the Colombian economy which are orientated towards a business history perspective and take the role of the diverse business actors – individuals, families, companies, business groups – as their unit of analysis. Nevertheless, a well-directed search may uncover some items of at least partial relevance to business history, even if they are scattered among sectoral treatments of the Colombian economy and may perhaps appear tangential. However, these studies should not be underestimated as means of understanding these actors and certain elements of their economic behaviour (innovation, risk taking, investment), their social con-ditions and business ethos. Bearing this in mind, the remainder of this paper reviews the historiography on foreign trade; the agricultural sector (coffee, tobacco, quinine, indigo, bananas, and rubber); mining and natural resources; and transport, communications and energy.

Turning first to foreign commerce, it was not until 1984 that a compre-hensive and rigorously documented work on Colombian foreign trade became available, with the publication of an excellent book by José A. Ocampo on the period between 1830 and 1910.[67] Along with Ocampo's important observations regarding the 'secondary periphery' nature of an economy weakly linked to world trade and a style of business behaviour which was based on speculative production (easy profits, the lack of reinvestment to develop the productive capacity of the land), the researcher interested in business history may also find information in this book on trading houses, mining companies, and prominent individual businessmen. This is due to the detailed examination which Ocampo undertakes of the export-import trade associated with the successive but short-lived economic bonanzas in tobacco, quinine, cotton, indigo and coffee which occurred during the second half of the nineteenth century. It will be recalled that

[67] José Antonio Ocampo, *Colombia y la economía mundial, 1830–1910* (Bogotá, 1984). It is interesting to note the comments of one well qualified critic, who stated a decade later that 'this book could already be considered a classic work on foreign trade and it had formed the basis for a transformation of the economic historiography': Oscar Rodríguez, 'La histo-riografía económica colombiana del siglo XIX', in Tovar (ed.), *La historia al final del milenio*, I, p. 201. See also José Antonio Ocampo, 'Comerciantes, artesanos y política económica, 1830–1880', *Boletín Cultural y Bibliográfico* 27 (1990), 20–45.

the majority of the work on businessmen in different regions which was discussed earlier in this paper highlighted their speculative behaviour and their adherence to a model of extremely diversified investments, normally covering the production of these exports and their articulation with commercial networks. This theme can be followed further in biographies of individual businessmen, which are discussed later. The negative context for capital and businessmen arising from the lack of protection for private property and personal security has been suggested by the German historian, Thomas Fischer, as a further factor, alongside geography and unfavourable commodity markets, to explain why the agro-export economy of nineteenth-century Colombia did not result in sustained growth.[68]

While there is an abundant bibliography on coffee and its role in economic development in Colombia, a 'coffee country' which was largely a monoexporter from the late nineteenth century until the 1960s, it has been rare for historians or economists to employ a micro approach to the study of plantations, coffee merchants, and the evolution of their business association, the Federación de Cafeteros.[69] The impressive account of the history of coffee between 1850 and 1970 written by Marco Palacios contributes to business history through its detailed analysis of the structures and operations of different types of coffee plantations and its examination of the initiative and capacity of merchants converted into planters and exporters of the crop.[70] When he published this book, however, there had been relatively little work in hacienda archives. A group of students at the Universidad de Antioquia later investigated the archives of three haciendas in Antioquia in order to examine their internal diversification, labour relations, and commercial practices in the period between 1880 and 1925.[71] Michael Jiménez also looked at the period between 1900 and 1930, relying on archival material in order to analyse business strategies (credit, labour, crop diversification, and transport costs) and the economic logic behind

[68] Thomas Fischer, 'Desarrollo hacia afuera y guerras civiles en Colombia, 1850–1910', *Ibero-Amerikanisches Archiv* 23: 1/2 (1997), 91–120. This is based on Fischer's doctoral thesis, 'Die vorlonen Dekaden: "Entwicklung nach Aussen" und ausländische Geschäfte in Kolumbien, 1870–1914' (Munich, 1997).

[69] The interest in Latin American rural history, which has been a dominant feature of the historiography of the region since 1970, has resulted in several comparative studies of coffee, for two reasons: first, it was the quintessential Latin American export crop and one in which Latin America, especially Brazil, dominated world markets between the late nineteenth and the mid-twentieth centuries, and second, it gave rise to a whole variety of social formations, ranging from large slave-operated plantations to smallholdings. For a recent and important collection of essays, which includes a fundamental paper on the growth and pattern of world demand and a chapter on Colombia, see William F. Roseberry et al. (eds), *Coffee, Society, and Power in Latin America* (Baltimore, 1995).

[70] Marco Palacios, *Coffee in Colombia (1850–1970): an economic, social, and political history* (Cambridge, 1980).

[71] Carlos A. Acebedo et al., 'La hacienda antioqueña: génesis y consolidación, 1880–1925' (thesis, Universidad de Antioquia, 1987).

them, and then relating this to the intense agrarian conflicts of the region. In a later paper he emphasised the boundaries of planter hegemony in the first third of the nineteenth century.[72] Prior to this, Malcolm Deas, the Oxford supervisor of some of the best research reviewed in this chapter, delved into the correspondence between an important absentee landlord and his hacienda administrator in order to gain an insight into the details of managing a large hacienda and the risks involved in doing so.[73] One invaluable source on individual landowners in the late nineteenth century is the work by Medardo Rivas, originally published in 1885 but still unsurpassed in its detail.[74] Although the work by Absalón Machado includes no detailed accounts of specific plantations, it does provide a useful analysis of the relationship between the interests of coffee growers and the Sociedad de Agricultores.[75] The study of Mariano Arango is also interesting for its analysis of the links between the big exporting houses dealing with coffee, the processors who carried out the hulling of coffee beans, and industry.[76] Finally, on coffee, one must not overlook the ground-breaking global study of Colombian coffee before 1940, carried out by Robert Beyer in 1947 but never published, nor that of Charles Bergquist, which is useful for understanding the links between politics and coffee-growers in the period between 1886 and 1910.[77] The few works on the powerful Federación de Cafeteros are mentioned later in the section on producers' associations.

Studies of tobacco, quinine, and indigo are rare, despite the fact that

[72] Michael Jiménez, '"Travelling Far in Grandfather's Car": the life cycle of central Colombian coffee estates: the case of Viota, Cundinamarca, 1900–1930', *Hispanic American Historical Review* 69 (1989), 185–219, and 'At the Banquet of Civilization: the limits to planter hegemony in early twentieth-century Colombia', in Roseberry *et al.* (eds), *Coffee, Society, and Power*, pp. 262–93. On conflict over colonisation in the same region, see Elsy Marulanda, *Colonización y conflicto: las lecciones del Sumapaz* (Bogotá, 1991).

[73] Malcolm Deas, 'A Colombian Coffee Estate: Santa Bárbara, Cundinamarca, 1870–1912', in Kenneth Duncan and Ian Rutledge (eds), *Land and Labour in Latin America: essays in the development of agrarian capitalism in the nineteenth and twentieth centuries* (Cambridge, 1973), pp. 269–98. Recently a Spanish version of this work has been printed as chapter 6 of a compilation of Deas's writings: Malcolm Deas, *Del poder y la gramática y otros ensayos sobre historia, política y literatura colombianas* (Bogotá, 1993). Deas writes at the end of this piece (p. 295 in the English version): 'No agricultural enterprise exists in an economist's vacuum: there were also present other risks and difficulties that must have their place in the agrarian history of nineteenth-century Latin America'.

[74] Medardo Rivas, *Los trabajadores de tierra caliente* (Bogotá, 1946).

[75] Absalón Machado, *El café: de la aparcería al capitalismo* (Bogotá, 1977).

[76] Mariano Arango, *Café e industria, 1850–1930* (Bogotá, 1977).

[77] Robert Beyer, 'The Colombian Coffee Industry: origins and major trends, 1740–1940' (PhD thesis, University of Minnesota, 1947); Charles Bergquist, *Coffee and Conflict in Colombia, 1886–1910* (Durham, NC., 1978). Bergquist went on to study labour in the coffee sector, within the context of a larger study of the working class in Latin America: see Charles Bergquist, *Labor in Latin America: comparative essays on Chile, Argentina, Venezuela, and Colombia* (Stanford, 1986), ch. 5.

tobacco was the main agro-export product during its rapid expansion (1849–57 and 1864–69). There are only four items of importance on tobacco: John Harrison's 1951 history of the sector between 1778 and 1849; a chapter in Safford's doctoral thesis which studies the business behaviour of two trading houses; a 1971 book which provides information on attempts by the principal tobacco company to control the quality of tobacco leaves; and a 1986 book which studies one of principal tobacco regions of Colombia during the eighteenth and nineteenth centuries.[78] The academic vacuum regarding quinine and indigo has yet to be filled; indeed, there is only one study on indigo between 1850 and 1880 as well as a regional study of quinine in the same period.[79]

The social conflicts in the banana region in 1928 have provoked the interest of various researchers in the last twenty years, LeGrand's work being the most solidly based.[80] In yet another book based on an Oxford thesis, Judith White offers a different emphasis in her analysis of United Fruit's operations between 1900 and 1940 and the company's links with the economy, politics, and society of the region.[81] Two of White's main themes, the monopolistic character of the company and its relationship with the government and local groups, are also examined by Fernando Botero and Alvaro Guzmán, but using different sources from those of White.[82] A recent study, based heavily on company archives, looks from inside the firm at the evolution of its costs and labour relations in the period between 1948 and 1968, and the transfer of its operations from one banana region, Santa Marta, to another, Urabá.[83] Another case study of

[78] John Harrison, 'The Colombian Tobacco Industry from Government Monopoly to Free Trade, 1778–1849' (PhD thesis, University of California at Berkeley, 1951); Safford, 'Commerce and Enterprise'; Luis F. Sierra, El tabaco en la economía colombiana del siglo XIX (Bogotá, 1971); Jesús A. Bejarano and Orlando Pulido, El tabaco en una economía regional: Ambalema, siglos XVIII y XIX (Bogotá, 1986).

[79] Francisco Alarcón and Daniel Arías, 'La producción y comercialización del añil en Colombia, 1850–1880', Anuario Colombiano de Historia Social y de la Cultura 15 (1987), 165–209; Yesid Sandoval and Camilo Echandía, 'La historia de la quina desde una perspectiva regional, Colombia, 1850–1882', Anuario Colombiano de Historia Social y de la Cultura 13/14 (1986), 153–87.

[80] Catherine LeGrand, 'Campesinos y asalariados en la zone bananera de Santa Marta, 1900–1935', Anuario Colombiano de Historia Social y de la Cultura (1983), 235–50, and 'El conflicto de las bananeras', in Nueva Historia de Colombia (Bogotá, 1989), III, 183–218. This violent episode was brought to world attention in a masterful way through fiction: see Gabriel García Márquez, Cien años de soledad (Buenos Aires, 1967), which was translated into English as One Hundred Years of Solitude (London, 1970).

[81] Judith White, Historia de una ignomia (Bogotá, 1978).

[82] Fernando Botero and Alvaro Guzmán, 'El enclave agrícola en la zone bananera de Santa Marta', Cuadernos Colombianos 3 (1977), 309–90.

[83] Marcelo Bucheli, Empresas multinacionales y enclaves agrícolas: el caso de la United Fruit en Magdalena y Urabá, 1948–1968 (Bogotá, 1994). See also Marcelo Bucheli, 'United Fruit in Colombia: impact of labor relations and governmental regulations on its operations, 1948–1968', Essays in Economic and Business History 17 (1997), 65–84.

the company in Colombia, aimed at an academic audience in the United States, was written by Maurice Brugardt.[84] However, other important twentieth-century crops such as cotton still await the attention of historians. There is just one solitary study of its evolution between 1960 and 1980.[85]

This has not quite been the case with rubber. There are three recent books, which were preceded by a couple of articles, on the exploitation of rubber in the Amazon region.[86] In addition a 1913 English polemic against the exploitation of the forest Indians in the Putumayo region, which was then disputed with Peru, was reissued in Colombia in 1995.[87] However, amongst the recent publications one should also include the memoirs of a pioneering nineteenth-century Colombian rubber entrepreneur, later the president of Colombia, who became involved in rubber after the collapse of the quinine trade.[88] Maybe one should also add that a more contemporary crop and agribusiness, namely cocaine, is located in much the same region as rubber. The business history of this sector remains to be written, of course, though there may be some useful primary sources when the criminal archives of various countries are opened to the public. Of course, since the middle of the 1980s a growing amount of information about the trade has been published in national and foreign periodicals and books intended for popular consumption. The principal academic writers on the relationship between the drugs trade and the Colombian economy and society contributed chapters to a recent book sponsored by the United Nations Development Programme.[89]

[84] Maurice Brugardt, 'The United Fruit Company in Colombia', in Henry Dethloff and Joseph Pusateri (eds), *American Business History: case studies* (Arlington Heights, 1990).

[85] Yesid Soler and Fabio Prieto, *Bonanza y crisis del oro blanco, 1960–1980* (Bogotá, 1982).

[86] Augusto Gómez, Ana Lesmes and Claudia Rocha, *Caucherías y conflicto Colombo-peruano: testimonios, 1904–1934* (Bogotá, 1995); Roberto Pineda and Beatriz Alzate (eds), *Pasado y presente del Amazonas: su historia económica y social* (Bogotá, 1993): some of the essays in this collection for the first time use registers (*libros de cuentas*) of the rubber companies to illustrate the differences between exploitation on the Amazon itself controlled by large exporters like the infamous Casa Arana and other rivers where entrepreneurs were smaller and used different labour practices; Roberto Pineda, *Ethnohistoria de las caucherías del Putumayo entre 1880 y 1932* (Bogotá, 1993); Augusto Gómez, 'El ciclo de caucho, 1850–1932', in *Colombia Amazónica* (Bogotá, 1988), pp. 183–212; Jorge Villegas and Fernando Botero, 'Putumayo: indígenas, caucho, y sangre', *Cuadernos Colombianos* 3 (1979), 529–65.

[87] A translation of *The Red Book of the Putumayo* (London, 1913), was published as *El Libro Rojo del Putumayo* (Bogotá, 1995) with a prologue by Roberto Pineda Camacho. Some scholarly attention has been given to the Putumayo affair in Britain, in part because the government's chief investigator was Sir Roger Casement, who later led the Irish nationalist Easter Rising in 1916: see Brian Inglis, *Roger Casement* (London, 1973). The basic source on the history of the Peruvian Rubber Company, the firm involved in the atrocities, remains the minutes of evidence taken before the House of Commons Select Committee investigating the affair: for these see Great Britain, House of Commons, *Parliamentary Papers*, 1913, XIV.

[88] Rafael Reyes, *Memorias, 1850–1885* (Bogotá, 1986).

[89] United Nations Development Programme / Ministerio de Justicia, *Drogas ilícitas en Colombia: su impacto económico, político y social* (Bogotá, 1997).

Since this review covers only the nineteenth and twentieth centuries no reference is made here to the impressive studies which have appeared on the colonial mining industry. However, an 1883 work by Vicente Restrepo, republished at the end of the 1970s, remains a classic and irreplaceable text that covers the technological, economic and business aspects of each individual silver and gold mine.[90] Much of the literature on the important mining industry in Antioquia was discussed earlier, in the section on the regional elites, but the work of Gabriel Poveda should also be mentioned.[91] In addition, there is a detailed unpublished study on the major mining company owned by local businessmen in Antioquia, together with a recent article on the role of assay offices and smelters in the commercialisation of gold.[92] On British investment there is a useful article by the US historian, Fred Rippy, and some very recent work by a German historian, Thomas Fischer, who uses a variety of primary and secondary sources, including British, French, and German diplomatic correspondence, to look at gold and silver mining in the light of Mira Wilkins' model of the free-standing company. Among the 75 companies he traced, those formed by British capitalists were dominant, but their performance was rather poor.[93] Dávila has also examined the causes of Britain's gloomy business record in the mining of precious metals as part of a general analysis of British investment in Colombia.[94] Despite the limitations of the sources these studies offer different accounts of individual companies.

Within the varied and polemical literature on petroleum, the most useful items for this survey are works on the relationship between businessmen, foreign companies, and politics. These themes are treated in books which are well documented from Colombian and foreign archives by the North American historians, Stephen Randall and René de la Pedraja. The former examines the links between the oil companies and the diplomacy of the United States between 1920 and 1940.[95] In his 1989 book, de la Pedraja

[90] Vicente Restrepo, *Estudio sobre las minas de oro y plata en Colombia* (Medellín, 1979).

[91] Gabriel Poveda, *Minas y mineros en Antioquia* (Bogotá, 1984). This is a collection of different authors and sources which offers a chronological description of mining in Antioquia. However, the lack of any rigorous referencing to the primary sources limits its usefulness.

[92] Luis F. Molina and Ociel Castaño, 'Titiribí y la empresa minera del Zancudo, 1750–1930' (thesis, Universidad de Antioquia, 1988); María Mercedes Botero, 'Los laboratorios de fundición y ensaye y su papel en el comercio de oro: Antioquia, 1850–1910', *Historia Crítica* 14 (1997), 53–58.

[93] J. Fred Rippy, 'British Investments in Colombian Mines', *Inter-American Economic Affairs* 7:3 (1953), 65–72. On the broader theme of foreign investment in Colombia besides the mining industry, see also his book, *The Capitalists and Colombia* (New York, 1940). For an application of recent theoretical advances in business history, see Thomas Fischer, 'Empresas extranjeras en el sector del oro y de plata en Colombia, 1870–1914: la *free-standing company* como modelo aplicado por inversionistas extranjeros', *Boletín Cultural y Bibliográfico* 39 (1995), 60–84.

[94] Carlos Dávila, 'Negocios y empresas británicas en Colombia, 1820–1940' (mimeo, 1990).

[95] Stephen James Randall, *The Diplomacy of Modernization: Colombian-American relations, 1920–1940* (Toronto, 1977). See also Randall's more recent work, *Hegemony and Dependence: Colombia and the United States since the wars for independence* (Athens, GA., 1992).

analysed Colombian policies on the development of energy resources (petroleum, electricity, and coal) after 1920; in the case of the electricity industry, he studies the evolution of the diverse types of companies that emerged in different cities in Colombia.[96] Indeed, the central part of de la Pedraja's first book was concerned with the history of the earliest energy companies, of one kind or another.[97] One should also mention an earlier book on petroleum by Jorge Villegas.[98] A later revisionist interpretation stressed the pioneering efforts of businessmen in the oil industry, in contrast to the normal view of them as *vendepatrias* (people who 'sold' the country).[99] It is probably too early for a history of oil expansion in the 1980s, in which British Petroleum has played a leading role. However, the evolution of Colombian government policies and foreign investment in coal mining was analysed at the time when the sector was in full growth.[100]

The historiography of transport

The historiography of the small Colombian rail network (2,500 kilometres were constructed in sixty years) has remained fundamentally in the hands of North American historians who have almost inevitably departed from an important primary source, two books by Alfredo Ortega, which illustrate how railway bosses, foreign and Colombian, became involved in a 'war of legal claims' rather than promoting further construction.[101] Between 1943 and 1951 several studies were published. In 1943 Rippy covered the period up to 1920, highlighting the role played by British and North American technology and capital.[102] This was followed by four doctoral theses. Theodore Hoffman looked at the evolution of the principal concessions for railway construction.[103] That of Robert Bayer, already mentioned in the

---

[96] René de la Pedraja, *Energy Politics in Colombia* (Boulder, 1989). See also Constanza Toro, 'Incursión privada en servicios públicos: el caso del alumbrado eléctrico de Bogotá y Medellín, 1899–1918', *Lecturas de Economía* 15 (1984).

[97] René de la Pedreja, *Historia de le energía en Colombia* (Bogotá, 1985).

[98] Jorge Villegas, *Petróleo, oligarquía e imperio* (Bogotá, 1968).

[99] José Isaza and Luis Salcedo, *Sucedió en la Costa Atlántica: los albores de la industria petrolera en Colombia* (Bogotá, 1993).

[100] Harvey F. Kline, 'The Coal of El Cerrejón: an historical analysis of major Colombian policy decisions and MNC activities', *Inter-American Economic Affairs* 35 (1981), 69–90, and also his *The Coal of El Cerrejón: dependent bargaining and Colombian policy-making* (University Park, 1987).

[101] Alfredo Ortega, *Ferrocarriles colombianos: resumen histórico* (2 vols, Bogotá, 1920), and *Ferrocarriles colombianos: la última experiencia ferroviaria del país, 1920–1932* (Bogotá, 1932).

[102] J. Fred Rippy, 'Dawn of the Railway Era in Colombia', *Hispanic American Historical Review* 23 (1943), 650–63. This paper is reprinted as J. Fred Rippy, 'Los comienzos de la era ferroviaria en Colombia', in José A. Bejarano (ed.), *El siglo XIX en Colombia visto por historiadores norteamericanos* (Bogotá, 1977), pp. 221–43. This book is a collection of a series of articles by US researchers, for the most part on railways.

[103] Theodore H. Hoffman, 'A History of Railway Concessions and Railway Development Policy in Colombia to 1943' (PhD thesis, The American University, 1947).

section on coffee, examined the interrelationship between the railways and the expansion of coffee.[104] Then, in 1951, Theodore Nichols demonstrated the crucial role played by transport (rail, river and sea) in the development of the three Colombian ports on the Caribbean, and offered more material than his predecessors on the involvement of North American and British entrepreneurs.[105] Both Nichols and, thirty five years later, Solano published articles on the connection between river transport and the development of Barranquilla.[106] In 1953 Donald Barnhart criticised the nationalisation of the railways in 1923 and the performance of public sector management, whilst failing to observe the rather undistinguished record of British businessmen before that time.[107] Seventeen years then passed without a single study worth mentioning here before a Peruvian historian, Hernán Horna, traced the history of Francisco Javier Cisneros, a prominent business pioneer, in his doctoral thesis. In this, together with his later works on related topics, Horna suggests a revisionist interpretation which supports the idea of a strong role for national businessmen and Colombian capital in the process of modernisation associated with the construction of railways directed towards the export economy.[108] A recent work on the Northern Railway covering the period between 1872 and 1930 demonstrated the high cost of the system of concessionaires that was utilised.[109] The Antioquia Railway was the subject of two books, in 1974 and 1980, whilst in the mid-1980s Gabriel Poveda produced a series of articles on engineers and railway bosses, and Jorge Arias examined the contribution made by an English engineer to the design of locomotives appropriate for the Colombian landscape.[110]

---

[104] Beyer, 'Transportation and the Coffee Industry'.

[105] Theodore Nichols, 'The Caribbean Gateway to Colombia: Cartagena, Santa Marta, and Barranquilla and their connections with the interior, 1820–1940' (PhD thesis, University of California at Berkeley, 1951). This was published in Spanish as *Tres puertos de Colombia: estudio sobre el desarrollo de Cartagena, Santa Marta y Barranquilla* (Bogotá, 1973).

[106] Theodore Nichols, 'The Rise of Barranquilla', *Hispanic American Historical Review* 34 (1954), 158–74; Sergio Paolo Solano, 'Comercio, transporte y sociedad en Barranquilla en la primera mitad del siglo XIX', *Boletín Cultural y Bibliográfico* 26 (1989), 24–34.

[107] Donald Barnhart, 'Colombian Transportation Problems and Policies, 1923–1948' (PhD thesis, University of Chicago, 1953). See also his article, 'Colombian Transport and the Reforms of 1931: an evaluation', *Hispanic American Historical Review* 38 (1958), 1–24.

[108] Hernán Horna, 'Francisco Javier Cisneros: a pioneer in transportation and economic development in Colombia' (PhD thesis, Vanderbilt University, 1970); 'La variedad de las actividades de Francisco Javier Cisneros', *Boletín de Historia y Antigüedades* 57 (1970), 195–212; 'Francisco Javier Cisneros: a pioneer in transportation and economic development in Latin America, 1857–1898', *The Americas* 30:1 (1973), 54–82; 'Transportation, Modernization and Entrepreneurship in Nineteenth-Century Colombia', *Journal of Latin American Studies* 14 (1982), 33–53; *Transportation, Modernization and Entrepreneurship in Nineteenth-Century Colombia: Cisneros and friends* (Uppsala, 1992).

[109] Andrea Junguito, 'Historia económica del ferrocarril del norte', *Historia Crítica* 14 (1997), 129–46.

[110] Gabriel Poveda, *Antioquia y el Ferrocarril de Antioquia* (Medellín, 1974); Roberto Tisnés and Heriberto Zapata, *El ferrocarril de Antioquia: historia de una empresa heroica* (Medellín,

More recently, Mejía examined some of the technical innovations linked to railway construction and operation, while Betancur and Zuluaga wrote a book on the evolution of railways in Colombia, which, despite its non-academic perspective, contributes an integrated synthesis as well as delving into the social and cultural aspects of the industry.[111]

Both the collapse of the Colombian railway system after 1960, when it was replaced by road transport, and the definitive decline of river transport between the interior and the Caribbean coast have yet to receive any academic attention. However, fluvial navigation during the nineteenth century involved a good deal of entrepreneurship. This was examined both by Gilmore and Harrison, and by Nichols, over forty years ago.[112] The subject was taken up again twenty years later in a paper by Zambrano and then in a series of short articles which offered useful information on companies and businessmen and paved the way for later research.[113] A recent book by Montaña attempts a general narrative history of river navigation including other routes besides the Magdalena and Cauca rivers.[114] Road construction in the difficult Colombian landscape, an odyssey even today, has only been the subject of two studies, the most recent in 1971.[115] In the case of air

1980); Gabriel Poveda, 'Los ferrocarriles y la ingeniería, primera parte', *Revista de la Universidad de Antioquia* 53 (1986), 4–35, and 'Los ferrocarriles y la ingeniería, segunda parte', *Revista de la Universidad de Antioquia* 54 (1987),53–70; Jorge Arias, 'Un momento estelar de la ingeniería mecánica en Colombia: los diseños de locomotoras de P. C. Dewhurst', *Boletín Cultural y Bibliográfico* 26 (1989), 53–72. See also Gustavo Arias, *La mula de acero* (Bogotá, 1986).

111 Carlos Mejía, 'Innovaciones tecnológicas y ferrocarriles', in Rainer Dombois and Carmen López (eds), *Cambio técnico, empleo y trabajo en Colombia: aportes a los estudios laborales en el VIII Congreso de Sociología* (Bogotá, 1993), pp. 187–98; Belisario Betancur and Conrado Zuluaga Osorio, *El tren y sus gentes: los ferrocarriles en Colombia* (Bogotá, 1995).

112 Robert L. Gilmore and John P. Harrison, 'Juan Bernardo Elbers and the Introduction of Steam Navigation on the Magdalena River', *Hispanic American Historical Review* 28 (1948), 335–59; Theodore Nichols, 'Cartagena and the Dique: a problem in transportation', *Journal of Transport History* 2 (1955), 22–34; see also Gustavo Bell, 'El Canal del Dique, 1810–1940: el viacrucis de Cartagena', *Boletín Cultural y Bibliográfico* 26: 21 (1989), 15–23.

113 On the river navigation companies of the Río Magdalena see Fabio Zambrano, 'La navegación a vapor por el río Magdalena', *Anuario Colombiano de Historia Social y de la Cultura* 9 (1979), 63–75; Eduardo Posada, 'Bongos, champanes y vapores en la navegación fluvial y colombiana en el siglo XIX', *Boletín Cultural y Bibliográfico* 26: 21 (1989), 3–14. The beginnings of navigation on the Cauca River at the end of the nineteenth century and the role of an important immigrant are studied in Germán Patiño, 'C. H. Simmonds y los comienzos de la navegación a vapor en el alto Cauca', *Boletín Cultural y Bibliográfico* 26: 21 (1989), 35–52.

114 Antonio Montaña, *A todo vapor* (Bogotá, 1996).

115 Both deal with the route to the Pacific. One of them is a North American doctoral thesis, which identifies the decisive role of the promoters of this road in the nineteenth century: James H. Neal, 'The Pacific Age Comes to Colombia: the construction of the Cali-Buenaventura route, 1854–1882' (PhD thesis, Vanderbilt University, 1971). The other is a narrative on the project during the twentieth century based on abundant primary sources: Mariano Arguelles, *La carretera al mar, 1926–1946* (Cali, 1946).

transport, which is worthy of attention since Colombia was one of the first countries to establish an airline in 1919 and which remains in full operation, there exist many works, for the most part non-academic accounts, which cover the whole sector and some dealing with its pioneers. Among them the works by Davies, Echavarría, Ardila, and García are worthy of attention. There is also a book on the history of the mail service.[116]

The historiography of industry

The economic rationality of industrialists, their formation as a sector of the ruling classes, their capacity for innovation, their behaviour regarding technological development, the limitations of their performance, their style of business management, and the ethos of specific business groups or sectors are subjects which have only occasionally provoked interest amongst the academics carrying out research on Colombian industry. Economists have not considered the entrepreneurial 'factor' within the models guiding the broad literature on Colombian industrialisation. Even today this variable is still considered part of a 'residual coefficient' (or a 'coefficient of ignorance'). As a result there are only a few relevant texts on business history within the literature which exists on the process of industrialisation in Colombia. The book by Luis Ospina Vásquez, published as long ago as 1955, remains an unsurpassed classic with abundant use of primary and secondary sources. This means that it has a broader significance than its title alone would suggest, and it offers valuable suggestions on the rationality with which the pioneers of industry in Colombia managed the risks involved in manufacturing.[117]

Useful chronological accounts of industrialisation at the level of individual firms may be found in the work produced by Gabriel Poveda in the late 1960s; his book on economic policies and technological innovation is

[116] R. E. G. Davies, *Airlines of Latin America since 1919* (Washington, 1984); Guillermo Echavarría, *De la mula al avión* (Medellín, 1989); Efraím Ardila García, *Camilo Daza, un hombre que nació por volar* (Bucaramanga, 1989); Miguel García, *Ernesto Cortissoz, conquistador de utopías* (Bogotá, 1994); On the history of mail, see Mario Arango *et al.*, *Comunicaciones y correos en la historia de Colombia y de Antioquia* (Bogotá, 1996).

[117] Luis Ospina Vásquez, *Industria y protección en Colombia* (Bogotá, 1955). On the history of protection, a subject that Ospina Vásquez initiated, José Antonio Ocampo added a qualitative analysis of tariff policies during the period between 1828 and 1906. See José Antonio Ocampo, 'Librecambio y proteccionismo en el siglo XIX', in José Antonio Ocampo and Santiago Montenegro (eds), *Crisis mundial, protección e industrialización* (Bogotá, 1984), pp. 235–95. The next essay in this volume, Santiago Montenegro, 'La política arancelaria en la primera fase de la industrialización, 1910–1945' (pp. 295–342), is also useful. The latter challenges some of the results of David Chu's doctoral dissertation comparing the effects of the Great Depression on industrialisation in Argentina and Colombia between 1930 and 1945: David S. Chu, 'The Great Depression and Industrialization in Latin America: response to relative price incentives in Argentina and Colombia, 1930–1945' (PhD thesis, Yale University, 1972).

also of value.[118] Alberto Mayor's two chapters on industrialisation between 1886 and 1968 link together technological factors, the formation of an industrial culture, and management techniques, with direct references to specific businessmen and businesses which go beyond Poveda.[119] The 'descriptive history' of Albert Berry, a North American economist, also serves as a good point of reference.[120] Juan José Echevarría provides useful information on the origin of the capital utilised by important industries in Colombia, besides analysing 'external shocks', the central theme of his study of industrialisation between 1920 and 1950.[121] His thesis concerning the *rentista* behaviour of Medellín's entrepreneurs has been challenged by Fernando Botero on the grounds that urban landownership was inextricably linked to commerce and other activities; it was not the chief source of accumulation.[122]

At the regional level the main studies include another book by Botero on the participation of Medellín traders in industry in Antioquia between 1900 and 1930; this was preceded by a polemical piece by Hugo López on the origins of manufacturing in the same region.[123] The literature on other regions is notoriously scarce, most obviously in the case of Bogotá, the capital city and the main industrial centre since the 1920s. On this there are only the works by Safford on the nineteenth century, which have already been mentioned, and a succinct and unfinished study by Zoilo Palleres on the 1900–1930 period which is solidly based on notarial archives.[124] On Caldas there is only the work of Manuel Rodríguez, which was discussed earlier in this paper. On the coast a recent book by Sergio

---

[118] Gabriel Poveda, 'Antecedentes y desarrollo de la industria en Colombia', *Revista Trimestral de la Andi* 4 (1967), 3–23; 'Historia de la industria en Colombia', *Revista Trimestral de la Andi* 11 (1970), 1–98; *Políticas económicas, desarrollo industrial y tecnología en Colombia. 1925–1950* (Bogotá, 1979).

[119] Alberto Mayor, 'Historia de la industria colombiana, 1886–1930' and 'Historia de la industria colombiana, 1930–1960', in Jorge O. Melo (ed.), *Nueva Historia de Colombia* (Bogotá, 1989), V, pp. 313–32 and 333–56.

[120] Albert Berry, ' A Descriptive History of Colombian Industrial Development in the Twentieth Century' (mimeo, 1979).

[121] Juan José Echavarría, 'External Shocks and Industrialization, Colombia, 1920–1950' (mimeo, Oxford, 1990). See also Echevarría's related article 'En la industrialización se ha sobreestimado el aporte antioqueño', *Revista Antioqueña de Economía y Desarrollo* 30 (1989), 81–96.

[122] Fernando Botero, *Medellín, 1890–1950: historia urbana y juego de intereses* (Medellín, 1996), esp. chapter 5.

[123] Fernando Botero, *La industrialización en Antioquia: génesis y consolidación, 1900–1930* (Medellín, 1985); see also Botero's thesis, 'Le processus d'industrialisation en Colombie: le cas de Medellín, 1900–1986' (thèse du troisième cicle, Paris, 1986); Hugo López, 'El desarrollo histórico de la industria en Antioquia: el período de consolidación', in Melo (ed.), *Los estudios regionales en Colombia*, pp. 187–210.

[124] Zoilo Pallares, 'Apreciaciones preliminares sobre el orígen de los empresarios en Bogotá', in ICFES, *Memoria del IV Congreso Nacional de Investigadores en Administración de Empresas* (Bogotá, 1984), pp. 231–50.

Solano and Jorge Conde studies the business elite, which was conditioned by its experience of having to do business with short-term time horizons, and the industrial development of Barranquilla.[125] An essay by Meisel examines the subsequent fragmentation of this industrial expansion.[126] On the industrialisation of Cali there are two ongoing research projects by Luis Ordóñez and Jairo Arroyo which have resulted in a book and several articles.[127] Both are focused on the role played by local entrepreneurs in this process.

The panorama regarding the historiography of specific industrial sectors is also one of extreme scarcity. Apart from the work already discussed in the section on petroleum, there are only a few studies of the textile, engineering, and iron and steel industries. The first to examine the textile industry was Enrique Echevarría's 1943 study, followed forty years later by Santiago Montenegro's analysis of the sector between 1900 and 1945, which emphasised the ways in which it was financed.[128] The origin and development of the textile industry in the specific case of Antioquia and in Colombia as a whole was researched by Carlos Londoño.[129] The literature on other key industrial sectors is equally scarce. The history of the metallurgical sector and its principal industrialists was studied by María Teresa Lopera while René de la Pedraja looked at Fedemetal, the employers' association they established.[130] The vicissitudes of the foundries established near Bogotá towards the end of the nineteenth century are the subject of two studies. Tatiana Machler highlights the diversity of the

[125] Sergio P. Solano and Jorge E. Conde, *Elite empresarial y desarrollo industrial en Barranquilla, 1875–1930* (Barranquilla, 1993). Before this book appeared there was an article by Jorge E. Conde, 'La industria en Barranquilla durante el siglo XIX', *Boletín Cultural y Bibliográfico* 28: 26 (1991), 41–56.

[126] Adolfo Meisel, '¿Por qué se disipó el dinamismo industrial de Barranquilla?', in Meisel and Posada (eds), *¿Por qué se disipó el dinamismo industrial?*, pp. 9–40.

[127] Luis A. Ordóñez, *Industrias y empresarios pioneros, Cali, 1910–1945* (Cali, 1995); Jairo Arroyo, 'Empresarios y empresas en Cali, 1920–1930' (thesis, Universidad del Valle, 1987); Jairo Arroyo, 'La modernización de Cali a comienzos del siglo XX', *Desarrollo Económico y Regional* 3 (1995), 15–50; Jairo Arroyo, 'Negociantes y comerciantes en Cali a comienzos del siglo XX', *Revista Cámara de Comercio de Buga* 3 (1994), 5–40. A synthesis of Cali's economic development in the twentieth century usefully sets the scene for the city's industrialisation: José Antonio Ocampo, 'El desarrollo económico de Cali en el siglo XX', in Ocampo and Montenegro (eds), *Crisis Mundial*, pp. 367–400.

[128] Enrique Echavarría, *Historia de los textiles en Antioquia* (Medellín, 1943); Santiago Montenegro, 'La industra textil en Colombia, 1900–1945', *Desarrollo y Sociedad* 8 (1982), 15–176; R. J. Brew, 'The Birth of the Textile Industry in Western Colombia', *Textile History* 8 (1977), 131–49; Santiago Montenegro, 'Breve historia de los principales textileros, 1900–1945', *Revista de la Universidad Nacional de Colombia (Medellín)*, 12 (1989).

[129] Carlos Londoño, *Orígen y desarrollo de la industria textil en Colombia y Antioquia* (Medellín, 1983).

[130] María Teresa Lopera, *El desarrollo de la industria metalúrgica colombiana hasta 1970* (Medellín, 1983); René de la Pedreja, *Fedemetal y la industrialización en Colombia* (Bogotá, 1986).

partners in one of the businesses, whilst Edgar Valero demonstrates the imbalances between the organisation of another ironworks and its technical advances.[131] Gabriel Poveda uses the evolution of technology as the central theme of a study of an important twentieth-century cement firm.[132]

The history of companies and businessmen

Fortunately business history is not merely confined to the study of individual companies and firms. If this were the case, then it would be a rather desolate field of research. Of course commemorative works on individual companies do exist, but they are generally official versions without very much academic rigour, and they tend to be distinctively anecdotal and eulogistic accounts. However, in Colombia their number is rather small. About sixty have been analysed for this paper, fifteen of which concern banking firms. These have not been included in this survey, though some may be useful sources for the academic researcher.[133] Interestingly, about ten such volumes were published in Medellín in three years in the mid-1990s. These concern firms owned by the largest economic groups in contemporary Colombia, and generally the commissions for them were awarded to academic researchers, indicating a shift in the trend prevailing in earlier decades. However, what is disappointing is that they have obliterated conflict and crisis, key ingredients in the life of the companies they study.[134] The fragility of the business memory, evident in the weak tradition which exists regarding the preservation of company archives in Colombia, has much to do with this situation. However, neither this loss of archives nor the problems of access to private sources can provide a definitive explanation for the nature of the historiography. The diligent researcher

[131] Tatiana Machler, 'La ferrería de Pacho: una ventana de aproximación', *Cuadernos de Economía* 6 (1984); Edgar Valero, 'La ferrería de Pacho: del empresario ingenuo al capitalismo (thesis, Universidad Nacional de Colombia, 1989); Victoria Peralta de Ferreira, 'Historia del fracaso de la ferrería de Samacá', *Universitas Humanística* 14: 24 (1983), 127–58.

[132] Gabriel Poveda, *Simesa: medio siglo de siderurgia* (Medellín, 1988).

[133] See Dávila, 'Historia empresarial en Colombia', pp. 47–53. Among these non-academic books those of E. Livardo Ospina stand out due to their use of internal company documents and other sources of information, but their referencing is not very systematic. See his books, *Una vida, una hecha, una victoria: monografía histórica de las empresas de servicios públicos de Medellín* (Medellín, 1966); *De la peña a las alturas: crónica de la Compañía de Cementos Argos en el cincuencentenario de su fundación* (Medellín, 1984); *Los hilos perfectos: crónica de Fabricato en sus 70 años* (Medellín, 1990).

[134] See, for eaxmple, Roberto Jaramillo *et al.*, *Compañía Suramericana de Seguros, 1944–1994* (Medellín, 1994); Santiago Londoño, *Horizontes de futuro: Compañía Nacional de Chocolates, 75 años* (Medellín, 1995). These two belong to leading groups within the so-called *Sindicato antioqueño*. See also the institutional history of Antioquia's development institute, Gloria Arango de Restrepo, *Idea para el porvenir: treinta años del IDEA* (Medellín, 1994). For the history of a company belonging to another of the big four economic groups see Cementos Caribe, *Cementos del Caribe S. A. 50 años de historia, 1944–1994* (Barranquilla, 1994).

can find sources if s/he searches for them. The major obstacle to further development of business history is the lack of interest that economists, historians, and sociologists in Colombia show in theoretical knowledge and the tradition of research into the evolution of business management and the corporate economy that exists at an international level.

Only a few studies remain for review here, therefore, those which have been inspired, at least in part, by the work of Alfred Chandler, and undertaken by researchers from the Universidad de Los Andes in Bogotá on themes such as business strategy, structure, and management hierarchies. Thus Enrique Ogliastri studied the one-hundred year history of a large brewing firm, emphasising the interrelationship between government economic policies and company strategy.[135] Carlos Dávila and his collaborators considered the strategies, organisational structures, management procedures, and inter-institutional relations of a public sector regional development corporation during its first twenty-five years.[136] Other works worth noting, written from different perspectives, include a study by the Posadas on another public sector corporation involved in regional development, a study of a state institution created in 1940 with the aim of promoting industry, and various banking histories.[137] Of the works on the central bank, which was established in 1923, the 1990 volume, which was intended fundamentally as a contribution to Colombian monetary history, is the more rigorous, though it says little about the evolution of the bank's internal organisation.[138] On credit institutions in Bogotá during the second half of the nineteenth century there are two studies, one by David Sowell on the artisans' savings bank which, like its counterparts in other Latin

[135] Enrique Ogliastri, *Cien años de Cerveza Bavaria* (Bogotá, 1990). This is part of a project initiated by Ogliastri at the end of the 1970s on the largest companies in Colombia. Another earlier history of this company remains unpublished: Roberto Junguito, 'Historia económica de Bavaria' (mimeo, 1980).

[136] Carlos Dávila et al., *La CAR, 25 años en el desarrollo regional, 1960–1985* (Bogotá, 1987). The CAR is the Corporación Autónoma Regional de la Sabana de Bogotá.

[137] Antonio Posada and Jeanne de Posada, *La CVC: un reto al subdesarrollo y al tradicionalismo* (Bogotá, 1966); Instituto de Fomento Industrial, *Instituto de Fomento Industrial, 1940–1995* (Bogotá, 1995). Banco de la República, *El Banco de la República: antecedentes, evolución y estructura* (Bogotá, 1990). A valuable work of reference published in 1994 contains the reports and press commentaries on the Kemmerer Mission which created the Banco de la República in 1923: see Adolfo Meisel, Alejandro López, and Francsico Ruiz (eds), *Kemmerer y el Banco de la República: diarios y documentos* (Bogotá, 1994). The classic work on the Kemmerer Missions is Paul W. Drake, *The Money Doctor in the Andes: the Kemmerer Missions, 1923–1933* (Durham, NC., 1989). Chapter 2 deals with Colombia.

[138] Banco de la República, *El Banco de la República: antecedentes, evolución y estructura* (Bogotá, 1990). A valuable work of reference published in 1994 contains the reports and press commentaries on the Kemmerer Mission which recommended the creation of this bank in 1923: see Adolfo Meisel, Alejandro López, and Francisco Ruiz (eds), *Kemmerer y el Banco de la República: diarios y documentos* (Bogotá, 1994). The classic work on Kemmerer is Paul W. Drake, *The Money Doctor in the Andes: the Kemmerer Missions, 1923–1933* (Durham, NC., 1989). Chapter 2 deals with Colombia.

American cities, filled a vacuum in banking for twenty years.[139] In the other, an analysis of the banks in Bogotá between 1870 and 1922, Carmen Romero concluded that their prudent and cautious behaviour was due to the influence of the businessmen who controlled them; previously she had also looked at a bank of issue at the end of the nineteenth century.[140] Other work on banking includes research by María Botero on the operations of banks in Antioquia during the same period; a book co-ordinated by Carlos Eslava on the Banco de Bogotá, the oldest private bank in the country; a study of a Medellín bank written by an economist, Jorge Valencia; and a history of a housing credit bank which was created in 1974 and which is part of the innovative Colombian system of indexed housing loans.[141] Francisco Piedrahita's detailed survey of the Medellín stock exchange between 1961 and 1986 is also a significant work on the financial history of Colombia.[142]

As in the case of company history, the analysis of biographies and autobiographies of businessmen in Colombia, over fifty of which were discovered in the course of research for this paper, reveals serious methodological deficiencies. As a consequence their utility lies not in considering them as academic works but as a valuable source for the researcher in business history.[143] They include memoirs, testimonies, opinions, and self-justifications all tinged with a degree of subjectivity, but it would be too simplistic to reject them on these grounds: rather they are sources which are awaiting the critical eye of a professional researcher. The majority of the studies on individual entrepreneurs and families included here are relatively short academic articles based on a variety of sources. As far as businessmen in Antioquia are concerned, for example, there is one text

---

[139] David Sowell, 'La Caja de Ahorros de Bogotá, 1846–1865: artisans, credit, development and savings in early national Colombia', *Hispanic American Historical Review* 73 (1993), 615–38.

[140] Carmen A. Rivero, 'La banca privada en Bogotá, 1870–1922', in Fabio Sánchez (ed.), *Ensayos de historia monetaria y bancaria de Colombia* (Bogotá, 1994), pp. 267–304. This volume makes a valuable contribution to monetary and banking history, and three of its six chapters are direct contributions to business history. See also Carmen A. Romero, 'La Regeneración y el Banco Nacional', *Boletín Cultural y Bibliográfico* 28: 26 (1991), 27–40.

[141] María Mercedes Botero, 'El Banco de Antioquia y el Banco de Sucre, 1872–1920', in Sánchez (ed.), *Ensayos de historia monetaria*, pp. 199–228; see also María Mercedes Botero, 'Los bancos locales en el siglo XIX: el caso del Banco de Oriente en Antioquia, 1883–1887', *Boletín Cultural y Bibliográfico* 25: 17 (1988), 76–93; Carlos Eslava *et al.*, *El Banco de Bogotá: 114 años en la historia de Colombia* (Bogotá, 1984); Fundación Antioqueña para los Estudios Sociales, *Banco Industrial Colombiano, 1945-1995* (Medellín, 1995); Carlos Dávila *et al.*, 'El desarrollo de la Corporación Social de Ahorro y Vivienda Colmena, 1974–1994 (mimeo, Bogotá, 1998).

[142] Francisco Piedrahita, *Bolsa de Medellín S. A., 25 años, 1961-1986* (Medellín, 1986). This is the work of an 'insider' with access to valuable archives.

[143] See, for example, Marco Restrepo, *El rey de la leña* (Buenos Aires, 1958); Remberto Burgos, *El general Burgos* (Bogotá, 1965); Hernán Mejía, *Don Gonzalo Mejía: 50 años de Antioquia* (Bogotá, 1984); Chaid Neme Hermanos S. A., *Pasos y huellas: testimonio de una obra* (Bogotá, 1993).

by a historian, an extensive monograph by a sociologist on an important family of businessmen who were also active in politics, a study of one of the pioneers of professional management, and a book based on a careful analysis of the diaries of a *patriarca antioqueño*.[144] With respect to the Atlantic Coast, there are works on two wealthy immigrants, an Italian and a North American, and a study of a pioneering family in the Barranquilla textile industry.[145] The studies of the Cauca Valley include an extensive and well documented biography of a sugar pioneer, some comparative biographical essays on a group of seven businessmen from the valley and Bogotá, an article about another immigrant, and a book on sugar planter whose business interests were highly diversified and who was, like most of the business figures in the literature reviewed here, also a political and employers' leader.[146] Part of Luis Ordóñez' book, which has already been mentioned, includes seven biographical essays on industrial pioneers in Cali.[147] Malcolm Deas also completed a scholarly biography of a British merchant, a 'tropical Victorian', who was also a well known writer.[148]

It must be stressed that in the historical writing on businessmen there is little attempt to relate it to theoretical concepts which might give it a greater analytical value. Such concepts might include Weberian ideas about the ethos of business, Sombart's idea of the bourgeois spirit, and those related to the social background, education, the role of the family, and the motivation of businessmen. The employment of some of these tools would allow the historian to move beyond a mere factual narrative and would open up some ways in which this type of study might be strengthened.

---

[144] Luis F. Molina and Omar Castaño, '"El burro de oro": Carlos Coroliano Amador, empresario antioqueño del siglo XIX', *Boletín Cultural y Bibliográfico* 24 (1988), 3–27; Luis F. Molina, 'El caso de don Leocadio María Arango', *Revista Antioqueña de Economía y Desarrollo* 32 (1990), 60–70; Ernesto Ramírez, 'La construcción del poder económico: la familia Ospina, 1850–1960', *Innovar* 8 (1996), 133–55; Alberto Mayor, 'Alejandro López, padre de la administración científica en Colombia', in Icfes, *Simposio de investigación sobre el empresariado colombiano: estado actual y perspectivas* (Bogota, 1987), pp. 11–103; Jorge Restrepo, *Retrato de un patriarca antioqueño: Pedro Antonio Restrepo Escovar, 1815–1899* (Bogotá, 1992).

[145] Luis F. Molina, '"El viejo Mainero": actividad empresarial de Juan Bautista Mainero y Trucco en Bolívar, Chocó, Antioquia, y Cundinamarca, 1860–1918', *Boletín Cultural y Bibliográfico* 25: 17 (1988), 3–29; Eduardo Posada, 'Karl C. Parrish, un empresario colombiano en los años veinte', *Boletín Cultural y Bibliográfico* 23: 8 (1986), 3–20; Sergio P. Solano, 'Familia empresarial y desarrollo industrial en el Caribe colombiano: el caso de la fábrica de tejidos Obregón', *Historia y Cultura* 1 (1993), 35–62.

[146] Phanor Eder, *Santiago M. Eder: recuerdos de su vida y acotaciones para la historia económica del Valle de Cauca* (Bogotá, 1959); Dávila, *El empresariado colombiano*; Alonso Valencia, 'Centu pur centu, moderata ganacia: Ernesto Cerutti, un comerciante italiano en el estado soberano del Cauca', *Boletín Cultural y Bibliográfico* 25: 17 (1988), 55–75; Oscar G. Ramos, *A la conquista del azúcar: Ingenio Riopaila S. A. y Central Castilla S. A. en homenaje a su fundador Hernando Caicedo* (Cali, 1990).

[147] Ordóñez, *Industrias y empresarios*, pp. 105–186.

[148] Malcolm Deas, *Vida y opiniones de Mr William Wills* (2 vols, Bogotá, 1996).

Miscellaneous

This final section will include some rather diverse works in terms of themes and methods which do not fit into the earlier parts of this essay. The role of education in the formation of the business values of the Bogotá elite during the nineteenth century is the main theme of Frank Safford's 1976 book.[149] An engineering school in Medellín, a similar breeding ground for businessmen and professional managers after the turn of the century, has been the subject of studies by a sociologist and a historian.[150] In 1994 an analysis of the evolution of accounting in Colombia was published.[151] However, despite the spread of business associations in the latter half of the twentieth century there are very few studies on their history: alongside the rather superficial but useful commemorative publications, there are no more than half a dozen academic works. In 1981 Miguel Urrutia's book provided an overall view of the growth of these organisations, from 22 in 1950 to 106 in 1980, along with a brief discussion of some of them, in which he argued that they were 'paper tigers' with very little influence on economic policy.[152] This is not a view that is shared by other analysts.[153] An earlier doctoral thesis had examined the powerful coffee producers' association and its development as an interest group, but there is still a need for a more comprehensive account of this body.[154] The changing influence of agricultural interests in relation to the state during a 100-year period is the main theme of Jesús Bejarano's well documented book on the Sociedad de Agricultores.[155] On the associations of large industrialists

[149] Frank Safford, *The Ideal of the Practical: Colombia's struggle to form a technical elite* (Austin, 1974).

[150] Mayor, *Etica, trabajo, y productividad en Antioquia*; Pamela Murray, 'Forging a Technocratic Elite in Colombia: a history of the Escuela Nacional de Minas de Medellín, 1887–1970' (PhD thesis, Tulane University, 1990), 'Engineering Development: Colombia's National School of Mines, 1887–1930', *Hispanic American Historical Review* 74 (1994), 63–82, and *Dreams of Development: Colombia's National School of Mines and its engineers, 1877–1970* (Birmingham, AL., 1997).

[151] Edgar Gracia *et al.*, *Historia de la contaduría pública en Colombia, siglo XX* (Bogotá, 1994).

[152] Miguel Urrutia, *Gremios, política económica y democracia* (Bogotá, 1983).

[153] Jonathan Hartlyn, 'Producers' Associations, the Political Regime, and Policy Processes in Contemporary Colombia', *Latin American Research Review* 20: 3 (1985), 111–38.

[154] B. E. Koffman, 'The National Federation of Coffee Growers of Colombia' (PhD thesis, University of Virginia, 1969). Other recent contributions in that direction include Rosemary Thorp, *Economic Management and Economic Development in Peru and Colombia* (Basingstoke, 1991); Rosemary Thorp and Francisco Durand, 'A Historical View of Business-State Relations: Colombia, Peru, and Venezuela compared', in Sylvia Maxfield and Ben Ross Schneider (eds), *Business and the State in Developing Countries* (Ithaca, 1997); Junguito and Pizano (eds), *Instituciones e instrumentos de política cafetera en Colombia*. This is perhaps the most complete account of the organisation, politics, finances, and activities of the Coffee Growers' Federation, written from the perspective of two insider economists.

[155] Jesús A. Bejarano, *Economía y poder: la SAC y el desarrollo agropecuario colombiano, 1871–1984* (Bogotá, 1985).

and their influence on the state between 1945 and 1950 there is a 1992 book which seems immersed in a rather Manichaen vision, as well as a recent institutional account: both are well documented.[156] There is also a study of the evolution of the associations representing small and medium-sized industry over a 35-year period, and a project in process on the association of merchants in relation to state economic policy.[157] This study does not share the simplistic view of the heroic businessman, and it also rejects the opposing view which sees him as irredeemably perverse and devious. Such perspectives, because of their ideological slant, diminish the contribution authors can make to critical business history. On the chambers of commerce two studies deserve a mention: one on Medellín between 1904 and 1930, the other on Bogota in the period 1878–1995.[158]

Without going into any great detail one should draw attention to the usefulness for the business historian, as sources more than anything else, of other types of literature: biographical dictionaries; testimonies of the few immigrant colonies in Colombia, particularly the Jewish colony; volumes on other groups such as the masons; the histories of social clubs which acted as means of socialisation and cohesion for the elite; and their educational institutions.[159]

Conclusion

In concluding this review of the literature on business history in Colombia it seems clear that the research remains in its early stages, even though the field has expanded since 1980 with the production of several new works and the appearance of new themes such as the formation of the business elite in regions other than Antioquia and the history of entrepreneurs. A number of themes, though, remain unresearched: the history of individual companies, whether national, foreign, or belonging to the public sector; the history of industry and of economic groups. The preferred period has been that between 1850 and 1930, with a lack of research on the diverse business actors of the later decades of the twentieth century.

If the existence of a recognised scientific community is used as an indicator of the state of an academic field, this is something that does not exist in the case of business history in Colombia. There are no identifiable

---

[156] Eduardo Sáenz, *La ofensiva empresarial: industriales, políticos y violencia en los años 40 en Colombia* (Bogotá, 1992); Fernando Botero, *1944 Andi cincuenta años 1994* (Medellín, 1994).

[157] Zoilo Pallares and Alberto Vargas, 'Historia de un gremio: la Asociación Colombiana Popular de Industriales (ACOPI), 1951–1986' (mimeo, 1988); Oscar Rodríguez, 'Interés gremial y regulación estatal: la formación de la Federación Nacional de Comerciantes, 1945–1970', *Anuario Colombiano de Historia Social y de la Cultura* 23 (1996), 171–218.

[158] Luis F. Molina, 'Cámara de Comercio de Medellín: la voz fuerte de Antioquia', *Revista Antioqueña de Economía y Desarrollo* 30 (1989), 13–25; Juan Camilo Rodríguez, *Historia de la Cámara de Comercio de Bogotá, 1878–1995* (Bogotá, 1995).

[159] More is said about these sources in Dávila, 'Historia empresarial', pp. 59–63.

theoretical trends to denote one school of thought or another which might provoke debate through the use of different approaches or interpretations. There is very little diffusion of the conceptual advances or methodology that business history has developed at an international level. The absence of this means that many studies in business history are distinctly descriptive rather than the result of using concepts and models from economics, sociology, and management. There are still no specialised business history journals or doctoral programmes in Colombia (the same is true of economic history) which might provide fertile ground for the development of business history. In historical congresses in Colombia business history is viewed still as being an undifferentiated part of economic history; and Colombians' links with the international academic community in business history remain weak. Paradoxically, there is a growing interest in the subject in terms of university teaching.[160]

As this chapter has shown, there are studies of good quality in several sub-fields of business history in Colombia. Nevertheless, it is clear that there is also a high degree of dispersion, fragmentation, and contributions from various disciplines, with the result that a critical mass of research has not yet been attained. Moreover, the contributions of foreign researchers continue to play a significant role. Interest in the formation of regional business elites has dominated and, in chronological terms, research on the final years of the century and the first three decades of the twentieth has been most common. In order to give further impetus to the field we need to address important questions and theoretically significant hypotheses; to utilise the analytical frameworks which exist; to possess the appropriate tools for the understanding of the internal technical, administrative, and financial processes of the companies we study; and to continue offering an open door to researchers from different disciplines. In addition, there is an urgent need to lay the ghosts that still wander around in certain academic circles and continue to see the businessman as someone who should be eulogised or demonised rather than studied critically.

---

[160] University courses in business history have existed for twenty-five years, having commenced in a private university, the Business School of the Universidad de los Andes. Since the middle of the 1980s they have spread to around ten public and private universities in different regions of the country. This provides a growing audience, not just of regular students of economics and management, but also of executives and businessmen participating in in-service programmes in business management. This is in contrast to the situation in other Latin American countries where similar audiences show very little interest in history. It seems that the British case is also rather different in that, despite a history of forty years of research in the field and a very large literature, business history has hardly managed to penetrate into business schools in that country.

CHAPTER SIX

Regional Studies and Business History in Mexico since 1975

Mario Cerutti

Research on the origins, development and activities of business groups in Mexico accelerated relatively quickly after the middle of the 1970s.[1] During the following decade it attained an obvious importance. An analysis of a large proportion of the published work allows one to pick out three significant features. First, developments in this particular field of historical research coincided with the growth of regional studies in Mexico. Second, from the very beginning these studies of businessmen were directly linked to the broader analysis of economic and social history. Third, if one adopts these two characteristics as the major points of reference, then one should also add that research interest has centred, above all, on the nineteenth and early twentieth centuries, with a particular concentration on the period between the 1840s and 1920.[2]

Before commencing the detailed analysis of the literature, one point must be emphasised. In contrast to several of the other chapters in this volume which review books and articles published both in Latin America and those published overseas, this discussion is based almost entirely on studies published in Mexico itself. In part this reflects the substantial volume of research produced in Mexico (in comparison with the work on business history in other countries). However, it also draws attention to the way in which the work undertaken in Mexico since the mid-1970s has changed perceptions of business history. It has resulted in conclusions quite unlike those of the general histories which were published before the 1980s. This emphasis also makes for a reading of Mexican business history which is rather different from that of many foreign scholars, especially in the United States, who often give little credence to the idea that domestic

---

[1] An earlier version of this paper was published in *Revista Interamericana de Bibliografía* 43 (1993), 375–93.

[2] The arguments in this chapter are based on extensive reading in the studies cited in the bibliography on Mexico at the end of the book. Rather than cluttering the text with extensive footnotes and citations, it seems preferable to refer the reader to the large number of regional studies cited in the bibliography which provide the evidence for the arguments developed here.

business elites, modern firms, and a style of development based on *local* capital could have grown up in Mexico or other Latin American societies. It also undermines the Latin American literature of the 1960s and 1970s which was composed more for reasons of ideology than of knowledge.

The nineteenth century and regional research

From the mid-1970s historical research dedicated to specific regional areas began to proliferate in Mexico. Historians started to focus their interest on projects which concentrated on rather smaller geographical areas than that which was eventually encompassed by the modern nation-state.

This trend coincided with a remarkable development of studies focusing on the nineteenth century, a period characterised by political, military, social, and economic processes of a regional nature. The idea of a unique *national* history, a process which emerged at exactly the same moment as the country achieved its independence, came to be seen as a weak and inefficient means of shedding light on the intense differences which distinguished the disparate regions of Mexico. The rhythms of growth in these areas, their interests, and their individual characteristics, varied widely. The differences among them appeared also in relation to the capital city, which at times seemed far distant from local and regional concerns.

It was historians working in research centres and universities in the interior of the country, in particular, who inspired this profound reorientation in the analysis of such a fundamental period in the history of Mexico. Forced to depend upon the local and provincial sources available to them, their conclusions began to diverge from those who took it for granted that Mexico had a much more homogeneous history in which the principal influences were the central government and the dominant role of Mexico City, features of the country which are so apparent in the late twentieth century.

One of the basic conclusions of the hundreds of seminar papers, articles, essays, theses, monographs, and edited collections which began to be published and circulated towards the end of the 1970s was that in nineteenth-century Mexico, at least up until the consolidation of the regime of Porfirio Díaz after the mid-1880s, one could not really speak of a genuine central power. Instead, the socio-political life of what was to become Mexico was distinguished by events and structures which were essentially regional. In some cases, these distinctive features became so acute that provinces escaped from the supposed control of Mexico City (in the case of Texas, in the north, in 1836), or else they reached the verge of doing so (such as Yucatán, in the south, during the same period).[3]

The structural weakness of the political and military forces based in the

---

[3] Between 1847 and 1855 the Maya Indians rebelled against the regional power in the so-called Guerra de las Castas.

central regions of Mexico, which were, of course, the most densely popu-
lated in the country, was evident in their inability to appropriate the
principal source of revenue that the national government possessed, the
customs duties levied on foreign trade. The experience of the years between
1855 and 1864 in the region that had now become the Northeast, following
the loss of over half of Mexico's territory in the war against the United
States, may serve as an example. During these ten years, the customs
houses located in strategic positions along the Río Bravo and on the Gulf
of Mexico passed on the income that they collected exclusively to the local
leaders and the local military.

The case of Governor Santiago Vidaurri, who effectively controlled
power in the frontier region in those years from his base in the city of
Monterrey, was one of the most striking. Although a supporter of the
Liberal cause, Vidaurri not only appropriated the customs revenues which
were collected in the Northeast, but even established a scale of tariffs which
contrasted sharply with those fixed by the national government in Mexico
City.[4] His ultra-liberal tariffs, which both preceded and coincided with the
Civil War in the United States, induced a spectacular boom in economic
activity in the Northeast. The prosperity enjoyed in this vast corner of
Mexico in those years, an area whose hinterland included the south of
Texas and stretched across the Gulf of Mexico as far as Havana, was far
removed from the endemic crisis which the south of the country was
suffering. The striking paradox is that war was the cause of both the boom
in the north and the crisis that was afflicting the centre of the country.

Economic history, business history

The research for one of the pioneering works of business history written
after 1975, Ciro Cardoso's edited collection on the formation and development of the bourgeoisie in nineteenth-century Mexico, was carried out
mainly in Mexico City.[5] Nevertheless, it was work undertaken in the regions
that really served to delineate the future pattern of the historiography. This
was for three reasons: first, the quantity and diversity of research projects
undertaken throughout the country (a phenomenon which has made this
regional work stand out in the field of Latin American history as a whole);
second, their focus, tightly linked to the regional dimension explained
above; and, third, because in the end they exerted a significant influence
on historians in the capital itself. In recent years the latter have started to
recognise that nineteenth-century Mexico City was little more than the
axis of an economic region situated in the geographical centre of Mexico.

[4] These were years of civil war in Mexico between the Liberals and Conservatives. After
1861 the latter were supported by French forces who remained in Mexico until they were
withdrawn by Napoleon III at the time of the Austrian-Prussian War of 1866.

[5] Ciro F. S. Cardoso (ed.), *Formación y desarrollo de la burguesía en México: siglo XIX*
(México, 1978).

After the mid-1970s studies of individual businessmen grew in keeping with the rate at which research on economic activity, and its principal protagonists, was expanding in the specialised centres and universities of the interior. In Puebla, Mérida, Guadalajara, Monterrey, Hermosillo, Jalapa, Durango, Morelia, and Ciudad Juárez, to take the most obvious cases, research efforts on the region in which these cities were situated were directed, at least in part, towards uncovering the economic world of the nineteenth century. Logically, therefore, historians had to become interested in those individuals who dominated the regional economy. Although, as a result, many of the studies which appear in the bibliography of business history in Mexico seem at times to concentrate more on mining, the railways, trade, agriculture, banking, or manufacturing industry, rather than on the men who ran them, the links between the history of economic activities in general and the narrower field of business history are clearly perceptible.

In other instances, the need to know more about and to explain the origins of the outstanding business groups of the present day, such as those in Chihuahua, Monterrey or Puebla, brought business history into contact with social history. In these studies, the initial priority was to explain the formation and development of the regional bourgeoisie which became dominant in the course of the nineteenth century, but the results were similar to those described in the previous paragraph. Of necessity research on the social origins of the elites had to incorporate material on the growth of their economic activities, and it thus ended up offering a wealth of information on various business sectors which were in the process of formation in the second half of the nineteenth century.

Yet whereas knowledge about the formation of particular sectors of business has improved markedly, research on individual firms has been less intense. The difficulties associated with obtaining access to business archives are well-known. In addition, the need for technical and theoretical knowledge, which scholars educated in departments of history and sociology have generally lacked, has led to a continuing scarcity of publications on individual enterprises. The technical ability required for this research still tends to be the property of economists. Apart from focusing on the regional research and the period between 1840 and 1920, the remainder of this paper will therefore concentrate on the origins and behaviour of individual entrepreneurs and the businesses that they controlled, rather than the internal evolution of the companies themselves.

Regional spaces, the business elite and investment

Just as the general historiography of Mexico before the mid-1970s suggested a unique national history, so the first studies on businessmen and the bourgeoisie, for their part, confused the members of the bourgeoisie who operated in Mexico City with the bourgeoisie in Mexico as a whole. Such

a perspective tended to marginalise what was happening in regional economic areas as different and distant as the Northwest (the states adjoining
California and Arizona), the Northeast (those adjacent to Texas), or, to
some extent, Yucatán, the state which displayed the most impressive growth
in agricultural production in nineteenth-century Mexico. After 1870 Yucatán is perhaps an exception, but this is more on account of the social and
racial consequences of growth than its economic and business aspects. In
reality, what stood out in this centralist perspective was the extent of
ignorance regarding the regional dynamics that played a major role in the
development of capitalist society in Mexico.[6]

These processes of change, and the inequalities they provoked, have now
been examined through the lens of regional research, especially with regard
to the centre and the north of the country. As a result there now exists
some quite detailed information about the emergence and development of
significant regional segments of the bourgeoisie during the nineteenth
century. Some of these groups, such as those in the north, have maintained
and even increased their importance in the twentieth century.

In Yucatán, Puebla, Veracruz, Jalisco, Chihuahua, Monterrey, Sonora,
and the cotton-growing region of La Laguna (which lies between the states
of Coahuila and Durango), the transformations which were becoming more
evident, especially after the liberal reforms of the mid-nineteenth century,
led to two results. First, clusters of specialised productive activities requiring
significant investments were established. Some of these were directed
towards the external market, others towards the internal market which was
then in the process of integration and consolidation. Second, there quickly
emerged individuals and firms, supported by capital accumulated in activities within their particular region, who were willing to take risks with the
capital, their properties, and the natural resources they possessed, in the
light of the demands and opportunities that were being presented.

The reaction to the stimulus of internal or external demand (or both at
the same time) influenced the bourgeois nature of these social agents.
Many of them, as will be noted later in this chapter, had acquired business
experience in one fundamental activity: commerce. Similarly, a substantial
number had been born overseas. However, although the immigrant entrepreneurs had arrived in Mexico under very different circumstances, in
almost all cases the capital which they employed had been accumulated
in defined regional areas of nineteenth-century Mexico. It was in these
same places that they made their principal investments after the 1870s and
1880s. In other words, this process began to occur even *before* the consolidation of Mexico as a nation-state and the parallel establishment of the
Porfirian order in the last quarter of the nineteenth century, and certainly
quite a long time *before* the entry of foreign capital began to intensify.

[6] Yucatán, the pricipal area of henequen cultivation, attracted particular attention from
both contemporary observers and later historians due to the profound social inequalities,
racial exploitation, and debt peonage associated with cultivation of this crop.

Commerce: a fundamental stepping stone

Like the majority of Latin American countries, as well as several in Europe, Mexico experienced a tumultuous history in the nineteenth century. The period was filled with political crises, internal and international wars, extreme institutional weakness, periods of regional influence as well as isolation, and many other such events which had a great influence in the formation of the nation-state. The future of the country was marked, moreover, by one of the greatest dramas in the history of the continent: the loss to the United States, in 1846–47, of over half of the territory inherited from Spain.

This overall picture explains why the most prominent sectors of the bourgeoisie, like their counterparts in other Latin American and European societies, attempted, above all, to employ their talents in the sphere of intermediation. The transfer of goods and capital into productive activities, in particular any that required substantial capital investments, would not come about until a new legal order, a certain degree of social and political stability, and a regular demand from international and national markets all appeared to be firmly grounded.

As far as historical research is concerned, the type of sources which were used, the historical period which was chosen, and the limited geographical extent of projects meant that work on this theme frequently followed the careers of the individuals who formed a substantial portion of the business elite of nineteenth-century Mexico in enormous detail, sometimes on an almost daily basis. Thus the role played by merchants, who were seen in the historiographical effervescence of the 1960s as an unproductive and parasitic group, has had to be revised. Recent studies have pointed out the strategic role of trade in three ways. First, it permitted the accumulation of significant amounts of capital which, towards the end of the century, provided the basis for other economic activities. Second, commercial enterprise encouraged the development of important credit mechanisms which in turn helped to stimulate production, at least between 1860 and 1900, after the liberal reforms had become firmly established. Third, involvement in trade resulted in the acquisition of business experience which, without any doubt, facilitated the transition towards other types of activity: manufacturing industry, banks, specialised agriculture, livestock ranching, forestry, transport, mining, and services.

Credit and banks

Particular emphasis must be laid on the development of credit mechanisms, which during the second half of the nineteenth century were largely dominated by trading houses. The role of the merchants, who converted themselves not only into money-lenders but also into providers of other financial services, was one of the key elements in the economic reconstruction that different regions experienced following the internal and international wars of the period between 1848 and 1867. The examples of Yucatán and La Laguna, where two of the most impressive processes of agricultural growth of the whole Porfirian era occurred, appear decisive in underlining this fact.

The arrival of the banks later in the century focuses attention on two further points. First, a high proportion of these institutions counted many of the traders and moneylenders who had been important in earlier periods amongst their founders. Second, the banks did not occupy the same space for credit operations which the merchant houses or individual money-lenders had previously monopolised. Indeed it seems that they hardly reduced the scope for this older type of operation.

The appropriation and use of land

While this was occurring, a significant proportion of the capital which had been accumulated in the regions was utilised for the acquisition of land. Bourgeois groups involved in commerce and the supply of credit converted themselves into landowners with enormous frequency. Liberal legislation, which encompassed both the redistribution of church and communal land (in a manner similar to that in Spain) and the colonisation of previously unsurveyed territory, opened the way for the appropriation of land and water rights by private interests, though on different scales in different regions.

This transfer of capital which had originated in commerce into land was another vital component of the process of economic recovery which could be observed from the middle of the 1870s. A large proportion of the lands which came from the Church, the municipalities, or the indigenous com-munities, from the cattle ranges of the North to the 'desert' and the land formerly occupied by semi-nomadic groups, including the largely inac-cessible slopes of the mountain regions, was now subjected to capitalist development. More intensive forms of livestock farming, the development of timber exploitation, and various types of commercial agriculture occu-pied numerous areas.

There were two other consequences of the advance of capital into landholding. First, urban and rural markets for land grew rapidly, and this in turn was a key factor in the shaping of the internal market of Mexico. Second, at the very end of the nineteenth century, when the *paz porfiriana* was at its height, the appropriation of land was stimulated even further by the possibility of gaining control of the subsoil, and the parallel connection with the development of mining.

The northern region and the United States' economy

Commercial activity was especially intense in the Northeast after the definition of the frontier with the United States in 1848. The dividing line, now fixed on the Río Bravo, offered spectacular opportunities for enrichment to individual businessmen and intermediary firms located on both sides of the river, just as much in times of war as of peace. The day-to-day relationship with the economy of the United States which evolved from the middle of the century provided the context in which powerful business groups in northern Mexico developed their activities.

Studies of northern Mexico, a block of around ten states that occupies more than half the national territory, and which has played a central role in domestic capitalist development, show how, when the liberal reforms began to have an effect and when, at roughly the same time, post-war economic construction became evident in both Mexico and the United States, a substantial part of the capital which had its origins in trade was now channelled into productive activities.

The slow but steady transformation of these merchants and money-lenders into mining, industrial, landowning, and banking entrepreneurs was closely connected with the extensive restructuring that the economy of northern Mexico experienced as a result of its exposure to the influence of one of the world's fastest growing markets, that of the United States. The social and political stability of the Porfiriato, a legal order that introduced such important novelties as the limited liability company, and the arrival of the railway reinforced the links between the North of Mexico and one of the greatest powers of the Second Industrial Revolution. The arrival of North American capital in Mexico itself stimulated these activities even more, and as the research shows in detail, expanded the opportunities for vigorous business groups like those in Monterrey and Chihuahua to develop further.

The Chihuahua–La Laguna–Monterrey axis

The spectacular development of productive activities in the North, a real frontier economy, thus had a significant impact on the formation and expansion of the national market. For the property-owning classes of the North a whole series of opportunities now emerged. Some were able to specialise in production for the growing and increasingly integrated domestic market. Examples are those involved in intensive cotton cultivation, coal mining, and industries such as soap manufacturing, beer, glass, cement, and steel. Others specialised in production for the US market (lead and copper mining and smelting, ranching, animal feedstuffs, and certain sectors of agriculture). Some took the opportunity to do both, in other words to operate in the internal and the external markets.

The vigour of these entrepreneurial groups was thus stimulated by two clusters of demand: the internal market, whose pace of growth was relatively slow but which possessed characteristics similar to countries such as Argentina, Brazil or Spain, and on the other hand, the demand for goods stemming from one of the centres of the Second Industrial Revolution, the east coast of the United States, which was driven by the more intense rhythms of the world economy. Chihuahua, the region of La Laguna, and Monterrey, the pivotal points of a geographical area which extended from Texas to the Gulf of Mexico, became active nurseries for businessmen between 1870 and the Revolution of 1910. Born and brought up in this dynamic frontier economy, a region which could be called an economic and territorial extension of the Second Industrial Revolution, the social agents who have been the subject of this research formed an entrepreneurial axis which spread down from Chihuahua, crossed La Laguna, and terminated in Monterrey. Based on the limited liability company (or *sociedad anónima*) the significance of this axis was evident in a series of collective projects, some of which had a great future. The most important of these were La Esperanza and its successor, the Compañía Industrial Jabonera de La Laguna (soap manufacturing), Vidrería Monterrey (glass), Cementos Hidalgo (cement), and various banking institutions (the Banco Minero de Chihuahua, the Banco de La Laguna, the Banco Mercantil de Monterrey, and the Banco Central Mexicano).

The centre, the south, and their markets

The industrial entrepreneurs of central Mexico, in contrast, responded almost entirely to the demands of the internal market, which was growing more slowly. This was particularly evident amongst those involved in the textile industry, which was especially dependent on the consumption of the popular sectors, a population which had a limited income. The most striking examples of growth in manufacturing emerged in Puebla, Veracruz the Valley of Mexico, and Jalisco. In addition to this there is another important point which research in the regions has brought to light, at least in the case of Puebla and its surroundings, namely the rural or semi-urban origins of much of the capital and the textile factories and other concerns which multiplied in number during the second half of the nineteenth century.

In contrast the businessmen who became involved in other specialised agricultural pursuits in central and southern Mexico, coffee and tobacco cultivation in Veracruz, for example, were stimulated by demands similar to those to which their counterparts in the North were responding. The principal purchasers of their products were located overseas, especially in the United States. A rather similar process occurred in the extreme Southeast.

The few studies of businessmen operating in the South of Mexico have been confined almost entirely to Yucatán. Here, too, it was the North American market that generated a striking transformation in agriculture. The emergence of the henequen plantations after the 1870s radically altered both the production systems and the social landscape of the north of the peninsula, and gave rise to an enormous accumulation of capital in the hands of the regional elite. The harsh critical tone present in many of these works, which for the most part condemn both the forms of social domination imposed by the Yucatán landowners and the expenditure on luxuries in which the resulting profits allowed them to indulge, has obscured the peculiarities of business development in the region. However, some of the more recent authors have clarified the means through which many of these planters became involved in the development of banking and railways in Yucatán, as well as the commercial origins of the capital which led to an explosion in henequen production.

Foreign surnames, regional capital

Perhaps one of the most notable aspects of the regional research concerned with economic and business activity in Mexico has been the study of the process by which capital was accumulated. The meticulous study of one, two, or more entrepreneurs or entrepreneurial families through decades of activity has produced results which require particular attention in this discussion of the state of the literature.

One of these has already been mentioned: the importance of commerce in the early stages of the formation both of capital and of the entrepreneurs themselves. Moreover, the research undertaken has illustrated the mechanisms through which fortunes which had their origins in trade were transformed into mining, banking, manufacturing and agricultural investments. Indeed, one of the most striking results of these projects which this review of the literature has emphasised is the *regional* and *local* origin of much of the elite wealth which the literature during the 1960s and 1970s considered without very much reflection, and with very little empirical justification, as *foreign*.

During the second half of the nineteenth century Mexico received relatively few immigrants. Unlike Argentina, Uruguay, or southern Brazil, where hundreds of thousands of Europeans arrived, only a small number entered Mexican territory. Of these, a considerable proportion came from Spain, especially from the North, but there was also an inflow of English, Irish, French, North American, Italian, and German migrants. The research on the regions has shown that quite a number of these immigrants enjoyed success, and accumulated large fortunes and holdings of property. However, it has also demonstrated several other significant points: on arrival in Mexico these men were normally very young with few resources of their own; the formative stage during which they obtained their capital and their business experience lasted years, often decades; and finally, their behaviour in the sphere of commerce or production did not differ substantially from that of their counterparts of Mexican origin.

The list of cases which has now been analysed appears sufficiently extensive for those who are specialists in business history to move beyond the common confusion between foreign *surnames* and foreign *capital*. As a result of their history (their birth, growth, and reproduction in a specific geographical area), their intensive involvement in day-to-day economic activity, and their tenuous relationship with the capitalist structure of the countries from which they had migrated, it would not be valid to apply the adjective *foreign* to these businessmen and their capital.

The businessmen of Spanish origin

In a manner which was perhaps unexpected, the most recent research in the regions has underlined with some force a further point which supports this argument, namely that the capital and property which were managed by businessmen of Spanish origin was particularly significant in the formation of domestic capitalism in Mexico. Originally suggested as a provisional conclusion, valid in principle for the northern and central Mexico, the presence of prominent businessmen of Spanish origin now seems widespread, a factor which had its roots in the middle of the century and acquires particular force between 1870 and 1910.

Three points regularly emerge from the cases that have been studied so far: the high proportion of immigrants coming from the north of the Iberian peninsula (the Basque region, Santander, and Asturias); the extremely young age at which they arrived in Latin America; and the lack of resources which marked the beginnings of their careers in Mexico. The latter two points must force historians to reject any interpretation which attempts to define the capital which these men managed decades later as foreign.

Conclusion

During the last twenty or so years research at the regional level has generated sufficient information for historians to refine or modify earlier interpretations of Mexico during the nineteenth and part of the twentieth century. One of the keys to this reappraisal lies in the fact that those undertaking the more recent research have adapted the scope of study to one appropriate for the time. This is a crucial methodological point for those who study a historical period during which the fundamental social, political, and economic processes were occurring not at the level on which the nation-state was eventually constructed but in more confined geographical areas. Another consequence is that research of this kind has shown Mexico City to be just one of the core areas of socio-economic and political development, the geographical centre of a country where regional trends were predominant, instead of presenting the capital city as the only decisive pivot of Mexico's history during this period.

Closely linked to the history of economic activity, business history in Mexico has developed in a particularly lively fashion and on the basis of a perspective that demands the intensive use of local primary sources. The results and conclusions have been summarised above, and they are supported by the extensive bibliography on Mexico which appears in the final section of this book.

When the consolidation of the Porfirian state began, in the middle of the 1880s, a large part of the transformations which would characterise this period of Mexican history were already developing strongly. As a consequence it is now necessary to emphasise the crucial importance of capital of regional origin in the structuring of capitalist society in Mexico, and to reassess the role ascribed to foreign capital in this formative period. Moreover, in view of the scale of economic activity in different parts of the country which was promoted by capital accumulation at a regional level, it is probable that the overall impact of the business groups located in Mexico City was rather less than that which the historiography suggested in the 1970s.

The most recent results from research into business history in Mexico also indicate a need to raise questions at a more general and more universal level. These would include the following. To what extent did the interpretations of Latin American entrepreneurs presented in the 1960s and 1970s underestimate or ignore the importance of capital accumulated and invested in the regions in the development of domestic capitalism? Were there in fact any historical grounds for speaking, with obvious ideological fervour but very little empirical evidence, of such a thing as a lumpenbourgeoisie?[7] Is it really possible to explain, in terms of cultural factors specific to the region, the behaviour of entrepreneurs and their failure to set off the longed for industrial revolution? Did the businessmen of nineteenth-century Latin America operate, with regards to capital accumulation and investment, with a different type of logic from their European and North American counterparts? What has been discovered in the case of Mexico, in the course of twenty years of research, implies a rather different history to that which was being written a couple of decades ago.

---

[7] The phrase is André Gunder Frank's. See his *Lumpenbourgeosie, Lumpendevelopment: dependence, class, and politics in Latin America* (New York, 1972).

CHAPTER SEVEN

Business History in Peru

Rory Miller

There are certain parallels between the task faced by a British business historian working on Latin America in the late twentieth century and the British businessman of the mid-nineteenth century who tried to apply the business techniques with which he was familiar in his home economy to a quite different environment. Both run the danger of overestimating the value of their own approach and imposing an alien agenda on a society and economy they only partially understand. It is worth stating at the outset, therefore, that there are many problems with the practice of business history in the United Kingdom. The field was founded on the company history, the classic example of which was Charles Wilson's two-volume history of Unilever.[1] Since 1954, when this was published, there has been a plethora of studies of individual companies in Britain, large and small, central and insignificant. The quality, of course, has been uneven, ranging from superficial and eulogistic narratives produced for a centenary or similar anniversary to sophisticated treatments which locate the company's history within a much broader set of problems and which demonstrate the theoretical and comparative awareness and technical expertise which characterise good historical writing. Nevertheless, the dominance of the company history or case study approach to business history, dictated in part by the constraints of finance and time, has attracted much criticism from leaders in the field in Britain, though it is not without some prominent defenders.[2]

Company history is not the same as business history, although it forms an important component of it. Nor is entrepreneurial history the same as business history, though many of the early studies in business history in Britain took this form. Unfortunately in Latin America the Spanish term

---

[1] Charles Wilson, *The History of Unilever: a study in economic growth and social change* (2 vols, London, 1954).

[2] Leslie Hannah, 'New Issues in British Business History', *Business History Review* 57 (1983), 165–74; Donald Coleman, 'The Uses and Abuses of Business History', *Business History* 29 (1987), 141–56; Stephen Nicholas, 'Locational Choice, Performance, and the Growth of British Multinational Firms', *Business History* 31 (1989), 122–41. For a defence, see Terry Gourvish, 'Business History: in defence of the empirical approach?', *Accounting, Business and Financial History* 5 (1995), 3–16.

historia empresarial, the phrase that is used most often to define the field, bears all three of these English-language meanings. This confusion perhaps symbolises the disjuncture between business history in Latin America and the same subject in North America or Great Britain. Since the time when Wilson was writing, or even the point a decade later when David Joslin was producing one of the first major case studies of foreign business activity in Latin America, the field has advanced enormously in North America, Europe, and Japan.[3] Under the influence of Alfred Chandler, and other business historians of international renown such as Mira Wilkins and Geoffrey Jones, the theoretically informed comparative study centred on a particular theme has become the device which has driven the subject forward. Without going into enormous depth about the way in which the subject has developed elsewhere, the consequence for historians of foreign and national business in Latin America ought to be to move the emphasis away from constructing narratives of an individual firm or entrepreneur, however significant these may be, and push it towards some of the central issues which might help to define and differentiate the history of capitalist business in Latin America. In the Latin American context the most important of these questions seem to be themes such as: the foundation of firms and their financing; the evolution of the structure and organisation of firms and the extent to which the managerial capitalism typical of the North Atlantic world developed in the nineteenth and twentieth centuries; the legal, institutional and economic environment within which entrepreneurs and firms developed and the opportunities and constraints that resulted; the strategies of owners and managers; and the outcomes (successes and failures, whether financial, technological or social), and the reasons for them.

It is inevitable that a British historian invited to survey the field of business history in Peru will have questions like these at the back of his mind. Yet clearly, if there have been problems in developing business history in Britain, where researchers have enjoyed a relative abundance of grants and well organised archives, as well as some sympathy on the part of leading businessmen for the task of the historian, one ought not to expect too much in Peru, given that it is one of the poorer countries of the western hemisphere and has suffered severe economic and political crises since the mid-1970s. In fact, business history in Peru has made some remarkable achievements, although it has also exhibited many problems similar to those found in Britain. The volume of literature is perhaps not as great as in some other Latin American countries, but the research undertaken in the final third of the twentieth century has provided some important insights into the way in which capitalist enterprise developed in Peru, highlighting some similarities and some differences with other Latin American countries.

---

[3] David Joslin, *A Century of Banking in Latin America: the Bank of London and South America, Ltd.* (London, 1963).

The background

Research in the economic history of Peru has suggested that two of the most significant characteristics of the Peruvian economy since the mid-nineteenth century have been its openness and the very high degree of regional and personal inequalities that have persisted. Export growth and cycles of foreign investment were the fundamental dynamic elements in the Peruvian economy until the 1960s, but however concentrated in particular geographical regions they might be they had ramifications throughout the country. Such an interpretation represents a move away from earlier dualistic models which depicted a modern capitalist sector based around well developed labour and product markets on the coast and a traditional precapitalist sector in the Andean sierra. It is clear now that few communities, except in the remote Amazon basin, were totally isolated from the market. This trend has also meant that the concept of an 'enclave economy', the idea Jonathan Levin used at the beginning of the 1960s to depict the guano economy of the mid-nineteenth century, is no longer sustainable in its original form.[4] Even though guano was exploited only on a handful of islands off the coast, the internal trade it generated, the government expenditure that it financed, and the capital accumulation that resulted had repercussions throughout the country.[5]

Although this trade dominates the economic historiography of mid-nineteenth century Peru, even at the peak of the guano period (1850–1870) Peru was in fact producing several other export products of importance from different regions of the country. These included silver, sugar, cotton, sheep's and alpaca wool, and, from the end of the 1860s, nitrate. Successive Peruvian governments were much more dependent on guano income than the economy as a whole. Of these other exports only nitrate, located in the far south, at all resembled an enclave; the remainder brought a stream of income and economic and social changes into their regions. The guano period in Peru thus raises many questions of interest to business historians: the process of creation of new business elites at both national and local levels; their social background and entrepreneurial and technical formation; the interplay among foreign firms, immigrant entrepreneurs, and local businessmen; the relationship of these different groups with the state; and businessmen's strategies, values, and ideologies.[6] Research since the mid-1960s has thrown some light on these issues. For a long time the nineteenth century had been the dark age of Peruvian economic history, and it was

[4] Jonathan Levin, *The Export Economies: their pattern of development in historical perspective* (Cambridge, Mass., 1960).

[5] W. M. Mathew, 'A Primitive Export Sector: guano production in mid-nineteenth century Peru', *Journal of Latin American Studies* 9 (1977), 35–57: Shane J. Hunt, 'Guano y crecimiento en el Perú del siglo XIX', *HISLA* 4 (1984), 35–92.

[6] On business ideologies at the time, see Paul Gootenberg, *Imagining Development: economic ideas in Peru's "fictitious prosperity" of guano, 1840–1880* (Berkeley, 1993).

assumed that a foreign-controlled guano enclave had little effect on the economy as a whole and on business ideologies. Thanks to detailed research in provincial archives and a reappraisal of the economic literature produced at the time such claims are no longer tenable.

The great watersheds in Peruvian economic history before the 1960s are the economic crisis of the mid-1870s and the Pacific War of 1879–1883 which followed. As a result Peru lost many of its most dynamic exports (including nitrate) and the power of the national governments in Lima disintegrated as state finances collapsed and the country's internal politics fell into turmoil. Due to the role government had played in the economy, through its dominance of the guano trade and then its partial nationalisation of the nitrate industry in the 1870s, the debacle left a legacy of distrust of state intervention in Peru. The collapse also brought changes to the foreign role in Peru, causing a radical shakeout amongst both local and foreign merchants, an end to foreign portfolio investment in the Peruvian economy until the 1920s, but also, in time, an influx of foreign direct investment into areas like railways, mining, and oil.[7] Foreign companies in railways and mining had important commercial implications in the interior, especially in the central sierra.

The Peruvian economy, and hence the environment in which business operated, now became characterised by a thriving export sector and a weak state.[8] In contrast to some of the other countries discussed in this book, which became dependent on single exports and fiscal linkages, Peru developed a range of exportable products with extensive backward linkages into regional economies. The initial recovery from the war was led by silver, but it was followed by copper and other non-ferrous metals, sugar and cotton, and petroleum. A rapid recovery from the depression of the early 1930s was fuelled by rising exports of precious metals and cotton, and after the Second World War the fishing industry developed rapidly. Not until the 1960s did the export sector of the economy cease to generate something new to replace products which were losing ground. The rapid recovery from the depression of the 1930s also meant that the state played a smaller role in the economy than in countries of comparable size (like Chile and Colombia), and there was less development of industry. The nationalist ideologies prevalent in Argentina, Brazil and Chile, which fuelled state intervention and deterred foreign investors, had much less impact in Peru in the immediate post-war period. Although industrial growth accelerated in the 1950s and 1960s, private sector enterprises,

[7] The epitome of this change was the signing of the Grace Contract, which transferred ownership of the state railways to the foreign bondholders: see Rory Miller, 'The Making of the Grace Contract: British bondholders and the Peruvian government, 1885–1890', *Journal of Latin American Studies* 8 (1976), 73–100.

[8] These are central themes of the standard economic history of the period: Rosemary Thorp and Geoffrey Bertram, *Peru, 1890–1977: growth and policy in an open economy* (London, 1978).

whether nationally or foreign-owned, were still the dominant business actors until 1968. This is not to say that nationalism was absent, for both the oil and mining firms came under attack, but the real target of many radicals in Peru was the small Lima business elite, the infamous oligarchy of thirty or forty families which was thought to dominate the country.

The other important element in the background to the development of business history is the academic environment. While many Peruvian historians in the mid-twentieth century exhibited rather traditional attitudes, researching the colonial period or political history and largely eschewing economic history, there were a handful of significant figures who did encourage research on economic and social themes.[9] Two well-known historians stand out in this respect. One was Jorge Basadre, whose monumental *Historia General de la República del Perú*, intermingled economic, social, and political themes, and who also published on business.[10] The other was Pablo Macera who, as Professor of History at the Universidad Nacional Mayor de San Marcos in the 1960s, began to encourage research in economic history by his students, especially agricultural enterprise. His stimulus inspired successive generations of younger historians, often trained abroad in the United States or in Paris, who changed the direction of Peruvian history towards socio-economic themes: amongst these were Heraclio Bonilla, Alberto Flores Galindo, Manuel Burga, Alfonso Quiroz, and José Deustua. Important also in this process was the foundation of the Instituto de Estudios Peruanos in the 1960s, the installation of Bonilla as its leading historian, and its development of an extensive publishing programme.[11] The political conjuncture made this an appropriate moment for the flowering of research on Peruvian economic history. There was a substantial audience eager to understand the roots of the country's problems and ready to consume works critical of the elite and their relationships with foreign companies, the state, and the popular classes. These developments also coincided with the rapid expansion of Latin American studies in the United States and Europe, and hence an influx of foreign scholars working on parallel themes. All this was aided by the almost total absence of academic repression under the military regime of 1968–1980. Just two caveats need to be added to this optimistic scenario for the development of economic and business history from the

[9] In one of the standard histories of modern Peru, published in 1967, Fredrick Pike comments that 'the writing of economic history has not yet reached a distinguished level ... No work that is even remotely satisfactory has appeared on the social history of Peru since independence': Fredrick B. Pike, *The Modern History of Peru* (London, 1967), p. 330.

[10] Jorge Basadre's magnum opus went through various editions; the most recent is *Historia de la República del Perú* (6th edition, Lima, 1968). For his excursion into business history, see Jorge Basadre y Rómulo A. Ferrero, *Historia de la Cámara de Comercio de Lima, 1888–1963* (Lima, 1963).

[11] For a survey of these developments see Heraclio Bonilla, 'The New Profile of Peruvian History', *Latin American Research Review* 16: 3 (1981), 210–24.

second half of the 1960s. First, this was an intellectual enterprise which, unlike Colombia or Mexico, was centred in the capital. For a long time little emerged from the provinces, although regional archives gained in organisation and accessibility throughout this period. Second, very few of the scholars involved would have considered themselves business historians pure and simple. Rather they were, for the most part, social, and to a lesser extent economic, historians whose political concerns drew them towards the study of business.

Business history in Peru

The bibliography on Peru in the appendix to this book offers an overall impression of the literature, in the form both of books and articles, which now exists on the business history of the country. It may be that the quantity, particularly for a relatively poor nation, is rather surprising, especially since the list excludes many more general works on social and economic history and is confined to studies which rely on primary sources of some kind: printed material (such as annual reports or official publications); manuscripts (whether the archives of the firm itself or else material in the public domain like notarial archives and, in the case of foreign companies, diplomatic correspondence); or interviews with managers and workers with a long period of service in the firms concerned. Nevertheless, a glance at the list shows up several problems in the historiography of business in Peru which have parallels both in the developed world and in the other Latin American countries discussed in this volume.

Histories of individual firms predominate. Comparative analysis, business history as opposed to company history, is comparatively rare, although there are quite a few broader sectoral studies. To state this is not to criticise those who have written company histories rather than business history in its broader sense, for without the company history as a basis, the development of business history proper is impossible. However, despite the number of interesting studies which have been published on individual firms, it is very difficult to imagine an adequate synthesis of the evolution of business in Peru being published within the immediate future because of the lack of studies on other significant themes, sectors, and enterprises. This will become very clear in considering the balance of books and articles on companies and business groups which have appeared.

Several significant imbalances are very evident. First, there is a disequilibrium in the themes covered. There has been much more emphasis on foreign companies, or else the Peruvian firms and business groups dedicated to export, than on those Peruvian firms whose interests were concentrated in the internal economy. These two categories (foreign firms or exporters) accounted for well over half of the studies in the bibliography which was initially prepared as a basis for this survey. Linked with this problem, there is also a very obvious chronological imbalance. Most of the studies published conclude before 1950, and many others follow themes established during the first half of the century up to the 1960s but no further. There is very little, therefore, on the transformation of the Peruvian economy which followed the depression of the early 1930s, whether on the export sector or on firms producing goods and services for domestic markets. Rather surprisingly, there is a reasonable amount of literature on the banks and other financial institutions during the first half of the twentieth century, but nothing has been published on the insurance companies, an important source of profits for the Lima elite following the withdrawal of the majority of the foreign companies at the turn of the century.[12] However, the Peruvian financial sector suffered major disruption in the early 1930s as a result of the collapse of the largest commercial bank, the Banco del Perú y Londres, and apart from in-house histories of the Banco del Crédito and the final sections of Alfonso Quiroz's work, there is very little on the banks which then came to the fore.[13] Studies of the banks from the 1930s onwards are lacking, and this is especially true of those which were later acquired by foreign interests such as the Banco Continental or else dominated by local elite families like the Banco Popular and the Banco Comercial. Financial groups such as the Wiese, Ferreyros, Prados, and Pardos, which had close links with banks and took control of important sectors of the Peruvian economy after 1930, have been rather neglected.[14] There is also a shortage of histories of manufacturing firms (apart from a handful of studies on the Backus and Johnston brewery and the alpaca spinning firms in Arequipa), companies in the fishmeal sector, and modern pressure groups such as ADEX (the Asociación de Exportadores). These facts, particularly the heavy focus on the export sector and the period before the 1930s, as well as conflicting ideological outlooks, helped to produce an abyss in Peru, as in Britain, between business history and schools of business administration. Business historians seem to produce little of relevance to the latter, with the exception, perhaps, of a few studies on relatively narrow themes such as industrial relations.[15] It would almost seem that the historians of the

[12] The foreign insurance companies opted to withdraw from Peru following the enactment of laws in 1897 and 1901 which stipulated minimum capital requirements for insurance firms and compelled them to invest in Peruvian real estate and government bonds: Alejandro Garland, *Peru in 1906* (Lima, 1908), pp. 306–07.

[13] Gianfranco Bardella, *Un siglo en la vida económica del Perú: Banco de Crédito, 1889–1989* (Lima, 1989); Alfonso W. Quiroz, *Domestic and Foreign Finance in Modern Peru, 1850–1950: financing visions of development* (London, 1993).

[14] One should, however, note a monograph on the Romero group: Germán Reaño and Enrique Vásquez, *El Grupo Romero: del algodón a la banca* (Lima, 1988). Vásquez further developed this work, adding studies of other groups like the Wiese, Brescia, Riva Agüero, and Bentín families, in his doctoral thesis: 'The Role, Origins and Strategies of Business Groups in Peru' (DPhil thesis, University of Oxford, 1995).

[15] Coleman notes this problem in the case of the British historiography, ascribing it to the secrecy of firms which impose a thirty-year limit on the release of their archives, but also to the lack of contacts between professional historians and businessmen. Given the intellectual

Instituto de Estudios Peruanos and the Lima universities on the one hand
and the staff of leading business schools like ESAN (the Escuela Superior
de Administración de Negocios) on the other never have any contact.

Why did this situation arise? The amount of research is, without doubt,
due to two connected factors: the interest shown in Peru by foreign scholars
after 1968 (the year in which the 'revolutionary' military government of
General Juan Velasco Alvarado took power), and also the intellectual
freedom that was maintained in the country, despite its serious political
problems, for many years.[16] However, the events which followed the
military had other significant consequences, both positive and negative,
for business history.

One unexpected benefit, apart from the growth in foreign academic
interest fuelled by research grants for Latin American studies and the
increase in Peruvian research activity in history and the social sciences in
a relatively non-repressive atmosphere, was the liberation of many of the
archives of the firms expropriated by the government (with the notable
exception of those banks which were nationalised).[17] As a result of the
Agrarian Reform of 1969 historians obtained access to the surviving papers
of many capitalist haciendas, both on the coast and in the sierra, which
were assembled in the Archivo del Fuero Agrario in Lima from late 1971
onwards.[18] Those who were able to establish good relations with senior
managers in the state enterprises which took over the assets of other
nationalised companies were also able to gain access to the archives of
certain key mining and petroleum firms, in particular those of the Cerro
de Pasco Corporation and the International Petroleum Company, which

and ideological hostility which has frequently existed between the two groups in Peru, this
has become an even more serious problem there and the reserve of businessmen towards the
social sciences seems even greater than in Britain.

[16] In contrast to military governments elsewhere in Latin America, Peru did not suffer
enormous repression in the 1970s, although a few intellectuals went into exile. Only in the
late 1980s, with the growth of Sendero Luminoso and an economic crisis which eroded
academic salaries, did certain well-known historians and social scientists emigrate in greater
numbers. For the most part those foreigners researching in Peru during the 1970s and 1980s
found a thriving community of historians and social scientists in both the universities and
independent research institutes.

[17] The reasons for this exception are probably straightforward: the need to protect commercial confidentiality regarding clients' accounts, and also the threat that revelations of
misdoing on the part of the management of an important bank might pose to the financial
stability of the institution and the country as a whole. Understandably, perhaps, banks have
been reluctant to open their archives, although both the retail and the merchant banks in
Britain have recently relaxed a little.

[18] Humberto Rodríguez Pastor, 'El Archivo del Fuero Agrario, Lima, Perú', Latin American
Research Review 14: 3 (1979), pp. 202–06. Unfortunately the civilian government which
followed the end of military rule in 1980 transferred this archive, which was in the care of
an experienced and knowledgeable group of historians, to the Archivo General de la Nación
where, as far as is known, it still remains. Since then it has been almost impossible to use it.

under the military became Centromín and Petroperú respectively.[19] Some historians, under the leadership of Heraclio Bonilla, also began research in the Lima and Arequipa archives of the former railway company, the Peruvian Corporation, which the military transformed into ENAFER (another part of this company's archive was already in University College, London).[20] In this way business history was stimulated by political events.

However, not all the consequences of the military takeover were beneficial. Serious problems for business historians arose as a result of this period of military rule. The expropriation of 'imperialist' firms and the continuing bitter conflict between the government and the old landholding families, the so-called 'oligarchy', led historians to concentrate their interest much more on the agrarian and mining enterprises which these groups had owned rather than on other areas of business in Peru. The liberation of the archives and the economic policy and rhetoric of the government thus led towards the same end. In contrast to the work on the export sectors or the railways nobody seems to have attempted serious research in the archives of other nationalised firms such as the telephone companies, the electricity and water utilities, or the banks, the very areas where the rhetoric of the government was much more conciliatory.[21] The result was that historical research became very heavily focused on certain economic activities, creating an obvious imbalance in the business history literature.

Moreover, the interventionist and apparently anti-capitalist policies of the military government put an end to a series of histories commissioned by the firms which remained in the private sector. Business historians are well aware of the limitations of such 'official' histories, especially when they are undertaken for motives of public relations. Nevertheless, they do at least they provide the historian who wishes to draw a more complete picture of the development of business with a chronology and certain key facts in the history of an enterprise. During the 1960s several such commemorative volumes had been published, often written by historians such as Jorge Basadre or Carlos Camprubí Alcázar with a well-deserved reputation for careful research, but this type of semi-official company 'biography' disappeared more or less completely after 1968.[22] This trend

---

[19] Nobody has done much with the archives of Petroperú, although several historians have received permission to consult them. It appears that they remain in a state of relative disorganisation, and it is difficult to know what may become of them following privatisation.

[20] See Janet Percival, *The Archives of the Peruvian Corporation* (London, 1980).

[21] It is unclear whether there was actually any attempt by any historian to gain access to papers; they simply appear not to have been of very great interest during the twelve years of the military government.

[22] See, for example, the work of Basadre and Ferrero, *Historia de la Cámara de Comercio*; Carlos Camprubí Alcazar, *Un siglo al servicio del ahorro, 1868–1968* (Lima, 1968), on the Caja de Ahorros de Lima (the Lima Savings Bank); Gianfranco Bardella, *Setenta y cinco años de vida económica del Perú, 1889–1964* (Lima, 1964). The one example published after 1968 for which I can find a reference is the rather weak book of Luís Alberto Sánchez, *Historia de una industria peruana: Cervicería Backus y Johnston S. A.* (Lima, 1978), but this deals with a

made the disequilibrium noted above much worse, because while important sectors of the economy, in particular manufacturing industry, commerce, and certain financial institutions, remained in the hands of the private sector, the owners of the companies still felt themselves threatened after the military coup. The private sector's distrust of the military increased sharply after the Industrial Law of 1970 which stipulated the formation of an 'Industrial Community' in each enterprise above a minimum size.[23]

The policies of the military government and the growth of economic problems and social conflicts in Peru after 1973 had further academic consequences. Both in the Peruvian universities and, at times, in the independent research institutes, the overall tenor of departments of modern history and other social sciences became increasingly antagonistic towards capitalist enterprise, thus creating even more barriers between historians and businessmen. In addition the strong influence of Marxist ideologies and dependency theories amongst both Peruvian academics and foreign researchers in the 1970s often made it much more difficult to reconcile preconceived ideas about the behaviour of both foreign and national firms with the empirical data found in the archives.[24]

company in an industrial sector to which the military government attached little importance. Even so, Sánchez states in his introduction that he completed the book at the end of 1971, but that its publication was delayed by difficulties with the Bentín Mújica family, the owners of the firm (pp. 16–17).

[23] The objective of this law was eventually to give workers in a firm a majority share in its ownership as well as participation in its management: see Peter T. Knight, 'New Forms of Economic Organization in Peru: towards workers' self-management', in Abraham F. Lowenthal (ed.), *The Peruvian Experiment: continuity and change within military rule* (Princeton, 1975), pp. 350–401; Anthony Ferner, 'The Industrialists and the Peruvian Development Model', in David Booth and Bernardo Sorj (eds), *Military Reformism and Social Classes: the Peruvian experience, 1968–1980* (London, 1983), pp. 40–71.

[24] These problems are very obvious in the otherwise interesting book produced by Manuel Burga and Wilson Reátegui on one of the leading Arequipa merchant houses involved in the wool trade: *Lanas y capital mercantil en el sur: la casa Ricketts, 1895–1935* (Lima, 1981). Following Immanuel Wallerstein, for example, the authors claim in the introduction that merchant capital was 'incapable of developing the internal market' (p. 16). The problem is not so straightforward, as they themselves show some time later in describing in some detail the agreements and conflicts between Ricketts and Peruvian textile mills, some of which were the property of other foreign merchant houses and attempting to substitute domestically produced goods for imports (pp. 131–148). Later still they affirm 'the existence of a strong link between manufacturing in Lima and the rural market of southern Peru via the merchant houses' (p. 180). Initially, too, they characterise the relations between the *rescatistas de lanas* (itinerant wool traders) and indigenous communities as 'the arena for speculation, abuse, and violent interchange' (p. 72), but they conclude, on the basis of Ricketts' correspondence, that the knowledge of the wool market that the Indians obtained alleviated or prevented full-scale exploitation by the *rescatista*: 'It was not so easy to trick them [the Indians]. Completely to the contrary ...' (pp. 105–106). And again they state: 'The exploitation and poverty of the peasant did not come about fundamentally as a result of the market, but within the haciendas'(p. 108). Nils Jacobsen, in reviewing this book, also criticised its internal contradictions: 'Comercio de lanas, estructura agraria y oligarquía en el sur del Perú', *Allpanchis* 19 (1982), 255–66.

These tendencies within the social sciences and history in Peru had another significant result. Leaving to one side the themes which were becoming central to business historians in the developed world, researchers in Peru began to concentrate on two subjects which, despite their significance, created yet more sources of imbalance within the historiography in the sense that it became more difficult to develop a balanced picture of the overall evolution of Peruvian business. These were, first, the debate over the links between foreign investment, the Peruvian oligarchy, and the state; and second, the emphasis, shared by historians in many other parts of the world in the 1970s and 1980s, on the history of subaltern groups both in the city and the countryside.[25] Both these lines of research can be represented diagramatically:

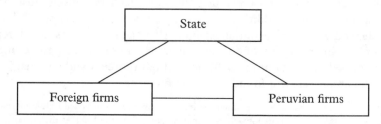

Figure 1 The debate over foreign investment and imperialism

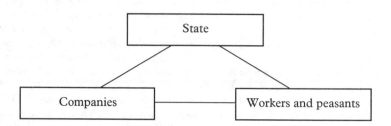

Figure 2 The debate over business and labour

Both these themes are, of course, important aspects of the history of business in Latin America, especially in a country like Peru which maintained a very open economy for many years and where the distribution of income remained one of the most inequitable in Latin America.[26] No business historian can ignore the complexities of inter-firm relationships; state-private sector interactions; or management-labour relations and conflicts. However, it is clear, bearing in mind the themes outlined in the introduction to this paper, that such an emphasis covers only part of the

[25] Until the mid-1990s 'the masses', or in Spanish 'las capas populares', would have been the preferred term.

[26] On income distribution, see Albert Berry, 'International Trade, Government, and Income Distribution in Peru since 1870', *Latin American Research Review* 25:2 (1990), 31–60.

subject matter with which business historians ought to be concerned. Bearing these limitations in mind, how has research in the subject developed and what can be learned from the case studies about the overall evolution of business in Peru?

The shape of business history in Peru: empirical studies

The business of guano exploitation itself attracted a good deal of research in the 1960s. The fundamental work on foreign interests in the trade was undertaken by W. M. Mathew utilising the extensive archives of Antony Gibbs & Sons in London, in part as a direct response to Levin's concept of an enclave economy dominated by foreign interests and the theories of informal imperialism developed in Britain by John Gallagher and Robert Robinson.[27] Heraclio Bonilla's use of the Dreyfus archives in Paris shed light on later negotiations between the Peruvian state and foreign interests over the trade.[28] The research both of Mathew, and later of Paul Gootenberg, highlighted the changing balance of power in the complex negotiations over the early guano contracts in the 1840s.[29] However, the key research in dispelling the myth of an enclave economy was a careful evaluation of the income flows arising from guano undertaken by an economist from the United States, Shane Hunt. This circulated as a working paper for a decade before being published both in Spanish and English in the mid-1980s.[30] By then, it was already clear that the guano period had seen major changes in business activity and organisation on the coast of Peru. Particularly important for outlining changes in coastal agriculture (sugar and cotton) were the works of Pablo Macera, John R. Engelsen, and Bill Bell.[31] On nitrate a detailed study by a Chilean

[27] W. M. Mathew, *The House of Gibbs and the Peruvian Guano Monopoly* (London, 1981); on questions of imperialism see two articles by Mathew: 'The Imperialism of Free Trade: Peru, 1820–1870', *Economic History Review* 21 (1968), 562–79; and 'Antony Gibbs & Sons, the Guano Trade, and the Peruvian Government, 1842–1861', in D. C. M. Platt (ed.), *Business Imperialism, 1840–1930: an inquiry based on British experience in Latin America* (Oxford, 1977), pp. 337–70.

[28] Heraclio Bonilla, *Guano y burguesía en el Perú* (Lima, 1974). There is some important data from the Schroder archives on the Dreyfus Contract of 1869 and the external loans of 1870 and 1872 in Richard Roberts, *Schroders: merchants and bankers* (London, 1992), pp. 86–92.

[29] W. M. Mathew, 'Foreign Contractors and the Peruvian Government at the Outset of the Guano Trade', *Hispanic American Historical Review* 52 (1972), 598–620; Paul Gootenberg, *Between Silver and Guano: commercial policy and the state in postindependence Peru* (Princeton, 1990).

[30] Hunt, 'Crecimiento y guano'; in English it appeared as 'Growth and Guano in Nineteenth-Century Peru', in Roberto Cortés Conde and Shane J. Hunt (eds), *The Latin American Economies: growth and the export sector* (New York, 1985), pp. 255–319.

[31] Pablo Macera, 'Las plantaciones azucareras andinas (1821–1875)', in *Trabajos de Historia* (4 vols, Lima, 1977), IV, 9–307; John R. Engelson, 'Social Aspects of Agricultural Expansion in Coastal Peru, 1821–1878' (PhD thesis, University of California at Los Angeles, 1977); William S. Bell, *An Essay on the Peruvian Cotton Industry, 1825–1920* (Liverpool, 1985).

historian, Oscar Bermúdez, for a long time remained the basic work of reference for changing ownership patterns in the industry, but this was later supplemented by some research using the Gibbs papers and other contemporary sources by foreign historians which reconsidered the Peruvian government's partial nationalisation of the industry in the mid-1870s.[32] An older work by Carlos Camprubí Alcazar also remains the most valuable reference on the banks which were founded in the 1860s on the basis of guano wealth.[33] The formation of a new business elite in Lima in the mid-nineteenth century deserves more study, but important contributions to the subject are Alfonso Quiroz's analysis of the consolidation of the Peruvian government's internal debt and Peter Blanchard's work on one of the leading businessmen of the time, Domingo Elías.[34] Another significant sector of the coastal market economy, many of whose interests suffered from the changes induced by guano, were the Lima artisans, and the political protests they engendered have drawn the attention of a couple of historians to their problems.[35]

It will be evident from this survey of the coast during the guano period that much of the literature takes the form of economic and social history broadly speaking, rather than research specifically directed at uncovering the history of Peruvian business, and this is true also of work on the sierra during the same period. The most important conclusion that business historians can draw from this work is the degree of entrepreneurial response to changing market opportunities in regions which were once considered to have possessed stagnant, traditional economies. Research has concentrated on two areas in particular, the south, where the early work of Alberto Flores Galindo was a precursor of the more substantial and detailed studies undertaken by Nils Jacobsen, and the centre, where the research of Peruvian historians has uncovered important information about the responses of mining entrepreneurs and landowners to business opportunities.[36] However,

[32] Oscar Bermúdez Miral, *Historia del salitre desde sus orígenes hasta la Guerra del Pacífico* (Santiago, 1963); Robert G. Greenhill and Rory M. Miller, 'The Peruvian Government and the Nitrate Trade, 1873–1879', *Journal of Latin American Studies* 5 (1973), 107–31; Thomas F. O'Brien, *The Nitrate Industry and Chile's Crucial Transition, 1870–1891* (New York, 1982).

[33] Carlos Camprubí Alcazar, *Historia de los bancos del Perú, 1860–1879* (Lima, 1957).

[34] Alfonso Quiroz, *La deuda defraudada: consolidación de 1850 y dominio económico en el Perú* (Lima, 1987); Peter Blanchard, 'The "Transitional Man" in Nineteenth-Century Latin America: the case of Domingo Elías of Peru', *Bulletin of Latin American Research* 15 (1996), 157–76.

[35] Margarita Giesecke, *Masas urbanas y rebelión en la historia: golpe de estado, Lima, 1872* (Lima, 1978), Paul Gootenberg, 'The Social Origins of Free Trade and Protectionism in Nineteenth-Century Lima', *Journal of Latin American Studies* 14 (1982), 329–58. On the Cuzco artisans in the same period, see Thomas Krüggeler, 'El doble desafío: los artesanos del Cuzco ante la crisis regional y la constitución del régimen repúblicano, 1824–1869', *Allpanchis* 23: 38 (1991), 13–66.

[36] Alberto Flores Galindo, *Arequipa y el sur andino, siglos XVIII–XX* (Lima, 1977); Nils Jacobsen, 'Cycles and Booms in Latin American Export Agriculture: the example of southern Peru's livestock economy, 1855–1920', *Review* 7 (1984), 443–507; and *Mirages of Transition:*

substantial gaps remain. There is, for example, no substantial work using available notarial registers and business archives of the merchants of Arequipa, Peru's second city, and the trading networks they created, and economic and business change in much of the rest of the sierra remains untouched by historians. The work of Lewis Taylor on the Cajamarca region is one of the few exceptions to this generalisation.[37]

Three themes have dominated research on business in Peru after the Pacific War: the role played by foreign companies; the nature of the local business elite; and social change in the sierra. The literature on the foreign merchant houses, which played an important role in financing and commercialising agricultural exports like sugar and cotton, was, for a long time, rather scanty as a result of the disappearance of the archives of the most important British firms.[38] However, in the late 1970s the papers of W. R. Grace & Co. were deposited in Columbia University in New York and opened to historians. This made possible some early work by Alfonso Quiroz on the Graces' activities during the War of the Pacific, and then a substantial company history by Lawrence Clayton, who also discovered and prepared for publication a forgotten biography of the firm by the award-winning journalist, Marquis James.[39] These added some new dimensions to earlier studies of the Grace Contract, one of the key negotiations between the Peruvian government and foreign interests, which had resulted in the transfer of the state railways and other assets to the Peruvian Corporation in 1890. This firm had itself left sizeable archives in London and Lima, but their content proved rather disappointing, and the only studies which resulted were rather insubstantial ones by Heraclio Bonilla and Rory Miller which did not take the company's history into the crucial years of the 1930s and 1940s.[40] The early business history of the oil industry

the Peruvian Altiplano, 1780–1930 (Berkeley, 1993); Carlos Contreras, Mineros y campesinos en los Andes (Lima, 1986); Nelson Manrique, Mercado interno y región: la sierra central, 1820–1930 (Lima, 1987); José Deustua, 'Mining Markets, Peasants, and Power in Nineteenth-Century Peru', Latin American Research Review 29: 1 (1994), 29–54, and 'Routes, Roads and the Silver Trade in Cerro de Pasco, 1820–1860: the internal market in nineteenth-century Peru', Hispanic American Historical Review 74 (1994), 1–32.

[37] See, for example, Lewis Taylor, 'Earning a Living in Hualgayoc, 1870–1900', in Rory Miller (ed.), Region and Class in Modern Peruvian History (Liverpool, 1987), pp. 103–24.

[38] Antony Gibbs & Sons, whose archive has been fundamental to reinterpretations of the guano period, withdrew from Peru during the War of the Pacific, and did not return until the 1920s.

[39] Alfonso W. Quiroz, 'Las actividades comerciales y financieras de la Casa Grace y la Guerra del Pacífico', Historia 7: 2 (1983), 214–54; Lawrence A. Clayton, Grace: W. R. Grace & Co., the formative years, 1850–1930 (Ottawa, IL., 1985); Marquis James, Merchant Adventurer: the story of W. R. Grace (Wilmington, 1993).

[40] Heraclio Bonilla, 'El impacto de los ferrocarriles: algunas proposiciones', Historia y Cultura 1 (1972), 93–120; Rory Miller, 'Railways and Economic Development in Central Peru, 1890–1930', in Rory Miller et al. (eds), Social and Economic Change in Modern Peru (Liverpool, 1976), pp. 27–52, and 'The Grace Contract, the Peruvian Corporation and Peruvian History', Ibero-Amerikanisches Archiv 9: 3/4 (1983), 319–48.

is also not particularly well-known, partly because the first company, the London and Pacific Petroleum Company, was never floated on the Stock Exchange in London, but there is some work with a business history focus both on this company after its transfer to Standard Oil of New Jersey and on the second company in the industry, Lobitos Oilfields Limited.[41] Just as the business history of Peruvian oil remains to be written, so does that of Peruvian mining, for there is no substantial study of the Cerro de Pasco Corporation, the most important enterprise in the industry in the first half of the twentieth century, let alone the many smaller firms. Instead, one has to make do with Elizabeth Dore's overall history of mining, which makes very sparse use of primary sources, and a series of studies which investigate labour recruitment and the social impact of the industry in the central sierra.[42] Of these, the work of Florencia Mallon and Fiona Wilson and the books by Bryan Roberts and Norman Long include much on the response of mestizo entrepreneurs to the commercial opportunities presented by the growth of the industry and the limitations of the businesses they established. On the overall impact of foreign business in Peru in this period there is an unpublished paper by Rory Miller on the British, and a chapter in a book on US business in Latin America by Thomas O'Brien.[43] The latter, inexplicably, says little about Standard Oil, but provides some important material both on Grace and on Cerro de Pasco.

The growing crisis of Peru in the 1960s and the military's attacks on the oligarchy after the 1968 coup stimulated a flood of literature on the business elite which was formed after the Pacific War, much of it, inevitably, in the intellectual climate of the times, concerned with debating the extent to which a 'national bourgeoisie' had been created in Peru. There is relatively little of this that is really of lasting interest to the business historian, but the work by Dennis Gilbert on three leading oligarchic

[41] Jonathan C. Brown, 'Jersey Standard and the Politics of Latin American Oil Production, 1911–1930', in John D. Wirth (ed.), *Latin American Oil Companies and the Politics of Energy* (Lincoln, 1985), pp. 1–50; Rory Miller, 'Small Business in the Peruvian Oil Industry: Lobitos Oilfields Limited before 1934', *Business History Review* 56 (1982), pp. 400–23.

[42] Elizabeth Dore, *The Peruvian Mining Industry: growth, stagnation and crisis* (Boulder, CO., 1988); Alberto Flores Galindo, *Los mineros del Cerro de Pasco, 1900–1930* (Lima, 1974); Dirk Kruijt and Menno Vellinga, *Estado, clase obrera y empresa transnacional: el caso de la minería peruana, 1900–1980* (Mexico, 1983); Julian Laite, *Industrial Development and Migrant Labour* (Manchester, 1981); Norman Long and Bryan Roberts (eds), *Peasant Cooperation and Capitalist Expansion in Central Peru* (Austin, 1978); Norman Long and Bryan Roberts, *Miners, Peasants, and Entrepreneurs: Regional Development in the Central Highlands of Peru* (Cambridge, 1984); Florencia E. Mallon, *The Defense of Community in Peru's Central Highlands: peasant struggle and capitalist transition, 1860–1940* (Princeton, 1983); Fiona Wilson, 'The Conflict between Indigenous and Immigrant Commercial Systems in the Peruvian Central Sierra, 1900–1940', in Miller (ed.), *Region and Class*, pp. 125–61.

[43] Rory Miller, 'Enterprise and Inertia: British business in Peru, 1850–1950' (mimeo, 1988); Thomas F. O'Brien, *The Revolutionary Mission: American enterprise in Latin America, 1900–1945* (Cambridge, 1996), pp. 109–59.

families and the synthesis by Manuel Burga and Alberto Flores Galindo, both completed at the end of the 1970s, stand out.[44] Also of interest to the business historian is a debate over the extent to which the coastal elite controlled the state during the so-called 'Aristocratic Republic' between Rory Miller and Michael Gonzales, both of whom used the papers of the Aspíllaga family, owners of the Cayaltí sugar hacienda.[45] Of even more relevance, though, is Alfonso Quiroz's reconstruction of the major family business groups of early twentieth-century Lima, and some work on leading interest group associations which can be found in Pablo Macera's study of the Compañía Administradora del Guano, using the papers of the Sociedad Nacional Agraria, and the commissioned history of the Cámara de Comercio de Lima.[46]

By the early twentieth century the leading businessmen in Peru combined commercial and financial activities in Lima with agriculture in the coastal valleys, the Prado family, who preferred manufacturing industry to agriculture, being a rare exception.[47] This has meant that there is much information on their business activities in the economic and social history literature on particular sectors, much of which used the hacienda archives which became available in the Archivo del Fuero Agrario. Sugar is best covered, with some early work by Peter Klaren on the businesses active in the Chicama Valley, and some later, much more detailed, research, using the hacienda archives which had become available by the mid-1970s, by Bill Albert and Michael Gonzales.[48] Despite its importance to the Peruvian economy as a whole and to many coastal valleys, cotton cultivation has been much less

[44] Dennis L. Gilbert, La oligarquía peruana: historia de tres familias (Lima, 1982); Manuel Burga and Alberto Flores Galindo, Apogeo y crisis de la República Aristocrática (Lima, 1979).

[45] Rory Miller, 'The Coastal Elite and Peruvian Politics, 1895–1919', Journal of Latin American Studies 14 (1982), 97–120; Michael J. Gonzales, 'Planters and Politics in Peru, 1895–1919', Journal of Latin American Studies 23 (1991), 515–42.

[46] Alfonso W. Quiroz, 'Financial Leadership and the Formation of Peruvian Elite Groups, 1884–1930', Journal of Latin American Studies 20 (1988), 49–81; Pablo Macera, 'El guano y la agricultura peruana de exportación, 1909–1945', in Trabajos de Historia, IV, 309–499; Basadre y Ferrero, Historia de la Cámara de Comercio.

[47] The Prados are one of the three clans studied in Gilbert's book on the oligarchy; see also Felipe Portocarrero, 'El imperio Prado, 1890–1970: ¿oligarquía o burguesía nacional?, Apuntes 19 (1986), 121–46. The title of this article illustrates some of the continuing preoccupations of Peruvian historians studying the business elite.

[48] Peter Klarén, Modernization, Dislocation, and Aprismo: origins of the Peruvian Aprista Party, 1870–1932 (Austin, 1973), and 'The Social and Economic Consequences of Modernization in the Peruvian Sugar Industry, 1870–1932', in Kenneth Duncan and Ian Rutledge (eds), Land and Labour in Latin America: essays on the development of agrarian capitalism in the nineteenth and twentieth centuries (Cambridge, 1977), pp. 229–52; William Albert, An Essay on the Peruvian Sugar Industry, 1880–1920, and the Letters of Ronald Gordon, Administrator of the British Sugar Company in Cañete, 1914–1920 (Norwich, 1976); Bill Albert, 'The Peruvian Sugar Industry, 1918–1939: response to world crisis', in Bill Albert and Adrian Graves (eds), The World Sugar Economy in War and Depression, 1914–40 (London, 1988), pp. 71–84 Michael J. Gonzales, Plantation Agriculture and Social Control in Northern Peru, 1875–1933 (Austin, 1985).

studied, especially after 1920, the period when it came to dominate the agriculture of many of the coastal valleys. There are, however, brief studies of the organisation of land and labour in the early stages of the industry by Gonzales, again using the Aspíllaga papers, and by Vincent Peloso.[49] Apart from Manuel Burga's research on the Jequetepeque valley in the north, there is nothing on other important agricultural pursuits in the coastal valleys such as rice and wine and alcohol production or the cultivation of foodstuffs for local markets.[50] For a long time the growth of financial services in Lima had also been neglected as a consequence of historians' preference for agrarian and social history. However, at the end of the 1980s work by Alfonso Quiroz on the archive of the defunct Banco del Perú y Londres provided a valuable complement to an earlier study by Carlos Camprubí of José Payán, the dominant financier in Lima at the turn of the century and the founder of this bank, and this should pave the way for further research on other financial institutions.[51] Manufacturing had also been neglected except for some passages using contemporary printed sources in Thorp and Bertram, but Francisco Durand's work on the immigrant role in industrial growth may help to encourage further studies.[52]

As far as business in the regions is concerned, historians have concentrated on those which were also the focus for the research on the mid-nineteenth century: the south, where wool remained the leading export, and the central sierra, especially the Mantaro valley which was deeply affected both by the growth of the mining economy and by labour migration to the coastal plantations and the growing urban economy of Lima. The principal items of literature on these two areas have already been mentioned, but research by two anthropologists, Gordon Appleby and Ben Orlove, and a case study of an Arequipa wool merchant by Manuel Burga and Wilson Reátegui are also important in understanding the business structures of southern Peru in this period.[53] This concentration on two

[49] Michael J. Gonzales, 'The Rise of Cotton Tenant Farming in Peru, 1890–1920: the Condor valley', *Agricultural History* 65 (1991), 51–71; Vincent C. Peloso, 'Cotton Planters, the State, and Rural Labor Policy: ideological origins of the Peruvian República Aristocrática, 1895–1908', *The Americas* 40: 2 (1983), 209–28.

[50] Manuel Burga, *De la encomienda a la hacienda capitalista: el valle del Jequetepeque del siglo XVI al XX* (Lima, 1976).

[51] Alfonso W. Quiroz, *Banqueros en conflicto: estructura financiera y economía peruana, 1884–1930* (Lima, 1989), and *Domestic and Foreign Finance in Modern Peru, 1850–1950: financing visions of development* (London, 1993); Carlos Camprubí Alcazar, *José Payán y de Reyna, 1844–1919: su trayectoria peruana* (Lima, 1967).

[52] Thorp and Bertram, *Peru, 1890–1977*, pp. 118–31, 190–95; Francisco Durand, 'Los primeros industriales y la inmigración extranjera en el Perú', *Estudios Migratorios Latinoamericanos* 3:9 (1988), 199–216.

[53] Gordon Appleby, 'Export Monoculture and Regional Social Structure in Puno, Peru', in Carol A. Smith (ed.), *Regional Analysis* (2 vols, New York, 1976), II, 291–308, and 'Exportation and its Aftermath: the spatioeconomic evolution of the regional marketing system in highland Puno, Peru' (PhD thesis, Stanford, 1978); Benjamin S. Orlove, *Alpacas, Sheep,*

regions means that large areas of business outside Lima have remained unstudied, including the urban economies of provincial cities, much of the rural economy of the coast and the sierra (although Lewis Taylor's work on Cajamarca again provides a partial exception), and the development of mining after the middle of the twentieth century.[54]

The shape of business history in Peru: interpretations

This survey of the trends in research since the 1960s shows up many problems and imbalances in Peruvian business history. However, taken together, they also suggest some important advances in interpretation, laying the foundations for a more sophisticated approach to the country's business history in the future. To be critical of imbalances in the historio-graphy should not be taken as implying an incapacity to recognise and appreciate its advances. Even though the majority of research may have been concentrated on the external sector, there have been many significant advances in interpretation of business structures and strategies. Before discussing these, however, a brief summary of the balance of research on the state – foreign firms – Peruvian firms triangle is in order.

As the more simplistic and conspiratorial interpretations of imperialism which were prevalent in the early 1970s have been undermined by empirical research, the tendency has been to emphasise the divergence of interests and conflicts among foreign companies.[55] Although many individual firms possessed quite strong leverage at particular times over the Peruvian gov-ernment, they acted as a bloc only on infrequent occasions, the main exceptions being when labour mobilisation was intense.[56] This ought to

and Men: the wool export economy and regional society in southern Peru (New York, 1977); Burga and Reátegui, *Lanas y capital mercantil.*

[54] Lewis Taylor, 'Main Trends in Agrarian Capitalist Development in Cajamarca, Peru, 1880–1976' (PhD thesis, University of Liverpool, 1979). There is some historical material on mining, specifically on the strategies of the Cerro de Pasco Corporation and the Southern Peru Copper Corporation in confronting nationalist attacks, in David G. Becker, *The New Bourgeoisie and the Limits of Dependency: mining, class, and power in "Revolutionary" Peru* (Princeton, 1983).

[55] A good example of the way in which the dominant intellectual trends of the dependency era led to particular interpretations of foreign and national business is Ernesto Yepes del Castillo, *Perú, 1820–1920: un siglo del desarrollo capitalista* (Lima, 1972).

[56] Examples discovered in my own research on British firms are the divergent commercial strategies of Lobitos Oilfields and the International Petroleum Company, the conflicts between the Peruvian Corporation and its customers such as Cerro de Pasco, the strong rivalry between Grace and Duncan Fox, the owners of the most important textile factories in the country, and the disputes among the Arequipa merchant houses: see Miller, 'Foreign Firms and the Peruvian Government, 1885–1930', in Platt (ed.), *Business Imperialism*, pp. 371–94, and 'British Business'. Hunt and Becker also point out how the response of foreign companies to the 'revolutionary' military government differed: Shane Hunt, 'Direct Foreign Investment in Peru: new rules for an old game', in Lowenthal (ed.), *The Peruvian Experiment*, pp. 302–48, and Becker, *The New Bourgeoisie and the Limits of Dependency*, chapters 5 and 6.

have given the Peruvian state much more leeway to negotiate with individual firms, and sometimes, it is clear, governments took advantage of these conflicting interests, for example in levying heavier taxation during the 1920s on the Compañía Petrolera Lobitos rather than allowing it to share in the lenient treatment of the Standard Oil subsidiary.[57] In the case of the Peruvian guano trade during the nineteenth century, Mathew concludes that in the end the Peruvian government had the power to replace Gibbs as consignee in 1861.[58] In 1869, similarly, the Balta administration was able to sign a contract with the Paris house of Dreyfus Frères for the sale of two million tons of guano, thus replacing the Peruvian consignees to whom its predecessors had awarded the contract eight years earlier. In the majority of cases, however, the Peruvian government appears to have acted weakly when confronted by a powerful foreign firm.

There were three reasons for this. First, on many occasions the state did not possess the bureaucratic or technical expertise to intervene more effectively, for example during the initial stages of the modern copper mining or petroleum industries after the War of the Pacific. Second,. it was always difficult to balance the desire of all governments to increase their tax revenues from established firms on the one hand and their need to attract new foreign investment on the other.[59] Until they learned more about the negotiating possibilities, many governments believed, like historians in the 1970s, that offending one powerful foreign firm would deter new investment by others. Third, on several occasions governments preferred to extract immediate advantages, for example the advance payment of taxes or aid in placing a foreign loan, rather than following a policy that would reap long-term benefits for the country. This tendency can be seen, for example, in the history of the Cerro de Pasco Corporation or IPC in the 1920s and 1930s.[60] It must be added that governments before that of General Velasco did almost nothing to control transfers of ownership among foreign companies, above all in the case of the sale of the petroleum deposits of La Brea y Pariñas by the London and Pacific Petroleum Company to Standard Oil of New Jersey in 1913. Nor did it do anything to halt foreign purchases of assets owned by Peruvian capitalists who, like

[57] Miller, 'Small Business', 414–23.

[58] Mathew, 'Antony Gibbs and Sons', pp. 348–49.

[59] This dilemma forms the basis for the excellent book of Theodore H. Moran on the Chilean *gran minería: Multinational Corporations and the Politics of Dependence: copper in Chile* (Princeton, 1974).

[60] A variation was the notorious agreement of 1922, popularly known as the *Laudo*, between the Leguía government and the International Petroleum Company, an affiliate of Standard Oil of New Jersey. This incorporated a one-off payment of one million dollars to the government in cash, together with Standard Oil's promise of aid in placing a loan with New York bankers, in exchange for the confirmation of its rights to disputed concessions and wide-ranging exemptions for the new taxes the government was levying on the exploitation and export of oil. On this see Thorp and Bertram, *Peru, 1890–1977*, p. 108–11 and Brown, 'Jersey Standard', pp. 18–20 who offer different views of the bargain.

their governments, frequently preferred to give away their future profits in exchange for an immediate and unexpected windfall.

The reluctance of the state to intervene in private business or take any serious steps to regulate the economy is an important feature of the environment within which the private sector operated in Peru. This is not to say that there was not government support for national businessmen. Empirical research in the 1970s and 1980s showed how agents of the state aided landowners in labour recruitment and control, and to a lesser extent how publicly funded construction projects were used to benefit private businessmen.[61] Early in the twentieth century subsidies and monopolies were used in order to aid national and foreign enterprise, while the state later took a much more active role with the creation of the Corporación del Santa to develop the Chimbote and the Ancash regions, and public sector enterprise in basic industries like steel, shipbuilding, and oil.[62] However, the accepted view was that the state should confine its role to supporting rather than leading. Before the 1960s the extent of state intervention was limited in comparison with other Latin American countries where the export sectors were foreign-owned, or where the state operated major public services like the railways. Confidence in state intervention in Peru had been undermined both by the ideological developments and the practical experiences of the guano period; at the end of the nineteenth century, too, an incipient movement for protection and state-led industrialisation had petered out. The rapid recovery of the Peruvian economy after the depression, the continued success of the export sectors, and a greater degree of balance of payments stability than most other Latin American countries enjoyed all combined to restrict the scope of state intervention in financial markets and foreign trade and to limit the growth of public sector enterprises, at least until the 1960s. This, in turn, meant that bureaucratic capacity remained at a low level, causing problems both in terms of developing the specialist expertise and negotiating skills required to deal with foreign companies and in terms of the strains which developed when the state's role in business rapidly expanded after 1968.[63] Such interpretations, which stress the openness of the economy and the limitations of the public sector, raise questions about the strategies followed both by businessmen and governments in Peru.

Doubts about the capacity of Peruvian business have been reinforced by studies of the internal economy, although there are few historians who

---

[61] In the early twentieth century foreign ownership of the railways restricted the extent to which the government could aid landowners by subsidising transport costs, in contrast to Chile and Brazil where there was much greater control. However, by the 1950s the state's regulation of freight tariffs under pressure from local business interests had become an important point of conflict between the government and the Peruvian Corporation.

[62] Thorp and Bertram, *Peru, 1890–1977*, pp. 261–69.

[63] An important comparative contribution to this discussion is Rosemary Thorp, *Economic Management and Economic Development in Peru and Colombia* (London, 1991).

would now deny the entrepreneurial qualities of the Peruvian elite. Although the role played by first and second generation immigrants gave rise to a debate in the 1970s and 1980s about the 'national' character of this elite, the point which appears most important for the growth of business is the progressive Peruvianisation of families like the Gildemeister, Wiese, Romeros, Gibsons, and Ricketts, and their concentration on the business possibilities which Peru offered them.[64] Immigrant families, it now seems, have been an important source of new enterprise and commerce a significant means of gathering both experience and capital in many Latin American economies. The problems lay rather in the forms of organisation the immigrants and the Peruvians from longer established families adopted, and the short-term nature of their business strategies.

Like the older entrepreneurs, the immigrants formed or became part of business groups, the central feature of Peruvian business structure since the second half of the nineteenth century. Such groups were normally based on one or two families linked together by close alliances, frequently through marriage.[65] Generally such groups developed interests in a number of economic activities (agriculture, industry, commerce), although in the majority of cases it is possible to identify one particular sector as the most important source of the family's wealth and prestige. During the twentieth century the distinctive feature of the most powerful and dynamic groups was normally the influence or direct control which they exercised over banks or other financial institutions. This enabled them to take advantage of the savings both of private individuals and other smaller companies, an important factor in a country where formal capital markets remained extremely underdeveloped. Control of a bank also permitted the business group to maintain a relatively high degree of liquidity within its activities as a whole, since it minimised its own capital commitments and facilitated the transfer of resources from one sector to another if economic conditions changed.

Strategy and long-term planning in business groups seem frequently to have been directed much more towards the preservation of liquidity than

[64] Of course there were other merchants such as the Graces (originally Irish but later North American) and Duncan Fox (British), which never became integrated into the Peruvian elite. Germans, Italians, and Spanish migrants tended to integrate more easily, while the Asians had little scope or desire to return to the Far East. The importance of immigrants in the formation of the Peruvian business elite in the nineteenth and twentieth centuries is hardly unusual. The important criteria in the distinctions between 'national', 'immigrant', and 'expatriate' businessmen are not their origins but the use they make of their profits and the extent to which they integrate socially and economically into the host economy.

[65] On this see especially Quiroz, 'Financial Leadership', Gilbert, La oligarquía peruana, and Felipe Portocarrero, 'Religión, familia, riqueza y muerte en la élite económica peruana, 1900–1930' (mimeo, 1990). An obvious example of a family group in mid nineteenth-century Peru is the Pardo-Barrera group: on Manuel Pardo and his ideas about development see Carmen McEvoy, Un proyecto nacional en el siglo XIX: Manuel Pardo y su visión del Perú (Lima, 1994).

to developing long-term investments. An alternative, if investments in fixed assets were unavoidable, was to secure a position of monopoly or oligopoly within the sector concerned. This was another significant feature of those groups which were oriented more towards the internal market, though not, of course, those who concentrated on export production and had to compete at a global level, and it is easy to understand the reasons behind such a strategy if one takes into account the limited size of the Peruvian market and the danger that overcapacity would lead to ruinous competition and losses. Behind a wall of protective tariffs it was thus possible to be sure of supernormal profits and to minimise risk.[66] This point can be supported by many examples, especially in basic manufacturing sectors such as food processing, beverages, and textiles: Nicolini and Field in the biscuit trade; Revoredo, Peral and Milne in flour milling; D'Onofrio in ice cream; Pilsen-Callao and Backus & Johnston, the two large companies which dominated brewing; or Grace and Duncan Fox in the cotton textile industry.

Greater understanding of these strategies and business structures has depended particularly on the research undertaken on the important families of Lima and the northern coast, above all sugar exporters like the Aspíllaga and other groups with industrial/financial interests such as the Prado family. The extent to which knowledge has advanced is impressive, but there remains a risk of imbalance in two senses. First, there is much less evidence on the development of influential groups in other sectors of the Lima economy, for example in urbanisation and construction. Second, it is important that as a consequence of the increasing economic dominance of Lima in the second half of the twentieth century historians should not overlook the development of middle-ranking firms and regional economies before then.

The extent to which relatively small-scale firms transformed key sectors of the Peruvian economy ought to be recognised. Good examples lie in inland passenger transport and cargo haulage at regional level, where new enterprises were frequently established by individuals using the capital that they had accumulated by working in the modern sector of the economy (mining, for example) or in commerce. Such stories are commonplace in the research of historians like Florencia Mallon, Fiona Wilson, Norman Long, Bryan Roberts, and their collaborators in the central *sierra*. During the first half of the twentieth century there was also quite a strong development of modern manufacturing industry in several of the largest provincial cities, as well as many local private investments in public services like electricity generation which were of little interest to foreign investors given the limited size and potential for expansion of cities other than Lima.

[66] It is worth noting that Stephen Haber finds the same tendency in his work on the development of manufacturing industry in Mexico, a market of much greater size than the Peruvian one: Stephen H. Haber, *Industry and Underdevelopment: the industrialization of Mexico, 1890–1940* (Stanford, 1989).

This form of expansion in provincial cities and regional economies was most common in the middle of the twentieth century, as Bryan Roberts shows in his study of industry in Huancayo between 1930 and 1970.[67] The northern coast, where the large sugar plantations in La Libertad and Lambayeque tended to internalise transactions and marginalise local commerce, may have been an exception, however. After the mid-twentieth century the potential for the expansion of business at this level seems to have become more limited.[68]

The evidence of the central sierra, where research has been greatest, suggests also that historians should distinguish between on the one hand the small businesses of an almost informal type that were established by local residents, and on the other the medium-sized firms which were often founded by immigrant traders in a particular region. The small businessmen, without much access to credit and modern technology, found it very difficult to expand their enterprise beyond the constraints imposed by the skills possessed by their immediate family and the locality where they lived. However, medium-sized entrepreneurs also seem to have been unwilling to expand too much, especially if it would mean the employment of a sizeable permanent labour force. Labour legislation and social security costs, which applied to all firms above a minimum size, and later the Industrial Community laws, which threatened the eventual loss of control over a business, deterred too rapid an expansion.[69] Frequently entrepreneurs preferred to operate a labour system dependent on subcontracting in order to reduce costs and facilitate the transfer of resources out of a business. This also avoided having to confront the industrial relations problems which might have arisen from the presence of trade unions. In the case of Huancayo, according to Roberts, immigrant entrepreneurs in the textile industry did not become permanently established in the region, and like the Lima oligarchy they preferred to maintain a high degree of personal liquidity rather than over-committing their resources to the business. They therefore financed their businesses by contracting rollover credits with the Lima banks, but this exacerbated their financial problems whenever a crisis arrived and interest rates rose.

It also seems likely, though the scarcity of research on firms in the provinces makes it difficult to draw more certain conclusions, that the

---

[67] Bryan R. Roberts, 'The Social History of a Provincial Town: Huancayo, 1890–1972', in Miller et al. (eds), Social and Economic Change, pp. 136–97.

[68] Much more research needs to be done on the evolution of business in the major towns in the south, especially Cuzco and Arequipa. There is some useful information on the latter in Baltazar Caravedo Molinari, Desarrollo desigual y lucha política en el Perú, 1948–1956: la burguesía arequipeña y el estado peruano (Lima, 1978).

[69] Corruption of government inspectors was one way of avoiding strict compliance with the labour legislation, but of course this still raised the employers' costs. For a brief comment on this, see David Chaplin, 'Blue Collar Workers in Peru', in David Chaplin (ed.), Peruvian Nationalism: a corporatist revolution (New Brunswick, NJ., 1976), pp. 214–15.

overall trend during the twentieth century was the subjugation of businessmen in the provinces to the interests of the banks and other large companies
in Lima. One scenario was for important regional groups to become
incorporated into those based in Lima. Another was that the most dynamic
entrepreneurs outside the capital found the constraints of provincial business curtailing their ambitions and thus relocated in Lima, one obvious
case being that of the Romeros who had originated as traders in Piura but
became one of the most important business groups at national level under
the military regime.[70] Peru never possessed a dynamic regional elite on the
scale found in Medellín, Monterrey, and São Paulo, not even in Arequipa,
where local businessmen maintained a degree of independence from Lima
for much of the period after independence.

This review of the research makes it clear that the triangles of interaction
which were described earlier in this paper as dominating research in the
1970s and early 1980s, when the influence of imperialism and dependency
was at its height, do not suffice for the analysis of business history in Peru.
Instead, it is necessary to visualise a much more complex and changing
image of the links among individual firms and between them and the
government in Lima, as demonstrated in Figure 3.

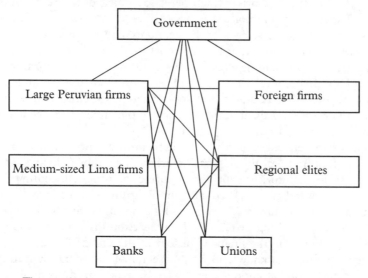

Figure 3 The complex inter-relationships between the state, the private sector, and labour

Even this, however, would not suffice as a basis for the development of
a more integrated business history of Peru, because the emphasis remains
on the interaction among different types of companies, their workers, and
governments. Missing from this picture is the analysis of other important
themes in business history such as the development of internal company

[70] Vásquez, 'The Role, Origins, and Strategies'.

structures, financial strategies, the diffusion of new techniques and marketing methods, and the growth of a cadre of professional managers and
engineers trained both in universities overseas and in the private universities
and postgraduate institutes in Lima.

The future

The research undertaken since the late 1960s by economic and social
historians, even if not specifically on business history, has enabled specialists
to identify some important features in the development of business in Peru.
However, the subject suffered for a long time from *a priori* conceptions
about the shortcomings of the private sector in Peru and the potential
success of state intervention, planning, and enterprise associated with the
ECLA school and dependency theories. It is without doubt that capitalism
in Peru has possessed its own peculiarities and shortcomings, not least the
eventual failure of the open economy, which had become evident by the
1960s, as well as the profound inequalities which persisted, and indeed
worsened, in the country. However, the preoccupation with a narrow
agenda of state – company – worker relations and the bias against private,
especially foreign, enterprise which pervaded much of the research of the
1970s obscured other important issues. Above all, it created an imbalance
in research with some sectors of the economy and regions of the country
being well covered and other being almost totally neglected. As a result a
need exists to formulate new research projects in order to confirm or reject
some of the hypotheses that emerged as a result of the research of the
1970s and 1980s There are several areas where research is required which
seem important in any attempt to correct the imbalances which mark
business history in Peru.

First, more detailed research is required on those firms whose interests
were concentrated in the internal market. The most obvious are the
manufacturing enterprises which grew during the twentieth century. There
is no history of industry in Peru comparable to those which exist for other
Latin American countries. There is nothing on important firms in sectors
such as food processing or textiles. It is clear too that, despite the efforts
of Alfonso Quiroz on the financial history of the first half of the twentieth
century, much less is known about this sector of the economy during the
second half. More attention might also be paid to companies of long
standing in other economic sectors, for example the long-distance bus
companies or the Cía de Aviación Faucett, which has dominated internal
air transport since the 1920s. Medium-scale mining enterprise also requires
much more investigation, for the published research, even for the period
before 1920, concentrates on the foreign takeover of the larger enterprises.[71]
Underlying all these comments, of course, is a wish for historians to liberate

---

[71] This sector is commonly referred to in Spanish as *mediana minería*.

themselves from the emphasis on the large exporting firms and foreign companies that characterises Peruvian business history.

Second, it will be necessary to recognise that multi-faceted business groups have been the dominant feature of business structure in Peru since at least the mid-nineteenth century. Originally these were often based on an alliance between two or three families, or else the descendants of a single businessman active at the beginning of the century. Several examples from the Lima elite have already been mentioned. But alongside these representatives of the capital the smaller provincial groups based in important cities like Arequipa, Cuzco, Huancayo, Trujillo, and Chiclayo should not be neglected, especially as ultimately they seem to have lacked the dynamism of comparable groups elsewhere in Latin America.[72] However, for most of the last century and the first half of the twentieth these groups possessed a relatively high degree of autonomy from the powerful Lima groups, acting as associates or representatives of foreign firms or agents of the Lima factories, and initiating their own ventures in their regions, especially in activities like public utilities and construction which were of little interest either to the *limeños* or foreign entrepreneurs. It seems probable that during the second half of the twentieth century the penetration of provincial markets by the manufacturing companies and banks owned by the Lima elite and by multinational firms made it opportune for these provincial groups to engage in closer alliances with those in the capital. The result was that some transferred the headquarters of their business to Lima, while others almost totally lost their autonomy and their influence. However, because of the lack of detailed research there is almost no information either to support or reject these hypotheses.[73]

Third, knowledge about employers' associations and other groups which have represented sectoral interests is also relatively patchy. Despite the publication of studies during the 1960s on some of the best-known such as the Sociedad Nacional Agraria (SNA) or the Lima Chamber of Commerce, there are no recent histories.[74] After its abolition by the Velasco government the papers of the SNA were deposited in Archivo del Fuero Agrario, and the Chamber of Commerce also possessed quite a voluminous archive and library. However, nobody has really utilised these resources. Under the Velasco regime new interest groups like ADEX grew up, and it is important to investigate their evolution and influence. A related point

[72] Some of the broader theoretical work which has arisen from business history elsewhere on the shortcomings of family enterprise might be useful here.

[73] One example is the association of Arequipa merchant houses after the late 1920s with foreign partners possessing greater access to networks of information and finance, Gibsons with Balfour Williamson, Ricketts with Antony Gibbs & Sons. In contrast to the British merchant houses in Lima, these firms of British origin in Arequipa ought to be considered immigrants rather than expatriates, and thus part of the local business elite.

[74] Macera, 'La Compañía Administradora del Guano'; Basadre and Ferrero, *Historia de la Cámara de Comercio*.

is the need to study the development of professional associations, for example those incorporating the various branches of engineering, in order to ascertain their organisation, influence, and contribution to the development of business in Peru.

Fourth, as the political mood in Peru has turned against state enterprise and the Fujimori regime has returned key sectors of the economy to private, often foreign, ownership during the 1990s, it has become urgent that historians should evaluate objectively the experience of public-sector enterprise in Peru. Just as the historians of the 1970s found it easy to dismiss the Peruvian-owned private sector and foreign business as exploitative, but without much regard to the nuances of their behaviour which the empirical evidence revealed, so it would be easy for historians in the 1990s to dismiss the experience of state firms as one of inefficiency simply because that is the assumption of most neoliberal reformers. To do so would be to undervalue the technical and managerial competence of many of those involved in firms like Petroperú, Centromín, or the state development and commercial banks, and to ignore the very real constraints under which they were forced to operate, especially as the economic environment deteriorated during the administrations of Fernando Belaúnde Terry and Alan García in the 1980s. The impact of these governments and the long-running Peruvian economic crisis on the private sector and the response they evoked also demands much greater consideration. As far as the public sector is concerned there was some attempt, in the early 1980s, to commence research on oil and mining, as well as internal distribution, but this line of enquiry seems subsequently to have petered out.[75]

Some critics may respond to these suggestions with two comments: first, that the sources to undertake such research are lacking; second, that because of the distrust shown by businessmen towards historians it would be impossible to obtain permission to use the private archives that still exist. However, if no-one searches for them, no-one will find them. The important point seems to be to determine the problems and hypotheses for research before becoming over-concerned about the availability of sources. The historiography of Peru in the last few decades is full of examples of research which has relied on documents whose existence was unknown at the beginning of the project. This has almost always been the case with research undertaken outside Lima. Yet good examples also exist of the discovery of unexpected archives in the capital which have permitted the development of important research projects: the use which Alfonso Quiroz was able to make of the papers of the defunct Banco del Perú y Londres, which he found in the offices of the Superintendencia de Banca y Seguros in Lima, and the analysis of the early twentieth-century elite

---

[75] Becker, *The New Bourgeoisie*, chapter 8; George Philip, *Oil and Politics in Latin America: nationalist movements and state oil companies* (Cambridge, 1982), chapter 20; Alfred W. Saulniers, 'ENCI: Peru's bandied monopolist', *Journal of Inter-American Studies and World Affairs* 22 (1980), 451–62.

which Felipe Portocarrero has been undertaking using probate records in the Lima archives.[76]

There are doubts, therefore, whether a lack of primary sources is a real obstacle to the progress of business history in Peru. For research on earlier periods there is a mass of data in the notarial archives and official reports (frequently the problem is that there is too much and that it is poorly organised and indexed, not that there is too little). For more recent history a large quantity of published reports, articles, and interviews exists, which might serve to establish the context for understanding primary sources obtained from the companies themselves, even though at times the latter may have to consist of semi-confidential interviews rather than written archives. The most important point is the historian's methods of working and the time available, since s/he needs to establish with some patience a network of personal contacts with businessmen and their employees as well as the willingness to undertake some basic tasks of archival organisation in return for permission to use them. The impression of over twenty years of personal research on both British firms in Peru and companies owned by nationals of the country is that in many cases the archives still exist, but in a poor state of organisation. If it is possible to establish some trust between the historian and key managers or directors, it is almost always possible to obtain permission to use the older papers, but at the cost of spending some weeks organising them before commencing research proper. On many occasions too, access is extended after the project has begun, especially if the historian discovers papers which the firm itself had forgotten.

A further point is that the flowering of social science research in Peru after the 1960s has provided historians with several significant advantages in commencing the task of constructing a modern business history of Peru. A couple of examples will serve to illustrate the point. Much data on ADEX, one of the key interest group associations which developed under the military government, was published in other sources in the 1970s and 1980s, for example in the early issues of *Actualidad Económica* and *¿Qué Hacer?*. As for the manufacturing firms, many studies on the contemporary situation of particular industries were undertaken after the 1960s, as a bibliography published some years ago by Francisco Durand demonstrates.[77] It was not very common for these research projects to use archives

[76] In 1972, in the course of an informal conversation with a leading figure in the business community in Arequipa, I was offered unconditional access to the archives of a major commercial firm which he had founded in the early 1930s. At the time this did not tie in with the subject of my PhD research, but I now deeply regret not having taken this opportunity then or later in the 1970s. It may be that foreign historians may be favoured when it comes to obtaining permission to use the papers of such firms, but they often do not have the connections that their Latin American counterparts possess in relation to local entrepreneurs. The important thing, whatever the nationality of the historian, is to construct the personal networks which aid mutual trust.

[77] Francisco Durand, 'La industrialización en el Perú: bibliografía', *Estudios Andinos* 17–18 (1981), 195–246.

or the other primary sources which the companies themselves possessed. In general they were directed at the sociological issues of the period, and there is normally little of a long-term historical perspective to the research. Nevertheless, several studies do exist which, owing to the copious contemporary data they contain, may provide a historian in the future with a useful point of departure.[78] Of course, numerous other primary sources exist, besides the archives and reports of the firms themselves, for example the reports published by the Banco Industrial, the Ministerio de Industria y Comercio, and the Sociedad Nacional de Industrias, as well as contemporary business periodicals like *Industria Peruana* and many theses undertaken in Peruvian universities.

Why, then, was the momentum of the 1970s and early 1980s not maintained? Relatively little new research of interest to business historians seems to have been initiated since the mid-1980s. For a long time the real problem in Peru was the lack of a political and economic climate in which such research could continue to flourish. Unlike other countries in Latin America, the problem was not repression, but political instability and economic collapse, which made many of these proposals for research something of a fantasy. The publications of the 1970s and early 1980s had pointed to many subjects and problems worth studying further. There was no doubt about the professional capacity of historians in Peru, many of whom possessed much better training and insight than their foreign counterparts. In abstract terms there was little doubt that it ought to be possible, as in other countries, to convince owners and managers of the interest they should take in the history of their company, and the contribution that this might make, not just in the field of public relations, to their firm's standing if they sponsored a well focused project. However, the economic and political trajectory of the country presented serious obstacles to the fulfilment of these dreams. Many companies simply could not rely on the financial resources to fund historical research, and there was certainly little chance of official funding, given the fiscal problems of Peru. From the mid-1970s, if not before, the strategic planning of firms in Peru hardly extended beyond the very short term. Why invest in historical research when there were such great doubts about whether the company itself could survive another five years? Moreover, the political and social crisis induced by the growing activities of Sendero Luminoso meant that several of the best Peruvian historians took the decision to migrate to the United States or other Latin American countries. At the same time the

---

[78] Examples are: David Chaplin, *The Peruvian Industrial Labor Force* (Princeton, 1967); Antony Ferner, 'The Dominant Class and Industrial Development in Peru', *Journal of Development Studies* 15 (1979), 268–88, and the same author's *La burguesía industrial en el desarrollo peruano* (Lima, 1982); Manuel Lajo, 'Agroindustria, transnacionales, y alimentos en el Perú', *Estudios Andinos* 17/18 (1981), 139–74; John Weeks, *Limits to Capitalist Development: the industrialization of Peru, 1950–1980* (Boulder, 1985); Frits Wils, *Industrialization, Industrialists and the Nation State in Peru: a comparative / sociological analysis* (Berkeley, 1980).

number of foreign historians prepared to research in Peru, especially in Lima and the central sierra, also declined. Thus many of the problems which impeded the development of business history in Peru resulted from the increasingly tragic history of the country, its social conflicts, and the political and economic incompetence of successive governments. In this light it is perhaps surprising that so much was achieved.

CHAPTER EIGHT

Economic and Business History in Venezuela

Ruth Capriles and Marisol Rodríguez de Gonzalo

In this chapter we take the risk of carrying out, perhaps for the very first time, an overall evaluation of the state of business history in Venezuela.[1] It is only recently that this theme has been considered by those working on it as an area of academic research which is both specific and distinctive. Business historians in Venezuela used to lack awareness of its dimensions and hardly realised the significance of the tasks in which they were engaged. They were simply researchers approaching an area of common interest from rather different directions. Nobody, including the authors of this paper, could claim to be a real authority in the field. Even today the body of literature on business history in Venezuela is still not clearly defined. However, it may be possible to analyse it now with a greater awareness of the significance of business history in contemporary Latin America, something that used to be done rather intuitively or using the tools of the general historian rather than those of the specialist.

This chapter will therefore analyse the state of economic and business history in Venezuela, considering questions such as the style of economic history that has been written, and the current trends in the subject. However, when it comes to discussing problems of method and knowledge we are very much dependent upon our own experience of research in this field. For reasons which will be explained, those scholars interested in business history have only recently gained a real consciousness of its particular nature and demands, and it is rather early to attempt a synthesis of the state of the field along the lines adopted in other chapters in this volume. Moreover, the central role played by the state in the economy of the country since the petroleum boom of the 1920s has created conditions for the development of economic and business history which do not have parallels elsewhere in Latin America.[2]

---

[1] We are extremely grateful to María Elena González Deluca for her collaboration in compiling the bibliography on which this paper is based.

[2] It should be emphasised that while we have attempted to include all the items on business history that we could find, the bibliography of Venezuelan economic history on which this chapter is based is not exhaustive. We have attempted only to outline a bibliographic typology

The general features of Venezuelan economic history

Venezuelan economic history shares certain characteristics that apply also to other countries in the region. It is not necessary to dwell on them here except to make the point that it is within this intellectual context that business and entrepreneurial history as such has developed, although not all research in business history has used economic history as its point of departure. One of the most striking features of economic history both in Venezuela, and in Latin America more generally, is the profusion of research, especially after the 1950s. This was a type of history that arose out of more theoretical work which was attempting to explain an idiosyncrasy, or rather, a peculiarity, of dependent capitalism, namely the existence of countries marked by uneven, unequal and under development. Latin American theories of underdevelopment, especially those which became known as the ECLA (or *cepalino*) and dependency theories, were really ad hoc attempts to fill the cracks in orthodox theories of capitalism, which seemed, in the early 1960s, to have been undermined by the unequal development of the countries in the region.[3] The traditions of economic thought that developed in Latin America after the late 1940s came to provide the orthodox framework for understanding economic events until the beginning of the 1980s.[4] Economic history thus became a history of events and phenomena that was undertaken in order to arrive at a diagnosis of the local peculiarities of general economic processes. The subject incorporated its own solutions for the problems of (under)development, solutions which, whether they came from the right or the left, fell neatly

on the basis of the consolidated bibliography arising from the work of three separate researchers, Marisol de Gonzalo, María Elena González, and Ruth Capriles. As the original listing of books was the outcome of our personal research on specific topics, the final result cannot pretend to be a complete listing. We recognise that there are undoubtedly several omissions which are bound to offend experts in the field. We offer apologies for any such major faults.

[3] One of the assumptions of classical economic liberalism, its universality, is constantly refuted by the realities of unequal development. Even now, when formerly socialist economies have been taken over by a belief in the theoretical assumptions and policies of capitalism, the universality of neoliberal thought is being refuted. Today more than ever we in Venezuela are far from development and the technological gulf between our own and more developed countries is becoming wider. The fact that the ideal of the socialist economy has disappeared does not mean that the only possible economic system is one of (neo) classical capitalism. Venezuela is an example of a different model, a system dominated by oligopolistic production and state capitalism. In this country the state has been the *homo economicus*. We will return to this point later in the chapter.

[4] The importance of ECLA and dependency theories in defining the contours for research on economic history in Latin America is highlighted in other chapters in this volume: see especially those on Brazil (pp. 44–48) and on Chile (pp. 61–66). For an overview of these theories and their significance the most accessible source in English is Cristóbal Kay, *Latin American Theories of Development and Underdevelopment* (London 1989).

under the heading of planning.[5] Economic history became the history of a process which had passed through various stages and which now provided a justification for state planning and intervention in a directed economy. Overall, it was believed, this process could have only one end result, one that became more attractive and yet more ambiguous over time: development. In retrospect, this was a history of utopias. It could perhaps be termed the prehistory of business.

However, these ideas left a clear mark on Venezuelans' interpretations of the economic process. These historians, who could well be economists, sociologists or anthropologists in terms of their academic training and discipline, based their arguments, perhaps unknowingly, on principles opposed to those of *laissez faire* liberalism. They assumed that if left to their own devices people in countries which were underdeveloped would not 'develop'. This perspective was something more than a simple Keynesian one, in that it was not just concerned with state intervention in order to correct the failures of market mechanisms, but rather with correcting the failures inherent in the entire economic system. This implied stimulating, managing, and controlling development by means of state planning. For the ECLA school, for example, 'development was equivalent to the deliberate direction of the process of import substitution industrialisation through the use of planning'.[6]

As far as historiography was concerned, this intellectual context resulted in a proliferation of general economic histories on the subject of economic development and the obstacles impeding it in Venezuela. It also had an interesting effect on our objectives here: self-analysis. Since so much was expected from state planning, considerable attention was given to evaluating the economic programmes already undertaken and stimulated by the state. As a result a whole series of studies was published on topics such as agrarian reform enterprise; small and medium sized industries; sugar mills; co-operatives; artisan programmes; and regional developments.

The weight of the state

The importance of both the state and the petroleum industry in the Venezuelan economy during the twentieth century has conditioned, and perhaps limited, research on private-sector business. This factor is also evident in the distortions introduced into important methodological questions such as the criteria used to determine periodisation.

This periodisation of Venezuelan history has generally been a function

[5] Research on national planning has been advanced by Jorge A. Giordiani in several works. See particularly Jorge A. Giordiani, 'Cuatro décadas de planificación nacional', *Cuadernos del CENDES* 13: 31 (1993) and 'Planning in Venezuela: from the national experience to the corporative oil plan' (mimeo, Istanbul, 1994).

[6] Clemy Machado and Nelly Arenas, 'Los orígenes de la Corporación Venezolana de Fomento' (mimeo, Caracas, n.d.)

of the growth of the oil industry or changes in government policies. The normal assumption is that there is a cause and effect relationship between the actions of the state and subsequent developments in the economy, ignoring other factors such as flows of capital, the potential for consumption, or the impact of technology, demography, and culture or psychology. Thus the fall of the Pérez Jiménez dictatorship in 1958, a political landmark, is seen as a major dividing line in the economic history of the twentieth century. The emergence of the petroleum industry during the 1920s is taken as a watershed in the economy, a criterion which is quite justified in terms of the undoubted importance of oil in the country's economy but one which, at the same time, obscures the development of business in Venezuela as a whole. The question of periodisation, as related to business, constitutes a methodological problem which historians in Venezuela are only now beginning to discuss and resolve.[7]

A further problem arises with the statistical information available to historians. Rather than reflecting the reality of business in the economy as a whole, most of the statistical data and macroeconomic indicators refer specifically to oil or to government. Moreover, the statistical information that does exist tends to be unreliable, contradictory, discontinuous, scattered, and difficult to compare over time due to changes in classification, normally initiated by government. The economic indicators usually employed by historians do not reveal anything about the true situation of the majority of businesses in Venezuela, as the global figures are affected above all by the factor of oil. For example, figures for per capita exports since 1925 reflect the rise in activity in the petroleum industry rather than any increase or fall in manufacturing production or any changes induced either by monetary policies (revaluations and devaluations of the *bolívar*) or by industrial and commercial policies.

Interpretations of Venezuelan economic history also often take as their point of departure the individual historian's preconceived views about the ideal relationship between the state and private business. Opinions on this range from those historians who have developed a critical appreciation regarding the influence of business interests in state action, to those who see the state as always tyrannising private business. Such interpretations are, of course, often influenced by the author's ideological inclinations, but they have been made more acute by the role of the state in the economy and the ambiguity which Venezuelans feel about it. The eternal dilemma is that Venezuelans wish to be liberals but have to accept that in Venezuela there is only one economic agent, the petroleum sector, which possesses the capacity to 'compete in the free market'.

Such a perspective has serious consequences for the historiography, not least of which is the frequency with which writers attribute the entire blame

[7] Marisol R. de Gonzalo, 'Consideraciones generales sobre la historia de la industria en Venezuela', in *Diccionario de historia de Venezuela* (2 vols, Caracas, 1988), II, 540–47.

for the failures of economic development to the state and, less frequently, to the private sector.[8] At the same time this implies a lack of interest in developing historical analysis of other aspects of the economy such as the behaviour of markets, variations in consumption, the process of investment, managerial elites, and changes in business organisation and entrepreneurship.

Types of economic history in Venezuela

One can use two criteria in order to distinguish between types of economic history in Venezuela.[9] One possibility is an essentially chronological approach, using the period when studies appeared during the second half of the twentieth century in order to define the historiography. The alternative is to group the research in terms of its subject matter. Clearly the chronological method is a difficult one to sustain. Early styles of economic history continue to reappear up to the present day. However, it is possible to observe some progression in terms of the emergence of different approaches from the first general economic histories up to the most recent business history.

The earliest general economic histories concentrated on the colonial period. They still remain basic works that contain extensive and comprehensive descriptions of the colonial economy. These now classic texts by Arellano Moreno, Arcila Farías and Brito Figueroa were almost all written at the end of the 1950s and during the 1960s.[10] Shortly afterwards, both these authors and others produced surveys of economic history that incorporated more recent periods, although it might be added that very soon their interpretations became tinged by the developmentalist and dependency approaches which became dominant amongst social scientists in Latin America.[11]

The modernisation theories that became central to the Alliance for Progress were of obvious influence in the writings of Venezuelan economic

8 During the last twenty years Venezuelans have heard repeated at regular intervals an interpretation which explains the country's incapacity for development in terms of the qualities of the Venezuelans themselves. This can be summarised simply as 'the workers are lazy and the businessmen lack any spirit of risk-taking enterprise'. See, for example, Carlos Rangel, *Del buen salvaje al buen revolucionario* (Caracas, 1976). This is not, properly speaking, a book on economics or business. It is more of an essayist diatribe on the historical and cultural destiny of Venezuelans by a well-known journalist and broadcaster. However, it is well written and reflects the sentiment of inadequacy common amongst Venezuelans.

9 The bibliography to this essay refers exclusively to 'contemporary' historiography, especially to works published since 1950 (although a few works from the 1940s are included).

10 Antonio Arellano Moreno, *Orígenes de la economía venezolana* (Madrid, 1960); Eduardo Arcila Farías, 'Evolución de la economía en Venezuela', in Fundación Eugenio Mendoza, *Venezuela independiente, 1810–1960* (Caracas, 1962), pp. 345–420; Federico Brito Figueroa, *La estructura económica y social de Venezuela: una estructura para su estudio* (2 vols, Caracas, 1966).

11 Federico Brito Figueroa, *Venezuela contemporánea, ¿país colonial?* (Caracas, 1972).

historians during the 1960s. Much of the literature of this period was linked with the initial stages of modernisation (the construction of roads, electricity, urban infrastructure, and industrialisation), and it offers evaluations of this process. However, during the 1960s, or more precisely from the late 1950s, the principal influence on the writing of general economic history in Venezuela came first from the ECLA school and then from dependency theories. Both were attempting to understand the problems which Latin American economies were facing as they lagged behind in their efforts to industrialise and modernise. They analysed the conditions of development on the periphery, and the possibilities of straightening out the journey towards progress by means of planning and state intervention.[12]

In the same decade, and under the same influences, the regional aspects of the Venezuelan economy provoked interest.[13] This gathered pace during the 1970s when ECLA redefined its model in order to apply it to individual sectors of the economy. The idea of a New International Economic Order further strengthened the generalist focus in the 1970s, when hopeful optimists began to turn their attention to the international sphere and the place of Venezuela within it.[14]

Finally, during the 1980s and 1990s, the renewed expansion of (neo) classical theories, the domination of macroeconomic perspectives, and the demands of economic globalisation and the opening of markets meant that sweeping economic approaches became dominant again. Even the reports of the principal economic ministries in Venezuela (Cordiplan, the Ministry of Development, and the Ministry of Finance) have incorporated analysis of the history of macroeconomic factors.[15]

Before concluding the discussion of general economic histories, the contribution of foreign scholars, and international and regional organisations, their specialised agencies in particular, deserves a special mention. These organisations tended towards a global and external vision of the economy.[16]

---

[12] Domingo Felipe Masa Zavala, *Hacia la independencia económica* (Caracas, 1960), and *Venezuela: una economía dependiente* (Caracas, 1962); Tomás Enrique Carrillo Batalla, *Desarrollo económico de Venezuela* (Caracas, 1963); Celso Furtado, 'El desarrollo reciente de la economía venezolana' (1957), republished in Banco Central de Venezuela, *La economía contemporánea de Venezuela* (2 vols, Caracas, 1990), I, 163–205.

[13] J. Chi-yi Chen, *Estrategia del desarrollo regional: caso de Venezuela* (Caracas, 1967); Salvador de la Plaza, *Desarrollo económico e industrias básicas* (Caracas, 1962); John Friedmann, *Regional Development Policy: a case study of Venezuela* (Cambridge, 1966).

[14] Guillermo Márquez, *La economía en la década del 70: algunas reflexiones* (Caracas, 1976).

[15] Cordiplan is, to give it its full title, the Oficina Central de Coordinación y Planificación de la Presidencia de la República.

[16] See, for example, International Bank for Reconstruction and Development, *The Economic Development of Venezuela* (Baltimore, 1961).

The history of individual sectors of the economy

In the early stages of the history of individual economic sectors, during the 1950s and the 1960s, research was linked, particularly in the case of industry, to the general process of industrialisation and modernisation taking place in Venezuela. In some cases these studies focused directly upon certain sub-sectors of industry like dairy products, fats and oils, and other products of agro-industry such as maize or rice.[17] For the most part, however, they analysed the general development of a broad sector of the economy, above all manufacturing industry. Included in this are the evaluations and studies published by the international and regional organisations which had specialised agencies for different types of industry or particular industrial sectors.[18] During the 1970s a more specific form of economic history was developed which, influenced perhaps by the sectoral perspective now adopted in ECLA plans, represented a whole new focus for interpreting the development of different economic sectors and the stages of development they had reached. Three crucial sectors of the economy should be distinguished in this respect: industry; commerce; and banking and finance.

The emphasis of the sectoral focus of the 1970s was, almost by definition given the emphasis of the prevailing development model, on the history of industry, particularly manufacturing (foodstuffs, textiles, etc.) and state enterprise such as electricity. The principal studies assess the state of development of the sector or sub-sector, and include some studies with a distinct spatial perspective.[19] Also around the mid-1970s small and medium-sized industries began to receive academic attention. This stimulated numerous studies, and continues to do so.

Although industrialisation had always been the central axis of the models of development (it should be recalled that throughout the 1960s and 1970s the orthodox development model in Latin America centred on import-substitution industrialisation), the history of the industrial sector has failed to prosper in the 1980s and the 1990s. In general, Venezuelan industry has not been studied in the depth or the detail it deserves. In fact, the same factor is in part responsible for this since the central role of industry in the development model had the result that almost all the studies were

[17] O. S. Hunziger and R. E. Hodgson, 'The Dairy Industry in Venezuela' (mimeo, US Department of Agriculture, Washington, 1942); Gumersindo Rodríguez, 'Una visión optimista del futuro económico y social de Venezuela', in Banco Central, *La economía contemporánea*, I.

[18] P. I. Aguerrevere, 'Industrial Development in Venezuela', *Proceedings of the United Nations Scientific Conference on the Conservation and Utilization of Resources* (New York, 1949); Thomas E. Eil *et al.*, *Area Handbook for Venezuela* (Washington, 1971).

[19] Meir Merhav, *Posibilidades de exportación de la industria venezolana* (Caracas, 1974); Fred Jongkind, 'Informe sobre investigación de la gran y mediana industria manufacturera en Venezuela: la participación nacional y extranjera en la industria' (mimeo, Caracas, 1977); Weine Karlsson, *Evolución y localización de la industria manufacturera en Venezuela* (Stockholm, 1979), and *Manufacturing in Venezuela: studies on development and location* (Stockholm, 1975).

dedicated to assessing the value added in the overall process of industrialisation, and very few examined particular industries or sub-sectors. The
reality is that Venezuelans possess an industry that they do not really
understand, even though it is the result of development plans and the
protectionist policies implemented by the state. For example, there are no
complete or detailed studies of the textile industry, the metallurgical and
engineering industries, or the automobile industry. There is not even a
global study of agro-industry in Venezuela, even though this is one of the
sub-sectors which received most attention. With regard to more microhis-
torical studies these seem to have been directed particularly towards
agricultural enterprises, banking, and commerce, all of which are better
analysed as a separate style of economic history. Given the current influence
of macroeconomics and the global economy, it is difficult to foresee a
revival of the sectoral history of the 1970s.

The history of commerce in Venezuela has experienced a rather different
development compared with that of industry. This sector was, in contrast,
subjected to much more micro-historical analysis and various case studies
such as those on commerce in Caracas and the Andes appeared, especially
in the late 1980s and 1990s.[20] However, there are still no general interpretations, but rather studies which are quite specific and confined in terms
of period. Only for the colonial period does the work of Arcila Farías offer
an overall view of the commercial sector.[21] It should be added, though,
that since its founding in the late 1960s the Instituto de Comercio Exterior
(ICE) has constituted the most important official source of material for
historians. The ICE has always been dedicated to the problems of integration, and within this context the commercial sector has been the subject
of numerous studies by the Planning Ministry, Cordiplan, and international
agencies.[22]

The banking and financial sector has always received frequent attention in
the economic historiography of Venezuela since the start of the century.
During the 1910s, and then again in the 1930s and 1940s, monetary questions were the dominant issue; in the 1950s and 1960s various studies of
the evolution of the Venezuelan banking and credit system were published.[23]

---

[20] Catalina Banko, *Contribución a la historia de la manufactura en Venezuela* (Caracas, 1990);
Catalina Banko, *El capital comercial en la Guaira y Caracas, 1821–1848* (Caracas, 1990); María
Elena González Deluca, *Los comerciantes de Caracas: cien años de acción y testimonio de la
Cámara de Comercio de Caracas* (Caracas, 1994).

[21] Eduardo Arcila Farías, *La economía colonial de Venezuela* (Mexico, 1946).

[22] Each national plan commissions research and consulting work. See, for example, ILPES,
'Estrategias de desarrollo de Venezuela para los años ochenta', in Cordiplan, *Jornadas de
Análisis sobre estrategias de desarrollo de Venezuela, años ochenta* (Caraballeda, 1980).

[23] Domingo Castillo, *La cuestión monetaria en Venezuela* (Amsterdam, 1912); Tomás E. Carrillo Batalla, *Moneda, crédito y banca en Venezuela* (2 vols, Caracas, 1964); Feliciano Pacanins,
Evolución bancaria de Venezuela (Caracas, 1962); Carlos Rafael Silva, 'Esbozo al desenvolvimiento institucional del sistema financiero venezolano, 1940–1965', in Banco Central de
Venezuela, *Economía venezolana en los últimos 25 años* (Caracas, 1966).

This focus on the overall development of this sector of the economy was reinforced by the sectoral perspective of the late 1960s and the 1970s, when various studies offering a clear perspective of the sector as independent from the remainder of the economy were published.

Micro or business history has played a continuous role in understanding the evolution of Venezuelan banking and finance. However, during the 1980s the business history of banking and finance seems to have become better defined and differentiated from the general or sectoral focus applied to other areas of the economy. In the cases where works of this kind were published in earlier years, it could hardly be said that the authors were consciously practising this kind of history. This is the case, for example, with regard to studies of the Banco de Venezuela, which began to appear in the 1920s and have continued up to the present day when this institution has come back into the financial news.[24] This firm was the leading bank in Venezuela. Though formed by private capital, it exercised the role of financial agent for the Venezuelan government for 42 years until the founding of the Central Bank in 1939. As other banks appeared, so did studies of them: the Banco Industrial, several regional banks (Maracaibo, Valencia), and the Banco Central itself.[25] There are also some studies of commercial banking.[26] Finally, it should also be noted that we can expect to see the publication of much more literature on the Venezuelan banking and financial system due to the crisis through which the country has been passing and which has led to a major reconsideration of the entire sector.

During the 1950s and 1960s a few general histories of the Venezuelan petroleum industry were published, together with some seminal analyses of state oil policy following the adoption of democratic government at the beginning of the 1960s.[27] Then, in the 1970s, these studies were expanded to include analyses of the linkages between the industry and the process of national capital accumulation and state finances, as well as issues of dependency.[28] However, it was only after the nationalisation of the oil

[24] Vicente Lecuna and Leopoldo Landaeta, *El Banco de Venezuela* (Caracas, 1924); Nikita Harwich Vallenilla, *Formación y crisis de un sistema financiero nacional: banca y estado en Venezuela, 1830–1940* (Caracas, 1986); Rafael Crazut, *El Banco de Venezuela: notas sobre su historia y evolución, 1940–1980* (Caracas, 1986).

[25] Banco Industrial de Venezuela, *Veinticinco años del Banco Industrial de Venezuela* (Caracas, 1962); David Belloso Rosell, *Historia del Banco de Maracaibo* (Madrid, 1974); Catalina Banko, 'Contribución a la historia del Banco de Maracaibo', *Revista Universitaria de Historia* 2 (1982), 79–123; Luis Taborda, *Apuntes históricos relacionados con la fundación y la vida de los bancos en Valencia* (Valencia, 1966).

[26] José M. Tejero and Henry Gómez, *La banca comercial en Venezuela* (Caracas, 1967); Dario Rico López, *Banca comercial venezolana: una metodología para su análisis* (Caracas, 1986).

[27] The classic English-language study is Edwin Lieuwen, *Petroleum in Venezuela: a history* (Berkeley, 1954). see also Federico G. Batista, *Historia de la industria petrolera en Venezuela* (Caracas, 1961)

[28] H. D. Montiel Camacho, *La explotación del petróleo en Venezuela y la capitalización nacional* (Mexico, 1967); Enrique A. Baloyra, 'Oil Policies and Budgets in Venezuela, 1938–1968',

industry in 1976 that interest in the study of the petroleum business in Venezuela really took off. The best studies of the oil industry were published after 1980, a period in which several excellent good first-hand accounts by participants in the industry also appeared.[29]

However, not enough has been published about this crucial economic sector, upon which Venezuela has depended since at least 1920. The majority of the published literature deals with the financial dependence of the Treasury and other sectors on the petroleum industry, and the stagnation and malfunctioning of the state as the administrator and distributor of this wealth. In short, there has been a tendency to analyse the negative effects of the oil industry as opposed to the way in which it operated. In our view much of the latter work has been undertaken most effectively in the form of theses written in the faculties of engineering, economics, chemistry, management, and law in the national universities. Although these theses are listed in a national database, they have not been published and it is often difficult for scholars to consult them.

Business in history

During the 1980s a significant change occurred in Venezuelan historiography. Some historians abandoned the study of large-scale economic processes, a retreat perhaps from the theories of the dependency school, and begin to turn to case studies, doing what might be called microhistory, though maybe without realising it. This appears to represent a new approach which instead of focusing on general or sectoral economic processes, assesses the role of business: its products, companies, activities, relations, capital investment, and specific events of importance.

In many ways this has created what might be termed a diversity of history related to business in Venezuela, since those concerned have studied the unfolding of different economic activities. However, it seems somewhat premature to say that business history exists as a discipline or a specific area of economic history in which it is possible to identify well-defined stages, tendencies, and influences. In general, even the most recent

Latin American Research Review 9:2 (1974), 28–72; Rómulo Betancourt, *Venezuela: política y petroleo* (Barcelona, 1979); Juan Pablo Pérez Alfonso, *Petróleo y dependencia* (Caracas, 1971).

[29] B. S. McBeth, *Juan Vicente Gómez and the Oil Companies in Venezuela, 1908–1935* (Cambridge, 1983); Stephen Rabe, *The Road to OPEC: United States relations with Venezuela, 1919–1976* (Austin, 1982); Jonathan C. Brown, 'Why Foreign Oil Companies Shifted their Production from Mexico to Venezuela in the 1920s', *American Historical Review* 90 (1985), 262–85; Edwin Lieuwen, 'The Politics of Energy in Venezuela', in John D. Wirth (ed.), *Latin American Oil Companies and the Politics of Energy* (Lincoln, 1985), pp. 189–225; Laura Randall, *The Political Economy of Venezuelan Oil* (New York, 1987); Aníbal R. Martínez, *Venezuelan Oil: development and chronology* (London, 1989); Juan C. Boué, *Venezuela: the political economy of oil* (Oxford, 1993); Jorge Salazar Carrillo, *Oil and Development in Venezuela during the Twentieth Century* (Westport, 1994); R. Vaez-Zadah, 'Oil Wealth and Economic Behavior: the case of Venezuela, 1963–1984', *IMF Staff Papers*. 36: 2 (1989), 343–84.

publications seem to indicate a lack of awareness of there being such a subject as business history possessing a specific focus; instead, the research might best be described as economic history or 'business in history'. Amongst the more recent publications one can find a little of everything: histories of plantations; haciendas; family farms; general industrial history; company history; the history of commercial and financial institutions; commercial credit; petroleum and other extractive industries; specific products such as cacao, coffee, tobacco, sugar, salt, chocolate, soap; the history of banking; agreements and contracts between private business and the state; public utilities such as gas, electricity, and the railways; commercial history; and one or two biographies of entrepreneurs. This type of history has attracted the attention of people who range from those with an amateur interest to those coming from quite different academic and professional backgrounds (journalists, historians, economists, businessmen, and technical experts), but who, paradoxically, seem to be following some calling for history, whether out of interest in the distant agro-exporting past (the research on products such as coffee and cacao or the German trading houses), or else out of the wish to understand the transition from an agrarian economy to one based on industry and finance.[30]

Nevertheless, there does seem to have been a recent change in this pattern of historiographical diversity and absence of disciplinary awareness. Researchers have begun to join forces in order to harmonise and give some coherence to the diverse and incomplete body of information they have uncovered. They are conscious of the gaps in their knowledge, in particular the need to develop conceptual tools that might permit a much broader assessment of the history of business in Venezuela, one free from ideological prejudice and *a priori* conceptions concerning the relationship between the state and private business. This seems a more pragmatic and reasoned approach. It avoids general histories and instead emphasises specific business activities, often in the form of case studies, and with some focus on issues like investment and the characteristics of businessmen and entrepreneurs. Generally speaking, it is possible to distinguish two main tendencies amongst this group of historians of business in Venezuela, although this categorisation is by no means exhaustive.

First, researchers who have come to this subject from the field of history and sociology are mainly concerned with the way in which businesses have evolved: their growth, diversification, processes of change and cycles; their growth strategies; an understanding of the key stages of transition in business organisation; the formulation and application of business policies; changes in the environment in which business was functioning; companies'

[30] See, for example, Alicia Ardao, *El café y las ciudades en los Andes venezolanos, 1870–1930* (Caracas, 1984); William Roseberry, *Coffee and Capitalism in the Venezuelan Andes* (Austin, 1983); Gastón Carvallo, *El hato venezolano, 1900–1980* (Caracas, 1985); Gastón Carvallo and Josefina Ríos de Hernández, *La hacienda venezolana* (Caracas, 1988).

capacity to adapt and the mechanisms for doing so; the motivation and creative responses of entrepreneurs; or the personal qualities of executives, managers, supervisors, and administrators. Even the relationship between the state and private enterprise has for the first time been analysed within a broader context which considers these two variables as being determined both by external conditions and the choices about this relationship made within Venezuela itself.[31]

Second, professional economists have turned their attention to history in order to uncover the origins and persistence of the problems and limitations of private business in Venezuela, and thus offer a diagnosis for change. This type of researcher is mainly interested in questions about organisation, management, the comparative advantage of the business sectors, competitiveness, entrepreneurial capacity, culture, and the possibilities for exports.[32]

Company history itself is a very recent development in Venezuela. Between 1950 and 1980 a few works of this kind, focusing on individual companies or businessmen, were published by the companies themselves once they had attained a reasonable size, generally for public relations purposes. For this reason they are normally quite superficial, lavishly illustrated accounts undertaken by journalists or publicists commissioned by the firm concerned and with the clear intention of painting a positive image of these companies. Only recently, and after struggling with some of the more atavistic fears of businessmen, is a new institutional history being developed, by the authors of this article amongst others, which results from companies employing professionals in business history. In other words, business history is no longer the work of journalists, or company public relations consultants. This change appears to be the result of the rapid process of investment and the maturing of businessmen in Venezuela, although, for this very reason, historical research has come up against numerous obstacles: distrust, fear, prejudice, changing alliances, and personalities who wish their role to be either minimised or praised.

It was unavoidable that many business historians, driven on most probably by factors such as those noted at the beginning of this paper, found their research concentrating on the relationship between the Venezuelan state and private business.[33] Those of us working in this field accepted the

---

[31] Clemy Machado de Assis, *La Reforma de La Ley de Hidrocarburos de 1943: un impulso hacia la modernización* (Caracas, 1990); Ruth Capriles Méndez, *Los negocios de Román Delgado Chalbaud* (Caracas, 1991); María Elena González Deluca, *Negocios y política en tiempos de Guzmán Blanco* (Caracas, 1991).

[32] See, for example, various works by Moisés Naím, 'El crecimiento de las empresas privadas en Venezuela: mucha diversificación, poca organización',and 'La empresa privada en Venezuela. ¿Qué pasa cuando se crece en medio de la riqueza y la confusión', in Moisés Naím *et al.* (eds), *Las empresas venezolanas: su gerencia* (Caracas, 1989), pp. 17–55 and 152–82 respectively; 'Evolución y desarrollo de grandes empresas venezolanas', in *I Congreso Venezolano de Ejecutivos de Finanzas* (Caracas, 1982);.

[33] In 1991 Dr Rogelio Pérez Perdomo assembled a group of specialist business historians

fact that it is impossible to understand, let alone to research business history in Venezuela, without first knowing the complex dynamics of economic policy and the intervention, guidance, and control of the state. Without an understanding of the policies of subsidies, quotas, and state finance, it is impossible to comprehend why some types of industry emerged at specific moments or why they developed a particular dynamic.

This is a condition that is as fundamental today as it must have been for the ECLA school. The difference is that now when historians study the two participants in the state-society relationship, they allow them to express their characteristics and dynamics without measuring them against a particular desired model of development. What those of us engaged in business history are attempting to achieve is a history that is both comprehensive and empathetic, one which might uncover the reasons why the Venezuelan economy developed in the way it did and not in a different fashion. In this sense it is a history directed towards the past when compared with the history influenced by dependency theories which looked towards a desirable future. This is an endeavour which is analytical rather than phenomenological, a micro history that studies the roles of public officials and entrepreneurs in the development of business in particular periods and circumstances.

This unorthodox focus allows us to appreciate that the relationship between the state and business or the state and the market is not one-way, or even two-way, but a multiple one, even when monopolistic or oligarchical processes are dominant. It has been possible, for example, to observe phenomena such as the ways in which economic interests influence public policy, and the effects and impact of public policy on business conditions and company behaviour. The latter is a fruitful area of research.

The interaction between the state and private enterprise has already produced various studies on subjects such as the oil industry and other public-sector industries, the effects of public expenditure, the impact of economic legislation and other state policies.[34] However, historians in Venezuela still have to produce many more studies, since the country's experience is special and could therefore make a significant contribution to business history as a whole. Venezuela ought to provide a basis for

in Venezuela in the Instituto de Estudios Superiores de Administración (IESA), with the intention of allowing us to relate our own research experiences. These meetings permitted us to appreciate the common factors in our approach and results. Individual studies written by members of the group that met in IESA include González Deluca, *Negocios y política*; Nikita Harwich Vallenilla, *Asfalto y Revolución: La New York and Bermudez Company* (Caracas, 1992); Capriles, *Los negocios de Román Delgado Chalbaud*. All of these form attempts to investigate this relationship between the public and private sectors.

[34] Antonio J. Azpúrua, 'The Role of the Guayana Development Corporation in Venezuelan Industrialization: diversification or vertical integration' (MA thesis, MIT, 1987); Isabel Boscán de Ruesta, *El 'holding' en la organización del sector público económico* (Caracas, 1975); Janet Kelly de Escobar, *Empresas del estado en América Latina* (Caracas, 1985).

producing an adequate interpretation of this peculiar type of economic development, a pseudo-capitalist style of production based on public enterprise and a state with an extraordinary capacity to invest. However, Venezuelans have yet to produce a rounded interpretation of their own country's economic development, the reasons for it, and its legitimacy. At least their concern shows that they are on the right track.

Another result of the search for the human volition behind business in Venezuela has been the deconstruction of historiographical myths. Companies which were traditionally regarded as 'the infamous incarnation of foreign capital' have turned out to be the result of the business activity of some national political leader or other influential figure.[35] Economic laws often attributed in the historical record to the arbitrary acts of a dictatorship have turned out to be the response of individuals other than the dictator who were both conscious of the needs of Venezuela and in positions of responsibility at crucial historic moments.[36]

Sources

Locating appropriate sources for business history is in itself a real challenge, since they tend to be scattered amongst the national archives, libraries, research centres, and private companies, the latter being particularly inaccessible.[37] As well as the usual problems of disarray, the loss of documents (due to fires, clearouts, removals, and insects), and the absence of any professional archival standards in many public depositories, there is also the problem that this new form of history requires a type of information (share registers, commercial records, operational files and the like) which were previously considered neither important nor 'historical', and were therefore not retained.

There are some well-kept national archives in Venezuela, especially those which are of specific importance such as the presidential archives. This, however, is not the case with municipal, industrial or commercial registers. There are sources of quantitative information such as the national accounts, government revenue, debt, and investments by branches of industry, and also several sources of this data such as Cordiplan and the Banco Central, which allow information to be collated provided one is not too demanding and also prepared to put up with loose methods of aggregation.

One of the most useful sources for business historians in recent years has been the North American and British consular and commercial reports, which were made available to researchers in Venezuela itself on microfilm

---

[35] This is the case, for example, of the Asphalt Company and Guzmán Blanco: see Harwich, *Asfalto y revolución*.

[36] This is the case, for example, of the *gomecista* banking laws passed in 1910–1911, studied by Capriles in *Los negocios de Román Delgado Chalbaud*.

[37] This point is heavily underlined by Vera Blinn Reber, 'Archival Sources for Latin American Business History', *Business History Review* 59 (1985), pp. 670–79.

at the Biblioteca Nacional after 1985. These reports contain an abundance of information and analysis regarding business, companies, investments and entrepreneurs, and they provide much information on commercial conditions and trends.

Oral and family history have also been a very useful source since Venezuela has numerous potential informants who, as well as being lovers of history, are also prepared to help reconstruct events in which they or their relations took part. Undoubtedly, this source has varying degrees of utility depending on the time that has lapsed and the amount of tradition conserved in the family memory.

Finally, there are problems with what might be termed 'the real invisible hand', that of capital.[38] In Venezuela this difficulty is especially acute as the capitalist generally prefers to hide away from history. This is not just because of the popularity of companies based on bearer shares, but also due to that very South American phenomenon, the use of front men, who act as mediators not just for foreign capital (something that was heavily criticised by the *dependentistas*), but also for national figures like presidents and civil servants, or shy and retiring businessmen who wish to avoid provoking social envy or resentment.

Two examples

The experience gained from research projects on two Venezuelan businesses allows for some theoretical and methodological reflections on the issues outlined in this paper. The two studies were a series of linked projects on the parent brewery company and subsidiaries of Empresas Polar, and a history of ILAPECA written for its thirtieth anniversary in 1990.[39] The latter is fundamentally a dairy products firm that experienced a rapid process of diversification. In both cases the company itself commissioned the research and the principal objective was to compile information in order to write a reliable account of its history.

It is worth noting that the companies selected professional historians to undertake the research, and that they offered every possible form of collaboration in obtaining information. This was all the more significant in view of the fact that one of the companies was extremely vulnerable to government policies and their managers had been exposed to fierce public criticism.

The principal sources for business history comprise the evidence of workers, employees, managers, and owners of the companies, as well as their associates, suppliers, distributors, customers, and consumers. These two research projects were based especially on information obtained from personal interviews. In undertaking theses interviews the methodology of

---

[38] Capriles, *Los negocios de Román Delgado Chalbaud.*

[39] Both these studies were unpublished; further details may be obtained from the authors.

oral history was modified in order to adapt to the particular circumstances of the business environment. Adapting oral history techniques to the peculiarities of the Venezuelan business environment led in turn to a process of learning. Rather than acting as a deterrent for the use of this methodology the adaptation enriched it and led to the conclusion that oral history was an indispensable tool in the equipment of the business historian which made it possible to capture the image and culture of the organisation, the company's experience, the functioning of the business, and the different operating areas within the company.

The other useful primary sources for the business historian in these two cases were the following: the records of shareholders' meetings, which contain information relating to the identity of the management, increases in capital, and changes in statutes; the minutes and reports of the board of directors, which were the main source allowing the historian to follow the company's policies and operation, and which contained important information on aspects of administration and organisation; and financial statements, which normally presented information reported with great continuity but with changing criteria.[40] This meant that figures had to be selected on the basis of definitions developed by the historian in order to permit comparisons between different periods. The statistical data and the form in which it was presented reflected the nature of the company during its different stages.

After consulting the information for the early stages of the companies' history five areas of research and sources of information were identified: production; sales and distribution; internal and external relationships; management and finance; and organisational structure. Initially this functional organisation was used as a means of organising and interpreting information, but in the course of the research it became evident that a simple functional division was an inconvenient means of data collection and analysis, since it led to unavoidable repetitions. An attempt was then made to divide the subject chronologically, commencing with decades and then using key turning points in the evolution of the company such as technological, commercial, and organisational landmarks. On reflection we believe that both criteria, the functional and chronological combined, allow the historian to capture the company's development in business time and space. However, significant difficulties appeared.

When one begins to assemble information on a company everything seems important: how and why it was formed; the characteristics and motivations of the shareholders, employees and workers; the amount of capital invested; the production process; the equipment acquired; the

[40] For example, in the case of the project on the Polar brewing firm, during the first decade of the company's history, the 1940s, there was abundant data on issues concerning production: the purchase of raw materials, equipment, and technical problems. After the 1950s the most voluminous data is concerned with sales: procedures, staffing, marketing systems, credits, and so on.

techniques employed; marketing, in terms of the company's staff and its methods; the type of advertising and so on. The information is heterogeneous but abundant, and although it is not exhaustive, the researcher can feel overwhelmed by it. Since it is impossible to incorporate everything, the historian must then decide what should and should not be included.

Despite the problems mentioned above, the researcher has to establish interpretative guidelines, having established a certain amount of knowledge of the facts and on the basis of the study of the documents and the interviews undertaken. One of the difficulties found in these projects when trying to establish interpretative criteria is the perception that the functional areas selected evolve according to different rhythms. How could one establish the relationship among them, as well as developing an appropriate periodisation? Equally, at some times the information collected points towards a focus and style of analysis which emphasises the taking of decisions and the activities and perceptions of certain individuals. On other occasions the technical and quantitative information points towards a more impersonal explanation. Are there aspects of a company's history which should be given priority? What is the best way to present such information? These questions remain open.

When researching a company which is still in operation, one of the other problems that arises is informing the management what a historian considers essential in order to explain the firm's evolution. For example, a significant alteration in shareholding might explain an abrupt change of policy and management style, but it could also be considered by the current management as not pertinent and indeed inconvenient to mention. This type of discrepancy may arise even when both sides, the businessman and the historian, are in agreement about the need to present a complete and truthful account. In this sense, there is a long way to go before businessmen become fully aware of the important role which company history can play.[41] One of these is the production of snapshots of the business at particular points in time which can be employed as induction material for the newly arrived senior executives, or as something to bear in mind in the training and development of personnel. In our experience, even when some executives were appreciative of the usefulness of the research, the general opinion in the company upon finishing the projects was that it was not convenient to divulge all the information contained in the research outside the firm. This constitutes a disincentive for the historian, unless it has been foreseen and the research undertaken with other ends in mind.

When research in business history is commissioned by the company itself or an organisation linked to it, such as an affiliate or a foundation, the objective of this 'contracted' work may seem remote from the real interests of the historian. This is another source of tension for which one

---

[41] An excellent synthesis of this problem can be found in Thomas C. Cochran, 'The Value of Company History: a review article', *Business History Review* 53 (1979), 79–84.

must be prepared. Obviously, the contractual objective must prevail over the academic aims; but it has been evident in these projects that maintaining two levels of interest may help the historian to give priority to the business objectives without sacrificing one's own interest in the research. If, on completing the research, the company decides to shelve the research report because public disclosure is considered not to be in the company's best interest at that specific moment, then the historian can still use the experience in order to reflect upon and undertake further research on business, industry and economic development in general. Even if one complies fully with the objectives of the business in commissioning the work, whether this has been done for publishing, public relations, or internal institutional reasons, and continues to respect the rights the company has established under the terms of the contract, the historian may still obtain information which in the medium term, though not immediately, can be used to formulate generalisations and interpretations of broader relevance than the specific interests of the company.

This experience of business history, in addition to a review of the literature on methods and theoretical models related to the discipline of business history, reveals that problems and difficulties exist which are inherent in its very nature. Being aware of the limitations helps the historian to identify the specific characteristics in the history of each company, to highlight the main features of its evolution, to assign the proper importance to individual people, events, and processes, and to avoid misinterpretations as far as possible. Our experience has also shown that, despite the limitations of the field, research on business history is a productive approach in the understanding of the economic phenomenon. To possess the rare opportunity of studying a company's evolution from within, consulting its documents, and being able to listen to the views of direct participants is enough to tempt any historian. However, this interest is stimulated still further if there exists the possibility of deriving useful conclusions for both the company and the discipline in general.

Bibliography

This bibliography was compiled by the authors of the individual chapters and sections on individual countries are divided according to criteria appropriate to each country. All Spanish- and Portuguese-language journals are published in the country concerned except where stated.

ARGENTINA

Raúl García Heras

Foreign Companies

Commercial houses

Gravil, Roger, 'British Retail Trade in Argentina, 1900–1940', *Inter-American Economic Affairs* 29: 2 (1970), pp. 3–26.

Reber, Vera Blinn, *British Mercantile Houses in Buenos Aires, 1810–1880*, Cambridge, Mass., Harvard University Press, 1979.

Railway companies

Fleming, William, *Regional Development and Transportation in Argentina: Mendoza and the Gran Oeste Argentino Railroad, 1885–1914*, New York, Garland, 1987.

——, 'Profits and Visions: British Capital and Railway Construction in Argentina, 1854–1886', in: *Railway Imperialism*, ed. Ronald E. Robinson, Clarence B. Davis y Kenneth E. Wilburn Jr., New York, Greenwood Press, 1991, pp. 71–84.

García Heras, Raúl, 'World War II and the Frustrated Nationalization of the Argentine British-owned Railways, 1939–1943', *Journal of Latin American Studies* 17 (1985), pp. 135–55.

——, 'Hostage Private Companies under Restraint: British Railways and Transport Coordination in Argentina during the 1930s', *Journal of Latin American Studies* 19 (1987), pp. 41–67.

——, 'Las compañas ferroviarias británicas y el control de cambios en la Argentina durante la gran depresión', *Desarrollo Económico* 29: 116 (1990), pp. 477–505.

Goodwin, Paul B., *Los ferrocarriles británicos y la U. C. R., 1916–1930*, Buenos Aires, La Bastilla, 1974.

Lewis, Colin M., 'British Railway Companies and the Argentine Government', in *Business Imperialism, 1840–1930: an Inquiry based on the British Experience in Latin America*, ed. D. C. M. Platt, Oxford, Clarendon Press, 1977, pp. 395–427.

——, *British Railways in Argentina, 1857–1914: a Case Study of Foreign Investment*, London, Athlone Press, 1983.

Ortiz, Ricardo M., *El ferrocarril en la economía argentina*, Buenos Aires, Problemas, 1946.

Regalsky, Andrés M., 'Las inversiones francesas en los ferrocarriles argentinos, 1887–1900', *Siglo XIX: Revista de Historia* (Monterrey, Mexico) 5 (1988), pp. 125–66.

——, 'Foreign Capital, Local Interests and Railway Development in Argentina: French Investments in Railways, 1900–1914', *Journal of Latin American Studies* 21 (1989), pp. 425–52.

Scalabrini Ortiz, Raúl, *Historia de los ferrocarriles argentinos*, Buenos Aires, Reconquista, 1940.

Wright, Winthrop R., *British-Owned Railways in Argentina: their Effect on the Growth of Economic Nationalism, 1857–1948*, Austin, University of Texas Press, 1974.

Zalduendo, Eduardo, *Libras y rieles: las inversiones británicas para el desarrollo de los ferrocarriles en Argentina, Brasil, Canadá e India durante el siglo XIX*, Buenos Aires, El Coloquio, 1975.

Motor Transport

Brennan, James P., 'El clasismo y los obreros: el contexto fabril del "Sindicalismo de Liberación" en la industria automotriz cordobesa, 1970–1975', *Desarrollo Económico* 32: 125 (1992), pp. 3–22.

——, *The Labor Wars in Córdoba, 1955–1976: Ideology, Work, and Labor Politics in an Argentine Industrial City*, Cambridge, Harvard University Press, 1994.

García Heras, Raúl, *Automotores norteamericanos, caminos y modernización urbana en la Argentina, 1918–1939*, Buenos Aires, Libros de Hispanoamérica, 1985.

Macdonald, Norbert, 'Henry J. Kaiser and the Establishment of the Automobile Industry in Argentina', *Business History* 30 (1988), pp. 329–45.

Nofal, María Beatriz, *Absentee Entrepreneurship and the Dynamics of the Motor Vehicle Industry in Argentina*, New York, Praeger Publishers, 1989.

Skupch, Pedro, 'Las consecuencias de la competencia de transportes sobre la hegemonía económica británica en la Argentina, 1919–1939', *Económica* 17 (1971), pp. 119–41.

Petroleum companies

Frondizi, Arturo, *Petróleo y política: contribución al estudio de la historia económica argentina y de las relaciones entre el imperialismo y la vida política nacional*, Buenos Aires, Raigal, 1954.

Kaplan, Marcos, *Economía y política del petróleo argentino, 1939–1956*, Buenos Aires, Praxis, 1957.

——, *Petróleo, estado y empresas en la Argentina*, Caracas, Síntesis Dosmil, 1972.

Liceaga, José V., *Reflexiones sobre el problema petrolero*, Buenos Aires, 1955.

Mayo, Carlos, Osvaldo Andino, and Fernando García Molina, *Diplomacia, política y petróleo en la Argentina, 1927–1930*, Buenos Aires, Ediciones Rincón, 1976.

Rumbo, Eduardo, *Petróleo y vasallaje*, Buenos Aires, Ediciones Hechos e Ideas, 1957.

Solberg, Carl, *Oil and Nationalism in Argentina*, Stanford, Stanford University Press, 1979.

Banks and finance

Amaral. Samuel, 'El empréstito de Londres de 1824', *Desarrollo Económico* 23: 92 (1984), pp. 559–87.

Burk, Kathleen, *Morgan Grenfell, 1838–1988: the Biography of a Merchant Bank*, Oxford, Oxford University Press, 1989.

Dawson, Frank Griffith, *The First Latin American Debt Crisis: the City of London and the 1822–25 Loan Bubble*, New Haven, Yale University Press, 1990.

Joslin, David, *A Century of Banking in Latin America: to commemorate the centenary in 1962 of the Bank of London and South America Ltd.*, London, Oxford Univesity Press, 1963.

Kynaston, David, *Cazenove & Co: a History*, London, Batsford, 1991.

Marichal, Carlos, 'Los banqueros europeos y los empréstitos argentinos: rivalidad y colaboración, 1880–1890', *Revista de Historia Económica* (Madrid) 2: 1 (1984), pp. 47–82.

———, *A Century of Debt Crises in Latin America: from Independence to the Great Depression*, Princeton, Princeton University Press, 1989.

Regalsky, Andrés, 'La evolución de la banca privada nacional en Argentina, 1860–1914: una introducción a su estudio', in *La formación de los bancos centrales en España y América Latina*, eds Pedro Tedde and Carlos Marichal, 2 vols, Madrid, Banco de España, 1994, Vol. II, pp. 35–59.

Roberts, Richard, *Schroders: Merchants and Bankers*, London, Macmillan, 1992.

Ziegler, Philip, *The Sixth Great Power: Barings, 1762–1929*, London, Collins, 1988.

Meat packing

Crossley, Colin and Robert Greenhill, 'The River Plate Beef Trade', in *Business Imperialism, 1840–1930: an Inquiry based on the British Experience in Latin America*, ed. D. C. M. Platt, Oxford, Clarendon Press, 1977, pp. 284–334.

Hanson, Simon G., *Argentine Meat and the British Market*, Stanford, Stanford University Press, 1938.

Smith, Peter H., *Politics and Beef in Argentina*, New York, Columbia University Press, 1969.

Other companies

Barbero, María Inés, 'Grupos empresarios, intercambio comercial e inversiones italianas en la Argentina: el caso de Pirelli, 1910–1920', *Estudios Migratorios Latinoamericanos* 15–16 (1990), pp. 311–42.

Cowen, Michael, 'Capital, Nation and Commodities: the Case of Forestal Land, Timber and Railway Company in Argentina and Africa, 1900–1945', in *Capitalism in a Mature Economy*, eds J. J. Van Helten and Y. Cassis, Aldershot, Edward Elgar, 1990, pp. 186–215.

Fuchs, Jaime, *La penetración de los trusts yanquis en la Argentina*, Buenos Aires, Cartago, 1959.

García Heras, Raúl, 'Capitales extranjeros, poder político y transporte urbano de pasajeros: la compañía de tranvías Anglo Argentina Ltda de Buenos Aires, Argentina, 1930–1943', *Desarrollo Económico* 32: 125 (1992), pp. 35–56.

Gori, Gastón, *La Forestal: la tragedia del quebracho colorado*, Buenos Aires, Platina/Stilcograf, 1965.

Míguez, Eduardo, *Las tierras de los ingleses en la Argentina*, Buenos Aires, Editorial de Belgrano, 1985.

Newton, Ronald C., *German Buenos Aires, 1900–1933: Social Change and Cultural Crisis*, Austin, University of Texas Press, 1977.

Phelps, Dudley Maynard, *Migration of Industry to South America*, New York, McGraw-Hill, 1936.

Sommi, Luis V., *El monopolio inglés del transporte en Buenos Aires*, Buenos Aires, Argumentos, 1940.

———, *Los capitales alemanes en la Argentina*, Buenos Aires, Claridad, 1945.

———, *Los capitales yanquis en la Argentina*, Buenos Aires, Monteagudo, 1949.

Argentine Private-Sector Firms

Amaral, Samuel, *The Rise of Capitalism on the Pampas: the estancias of Buenos Aires, 1785–1870*, Cambridge, Cambridge University Press, 1998.

Brown, Jonathan, 'A Nineteenth Century Cattle Empire', *Agricultural History* 52 (1978), pp. 160–78.

Carretero, Andrés, *Los Anchorena: política y negocios en el siglo XIX*, Buenos Aires, Octava Década, 1970.

Cochran, Thomas C. and Rubén E. Reina, *Entrepreneurship in Argentine Culture: Torcuato Di Tella and Siam*, Philadelphia, University of Pennsylvania Press, 1962.

Fleming, William J., 'The Cultural Determinants of Entrepreneurship and Economic Development: A Case Study of Mendoza Province, Argentina, 1861–1914', *Journal of Economic History* 39 (1979), pp. 211–24.

Girbal de Blacha, Noemí, 'Ajustes de una economía regional: inserción de la vitivinicultura cuyana en la Argentina agroexportadora, 1885–1914', *Investigaciones y Ensayos* 35 (1987), pp. 409–42.

——, 'Estado, modernización azucarera y comportamiento empresario en la Argentina, 1876–1914: expansión y concentración de una economía regional', *Anuario de Estudios Americanos* (Sevilla) 45 (1988), pp. 383–417.

Gutiérrez, Leandro and Juan Carlos Korol, 'Historia de empresas y crecimiento industrial en la Argentina: el caso de la Fábrica Argentina de Alpargatas', *Desarrollo Económico* 28: 111 (1988), pp. 401–24.

Guy, Donna, *Argentine Sugar Politics: Tucumán and the Generation of Eighty*, Tempe, AZ., Center for Latin American Studies, 1980.

——, 'Refinería Argentina, 1888–1930: límites de la tecnología azucarera en una economía periférica', *Desarrollo Económico* 28: 111 (1988), pp. 353–73.

Regalsky, Andrés, 'La evolución de la banca privada nacional en la Argentina, 1880–1914', in *La formación de los bancos centrales en España y América Latina: siglos XIX y XX*, ed. Pedro Tedde and Carlos Marichal, 2 vols, Madrid, Banco de España, 1994, Vol. 2, pp. 35–60.

Schenkolewski-Kroll, Silvia, 'Los archivos de S.I.A.M. Di Tella S. A.: primera organización de fuentes en la historia de las empresas argentinas', *Estudios Interdisciplinarios de América Latina y el Caribe* 3: 2 (1992), pp. 105–22.

Schvarzer, Jorge, *Bunge y Born: crecimiento y diversificación de un grupo económico*, Buenos Aires, Latinoamericano, 1988.

Sebrelli, Juan José, *La saga de los Anchorena*, Buenos Aires, Sudamericana, 1985

Socolow, Susan Migden, *The Merchants of Buenos Aires, 1778–1810*, Cambridge, Cambridge University Press, 1978.

State Enterprise

Angueira, María del C. and Alicia del C. Tonini, *Capitalismo de estado, 1927–1956*, Buenos Aires, Centro Editor de América Latina, 1986.

Esteban, Juan Carlos and Luis Ernesto Tassara, *Valor industrial y enajenación de DINIE*, Buenos Aires, Ediciones de la Cátedra Lisandro de la Torre, 1958.

Favaro, Orietta and Marta B. Morinelli, *Petróleo, estado y nación*, Buenos Aires, Centro Editor de América Latina, 1991.

Ferrer, Aldo, *El estado en el desarrollo económico*, Buenos Aires, Raigal, 1956.

García Heras, Raúl, 'State Intervention in Urban Passenger Transportation: the Transport Corporation of Buenos Aires, Argentina, 1939–1962', *Hispanic American Historical Review* 74 (1994), pp. 83–110.

Kaplan, Marcos, 'El estado empresario en la Argentina', *Aportes* 10 (1968), pp. 34–69.

Maldifessi, José O. and Pier A. Abetti, *Defense Industries in Latin American Countries: Argentina, Brazil, and Chile*, New York, Praeger, 1994.

Novick, Susana, *IAPI: auge y decadencia*, Buenos Aires, Centro Editor de América Latina, 1986.

Ortiz, Ricardo M., *El ferrocarril en la economía argentina*, 2nd edition, Buenos Aires, Ediciones Cátedra Lisandro de La Torre, 1958.

Panaia, Marta and Ricardo Lesser, 'Las estrategias militares frente al proceso de industrialización, 1943–1947' in *Estudios sobre los orígenes del peronismo*, eds Marta Panaia, Ricardo Lesser y Pedro Skupch, 2 volumes, Buenos Aires, Siglo XXI, 1975, II, pp. 95–164.

Páramo, Marta Susana, *Un fracaso hecho historia: la Corporación de Transportes de la Ciudad de Buenos Aires*, Mendoza, Universidad Nacional de Cuyo, 1991.

Sábato, Jorge A., *SEGBA: Cogestión y Banco Mundial*, Buenos Aires, Juárez Editor, 1971.

Schvarzer, Jorge, 'Empresas públicas y desarrollo industrial en Argentina', *Economía de América Latina* (México) 3 (1979), pp. 45–68.

Solberg, Carl, 'Entrepreneurship in Public Enterprise: General Enrique Mosconi and the Argentine Petroleum Industry', *Business History Review* 56 (1982), pp. 380–99.

——, 'YPF: The Formative Years of Latin America's Pioneer State Oil Company, 1922–39' in *Latin American Oil Companies and the Politics of Energy*, ed. John Wirth, Lincoln, University of Nebraska Press, 1985, pp. 51–102.

Interest Groups

Acuña, Carlos H., 'Business Interests, Dictatorship and Democracy in Argentina', in *Business and Democracy in Latin America*, ed. Leigh A. Payne, Pittsburgh, University of Pittsburgh Press, 1995, pp. 3–48.

Acuña, Marcelo Luis, *Alfonsín y el poder económico: el fracaso de la concentración y los pactos corporativos entre 1983 y 1989*, Buenos Aires, Corregidor, 1995.

Azpiazu, Daniel, Miguel Khavisse and Eduardo M. Basualdo, *El nuevo poder económico*, Buenos Aires, Hyspamérica, 1986.

Barbero, María Inés and Susane Felder, 'Industriales italianos y asociaciones empresariales en la Argentina: el caso de la UIA, 1887–1930', *Estudios Migratorios Latinoamericanos* 6–7 (1987), pp. 163–77.

Brennan, James P., 'Industrialists and "Bolicheros": Business and the Peronist Populist Alliance, 1943–1976', in *Peronism and Argentina: Essays on the Democratic Transition*, eds James P. Brennan and Juan Carlos Torre, New York, Scholarly Resources, 1997.

Cornblit, Oscar, 'Inmigrantes y empresarios en la política argentina', *Desarrollo Económico* 6: 24 (1967), pp. 641–91.

Cúneo, Dardo, *Comportamiento y crisis de la clase empresarial*, Buenos Aires, Pleamar, 1967.

Freels, John William, *El sector industrial en la política nacional*, Buenos Aires, Editorial Universitaria de Buenos Aires, 1970.

Lewis, Colin M., 'Immigrant Entrepreneurs, Manufacturing and Industrial Policy in the Argentine, 1922–28', *Journal of Imperial and Commonwealth History* 16: 1 (1987), pp. 77–108.

Lindenboim, Javier, 'El empresariado industrial argentino y sus organizaciones gremiales entre 1930 y 1946', *Desarrollo Económico* 16: 62 (1976), pp. 163–201.

Manzetti, Luigi, 'The Evolution of Agricultural Interest Groups in Argentina', *Journal of Latin American Studies* 24 (1992), pp. 585–616.

Niosi, Jorge, *Los empresarios y el estado argentino, 1955–1969*, Buenos Aires, Siglo XXI, 1974.

Nun, José and Mario Lattuada, *El gobierno de Alfonsín y las corporaciones agrarias*, Buenos Aires, Ediciones Manantial, 1991.

Ostiguy, Pierre, *Los capitanes de la industria: grandes empresarios, política y economía en la Argentina de los años 80*, Buenos Aires, Legasa, 1990.

Palomino, Mirta L. de, *Tradición y poder: la Sociedad Rural Argentina, 1955–1983*, Buenos Aires, CISEA/Grupo Editor Latinoamericano, 1988.

Schvarzer, Jorge, *Empresarios del pasado: la Unión Industrial Argentina*, Buenos Aires, CISEA/Imago Mundi, 1991.

——, *La industria que supimos conseguir*, Buenos Aires, Planeta, 1996.

BRAZIL

Colin M. Lewis

General Works

Abreu, Marcelo de Paiva (ed.), *A ordem do progresso; cem anos de política economica republicana, 1889–1989*, Rio de Janeiro, Campus, 1989.

Baer, Werner, *The Brazilian Economy: Growth and Development*, 3rd edition, New York, Praeger 1986.

Bethell, Leslie (ed.), *Brazil: Empire and Republic*, Cambridge, Cambridge University Press, 1989.

Buescu, Mircea, *Brasil: problemas econômicas e experiência histórica*, Rio de Janeiro, Forense-Universitária, 1985.

Castro, Ana C., *As empresas extrangeiras no Brasil, 1860–1913*, Rio de Janeiro, Zaher, 1979.

Costa, Emilia Viotti da, *The Brazilian Empire: Myths and Histories*, Chicago, Chicago University Press, 1985.

Faoro, Raymundo de, *Os donos do poder: formação do patronato político brasileiro*, 2nd edition, Pôrto Alegre, Editorial Globo, 1975.

Fritsch, Winston, *External Constraints on Economic Policy in Brazil, 1889–1930*, London, Macmillan, 1988.

Furtado, Celso, *The Economic Growth of Brazil*, Berkeley, University of California Press, 1971.

Neuhaus, Paulo (ed.), *Economia brasileira: uma visão histórica*, Rio de Janeiro, Campus, 1980.

Topik, Steven, *The Political Economy of the Brazilian State, 1889–1930*, Austin, University of Texas Press, 1987.

Villela, Anibal V. and Suzigan, Wilson, *Política do govêrno e crescimento da economia brasileira*, Rio de Janeiro, IPEA/INPES, 1975.

Agriculture

Canabrava, Alice P., *O algodão em São Paulo, 1861–1875*, 2nd edition, São Paulo, T. A. Queiroz, 1984.

Dean, Warren, *Rio Claro: a Brazilian Plantation System, 1820–1920*, Stanford, Stanford University Press, 1976.

——, *Brazil and the Struggle for Rubber: a Study in Environmental History*, Cambridge, Cambridge University Press, 1987.

Eisenberg, Peter L., 'The Consequences of Modernization for Brazil's Sugar Plantations in the Nineteenth Century'. in *Land and Labour in Latin America: Essays in Agrarian Capitalism*, eds Kenneth Duncan and Ian Rutledge, Cambridge, Cambridge University Press, 1977, pp. 345–68.

——, *The Sugar Industry in Pernambuco: Modernization without Change, 1840–1910*, Berkeley, University of California Press, 1974.

Galloway, John H., 'The Sugar Industry of Pernambuco during the Nineteenth Century', *Annals of the Association of American Geographers* 58: 2 (1968), pp. 285–303.

Graham, Richard, *Britain and the Onset of Modernization in Brazil, 1850–1914*, Cambridge, Cambridge University Press, 1968.

Holloway, Thomas H., *Immigrants on the Land: Coffee and Society in São Paulo, 1886–1934*, Chapel Hill, NC., University of North Carolina Press, 1980.

Peláez, Carlos M. (ed.), *Essays on Coffee and Economic Development*, Rio de Janeiro, Instituto Brasileiro do Café, 1973.

Reis, Jaime, 'From *Bangué* to *Usina*: Social Aspects of Growth and Modernization in the Sugar Industry of Pernambuco, Brazil, 1850–1920' in *Land and Labour in Latin America: Essays in Agrarian Capitalism*, eds Kenneth Duncan and Ian Rutledge, Cambridge, Cambridge University Press, 1977, pp. 369–96.

Resor, Randolph R., 'Rubber in Brazil: Dominance and Collapse, 1876–1945', *Business History Review* 51 (1977), pp. 341–66.

Stein, Stanley J., *Vassouras: a Brazilian Coffee County, 1850–1900*, Cambridge, Mass., Harvard University Press, 1957.

Szmrecsányi, Tamás, *Pequena história da agricultura no Brasil*, São Paulo, Contexto, 1990.

Weinstein, Barbara, *The Amazon Rubber Boom, 1850–1920*, Stanford, Stanford University Press, 1983.

Banking, Investment, and Credit

Azevedo, Thales de and Lins, Vieira E. Q., *História do Banco da Bahia, 1858–1958*, Rio de Janeiro, J. Olimpio,1969.

Franco, Gustavo H. B., *Reforma monetária e instabilidade durante a transição republicana*, Rio de Janeiro, BNDES, 1983.

Goldsmith, Raymond W., *Brasil, 1840–1950: desenvolvimento financiero sob um século de inflação*, São Paulo, Banco Bamerindus do Brasil / Editores Harper & Row do Brasil, 1986.

Haber, Stephen, *The Efficiency Consequences of Institutional Change: Financial Market Regulation and Industrial Productivity Growth in Brazil, 1866–1934*, Cambridge, Mass., National Institute of Economic and Social Research, 1996.

Levy, María Bárbara, *História da Bolsa de Valores do Rio de Janeiro*, Rio de Janeiro, IBMEC, 1977.

——, 'El sector financiero y el desarrollo bancario en Rio de Janeiro, 1850–1888' in *La formación de los bancos centrales en España y America Latina: siglos XIX y XX*, eds Pedro Tedde y Carlos Marichal, 2 vols, Madrid, Banco de España, 1994, II.

Peláez, Carlos M., 'The Establishment of Banking Institutions in a Backward Economy', *Business History Review* 40 (1975), pp. 446–72.

—— and Wilson Suzigan, *História monetária do Brasil: analise da política, comportamento e instituções monetárias*, Rio de Janeiro, 1976.

Saes, Flávio A. Marquês de, *Crédito e bancos no desenvolvimento da economica paulista, 1850–1930*, São Paulo, Instituto de Pesquisas Econômicas, 1986.

Triner, Gail, 'The Formation of Modern Brazilian Banking, 1906–1930: Opportunities and Constraints Presented by the Public and Private Sectors', *Journal of Latin American Studies* 28 (1996), 49–74.

Versiani, Flávio R., 'Industrial Investment in an "Export" Economy: the Brazilian Experience before 1914', *Journal of Development Economics* 7 (1980), pp. 307–27.

Merchants and Trade

Greenhill, Robert G., 'The Brazilian Coffee Trade', in *Business Imperialism, 1840–1930: an Inquiry based on British Experience in Latin America*, ed. D. C. M. Platt, Oxford, Clarendon Press1977, pp. 198–230.

Sweigart, Joseph E., *Coffee Factorage and the Emergence of a Brazilian Capital Market, 1850–1888*, London, Garland, 1987.

Businessmen and Economic Interest Groups

Barros, Eudes, *A Associação Commercial no Império e na República*, Rio de Janeiro, 1975.

Birchal, Sérgio de O., 'Empresarios brasileiros: um estudo comparativo', *VII Seminario sobre Economia Mineiria*, Belo Horizonte, 1995, pp. 393–427.

Bresser Pereira, Luis C., *Empresários e administradores no Brasil*, São Paulo, 1974.

Cardoso, Fernando Henrique, *Empresario industrial e desenvolvimento econômico no Brasil*, São Paulo, Difusão Europeia do Livro, 1964.

Cardoso de Mello, Zelia M., *Metamorfoses da riqueza: São Paulo, 1845–1895*, São Paulo, Hucitec, 1990.

Diniz, Eli and Boschi, Renato R. (eds), *Empresariado nacional e estado no Brasil*, Rio de Janeiro, Forenze-Universitária, 1978.

Faria, Alberto de, *Mauá: Irenêo Evangelista de Souza, Barão e Visconde de Mauá, 1813–1889*, São Paulo, Companhia Editora Nacional, 1933.

Marchant, Anyda, *Viscount Mauá and the Empire of Brazil: a Biography of Irinêo Evangelista de Sousa, 1813–1889*, Berkeley, University of California Press, 1965.

Martins, José de Souza, *Empresário e empresa na biografia do Conde Matarazzo*, Rio de Janeiro, Instituto de Ciências Socais, 1967.

Ridings, Eugene, *Business Interest Groups in Nineteenth-Century Brazil*, Cambridge, Cambridge University Press, 1994.

Weinstein, Barbara, 'The Industrialists, the State and the Issues of Worker Training and Social Services in Brazil, 1930–50', *Hispanic American Historical Review* 70 (1990), pp. 379–404.

Slavery and the Labour Force

Cardoso, Fernando Henrique, *Capitalismo e escravidão no Brasil meridional*, São Paulo, Difusão Europeia do Livro,1962.

Conrad, Robert, 'The Planter Class and the Debate over Chinese Immigration to Brazil, 1850–1893', *International Migration Review* 9 (1975), pp. 41–55.

Eisenberg, Peter L., 'Escravo e proletario na história do Brasil', *Estudos Econômicos* 13:1 (1983), pp. 55–69.

Giroletti, Domingos A., *Fábrica: convento e disciplina*, Belo Horizonte, Imprensa Oficial do Estado de Minas Gerais, 1991.

Lamounier, M. Lúcia, *Da escravidão ao trabalho livre*, Campinas, Papirus, 1988.

Libby, Douglas C., *Transformação e trabalho em una economia escravista: Minas Gerais no século XIX*, São Paulo, Editorial Brasiliense, 1988.

Maram, Sheldon L., *Anarquistas, imigrantes e o movimento operário brasileiro*, Rio de Janeiro, Paz e Terra, 1979.

Pang, Eul-Soo, 'Modernization and Slavocracy in Nineteenth-Century Brazil', *Journal of Interdisciplinary History* 9 (1979), pp. 667–88.

Pena, Maria V. J., *Mulheres e trabalhadoras: presença feminina na constitução do sistema fabril*, Rio de Janeiro, Paz e Terra, 1981.

Pinheiro, Paulo S. and Michael Hall, *A clase operária no Brasil: docomentos, 1889–1930*, 2 vols, São Paulo, Alfa-Omega, 1979–1981.

Slenes, Robert W., *The Demography and Economics of Brazilian Slavery*, Ann Arbor, University Microfilms International, 1977.

Soares de Galliza, Diana, *O declínio da escravidão na Paraíba, 1850–1888*, João Pessoa, Editora Universitária/ UFPB, 1979.

Railways and Public Utilities

Duncan, Julian S. *Public and Private Operation of Railways in Brazil*, New York, Columbia University Press, 1932.

El-Kareh, Almir C., *Filha branca de mãe preta: a companhia da estrada de ferro D. Pedro II, 1855–1865*, Petrópolis, Vozes, 1982.

Giroletti, Domingos A. and Herminio, Antonio, *A companhia e a rodovia União e Indústria e o desenvolvimento de Juiz de Fora, 1850–1900*, Belo Horizonte, 1980.

Lewis, Colin M., *Public Policy and Private Initiative: Railway Building in São Paulo, 1860–1889*, London, Institute of Latin American Studies, 1991.

Mattoon, Robert H., 'Railroads, Coffee, and Big Business in São Paulo, Brazil', *Hispanic American Historical Review* 57 (1977), pp. 273–92.

Nogueira de Matos, Odilon, *Café e ferrovias: a evolução ferroviária de São Paulo e o desenvolvimento da cultura cafeeira*, 2nd edition, São Paulo, Alfa-Omega, 1974.

Saes, Flávio A. Marquês de, *As ferroviarias de São Paulo*, São Paulo, Hucitec, 1981.

——, *A grande emprêsa de serviços publicos na economia cafeeira*, São Paulo, Hucitec, 1986.

Industry

Cano, Wilson, *Raízes da concentração industrial em São Paulo*, Rio de Janeiro, Difel, 1977.

Dean, Warren, *The Industrialization of São Paulo, 1880–1945*, Austin, University of Texas Press, 1969.

Fishlow, Albert, 'Origins and Consequences of Import Substitution in Brazil', in *International Economics and Development: Essays in Honor of Raúl Prebisch*, ed. Luiz M. di Marco, New York, Academic Press, 1972, pp. 311–65.

Giroletti, Domingos A., *Industrializção de Juiz de Fora, 1850–1930*, Juiz de Fora, Universidade Federal de Juiz de Fora, 1988.

Hilton, Stanley J., 'Vargas and Brazilian Economic Development, 1930–1945: a Reappraisal of his Attitude towards Industrialization and Planning', *Journal of Economic History* 35 (1975), pp. 754–78.

Lewis, Colin M., 'Railways and Industrialization: Argentina and Brazil, 1870–1929', in *Latin America: Economic Imperialism and the State: the Political Economy of the External Connection from Independence to the Present*, eds Christopher Abel and Colin M. Lewis, London, Athlone, 1985, pp. 199–230.

Libby, Douglas C., 'Proto-Industrialization in a Slave Society: the Case of Minas Gerais', *Journal of Latin American Studies* 23 (1991), pp. 1–35.

Lobo, Eulália M. L., *História do Rio de Janeiro: do capital comercial ao capital industrial e financiero*, Rio de Janeiro, Instituto Brasileiro do Mercado de Capitais, 1978.

Luz, Nícia V., *A luta pela industrialização do Brasil, 1808 a 1930*, São Paulo, Difusão Europeia do Livro, 1975.

Reichel, Heloisa J., *A indústria têxtil do Rio Grande do Sul, 1910–1930*, Porto Alegre, 1980.

Silva, Sérgio, *Expansão cafeeira e origems da industria no Brasil*, São Paulo, Alfa-Omega, 1976.

Soares, Luis C., *A manufactura na formação econômica e social escravista no sudeste: um estudo das actividades manufactureieras na regão fluminense, 1840–1880*, Niteroi, 1980.

Stein, Stanley J., *The Brazilian Cotton Manufacture: textile enterprize in an underdeveloped area, 1850–1950*, Cambridge, Mass., Harvard University Press, 1957.

Suzigan, Wilson, *Indústria brasileira: origems e desenvelvimento*, São Paulo, Brasiliense, 1986.

Suzigan, Wilson and Tamás Szmrecsányi, 'Os investimentos estrangeiros no início da industralização no Brasil', in *História econômica da Primera República*, eds Sérgio S. Silva and Tamás Szmrecsányi, São Paulo, Hucitec, 1996, pp. 261–83.

Vaz, Alisson M., *Cia. Cedro e Cachoeira: história de uma empresa familiar, 1883–1987*, Belo Horizonte, 1990.

Versiani, Flávio R., 'Before the Depression: Brazilian Industry in the 1920s', in *Latin America in the 1930s: the Role of the Periphery in World Crisis*, ed. Rosemary Thorp, London, 1984, pp. 163–87.

Versiani, Flávio R. and Jose R. Mendonça de Barros (eds), *Formação econômica do Brasil: a experiência de industrialização*, São Paulo, Edição Saraiva, 1977.

Weid, Elisabeth von der and Ana M. Rodriques Bastos, *O fio da meada: estratégia de expansão de uma indústria têxtil – Companhia América Fabril*, Rio de Janeiro, FCRB/CNI, 1986.

Weinstein, Barbara, *For Social Peace in Brazil: Industrialists and the Remaking of the Working Class in São Paulo*, Chapel Hill, University of North Carolina Press, 1997.

Mining

Eakin, Marshall C., *British Enterprise in Brazil; the St. John d'el Rey Mining Company and the Morro Velho gold mine, 1830–1960*, Durham, NC, Duke University Press, 1989.

Libby, Douglas C., *Trabalho escravo e capital estrangeiro no Brasil: o caso de Morro Velho*, Belo Horizonte, Itatiaia, 1984.

CHILE

Luis Ortega

General

AA. VV., *Empresa Privada*, Valparaíso, Escuela de Negocios de Valparaíso, no date.

Aránguiz, Horacio, 'La situación de los trabajadores agrícolas en el siglo XIX', *Estudios de las Instituciones Políticas y Sociales*, 2 (1967), pp. 5–31.

Cademártori, José, *La economía chilena: un enfoque marxista*, Santiago, Editorial Universitaria, 1970.

Cariola, Carmen and Osvaldo Sunkel, *Un siglo de historia económica de Chile, 1830–1930: dos ensayos y una bibliografia*, Madrid, Instituto de Cooperación Iberoamericana, 1982.

Collier, Simon, 'The Historiography of the "Portalian" Period (1830–1891) in Chile', *Hispanic American Historical Review* 57 (1977), pp. 660–90.

Drake, Paul W., 'El impacto académico de los terremotos políticos: investigaciones de historia chilena en inglés, 1977–1983', *Alternativas* 2 (1983), pp. 56–78.

Ellsworth, P. T., *Chile: an economy in transition*, New York, Macmillan Co., 1945.

Encina, Francisco, *Nuestra inferioridad económica*, Santiago, 1911.

Estrada, Baldomero, 'Tesis sobre historia de Chile realizadas en Gran Bretaña, Estados Unidos y Francia', *Nueva Historia* (London) 8 (1983), pp. 251–75.

Góngora, Mario, *Ensayo crítico sobre la noción de Estado en Chile en los siglos XIX y XX*, Santiago, Ediciones La Ciudad, 1981.

Hurtado, Carlos, *Concentración de población y desarrollo económico: el caso chileno*, Santiago, Universidad de Chile, 1966.

Jobet, Julio César, *Ensayo crítico del desarrollo económico y social de Chile*, Santiago, Editorial Universitaria, 1955.

Lagos, Ricardo, *La concentración del poder económico*, Santiago, Editorial del Pacífico, 1960.

Mamalakis, Markos, *The Growth and Structure of the Chilean Economy: From Independence to Allende*, New Haven, Yale University Press, 1976.

Meller, Patricio, *Un siglo de economía política chilena (1890–1990)*, Santiago, 1996.

Montero, Cecilia, *La revolución empresarial chilena*, Santiago, 1997.

Muñoz, Oscar, *Los inesperados caminos de la modernización económica*, Santiago, 1995.

Pérez de Arce, Hermógenes (ed.), *Los Pioneros*, Santiago, Instituto de Estudios Generales, 1974.

Pinto, Aníbal, *Chile, un caso de desarrollo frustrado*, Santiago, 1958.

Ramos, Sergio, *Chile ¿una economía en transición?*, Santiago, Austral, 1973.

Ramírez, Hernán, *Antecedentes económicos de la Independencia de Chile*, Santiago, Editorial Universitaria, 1969.

——, *Historia del movimiento obrero en Chile: siglo XIX*, Santiago, Austral, 1956.

——, *Historia del imperialismo en Chile*, Santiago, Austral, 1960.

——, *Balmaceda y la contrarrevolución de 1891*, Santiago, Editorial Universitaria, 1969.

Salazar, Gabriel, 'El movimiento teórico sobre desarrollo y dependencia en Chile, 1950–1975', *Nueva Historia* (London) 4 (1982)

——, 'Empresariado popular e industrialización: la guerrilla de los mercaderes (Chile, 1830–1885)', *Proposiciones* 20 (1991), pp. 180–231.

Segall, Marcelo, *El desarrollo del capitalismo en Chile: cinco ensayos dialécticos*, Santiago, Editorial del Pacífico, 1953.

Silva, Fernando, 'Comerciantes, habilitadores y mineros: una aproximación al estudio de la mentalidad empresarial en los primeros años de Chile republicano (1817–1840)', in AA. VV, *Empresa Privada*, pp. 37–71.

——, 'Notas sobre la evolución empresarial chilena en el siglo XIX', in AA. VV, *Empresa Privada*, pp. 73–91.

Vargas, Juan and Gerardo Martínez, 'José Romás Ramos Font: una fortuna chilena del siglo XIX', *Historia* 18 (1982), pp. 355–92.

Vargas, Juan, *José Tomás Ramos Font: una fortuna chilena del siglo XIX*, Santiago, Ediciones de la Universidad Católica de Chile, 1988.

Vial, Gonzalo, *Historia de Chile (1891–1973)*, Santiago, Editorial Santillana, 1981.

——, 'Tradición y mentalidad industrial en Chile', in Ceppi, Sergio, et. al., *Chile: 100 años de industria (1883–1983)*, Santiago, Sociedad de Fomento Fabril, 1983.

Villalobos, Sergio, 'Sugerencias para un enfoque del siglo XIX', *Colección Estudios Cieplan* 12 (1984), pp. 9–36.

——, *Orígen y ascenso de la burguesía chilena*, Santiago, Editorial Universitaria, 1987.

Vitale, Luis, *Interpretación marxista de la historia de Chile*, 5 vols, various publishers, 1967–1982.

Zeitlin, Maurice, *The Civil Wars in Chile (or the bourgeois revolutions that never were)*, Princeton, Princeton University Press, 1984.

Merchants and Trade

Cavieres, Eduardo, 'Estructura y funcionamiento de las sociedades comerciales de Valparaíso durante el siglo XIX, 1820–1880', *Cuadernos de Historia* 4 (1984), pp. 61–86.

——, *Comercio chileno y comerciantes ingleses, 1820–1880: un ciclo de historia económica*, Valparaíso, Universidad Católica de Valparaíso, 1988.

Kirsch, Henry W. *Balmaceda y la burguesía nacional realidad o utopía*, Santiago, mimeo, 1970.

Mayo, John, 'Before the Nitrate Era: British Commission Houses and the Chilean Economy, 1851–1880', *Journal of Latin American Studies* 11 (1979), pp. 283–302.

Mayo, John, *British Merchants and Chilean Development, 1851–1886*, Boulder, Westview, 1987.

Agriculture

Ballesteros, Mario, 'Desarrollo agrícola chileno, 1910–1955', *Cuadernos de Economía* 2 (1965), pp. 153–76.

Baraona, Rafael, *et al.*, *Valle de Putaendo: estudio de estructura agraria*, Santiago, Universidad de Chile, 1961.

Bauer, Arnold J., 'Expansión económica en una sociedad tradicional: Chile central en el siglo XIX', *Historia* 9 (1970), pp. 137–232.

——, 'The Hacienda 'El Huique' in the Agrarian Structure of Nineteetnth-Century Chile', *Agricultural History*, 46 (1972), pp. 455–70.

——, *Chilean Rural Society: from the Spanish Conquest to 1930*, Cambridge, Cambridge University Press, 1975.

Bauer, Arnold J. and Anne H. Johnson 'Land and Labour in Rural Chile, 1850–1935', in *Land and Labour in Latin America: Essays on the Development of Agrarian Capitalism in the Nineteenth and Twentieth Centuries*, eds Kenneth Duncan y Ian Rutledge, Cambridge, Cambridge University Press, 1977; pp. 83–102.

Bengoa, José, *El poder y la subordinación: historia social de la agricultura chilena*, Santiago, Ediciones Sur, 1988.

Carrière, Jean, *Landowners and Politics in Chile: a Study of the Sociedad Nacional de Agricultura*, Amsterdam, CEDLA, 1980.

Hernández, Silvia, 'Transformaciones tecnológicas en la agricultura de Chile central: siglo XIX', *Cuadernos del Centro de Estudios Socioeconómicos* 3 (1966), pp. 103–39.

Izquierdo, Gonzalo, *Un estudio de las ideologías chilenas: la Sociedad Nacional de Agricultura en el siglo XIX*, Santiago, Universidad de Chile, 1968.

Kay, Cristóbal, 'The Development of the Chilean Hacienda System, 1850–1973', in *Land and Labour in Latin America: Essays on the Development of Agrarian Capitalism in the Nineteenth and Twentieth Centuries*, eds Kenneth Duncan and Ian Rutledge, Cambridge, Cambridge University Press, 1977, pp. 103–39.

Wright, Thomas C., *Landowners and Reform in Chile: the Sociedad Nacional de Agricultura, 1919–1940*, Urbana, University of Illinois Press, 1982.

Mining

General

Pederson, Leland R., *The Mining Industry of the Norte Chico, Chile*, Evanston, Northwestern Universty, 1966.

Pinto, Julio and Luis Ortega, *Expansión minera y desarrollo industrial: un caso de desarrollo asociado (Chile 1850–1914)*, Santiago, Universidad de Santiago de Chile, 1991.

Vayssière, Pierre, *Un siècle de capitalisme minier au Chili, 1830–1930*, París, Editions du Centre National de Recherches Scientifiques, 1980.

Copper

Culver, William W. and Cornel J. Reinhart, 'The Decline of a Mining Region and Mining Policy: Chilean Copper in the Nineteenth Century', in *Miners and Mining in the Americas*, eds Thomas Greaves y William W. Culver, Manchester, Manchester University Press, 1985, pp. 68–81.

——, 'Capitalist Dreams: Chile's Response to Nineteenth-Century World Copper Expansion', *Comparative Studies in Society and History* 31 (1989), pp. 722–44.

Mayo, John, 'Commerce, Credit and Control in Chilean Copper Mining before 1880', in *Miners and Mining in the Americas*, eds Thomas Greaves and William W. Culver, Manchester, Manchester University Press, 1985, pp. 29–46.

Nazer, Ricardo, *José Tomás Urmeneta: un empresario del siglo XIX*, Santiago, Dirección de Bibliotecas, Archivos y Museos, 1993.

Przeworski, Joanne Fox, *The Decline of the Copper Industry in Chile and the Entrance of North American Capital*, New York, New York University Press, 1980.

Reynolds, Clark W., 'Development Problems of an Export Economy: the Case of Copper and Chile', in *Essays on the Chilean Economy*, eds Markos J. Mamalakis and Clark W. Reynolds, Homewood, IL., Richard D. Irwin Inc., 1965, pp. 203–398.

Valenzuela, Luis, 'The Copper Smelting Company "Urmaneta y Errázuriz" of Chile: an Economic Profile', *The Americas* 53 (1996), pp. 235–72.

Volk, Steven S., 'Mine Owners, Money Lenders, and the State in Mid-Nineteenth Century Chile', *Hispanic American Historical Review* 73 (1993), pp. 67–98.

Nitrate

Bermúdez, Oscar, *Historia del salitre desde sus orígenes hasta la Guerra del Pacífico*, Santiago, Editorial Universitaria, 1963.

——, *Historia del salitre desde la Guerra del Pacífico a la revolución de 1891*, Santiago, Ediciones Pampa Desnuda, 1984.

Blakemore, Harold, *British Nitrates and Chilean Politics, 1886–1896: Balmaceda and North*, London, 1974.

Fernández, Manuel, 'El enclave salitrero y la economía chilena, 1880–1914', *Nueva Historia* (London) 3 (1981), pp. 2–42.

Mayo, John, 'La Compañía de Salitres de Antofagasta y la Guerra del Pacífico', *Historia* 14 (1979), pp. 71–102.

Monteon, Michael, *Chile in the Nitrate Era: the Evolution of Economic Dependence, 1880–1930*, Wisconsin, University of Wisconsin Press, 1982.

O'Brien, Thomas F., 'The Antofagasta Company: a Case Study of Peripheral Capitalism', *Hispanic American Historical Review* 60 (1980), pp. 1–31.

——, *The Nitrate Industry and Chile's Crucial Transition, 1879–1891*, New York, New York University Press, 1982.

Coal

Duncan, Roland E., 'Chilean Coal and British Steamers: the Origin of a South American Industry', *Mariner's Mirror* 60 (1975), pp. 271–81.

Ortega, Luis, 'The First Four Decades of the Chilean Coal Mining Industry', *Journal of Latin American Studies* 14 (1982), pp. 1–32 ...

——, *La industria del carbón de Chile, 1840–1880*, Santiago, Universidad de Santiago de Chile, 1988.

Transport and Communications

Blakemore, Harold, *From the Pacific to La Paz: the Antofagasta (Chili) and Bolivia Railway Company, 1888–1988*, London, Lester Crook, 1989.

Duncan, Roland E., 'William Wheelwright and Early Steam Navigation in the Pacific', *The Americas* 32: 2 (1975), pp. 257–81.

Johnson, J. J., *Pioneer Telegraphy in Chile, 1852–1876*, Stanford, Stanford University Press, 1948.

Oppenheimer, Robert B., 'National Capital and National Development: Financing Chile's Central Valley Railroads', *Business History Review* 56 (1982), pp. 54–75.

Véliz, Claudio, *Historia de la marina mercante*, Santiago, Editorial Universitaria, 1961.

Public Utilities

Jones, Linda, Charles Jones, and Robert Greenhill, 'Public Utility Companies', in *Business Imperialism, 1840–1930: an Inquiry based on British Experience in Latin America*, ed. D. C. M. Platt, Oxford, Clarendon Press, 1977, pp. 77–118.

Kinsbruner, Jay, 'Water for Valparaíso: a Case of Entrepreneurial Frustration', *Journal of Inter-American Studies* 10 (1968), pp. 635–61.

Industry

Bauer, Arnold J., 'Industry and the Missing Bourgeoisie: Consumption and Development in Chile, 1850–1950', *Hispanic American Historical Review* 70 (1990), pp. 227–53.

Carmagnani, Marcello, *Sviluppo Industriale e Sottosviluppo Economico. II caso cileno (1860–1920)*, Torino, Luigi Einaudi, 1971.

Ceppi, Sergio, et. al., *Chile: 100 años de industria (1883–1983)*, Santiago, Sociedad de Fomento Fabril, 1983.

Góngora, Alvaro, 'Políticas económicas, agentes económicos y desarrollo industrial en Chile hacia 1870–1900', in *Dimensión Histórica de Chile*, I.

Kirsch, Henry W., *Industrial Development in a Traditional Society: the Conflict Between Entrepreneurship and Modernization in Chile*, Gainesville, University Presses of Florida, 1977.

Lagos, Ricardo, *La industria en Chile: antecedentes estructurales*, Santiago, Universidad de Chile, 1966.

Marshall, Jorge, *La nueva interpretación de los orígenes de la industrialización chilena*, Santiago, 1988.

Muñoz, Oscar, *Crecimiento industrial de Chile, 1914–1965*, Santiago, Universidad de Chile, 1968.

——, *Proceso a la industrialización chilena*, Santiago, Universidad Católica de Chile, 1972.

——, *Estado e industrialización en el ciclo de expansión del salitre*, Santiago, Cieplan, 1977.

——, *Chile y su industrialización: pasado, crisis y opciones*, Santiago, Cieplan, 1986.

Ortega, Luis, 'Acerca de los orígenes de la industrialización chilena, 1860–1879', *Nueva Historia* (London) 2 (1981).

——, 'El proceso de industrialización en Chile, 1850–1930', *Historia* 26 (1991–1992), pp. 213–46.

——, 'Los límites de la industrialización en Chile, 1850–1880', *Revista de Historia Industrial* (Barcelona), 5 (1995), pp. 73–91.

Palma, Gabriel, 'Chile 1914–1935: de economía exportadora a sustitutiva de importaciones', *Nueva Historia* (London) 7 (1983), pp. 165–92.

Vargas, Juan, 'La Sociedad de Fomento Fabril, 1883–1920', *Historia* 13 (1976), pp. 5–53.

Public Sector Enterprise

Mamalakis, Markos, 'An Analysis of the Financial and Investment Activities of the Chilean Development Corporation, 1939–1974', *Journal of Development Studies* 5 (1977), pp. 118–37.

Ortega, Luis, et. al., *50 años de realizaciones: Corfo 1939–1989*, Santiago, Corporación de Fomento de la Producción, 1989.

COLOMBIA

Carlos Dávila

General

Bejarano, Jesús Antonio, *Historia económica y desarrollo: la historiografía económica sobre los siglos XIX y XX en Colombia*, Bogotá, Cerec, 1994.

Chandler, Alfred, *Strategy and Structure: Chapters in the History of the Industrial Enterprise*, Cambridge, MA, MIT Press, 1962.

——, *The Visible Hand: the Managerial Revolution in American Business*, Cambridge, MA, Harvard University Press, 1977.

——, *Scale and Scope: the Dynamics of Industrial Capitalism*, Cambridge, MA, Harvard University Press, 1990.

Colmenares, Germán, 'Estado de desarrollo e inserción social de la historia en Colombia', in Ministerio de Educación Nacional, Misión de Ciencia y Tecnología, *La conformación de comunidades científicas en Colombia*, 2 vols, Ministerio de Educación Nacional, Bogotá, 1990, II.

Dávila, Carlos, 'Dominant Classes and Elites in Economic Development: A Comparative Study of Eight Urban Centers in Colombia', PhD thesis, Northwestern University, 1976.

——, *Historia empresarial de Colombia: estudios, problemas y perspectivas*, Bogotá, Universidad de los Andes, 1991.

Fischer, Thomas, 'Desarrollo hacia afuera y guerras civiles en Colombia. 1850–1910', *Ibero-Amerikanisches Archiv* 23: 1/2, 1997, pp. 91–120.

——, 'Die vorlonen Dekaden: "Entwickung nach aussen und ausländische Geschäfte in Kolumbien, 1870–1914', doctoral thesis, Munich, 1997.

Johnson, David, 'Reyes González Hermanos: la formación de capital durante la regeneración en Colombia', *Boletín Cultural y Bibliográfico*, 23: 9 (1986), pp. 25–43.

Melo, Jorge Orlando, 'La literatura histórica en la última década', *Boletín Cultural y Bibiográfico*, 25: 15 (1988).

Ogliastri, Enrique and Carlos Dávila, 'Estructura de poder y desarrollo en once ciudades intermedias de Colombia', *Desarrollo y Sociedad* 12 (1983), pp. 149–88.

——, 'The Articulation of Power and Business Structures: A Study of Colombia', in *Inter-corporate Relations: the Structural Analysis of Business*, eds Mark Mizruchi and Michael Schwartz, Cambridge, Cambridge University Press, 1987, pp. 233–63.

Rodríguez, Oscar, ' La historiografía económica colombiana del siglo XIX', in *La historia al final del milenio: ensayos de historiografía colombiana y latinoamericana*, ed. Bernardo Tovar Zambrano, 2 vols, Bogotá, Editorial Universidad Nacional de Colombia (1994), pp. 187–250.

Safford, Frank, 'Commerce and Enterprise in Central Colombia, 1821–1870', PhD thesis, Columbia University, 1965.

——, 'Foreign and National Enterprise in Nineteenth-Century Colombia', *Business History Review* 39 (1965), pp. 503–26.

——, 'Empresarios nacionales y extranjeros en Colombia durante el siglo XIX', *Anuario Colombiano de Historia Social y de la Cultura* 4 (1969), pp. 87–111.

——, 'Significación de los antioqueños en el desarrollo económico colombiano: un examen crítico de las tesis de Everett Hagen', *Anuario Colombiano de Historia Social y de la Cultura* 3 (1967), pp. 49–69.

Tovar Zambrano, Bernardo (ed.), *La historia al final del milenio: ensayos de historiografía colombiana y latinoamericana*, 2 vols, Bogotá, Editorial Universidad Nacional de Colombia, 1994.

The Regional Business Elites and Entrepreneurship

Antioquia

Botero, Fabio, 'Las vías de comunicación y el transporte', in *Historia de Antioquia*, ed. Jorge Orlando Melo, Medellín, Suramericana de Seguros, 1988, pp. 287–298.

Botero, María Mercedes, 'Comercio y bancos, 1850–1923', in *Historia de Antioquia*, ed. Jorge Orlando Melo, Medellín, Suramericana de Seguros, 1988, pp. 243–248.

——, 'De cómo los comerciantes también se hicieron banqueros: el surgimiento de la élite bancaria en Antioquia, 1905–1923', *Revista Antioqueña de Economía y Desarrollo* 30 (1989), pp. 61–71

——, 'Antecedentes del desarrollo de la economía exportadora. Antioquia, 1850–1890', master's thesis, Universidad Nacional de Colombia, 1994.

——, 'Comercio, comerciantes y circuitos mercantiles: Antioquia, 1850–1930', mimeo, Bogotá, Universidad de los Andes, 1996.

Brew, Roger, 'The Economic Development of Antioquia from 1850 to 1920', DPhil thesis, University of Oxford, 1973.

——, *El desarrollo económico de Antioquia desde la independencia hasta 1920*, Bogotá, Banco de la República, 1977.

Casas, A. L., 'Medellín en el siglo XVIII: Valle de Mercaderes', *Revista Antioqueña de Economía y Desarrollo* 30 (1989), pp. 26–38.

Dávila, Carlos, 'Ciencia y ficción sobre el desarrollo de Antioquia: notas extemporáneas sobre el libro de Everett Hagen', *Revista Universidad Eafit- Temas Administrativos* 41 (1981), pp. 47–68.

——,'El empresariado antioqueño, 1760–1920: de las interpretaciones psicológicas a los estudios históricos', *Siglo XIX: Revista de Historia* (Monterrey, Mexico) 5: 9 (1990), pp. 11–74.

Echavarría, Juan Fernando, 'Bancos y finanzas en el siglo XX', in *Historia de Antioquia*, ed. Jorge Orlando Melo, Medellín, Suramericana de Seguros, 1988, pp. 257–266.

Fajardo, Luis H., *¿La moralidad protestante de los antioqueños? Estructura social y personalidad*, Cali, Universidad del Valle, 1968.

Fenalco-Antioquia, *El comercio en Medellín, 1900–1930*, Medellín, 1982.

Ferro Medina, Germán, *A lomo de mula*, Bogotá, Fondo Cultural Cafetero, 1994.

Hagen, Everett, *On the Theory of Social Change*, Homewood, Dorsey, 1962. The chapter on Antioquia was translated as *El cambio social en Colombia: el factor humano en el desarrollo*, Bogotá, Tercer Mundo, 1963.

Jaramillo, Roberto Luis, 'La colonización', in *Historia de Antioquia*, ed. Jorge Orlando Melo, Medellín, Suramericana de Seguros, 1988, pp. 177–208

Instituto de Estudios Colombianos, *Historia económica de Colombia: un debate en marcha*, Bogotá, Biblioteca Banco Popular, 1979.

Koonings, Kees y Menno Vellinga, 'Origen y consolidación de la burguesía industial en Antioquia', in *Burguesía e industria en América Latina y Europa Meridional*, eds Mario Cerutti and Menno Vellinga, Madrid, Alianza Editorial, 1989, pp. 55–104.

Londoño, Santiago, 'Así ha evolucionado el comercio interior en Antioquia, 1954–1980', *Revista Antioqueña de Economía y Desarrollo* 5 (1982).

López Toro, Alvaro, *Migración y cambio social en Antioquia durante el siglo XIX*, Bogotá, Universidad de los Andes, Cede, 1970.

Mayor Alberto, *Etica, trabajo y productividad en Antioquia: una interpretación sociológica sobre la influencia de la Escuela Nacional de Minas en la vida, costumbres e industrialización regionales*, Bogotá, Tercer Mundo, 1984.

——, 'La profesionalización de la administración de empresas en Colombia', in *En búsqueda de una administración para América Latina*, eds Rubén Darío Echeverry, Alain Chanlat y Carlos Dávila, Bogotá, Oveja Negra-Universidad del Valle, 1990, pp. 97–109.

——, 'Industrialización colombiana y diferenciación de las profesiones liberales', *Sol naciente*, 1 (1990), pp. 12–23.

McGreevey, William Paul, *An Economic History of Colombia, 1845–1930*, Cambridge, Cambridge University Press, 1971.

Melo, Jorge Orlando (ed.), *Historia de Antioquia*, Medellín, Suramericana de Seguros, 1988.

Ocampo, José Fernando, *Dominio de clase en la ciudad colombiana*, Medellín, Oveja Negra, 1972.

Palacios, Marco, 'El café en la vida de Antioquia', in *Los estudios regionales en Colombia: el caso de Antioquia*, eds Moisés Melo and Fundación Antioqueña para los Estudios Sociales (FAES), Medellín, Fondo Rotatorio de Publicaciones FAES, 1982.

Parsons, James, *Antioqueño Colonization in Western Colombia*, Berkeley, University of California Press, 1949.

——, *La colonización antioqueña en el occidente de Colombia*, Bogotá, Carlos Valencia Editores, 1979.

——, *Antioquia's Corridor to the Sea: an Historical Geography of the Settlement of Urabá*, Berkeley, University of California Press, 1967.

Poveda, Gabriel, 'Breve historia de la minería', in *Historia de Antioquia*, ed. Jorge Orlando Melo, Medellín, Suramericana de Seguros, 1988, pp. 209–24.

Restrepo, Manuel, 'La historia de la industria antioqueña 1880–1950', in *Historia de Antioquia*, ed. Jorge Orlando Melo, Medellín, Suramericana de Seguros, 1988, pp. 257–67.

Twinam, Ann, 'De judío a vasco: mitos étnicos y espíritu empresarial antioqueño', *Revista de Extensión Cultural* 9/10 (1981).

——, 'Comercio y comerciantes en Antioquia', in *Los estudios regionales en Colombia: el caso de Antioquia*, eds Moisés Melo and Fundación Antioqueña para los Estudios Sociales (FAES), Medellín, Fondo Rotatorio de Publicaciones FAES, 1982.

——, *Miners, Merchants and Farmers in Colonial Colombia*, Austin, University of Texas Press, 1982.

Uribe de Hincapié, María Teresa, 'Bajo el signo del mercurio: la influencia de los comerciantes de Medellín en la segunda mitad del siglo XIX', *Revista Antioqueña de Economía y Desarrollo* 30 (1989), pp. 30–50.

Zuleta, Luis Alberto, 'El comercio en el siglo XX', in *Historia de Antioquia*, ed. Jorge Orlando Melo, Medellín, Suramericana de Seguros, 1988, pp. 249–56.

Viejo Caldas

Christie, Keith, 'Oligarchy and Society in Old Caldas, Colombia', DPhil thesis, University of Oxford, 1974.

——, 'Antioqueño Colonization in Western Colombia: a Reappraisal', *Hispanic American Historical Review* 58 (1978), pp. 260–83.

——, *Oligarcas, campesinos y política en Colombia: aspectos de la historia socio-política de la frontera antioqueña*, Bogotá, Universidad Nacional de Colombia, 1986.

Junguito, Roberto and Diego Pizano, *Instituciones e instrumentos de política cafetera, 1927–1997*, Bogotá, 1997.

LeGrand, Catherine, *Frontier Expansion and Peasant Protest in Colombia, 1850–1936*, Albuquerque, University of New Mexico Press, 1986.

Restrepo, Ignacio, *50 años del desarrollo económico en Manizales*, Manizales, 1995.

Rodríguez, Manuel. *El empresario industrial del Viejo Caldas*, Bogotá, Universidad de los Andes, 1983.

Valencia, Albeiro, *Manizales en la dinámica colonizadora (1846–1930)*, Manizales, Fondo Editorial Universidad de Caldas, 1990.

——, *Colonización: fundaciones y conflictos agrarios*, Manizales, Imprenta Departamental de Caldas, 1994.

——, *Vida cotidiana y desarrollo regional en la colonización antioqueña*, Manizales, 1996.

The east of Colombia

Arenas, Emilio, *La casa del diablo. Los Puyana: tenencia de tierras y acumulación de capital en Santander*, Bucaramanga, Urbanas S. A., 1982.

Dávila, Carlos, *El empresariado colombiano: una perspectiva histórica*, Bogotá, Universidad Javeriana, 1986.

Fischer, Thomas, 'El caso Cerruti. Eine Fallstudie zum Verhältnis von staatlicher Autorität und ausländischer Einflussnahme in Kolumbien im ausgehenden 19. Hahrhundert', in *Lateinamerika zwischen Europa und den USA. Wechslewirkungen und Transformationprozesse in Politik, Ökonomie und Kultur*, eds Ute Guthunz and Thomas Fischer, Frankfurt-am-Main, Vervuert, 1995, pp. 57–85.

——, 'Craftsmen, Merchants, and Violence in Colombia: the *sucesos de Bucaramanga* of 1879', *Itinerario* 20: 1, 1996, pp. 79–99.

Garnica, Manuel, 'Guarapo, champaña y vino blanco', *Boletín Cultural y Bibliográfico* 29, 1992, pp. 41–59.

Gómez, Ramiro, 'Primera fábrica de hilados y tejidos del Socorro', *Boletín de Historia y Antigüedades* 68: 733, 1981, pp. 509–17.

Johnson, David, 'Social and Economic Change in Nineteenth Century Santander', PhD thesis, University of California at Berkeley, 1975.

——, 'Reyes González Hermanos: la formación del capital durante la regeneración en Colombia', *Boletín Cultural y Bibliográfico* 23: 9 (1986), pp. 25–43.

Pabón, Silvano, Carmen Ferreira *et al.*, *Ensayos de historia regional*, Bucaramanga, 1995.

Palacios, Marco, 'La fragmentación regional de las clases dominantes en Colombia: una perspectiva histórica', *Revista Mexicana de Sociología* 42 (1980), pp. 1663–89.

Raymond, Pierre, *Hacienda tradicional y aparcería*, Bucaramanga, 1997.

Rodríguez, Horacio, *La inmigración alemana al estado soberano de Santander en el siglo XIX: repercusiones socio-económicas de un proceso de transculturación*, Bogotá, 1968.

Safford, Frank, 'Empresarios ingenuos: organización, capital y conocimientos técnicos en las fábricas de Bogotá, 1814–1850', *Revista de Investigaciones* 1: 2 (1986).

Valle del Cauca

Collins, Charles, 'Formación de un sector de clase social: la burguesía en el Valle del Cauca durante los años treinta y cuarenta', *CIDSE* 14–15 (1985), pp. 35–90.

Colmenares, Germán, *Sociedad y economía en el Valle del Cauca: terratenientes, mineros y comerciantes, siglo XVIII*, Bogotá, Biblioteca Banco Popular, 1983.

Escorcia, José, *Sociedad y economía en el Valle del Cauca: desarrollo económico, social y político, 1800–1854*, Bogotá, Biblioteca Banco Popular, 1983.

Hyland, Richard P., 'A Fragile Prosperity: Credit and Agrarian Structure in the Cauca Valley, Colombia', *Hispanic American Historical Review* 62 (1982), pp. 369–406.

——, *Sociedad y economía en el Valle del Cauca: el crédito y la economía, 1851–1880*, Bogotá, Biblioteca Banco Popular, 1983.

Mejía, Eduardo and Armando Moncayo, 'La transición de hacienda a ingenio azucarero industrializado en el valle geográfico del río Cauca, 1850–1923', thesis, Universidad del Valle, 1986.

Rojas, José María, *Sociedad y economía en el Valle del Cauca: empresarios y tecnología en la formación del sector azucarero en Colombia, 1860–1980*, Bogotá, Biblioteca Banco Popular, 1983.

Valencia, Alonso, *Empresarios y políticos en el estado soberano del Cauca*, Cali, Universidad del Valle, 1993.

——, ed., *Historia del Gran Cauca: historia regional del Suroccidente colombiano*, Cali, 1994.

The Atlantic Coast

Bell, Gustavo, 'Regional Politics and the Formation of the National State: the Caribbean coast of Colombia in the first years of independence', DPhil thesis, Oxford, 1997.

Echeverri, Luz Elena, 'Los trabajadores de Marta Magdalena: una hacienda ganadera al suroeste del departamento de Bolívar, 1912–1956', thesis, Universidad Nacional de Colombia (Medellín), 1993.

Fawcett de Posada, Lousie, *Libaneses, palestinos y sirios en Colombia*, Barranquilla, Universidad del Atlántico, 1991.

Hakim Murad, Eduardo, *El murmullo de los cedros*, Bogotá, 1993.

Lotero, Amparo, 'Franceses en el Sinú: un *affaire* olvidado', *Boletín Cultural y Bibliográfico* 29 (1992), pp. 60–72.

Machado, Adalberto, 'La exportación de carnes y el Packing House de Coveñas, 1918–1938', thesis, Corporación Tecnológica de Bolívar, 1989.

Meisel, Adolfo, 'Los bancos de Cartagena', *Lecturas de Economía* 32–33 (1990), pp. 69–96.

Meisel, Adolfo and Posada, Eduardo (eds), *¿Por qué se disipó el dinamismo industrial de Barranquilla? Y otros ensayos de historia económica de la Costa Caribe*, Barranquilla, Ediciones Gobernación del Atlántico, 1993.

——, 'Bancos y banqueros de Barranquilla 1873–1925', in *¿Por qué se disipó el dinamismo industrial de Barranquilla? Y otros ensayos de historia económica de la Costa Caribe*, eds Adolfo

Meisel and Eduardo Posada, Barranquilla, Ediciones Gobernación del Atlántico, 1993, pp. 41–67.

Ocampo, Gloria Isabel, 'Hacienda, parentesco y mentalidad: la colonización antioqueña en el Sinú', *Revista Colombiana de Antropología* 36 (1986–1988), pp. 5–42.

Posada, Eduardo, 'La hacienda Berástegui: notas para una historia rural de la Costa Atlántica', *Huellas* 17 (1986), pp. 4–7.

——, *Una invitación a la historia de Barranquilla*, Bogotá, Cerec, 1987.

——, 'La ganadería en la Costa Atlántica colombiana, 1870–1950', *Coyuntura Económica* 8: 3 (1988).

——, *The Colombian Caribbean: a Regional History*, Oxford, Clarendon Press, 1996.

Restrepo, Jorge y Manuel Rodríguez, 'La actividad comercial y el grupo de comerciantes de Cartagena a fines del siglo XIX', *Estudios Sociales* 1 (1986), pp. 43–109.

Rodríguez, Manuel and Jorge Restrepo, 'Los empresarios extranjeros de Barranquilla, 1820–1900', *Desarrollo y Sociedad* 8 (1982), pp. 77–114.

Business Sectors

Foreign Trade

Ocampo, José Antonio, *Colombia y la economía mundial, 1830–1910*, Bogotá, Siglo XXI-Fedesarrollo, 1984.

——, 'Comerciantes, artesanos, y política económica, 1830–1880', *Boletín Cultural y Bibliográfico* 27, 1990, pp. 20–45.

Coffee

Acebedo, Carlos A., José Rodrigo Arango, Mario Alberto Gaviria and José A. Muñoz, 'La hacienda antioqueña: génesis y consolidación, 1880–1925', thesis, Universidad de Antioquia, 1987.

Arango, Mariano, *Café e industria, 1850–1930*, Bogotá, Carlos Valencia Editores, 1977.

Bergquist, Charles, *Coffee and Conflict in Colombia, 1886–1910*, Durham, NC., Duke University Press, 1978.

Beyer, Robert, 'The Colombian Coffee Industry: Origins and Major Trends, 1740–1940', PhD thesis, University of Minnesota, 1947.

Deas, Malcolm, 'A Colombian Coffee Estate: Santa Bárbara, Cundinamarca, 1870–1912', in *Land and Labour in Latin America: Essays on the Development of Agrarian Capitalism in the Nineteenth and Twentieth Centuries*, eds Kenneth Duncan and Ian Rutledge, Cambridge, Cambridge University Press, 1977, pp. 269–98.

Jiménez, Michael, '"Traveling Far in Grandfather's Car". The Life Cycle of Central Colombian Coffee Estates: the Case of Viota, Cundinamarca (1900–30)', *Hispanic American Historical Review* 69 (1989), pp. 185–219.

Machado, Absalón, *El café: de la aparcería al capitalismo*, Bogotá, Punta de Lanza, 1977.

Marulanda, Elsy, *Colonización y conflicto: las lecciones del Sumapaz*, Bogotá, Tercer Mundo, 1991.

Palacios, Marco, *Coffee in Colombia, 1850–1970: an Economic, Social and Political History*, Cambridge, Cambridge University Press, 1980.

Rivas, Medardo, *Los trabajadores de tierra caliente*, Bogotá, Biblioteca de Cultura Popular, 1946.

Tobacco, Quinine, and Indigo

Alarcón, Francisco and Daniel Arias, 'La producción y comercialización del añil en Colombia, 1850–1880', *Anuario Colombiano de Historia Social y de la Cultura* 15 (1987), pp. 165–209.

Bejarano, Jesús A. and Orlando Pulido, *El tabaco en una economía regional: Ambalema, siglos XVIII y XIX*, Bogotá, Editorial Universidad Nacional de Colombia, 1986.

Harrison, John, 'The Colombian Tobacco Industry from Government Monopoly to Free Trade, 1778–1849', PhD thesis, University of California, Berkeley, 1951.

Sandoval, Yesid and Camilo Echandía, 'La historia de la quina desde una perspectiva regional, Colombia, 1850–1882', *Anuario Colombiano de Historia Social y de la Cultura* 13–14 (1986), pp. 153–87.

Sierra, Luis F., *El tabaco en la economía colombiana del siglo XIX*, Bogotá, Universidad Nacional de Colombia, 1971.

Bananas, Rubber and Cotton

Botero, Fernando and Alvaro Guzmán, 'El enclave agrícola en la zona bananera de Santa Marta', *Cuadernos Colombianos* 3: 11 (1977).

Brugardt, Maurice, 'The United Fruit Company in Colombia', in *American Business History: Case Studies*, eds Henry Dethloff and Joseph Pusateri, Arlington Heights, H. Davidson, 1990.

Bucheli, Marcelo, *Empresas multinacionales y enclaves agrícolas: el caso de la United Fruit en Magdalena y Urabá (1948–1968)*, Bogotá, Universidad de los Andes, 1994.

——, 'United Fruit in Colombia: impact of labor relations and governmental regulations on its operations, 1948–1968', *Essays in Economic and Business History* 17, 1997, pp. 65–84.

Gómez, Augusto, 'El ciclo del caucho, 1850–1932', in *Colombia Amazónica*, Bogotá, Universidad Nacional de Colombia, 1988, pp. 183–212.

Gómez, Augusto, Ana Lesmes, and Claudia Rocha, *Caucherías y conflicto colombo-peruano: testimonios, 1904–1934*, Bogotá, Disloque, 1995.

LeGrand, Catherine, 'Campesinos y asalariados en la zona bananera de Santa Marta: 1900–1935', *Anuario de Historia Social y de la Cultura* 11 (1983).

——, 'El conflicto de las bananeras', in *Nueva Historia de Colombia*, ed. Jorge O. Melo, Bogotá, Planeta, 1989, III.

Pineda, Roberto, *Ethnohistoria de las caucherías del Putumayo entre 1880 y 1932*, Bogotá, 1993.

Pineda, Roberto, and Beatriz Alzate, eds, *Pasado y presente del Amazonas: su historia económica y social*, Bogotá, 1993.

Reyes, Rafael. *Memorias 1850–1885*, Bogotá, Fondo Cultural Cafetero, 1986.

Soler, Yesid and Fabio Prieto, *Bonanza y crisis del oro blanco, 1960–1980*, Bogotá, Editográficas, 1982.

Villegas, Jorge and Fernando Botero, 'Putumayo: indígenas, caucho y sangre', *Cuadernos Colombianos* 3: 12 (1979), pp. 529–65.

White, Judith, *Historia de una ignominia*, Bogotá, Presencia, 1978.

Mining and Natural Resources

Dávila, Carlos, 'Negocios y empresas británicas en Colombia, 1820–1940', mimeo, 1990.

De la Pedraja, René, *Energy Politics in Colombia*, Boulder, Colorado, Westview Press, 1989.

——, *Historia de la energía en Colombia*, Bogotá, El Ancora, 1985.

Fischer, Thomas, 'Empresas extranjeras en el sector del oro y de plata en Colombia, 1870–1914: la *free-standing company* como modelo aplicado por inversionistas extranjeros', *Boletín Cultural y Bibliográfico* 39, 1995, pp. 60–84.

Isaza, José, and Luis Salcedo, *Sucedió en la Costa Atlántica: los albores de la industria petrolera en Colombia*, Bogotá, Ancora, 1993.

Kline, Harvey F., 'The Coal of El Cerrejón: an historical analysis of major Colombian policy decisions and MNC activities', *Inter-American Economic Affairs* 35, 1981, pp. 69–90.

——, *The Coal of El Cerrejón: Dependent Bargaining and Colombian Policy-Making*, University park, Pennsylvania State University Press, 1987.

Mercedes Botero, María, 'Los laboratorios de fundición y ensaye y su papel en el comercio del oro: Antioquia, 1850–1910', *Historia Crítica* 14, 1997, pp. 53–58.

Molina, Luis F., and Ociel Castaño, 'Titiribí y la empresa minera del Zancudo, 1750–1930', thesis, Universidad de Antioquia, 1988.

Poveda, Gabriel, *Minas y mineros de Antioquia*, Bogotá, Banco de la República, 1984.

Randall, James S., *The Diplomacy of Modernization: Colombian-American Relations 1920–1940*, Toronto, University of Toronto Press, 1977.

Restrepo, Vicente, *Estudio sobre las minas de oro y plata en Colombia*, Medellín, FAES, 1979.

Rippy, J. Fred, *The Capitalists and Colombia*, New York, Vanguard Press, 1940.

——, 'British Investments in Colombian Mines', *Inter-American Economic Affairs* 7: 3 (1953), pp. 65–72.

Villegas, Jorge, *Petróleo, oligarquía e imperio*, Bogotá, Ediciones Ese, 1968.

Transport

Arango, Mario et al., *Comunicaciones y correos en la historia de Colombia y de Antioquia*, Bogotá, Gente Nueva, 1996.

Ardila García, Efraím, *Camilo Daza, un hombre que nació para volar*, Bucaramanga, Biblioteca Academia de Historia de Santander, 1989.

Arguelles, Mariano, *La carretera al mar, 1926–1946*, Cali, Imprenta Departamental, 1946.

Arias, Gustavo, *La mula de acero*, Bogotá, Carlos Valencia Editores, 1986.

Arias, Jorge, 'Un momento estelar de la ingeniería mecánica en Colombia: los diseños de locomotoras de P. C. Dewhurst', *Boletín Cultural y Bibliográfico* 26: 21 (1989), pp. 53–72.

Barnhart, Donald, 'Colombian Transportation Problems and Policies, 1923–1948', PhD thesis, University of Chicago, 1953.

——,'Colombian Transport and the Reforms of 1931: an Evaluation', *Hispanic American Historical Review* 38 (1958), pp. 1–24.

Bell, Gustavo, 'El Canal del Dique 1810–1940: el viacrucis de Cartagena', *Boletín Cultural y Bibliográfico* 26: 21 (1989), pp. 15–23.

Betancur, Belisario, and Conrado Zuluaga, *El tren y sus gentes: los ferrocarriles en Colombia*, Bogotá, Navegante / Bancafé, 1995.

Davies, R. E. G., *Airlines of Latin America*, Washington, Smithsonian Institution, 1984.

Echavarría, Guillermo, *De la mula al avión*, Medellín, 1989.

García. Miguel, *Ernesto Cortissoz, conquistador de utopías*, Bogotá, 1994.

Gilmore, Robert L. and John P. Harrison, 'Juan Bernardo Elbers and the Introduction of Steam Navigation in the Magdalena River', *Hispanic American Historical Review* 28 (1948), pp. 335–59.

Hoffman, Theodore H., 'A History of Railway Concessions and Railway Development Policy in Colombia to 1943', PhD thesis, American University, 1947.

Horna, Hernán, 'Francisco Javier Cisneros: a Pioneer in Transportation and Economic Development in Colombia', PhD thesis, Vanderbilt University, 1970.

——, 'La variedad de las actividades de Francisco Javier Cisneros', *Boletín de Historia y Antiguedades* 57 (1970), pp. 195–212.

——, 'Francisco Javier Cisneros: a Pioneer in Transportation and Economic Development in Latin America, 1857–1898', *The Americas* 30: 1 (1973), pp. 54–82.

—— 'Transportation, Modernization and Entrepreneurship in Nineteenth-Century Colombia', *Journal of Latin American Studies* 14 (1982), pp. 33–53.

——, *Transport Modernization and Entrepreneurship in Nineteenth Century Colombia: Cisneros & Friends*, Uppsala, Actas Universitatis Upsaliensis, 1992.

Junguito, Andrea, 'Historia económica del ferrocarril del norte', *Historia Crítica* 14 (1997), pp. 129–46.

Mejía, Carlos, 'Innovaciones tecnológicas y ferrocarriles', in *Cambio técnico, empleo y trabajo en Colombia: aportes a los estudios laborales en el VIII Congreso de Sociología*, eds, Rainer Dombois and Carme López, Bogotá, 1993, pp. 187–98.

Montaña, Antonio, *A todo vapor*, Bogotá, Fondo Cultural Cafetero, 1996.

Neal, James H., 'The Pacific Age Comes to Colombia: The Construction of the Cali-Buenaventura Route, 1854–1882', PhD thesis, Vanderbilt University, 1971.

Nichols, Theodore, 'The Caribbean Gateway to Colombia: Cartagena, Santa Marta and Barranquilla and their Connections with the Interior, 1820–1940', PhD thesis, University of California, Berkeley, 1951.

——, 'The Rise of Barranquilla, *Hispanic American Historical Review* 34 (1954), pp. 158–74.

——, 'Cartagena and the Dique: a Problem in Transportation', *Journal of Transport History* 2 (1955), pp. 22–34.

Ortega, Alfredo, *Ferrocarriles colombianos: resumen histórico*, Bogotá, Biblioteca de Historia Nacional, 1920.

——, *Ferrocarriles colombianos: la última experiencia ferroviaria del país, 1920–1932*, Bogotá, Biblioteca de Historia Nacional, 1932.

Patiño, Germán, 'C. H. Simmonds y los comienzos de la navegación a vapor en el alto Cauca', *Boletín Cultural y Bibliográfico* 26: 21 (1989), pp. 35–52.

Posada, Eduardo, 'Bongos, champanes y vapores en la navegación fluvial y colombiana en el siglo XIX', *Boletín Cultural y Bibliográfico* 26:21 (1989), pp. 3–14.

Poveda, Gabriel, *Antioquia y el Ferrocarril de Antioquia*, Medellín, Gráficas Vallejo, 1974.

——, 'Los ferrocarriles y la ingeniería', primera parte, *Revista Universidad de Antioquia*, 53: 206 (1986), pp. 4–35.

——, 'Los ferrocarriles y la ingeniería', segunda parte, *Revista Universidad de Antioquia*, 54: 207 (1987) 53–70.

Rippy, J. Fred, 'The Dawn of the Railway Era in Colombia', *Hispanic American Historical Review* 23 (1943), pp. 650–63.

Solano, Sergio Paolo, 'Comercio, transporte y sociedad en Barranquilla, en la primera mitad del siglo XIX', *Boletín Cultural y Bibliográfico* 26: 21 (1989), pp. 24–34.

Tisnés, Roberto and Heriberto Zapata, *El ferrocarril de Antioquia: historia de una empresa heroica*, Medellín, Imprenta Departamental, 1980.

Toro, Constanza, 'Inversión privada en servicios públicos: el caso del alumbrado eléctrico de Bogotá y Medellín, 1889–1918', *Lecturas de Economía*, 15 (1984).

Zambrano, Fabio, 'La navegación a vapor por el río Magdalena', *Anuario Colombiano de Historia Social y de la Cultura* 9 (1979), pp. 63–75.

Industry

Arroyo, Jairo, 'Empresarios y empresas en Cali, 1920–1930', thesis, Universidad del Valle, 1987.

——, 'Negociantes y comerciantes en Cali a comienzos del siglo XX', *Revista Cámara de comercio de Buga* 3 (1994), pp. 5–40.

——, 'La modernización de Cali a comienzos del siglo XX', *Desarrollo Económico y Regional* 3 (1995), pp. 15–50.

Berry, Albert, 'A Descriptive History of Colombian Industrial Development in the XXth Century', Fedesarrollo, mimeo, 1979.

Botero, Fernando, *La industrialización en Antioquia: génesis y consolidación, 1900–1930*, Medellín, Universidad de Antioquia, 1984.

——, 'Le processus d'industrialisation en Colombie: le cas de Medellín, 1900–1986', thèse du troisième cicle, Paris, 1986.

——, *Medellín, 1890–1950: historia urbana y juego de intereses*, Medellín, 1996.

Brew, R. J., 'The Birth of the Textile Industry in Western Colombia', *Textile History* 8 (1977), pp. 131–49.

Conde, Jorge E. 'La industria en Barranquilla durante el siglo XIX', *Boletín Cultural y Bibliográfico* 28: 26 (1991), pp. 41–56.

De la Pedraja, René, *Fedemetal y la industrialización en Colombia*, Bogotá, Fedemetal, 1986.

Echavarría, Enrique, *Historia de los textiles en Antioquia*, Medellín, Bedout, 1943.

Echavarría, Juan José, 'External Shocks and Industrialization: Colombia, 1920–1950', mimeo, University of Oxford, 1990.

——, 'En la industrialización se ha sobreestimado el aporte antioqueño', *Revista Antioqueña de Economía y Desarrollo* 30 (1989), pp. 81–96.

Londoño, Carlos, *Origen y desarrollo de la industria textil en Colombia y Antioquia*, Medellín, Universidad de Antioquia, 1983.

Lopera, María Teresa, *El desarrollo de la industria metalúrgica colombiana hasta 1970*, Medellín, Universidad de Antioquia, 1983.

López, Hugo, 'El desarrollo histórico de la industria en Antioquia: el período de la consolidación', in *Los estudios regionales en Colombia: el caso de Antioquia*, eds Moisés Melo and Fundación Antioqueña para los Estudios Sociales (FAES), Medellín, Fondo Rotatorio de Publicaciones FAES, 1982, pp. 187–210.

Machler, Tatiana, 'La ferrería de Pacho: una ventana de aproximación', *Cuadernos de Economía* 6: 7 (1984).

Mayor, Alberto, 'Historia de la industria colombiana, 1886–1930', in *Nueva Historia de Colombia*, ed. Jorge O. Melo, Bogotá, Planeta, 1989, V, pp. 313–32

——, 'Historia de la industria colombiana, 1930–1960', in *Nueva Historia de Colombia*, ed. Jorge O. Melo, Bogotá, Planeta, 1989, V, 333–56.

Meisel, Adolfo, '¿Por qué se disipó el desarrollo industrial de Barranquilla?', in *¿Por qué se disipó el dinamismo industrial de Barranquilla? Y otros ensayos de historia económica de la Costa Caribe*, eds Adolfo Meisel and Eduardo Posada, Barranquilla, Ediciones Gobernación del Atlántico, 1993, pp. 9–40.

Montenegro, Santiago, 'La industria textil en Colombia, 1900–1945', *Desarrollo y Sociedad* 8 (1982).

——, 'La política arancelaria en la primera fase de la industrialización 1910–1945', in *Crisis mundial, protección e industrialización*, eds José Antonio Ocampo and Santiago Montenegro, Bogotá, Cerec, 1984, pp. 295–342.

——, 'Breve historia de los principales textileros, 1900–1945', *Revista Universidad Nacional de Colombia* (Medellín), 12 (1989).

Ocampo, José Antonio, 'Librecambio y proteccionismo en el siglo XIX', in *Crisis mundial, protección e industrialización*, eds José Antonio Ocampo and Santiago Montenegro, Bogotá, Cerec, 1984, pp. 235–95.

Ordóñez, Luis A., *Industrias y empresarios pioneros: Cali 1910–1945*, Cali, Universidad del Valle, 1995.

Ospina Vásquez, Luis, *Industria y protección en Colombia, 1810–1930*, Bogotá, Editorial Santa Fé, 1955.

Pallares, Zoilo, 'Apreciaciones preliminares sobre el origen de los empresarios en Bogotá', in Icfes, *Memoria: IV Congreso Nacional de Investigadores en Administración de Empresas*, Bogotá, Icfes, 1984, pp. 231–50.

Poveda, Gabriel, 'Antecedentes y desarrollo de la industria en Colombia', *Revista Trimestral de la Andi* 4 (1967), pp. 3–23.

——, 'Historia de la industria en Colombia', *Revista Trimestral de la Andi* 11 (1970), pp. 1–98.

——, *Políticas económicas, desarrollo industrial y tecnología en Colombia, 1925–1950*, Bogotá, Colciencias, 1979.

Solano, Sergio P. and Jorge E. Conde, *Elite empresarial y desarrollo industrial en Barranquilla, 1875–1930*, Barranquilla, Ediciones Uniatlántico, 1993.

Valero, Edgar, 'La ferrería de Pacho: del empresario ingenuo al capitalismo', thesis, Universidad Nacional de Colombia, 1989.

Company History

Arango, Luz Gabriela, *Mujer, religión e industria: Fabricato 1923–1982*, Medellín, Editorial Universidad de Antioquia-Universidad Externado de Colombia, 1991.

Banco de la República, *El Banco de la República: antecedentes, evolución y estructura*, Bogotá, Editorial Banco de la República, 1990.

Botero, María Mercedes, 'El Banco de Antioquia y el Banco de Sucre 1872–1920', in *Ensayos de historia monetaria y bancaria de Colombia*, ed. Fabio Sánchez, Bogotá, Tercer Mundo-Fedesarrollo-Asobancaria, 1994, pp. 199–228.

——, 'Los bancos locales en el siglo XIX: el caso del Banco de Oriente en Antioquia, 1883–1887', *Boletín Cultural y Bibliográfico* 25: 17 (1988), 76–93.

Cementos Caribe, *Cementos del Caribe S. A. 50 años de historia*, Barranquilla, 1994.

Dávila, Carlos, *et al.*, 'La CAR, 25 años en el desarrollo regional, 1960–1985', mimeo, Bogotá, Universidad Javeriana, 1987.

——, 'El desarrollo de la Corporación Social de Ahorro y Vivienda Colmena, 1974–1994, mimeo, Bogotá, Universidad de los Andes, 1998.

Eslava, Carlos (with the collaboration of Germán Mejía, Juan C. Eastman and Augusto Gómez), *El Banco de Bogotá: 114 años en la historia de Colombia*, Bogotá, OP Gráficas, 1984.

Fundación Antioqueña para los Estudios Sociales, *Banco Industrial Colombiano, 1945–1995*, Medellín, 1995.

Jaramillo, Roberto et al., *Compañía Suramericana de Seguros, 1944–1994*, Medellín, 1994.

Junguito, Roberto, 'Historia económica de Bavaria', Bogotá, mimeo, 1980.

Londoño, Rocío and Gabriel Restrepo, *Diez historias de vida: las 'Marías'*, Bogotá, Fundación Social, 1995.

Londoño, Santiago, *Horizontes del futuro: Compañía Nacional de Chocolates, 75 años*, Medellín, 1995.

Meisel, Adolfo, Alejandro López and Francisco Ruiz (eds), *Kemmerer y el Banco de la República: diarios y documentos*, Bogotá, Banco de la República, 1994.

Ogliastri, Enrique, *Cien años de Cerveza Bavaria*, Bogotá, Universidad de los Andes, 1990.

Ospina, E. Livardo, *Una vida, una lucha, una victoria: monografía histórica de las empresas de servicios públicos de Medellín*, Medellín, Empresas Públicas de Medellín, 1966.

——, *De la peña a las alturas: crónica de la Compañía de Cementos Argos en el cincuencentenario de su fundación*, Medellín, Compañía de Cementos Argos, 1984.

——, *Los hilos perfectos: crónica de Fabricato en sus 70 años*, Medelín, Fabricato, 1990.

Piedrahita, Francisco, *Bolsa de Medellín S. A., 25 años, 1961–1986*, Medellín, Bolsa de Medellín, 1986.

Posada, Antonio and Jeanne de Posada, *La CVC: un reto al subdesarrollo y al tradicionalismo*, Bogotá, Tercer Mundo, 1966.

Poveda, Gabriel, *Simesa: medio siglo de siderurgia*, Medellín, Editorial Colina, 1988.

Romero, Carmen A., 'La Regeneración y el Banco Nacional', *Boletín Cultural y Bibliográfico*, 28: 26 (1991), pp. 27–40

——, 'La banca privada en Bogotá: 1870–1922', in *Ensayos de historia monetaria y bancaria de Colombia*, ed. Fabio Sánchez, Bogotá, Tercer Mundo-Fedesarrollo-Asobancaria, 1994, pp. 267–304.

Sowell, David, 'La Caja de Ahorros de Bogotá, 1846–1865: Artisans, Credit, Development, and Savings in Early National Colombia', *Hispanic American Historical Review* 73 (1993), 615–38.

The History of Entrepreneurs

Burgos, Remberto, *El general Burgos*, Bogotá, 1965.

Deas, Malcolm, *Vida y opinión de Mr William Wills*, Bogotá, 1996.

Eder, Phanor, *Santiago M. Eder: recuerdos de su vida y acotaciones para la historia económica del Valle del Cauca*, Bogotá, Antares, 1959.

Mayor, Alberto, 'Alejandro López: padre de la administración científica en Colombia', in Icfes, *Simposio la investigación sobre el empresariado colombiano: estado actual y perspectivas*, Bogotá, Icfes, 1987, pp. 11–103.

Mejía, Hernán, *Don Gonzalo Mejía: 50 años de Antioquia*, Bogotá, 1984.

Molina, Luis F., 'El caso de don Leocadio María Arango', *Revista Antioqueña de Economía y Desarrollo* 32: 2 (1990), pp. 60–70.

——, '"El viejo Mainero": actividad empresarial de Juan Bautista Mainero y Trucco en Bolívar, Chocó, Antioquia, y Cundinamarca, 1860–1918', *Boletín Cultural y Bibliográfico* 25: 17 (1988), pp. 3–29.

—— and Omar Castaño, 'El "burro de oro": Carlos Coroliano Amador, empresario antioqueño del siglo XIX', *Boletín Cultural y Bibliográfico* 24 (1988), pp. 3–27.

Posada, Eduardo, 'Karl C. Parrish, un empresario colombiano en los años veinte', *Boletín Cultural y Bibliográfico* 23: 8 (1986), pp. 3–20.

Ramírez, Ernesto, 'La construcción del poder económico: la familia Ospina, 1850–1960', *Innovar* 8 (1996), pp. 133–55.

Ramos, Oscar G., *A la conquista del azúcar: Ingenio Riopaila S. A. y Central Castilla S. A. en homenaje a su fundador Hernando Caicedo*, Cali, Impresora Feriva, 1990.

Restrepo, Jorge, *Retrato de un patriarca antioqueño: Pedro Antonio Restrepo Escovar, 1815–1899*, Bogotá, 1992.

Restrepo, Marco, *El rey de la leña*, Buenos Aires, 1958.

Solano, Sergio P., 'Familia empresarial y desarrollo industrial en el Caribe colombiano: el caso de la fábrica de tejidos Obregón', *Historia y Cultura* 1: 1 (1993), pp. 35–62.

Valencia, Alonso, 'Centu per centu, moderata ganacia: Ernesto Cerutti, un comerciante italiano en el estado soberano del Cauca', *Boletín Cultural y Bibliográfico* 25: 17 (1988), pp. 55–75.

Miscellaneous

Bejarano, Jesús A., *Economía y poder: la SAC y el desarrollo agropecuario colombiano, 1871–1974*, Bogotá, Sociedad de Agricultores de Colombia y Centro Estudios de la Realidad Colombiana, 1985.

Botero, Fernando, *Andi: cincuenta años, 1944–1994*, Medellín, Asociación Nacional de Industriales, 1994.

Gracia, Edgar at al., *Historia de la contaduría pública en Colombia, siglo XX*, Bogotá, Fundación Universidad Central, 1994.

Hartlyn, Jonathan, 'Producers' Associations, the Political Regime, and Policy Processes in Contemporary Colombia', *Latin American Research Review* 20: 3 (1985), pp. 111–38.

Junguito, Roberto, and Diego Pizano, eds, *Instituciones e instrumentos de política cafetera en Colombia*, Bogotá, 1997.

Koffman, B. E., 'The National Federation of Coffee-Growers of Colombia', PhD thesis, University of Virginia, 1969.

Molina, Luis F., 'Cámara de Comercio de Medellín: la voz fuerte de Antioquia', *Revista Antioqueña de Economía y Desarrollo* 30 (1989), pp. 13–25.

Murray, Pamela, 'Forging a Technocratic Elite in Colombia: A History of the Escuela Nacional de Minas de Medellín, 1887–1970', PhD thesis, Tulane University, 1990.

——, 'Engineering Development: Colombia's National School of Mines, 1887–1930', *Hispanic American Historical Review* 74 (1994), pp. 63–82.

——, *Dreams of Development: Colombia's National School of Mines and its engineers, 1887–1930*, Birmingham, University of Alabama Press, 1997.

Pallares, Zoilo and Alberto Vargas, 'Historia de un gremio: la Asociación Colombiana Popular de Industriales, Acopi, 1951–1986', Bogotá, mimeo, 1988.

Restrepo, Gloria Arango de, *Idea para el porvenir: treinta años del IDEA*, Medellín, 1994.

Rodríguez, Juan Camilo, *Historia de la Cámara de Comercio de Bogotá, 1878–1995*, Bogotá, Universidad Externado de Colombia, 1995.

Rodríguez, Oscar, 'Interés gremial y regulación estatal: la formación de la Federación Nacional de Comerciantes, 1945–1970', *Anuario Colombiano de Historia Social y de la Cultura* 23 (1996), pp. 171–218.

Sáenz, Eduardo, *La ofensiva empresarial: industriales, políticos y violencia en los años 40 en Colombia*, Bogotá, Tercer Mundo-Ediciones Uniandes, 1992.

Thorp, Rosemary, *Economic Management and Economic Development in Peru and Colombia*, Basingstoke, Macmillan, 1991.

Thorp, Rosemary, and Francisco Durand, 'A Historical View of Business-State Relations: Colombia, Peru, and Venezuela compared', in *Business and the State in Developing Countries*, eds Sylvia Maxfield and Ben Ross Schneider, Ithaca, Cornell University Press, 1997.

Urrutia, Miguel, *Gremios, política económica y democracia*, Bogotá, Fondo Cultural Cafetero, 1983.

MEXICO

Mario Cerutti

Author's note

The list of works cited in this bibliography of regional history in Mexico is selective, not exhaustive, given the restricted circulation of several of the research results. It is sufficient, nevertheless, to indicate the volume and variety of regional studies which have been undertaken in Mexico since the late 1970s. Taken together, these works offer an enormous amount of useful information for someone to write a history of business in Mexico between the early 1840s, the eve of the war with the United States, and the 1920s, the aftermath of the civil war of the previous decade. Some address issues in business history directly; others are significant because of their discussion of broader economic trends.

For the most part, the authors cited undertook their work in research institutes in the interior of Mexico. The studies of a general nature, those which focus on the country as a whole, are included because of the information that they provide from the point of view of the review of the literature undertaken here. Work produced by foreigners resident in Mexico has also been included. However, the work of non-Mexicans who live and work elsewhere has normally been excluded. It is important to recognise, however, that some foreigners have made significant contributions to the study of the business history of Mexico in the period covered here, and so some items by historians such as Walther Bernecker, Stephen H. Haber, Gilbert M. Joseph, Manuel Plana, Alex Saragoza, David Walker, Mark Wasserman, and Allen Wells are included.

Further details of additional unpublished papers (which have not been included here since they are unlikely to be easily available to readers based overseas), can be found in Mario Cerutti, 'Estudios regionales e historia empresarial en México (1840–1920): quince años de historiografía', Revista Interamericana de Bibliografi 43: 3 (1993) pp. 375–93.

Aguilar Aguilar, Gustavo and Wilfrido Ibarra, 'El establecimiento de la sucursal Culiacán del Banco de Sonora (1910–1912)', *Memoria del XV Simposio de Historia y Antropología de Sonora*, Hermosillo, Universidad de Sonora, 1991, I.

Aguilar Sánchez, Martín and Leopoldo Alafita Nartínez, 'El istmo veracruzano: la construcción de una región', in *Economía y sociedad en las regiones de México: siglo XIX*, ed. Jaime Olveda, Guadalajara, Colegio de Jalisco / Universidad de Guadalajara, 1996.

Aguirre Anaya, Carmen, *Personificaciones del capital: siete propiedades en la sociedad e industria textil de Puebla durante el siglo XIX*, Puebla, Cuadernos de la Casa Presno, Universidad Autónoma de Puebla, 1987.

——, 'Capitales y textiles en la ciudad de Puebla: nueve patrimonios durante el siglo XIX', in *Espacios y perfiles: historia regional del siglo XIX*, ed. Carlos Contreras Cruz, Puebla, Universidad Autónoma de Puebla/ Consejo Mexicano de Ciencias Sociales, 1989.

——, 'Industria y tecnología: motricidad en los textiles de algodón en el siglo XIX', *Siglo XIX: Cuadernos de Historia* 6 (1993).

——, 'Jesús Rivero Quijano: industrial e ideólogo del desarrollo tecnológico de México', doctoral thesis, Universidad Nacional Autónoma de México, 1995.

——, and Alberto Carabarín García, 'Formas artesanales y fabriles de los textiles de algodón en la ciudad de Puebla: siglos XVIII y XIX', in *Puebla, de la colonia a la Revolución. estudios de historia regional*, Puebla, Universidad Autónoma de Puebla, 1987.

Alafita Méndez, Leopoldo, 'La administración privada de las empresas petroleras, 1880–1937', *Anuario* 5 (1988).

Alba Vega, Carlos and Dirk Kruijt, *Los empresarios y la industria en Guadalajara*, Guadalajara, El Colegio de Jalisco, 1988.

——, 'Las regiones industriales y los empresarios en México', in *Los empresarios mexicanos, ayer y hoy*, eds Cristina Puga and Ricardo Tirado, México, 1992.

Aldana Rendón, Mario, 'De la Restauración al porfiriato: una nueva era dorada en Jalisco', in *De los borbones a la revolución: ocho estudios regionales*, ed. Mario Cerutti, México, GV Editores -Consejo Mexicano de Ciencias Sociales (COMECSO) – Universidad Autónoma de Nuevo León, 1986.

Arellanes, Anselmo, 'La reestructuración de la propiedad agraria en el sur de México', in *Economía y sociedad en las regiones de México: siglo XIX*, ed. Jaime Olveda, Guadalajara, Colegio de Jalisco / Universidad de Guadalajara, 1996.

Barceló Quintal, Raquel Ofelia, 'El desarrollo de la banca en Yucatán: el henequén y la oligarquía henequenera', *Yucatán: Historia y Economía* 29 (1982).

——, 'El desarrollo de la banca en Yucatán: el henequén y la oligarquía henequenera', in *Banca y poder en México (1800–1925)*, eds Leonor Ludlow and Carlos Marichal, México, Enlace-Grijalbo, 1986.

Barragán, Juan, 'El Archivo Brittingham: fuente para la historia industrial y bancaria de México', *Boletín de Fuentes para la Historia Económica de México* 8 (1992).

——, 'Empresarios del norte e importación de tecnología a principios del siglo XX', *Siglo XIX: Cuadernos de Historia* 6 (1993).

—— and Mario Cerutti, *Juan Brittingham y la industria en México*, Monterrey, Urbis Internacional, 1993.

Bátiz V., José Antonio, 'Aspectos financieros y monetarios (1821–1880)', in *México en el siglo XIX (1821–1910): historia económica y de la estructura social*, ed. Ciro Cardoso, México, Nueva Imagen, 1980.

——, 'Trayectoria de la banca en México hasta 1910', in *Banca y poder en México (1800–1925)*, eds Leonor Ludlow and Carlos Marichal, México, Enlace-Grijalbo, 1986.

—— and Enrique Canudas Sandoval, 'Aspectos financieros y monetarios', in *México en el siglo XIX (1821–1910): historia económica y de la estructura social*, ed. Ciro Cardoso, México, Nueva Imagen, 1980.

Beato, Guillermo, 'La casa Martínez del Río: del comercio colonial a la industria fabril. 1829–1864', in *Formación y desarrollo de la burguesía en México: siglo XIX*, ed. Ciro F. S. Cardoso, México, Siglo XXI Editores, 1978.

——, 'Jalisco: economía y estructura social en el siglo XIX', in *El siglo XIX en México: cinco procesos regionales*, ed. Mario Cerutti, México, Claves Latinoamericanas, 1985.

——, 'Los inicios de la gran industria y la burguesía en Jalisco', *Revista Mexicana de Sociología* 48: 1 (1986).

Beato, Guillermo and Domenico Sindico, 'Formas de comercialización de mercancías de la hacienda azucarera', in *Los lugares y los tiempos: ensayos sobre las estructuras regionales del siglo XIX en México*, eds Alejandra García Quintanilla and Abel Juárez, México, Nuestro Tiempo, 1989.

Benitez Juárez, Mirna Alicia and Leopoldo Alafita Méndez, 'La industria petrolera como frontera interna en el estado de Veracruz, 1900–1930', in *Veracruz, un tiempo para contar*, México, Universidad Veracruzana/Instituto Nacional de Antropología e Historia, 1989.

Bernecker, Walter L., *De agiotistas a empresarios: en torno a la temprana industrialiización mexicana (siglo XIX)*, Mexico, 1992.

Blázquez Domínguez, Carmen, 'Los grupos empresariales y el proyecto de estado-nación, 1867–1876; esbozo de una perspectiva regional', in *El dominio de las minorías: república restaurada y porfiriato*, México, Colegio de México, 1989.

——, 'Juan Antonio Lerdo de Tejada: las raíces regionales de una familia liberal, 1800–1850', in *Espacios y perfiles: historia regional del siglo XIX*, ed. Carlos Contreras Cruz, Puebla, Universidad Autónoma de Puebla/Consejo Mexicano de Ciencias Sociales, 1989.

——, 'Comerciantes jalapeños: 1800–1830: generalidades sobre la conformación de un grupo social', in *Veracruz, un tiempo para contar*, México, Universidad Veracruzana/Instituto Nacional de Antropología e Historia, 1989).

——, 'Comercio y política: Bernardo Sáyago, 1830–1850', in *El poder y el dinero: grupos y regiones mexicanos en el siglo XIX*, ed. Beatriz Rojas, México, Instituto de Investigaciones Dr. Mora, 1994.

——, 'Empresarios y financieros en el puerto de Veracruz y Xalapa, 1870–1890', in *Una inmigración privilegiada: comerciantes, empresarios y profesionales españoles en México en los siglos XIX y XX*, ed. Clara Lida, Madrid, Alianza, 1994.

Burnes, Arturo, 'Minería e intervencionismo estatal en el México decimonónico: el caso de Zacatecas, 1821–1876', in *Economía y sociedad en las regiones de México: siglo XIX*, ed. Jaime Olveda, Guadalajara, Colegio de Jalisco / Universidad de Guadalajara, 1996.

Camarena Ocampo, Mario, 'Fábricas, naturaleza y sociedad en San Angel, 1850–1910', in *Tierra, agua y bosques: historia y medio ambiente en el México central*, ed. Alejandro Tortolero Villaseñor, México, 1996.

Cano Cooley, Gloria, 'La industria del hierro: apuntes para la realización de una pieza más acabada', *Transición* 1 (1989).

——, '*La explotación del hierro en Durango (1889–1905)*', *Transición* 2 (1989).

——, 'La montaña que tirando a rojo ... construyó la vía de la dependencia económica durangueña', *Transición* 4 (1990).

—— and Miguel Vallebueno, 'El campo y la tenencia de la tierra durante el porfiriato', in *Durango (1840–1915): banca, transportes, tierra e industria*, Monterrey, Universidad Autónoma de Nuevo León/ Universidad Juárez del Estado de Durango, 1995.

——, María Guadalupe Rodríguez and Mauricio Yen Fernández, *Empresarios de Durango en el siglo XIX*, Durango, Universidad Juárez de Durango, 1990.

Cardoso, Ciro F. S., ed., *Formación y desarrollo de la burguesía en México: siglo XIX*, México, 1978.

Cariño O., Martha Micheline, 'La pesca y el cultivo de perlas en la región de La Paz (1870–1940): su impacto socioeconómico', *Siglo XIX: Cuadernos de Historia* 13 (1995).

——, 'Concesiones territoriales a la inversión extranjera en Sudcalifornia durante el siglo XIX', in *Inversiones y empresarios extranjeros en el noroccidente de México: siglo XIX*, ed. Jaime Olveda, Zapopán, El Colegio de Jalisco, 1996.

Castañeda, Carmen and María de la Luz Ayala, 'Universidad y comercio: los dominios de la élite en Guadalajara, 1792–1821', *Actas del Segundo Congreso de Historia Regional Comparada. 1990*, Ciudad Juárez, Universidad Autónoma de Ciudad Juárez, 1991.

Castellón Fonseca, Javier, *et al.*, 'El fin del siglo XIX y el ocaso de la industria regional: el caso de las tabacaleras nayaritas', *Secuencia* 9 (1987).

Cerutti, Mario, 'Estudios regionales e historia empresarial en México (1840–1920): quince años de historiografía', *Revista Interamericana de Bibliografía*, 43: 3 (1993).

——, 'Patricio Milmo, empresario regiomontano del siglo XIX', in *Formación y desarrollo de la burguesía en México: siglo XIX*, ed. Ciro F. S. Cardoso, Mexico, Siglo XXI, 1978.

——, *Burguesía y capitalismo en Monterrey (1850–1910)*, México, Claves Latinoamericanas, 1983.

——, *Economía de guerra y poder regional en el siglo XIX*, Monterrey, Archivo General del Estado de Nuevo León, 1983.

——, 'División capitalista de la producción, industrias y mercado interior. Un estudio regional: Monterrey (1890–1910)', in *El siglo XIX en México: cinco procesos regionales*, México, Claves Latinoamericanas, 1985.

——, 'El préstamo prebancario en el noreste de México: la actividad de los grandes comerciantes de Monterrey (1855–1890)', in *Banca y poder en México (1800–1925)*, eds Leonor Ludlow and Carlos Marichal, México, Enlace-Grijalbo, 1986.

——, 'Producción capitalista y articulación del empresariado en Monterrey (1890–1910)', in *Grupos económicos y organizaciones empresariales en México*, ed. Julio Labastida, México, Alianza Editorial/Universidad Nacional Autónoma de México, 1986.

——, 'Formación y consolidación de una burguesía regional en el norte de México. Monterrey: de la Reforma a la industria pesada (1850–1910)', in *Burguesías e industria en América Latina y Europa meridional*, eds Mario Cerutti and Menno Vellinga, Madrid, Alianza, 1989.

——, 'Historia económica y empresarial del gran norte oriental: dos fuentes en Monterrey', *Boletín de fuentes para la historia económica de México* 2 (1990).

——, *Burguesía, capitales e industria en el norte de México: Monterrey y su ámbito regional (1850–1910)*, México, Alianza Editorial-Universidad Autónoma de Nuevo León, 1992.

——, 'Españoles, gran comercio y brote industrial en el norte de México (1850–1910)', *Siglo XIX: Cuadernos de Historia* 2 (1992).

——, 'Comerciantes y generalización del crédito laico en México (1860–1910): experiencias regionales', *Anuario IEHS* (Tandil, Argentina) 7 (1992).

——, Industria pesada y reestructuración económica: la Fundidora de Fierro y Acero de Monterrey (1917-1930)', in *México en los años 20: procesos políticos y reconstrucción económica*, ed. Mario Cerutti, México, Claves Latinoamericanas/Universidad Autónoma de Nuevo León, 1993.

——, 'Crédito y transformaciones económicas en el norte de México (1850–1920): gran comercio, banca e industria en Monterrey', in *La formación de los bancos centrales en España y América Latina. Siglos XIX y XX*, eds Pedro Tedde and Carlos Marichal, Madrid, Banco de España, 1994.

——, 'Investigación regional e historia económica y empresarial del norte de México (1850–1925)', *Revista de Historia* (Neuquén, Argentina) 4 (1994).

——, 'Empresarios y sociedades empresariales en el norte de México (1870–1920)', *Revista de Historia Industrial* (Barcelona) 6 (1994).

——, 'Entre el río Bravo y la Habana: los comerciantes en la Guerra de Secesión (1861–1865)', in *Una inmigración privilegiada: comerciantes, empresarios y profesionales españoles en México en los siglos XIX y XX*, ed. Clara Lida, Madrid, Alianza Editorial, 1994.

——, *Empresarios españoles y sociedad capitalista en México (1840–1920)*, Colombres (Spain), Fundación Archivo de Indianos, 1995.

——, 'El Norte de México, Texas y el comercio atlántico, 1850–1875', *Ibero-Amerikanisches Archiv* 22 (1996).

——, 'Empresarios de origen vasco en el norte de México: entre Monterrey y el Bravo (1850–1915), in *Los vascos en las regiones de México: siglos XIX al XX*, ed. Amalia Garritz, Mexico, UNAM / Ministerio de Cultura del Gobierno Vasco, 1996.

——, and Miguel González Quiroga, 'Guerra y comercio en torno al río Bravo (1855–1867). Línea fronteriza, espacio económico común', *Historia Mexicana* 40: 2 (1990).

——, and Miguel González Quiroga, *Frontera e historia económica: Texas y el norte de México (1850–1865)*, México, Instituto de Investigaciones Dr. Mora/Universidad Autónoma Metropolitana 1993.

——, and Carlos Marichal, eds, *Historia de las grandes empresas en México (1840–1930)*, Mexico, Fondo de Cultura Económica / Universidad Autónoma de Nuevo León, 1997.

Collado, María del Carmen, *El emporio Braniff y su participación política, 1865–1920*, México, Siglo XXI Editores, 1987.

Colón Reyes, Linda Ivette, *Los orígenes de la burguesía y el Banco de Avío*, México, Ediciones El Caballito, 1982.

Crespo, Horacio, 'El azúcar en el mercado de la ciudad de México. 1885–1910', in *Morelos: cinco siglos de historia regional*, ed. Horacio Crespo, México, Centro de Estudios Históricos del Agrarismo – Universidad Autónoma de Morelos, 1985.

Díaz-Polanco, Héctor, *Formación regional y burguesía agraria en México (Valle de Santiago)*, México, Ediciones Era, 1982.

——, and Laurent Guye Montandon, *Agricultura y sociedad en el Bajío (siglo XIX)*, México, Juan Pablos Editor, 1984.

Durand, Jorge, 'Siglo y medio en el camino de la industrialización', in *Guadalajara, la gran ciudad de la pequeña industria*, ed. Patricia Arias, Zamora, El Colegio de Michoacán, 1985.

Favret Tondato, Rita, *Tenencia de la tierra en el estado de Coahuila (1880–1987)*, Saltillo, Universidad Autónoma Agraria Antonio Narro, 1992.

Fernández de Castro, Patricia, 'Comercio y contrabando en la frontera noreste (1861–1865)', *Frontera Norte* 6: 11 (1994).

Flores Clair, Eduardo, *Conflictos de trabajo de una empresa minera: Real del Monte y Pachuca, 1872–1877*, Mexico, Instituto Nacional de Antropología e Historia, 1991.

Flores Hernández, Ivonne, *Cusihuiarachi: minería e historia regional*, Ciudad Juárez, Universidad Autónoma de Ciudad Juárez, 1992.

Flores Torres, Oscar, 'De la edad del acero a los tiempos revolucionarios. Dos empresas industriales regiomontanas (1909–1923)', in *Monterrey, Nuevo León, el Noreste: siete estudios históricos*, ed. Mario Cerutti, Monterrey, Universidad Autónoma de Nuevo León, 1987.

——, 'La contrarrevolución en Monterrey: la Cámara Nacional de Comercio, 1915–1917', in *Espacios y perfiles: historia regional del siglo XIX*, ed. Carlos Contreras Cruz, Puebla, Universidad Autónoma de Puebla/Consejo Mexicano de Ciencias Sociales, 1989.

——, 'Revolución mexicana y diplomacia española: la burguesía de Monterrey y los *gachupines* en el Nuevo Léon de 1914', *Siglo XIX: Revista de Historia* 9 (1990).

——, *Burguesía, militares y movimiento obrero en Monterrey, 1909–1923*, Monterrey, Universidad Autónoma de Nuevo León, 1991.

——, 'Revolución mexicana y diplomacia española: contrarrevolución y oligarquía hispana en México (1909–1920)', doctoral thesis, Universidad Complutense de Madrid, 1991.

——, 'Empresarios, revolución y conflictos laborales en Monterrey. La industria metalúrgica (1920–1923)', *Siglo XIX: Cuadernos de Historia* 9 (1994).

——, 'Reportes diplomáticos y estructura económico-social villista', in *Economía y sociedad en las regiones de México: siglo XIX*, ed. Jaime Olveda, Guadalajara, Colegio de Jalisco / Universidad de Guadalajara, 1996.

——, 'Evolución, diplomacia y grupos económicos hispanos en el norte de México (1910–

1917', in *Historia económica del norte de México (siglos XIX y XX)*, IV, Monterrey, Universidad Autónoma de Nuevo León / Universidad de Monterrey, 1997.

Florescano Mayet, Sergio, 'El agua y la industrialización de Xalapa y su región durante el siglo XIX: usos, destinos, conflictos', *Deslinde* 15 (1986).

——, 'El tránsito a la manufactura en la región de Orizaba y el surgimiento de su primera fábrica textil: Cocolapán, 1837–1845', *Anuario* 7 (1990).

Franco Cáceres, Iván, 'Familias, oligarquía y empresarios en Yucatán (1879–1906)', *Siglo XIX: Cuadernos de Historia* 7 (1993).

Gamboa Ojeda, Leticia, 'Ascenso y declinación de una familia empresarial: los Conde y Conde, 1897–1918', *Boletín de Investigaciones del Movimiento Obrero* 5 (1982).

——, *Los empresarios de ayer: el grupo dominante en la industria textil de Puebla, 1906–1929*, Puebla, Universidad Autónoma de Puebla, 1985.

——, 'La trayectoria de una familia empresarial en la industria textil de Puebla: los Quijano-Rivero', in *Grupos económicos y organizaciones empresariales en México*, ed. Julio Labastida, México, Alianza Editorial/Universidad Nacional Autónoma de México, 1986.

——, 'La movilidad geográfica de los obreros textiles en Atlixco, Puebla (1899–1909)', *Deslinde* 21 (1988).

——, 'Industria y trabajadores del tabaco en la ciudad de Puebla (los años de la revolución)', *Anuario* 6 (1989).

——, 'Formas de asociación empresarial en la industria textil poblana' in *Los negocios y las ganancias: de la Colonia al México moderno*, eds Leonor Ludlow and Jorge Silva Riquer, Instituto de Investigaciones Dr. Mora / Universidad Nacional Autónoma de México, 1993.

——, 'Los españoles en la ciudad de Puebla hacia 1930', in *Una inmigración privilegiada: comerciantes, empresarios y profesionales españoles en México en los siglos XIX y XX*, ed. Clara Lida, Madrid, Alianza, 1994.

—— and Rosalina Estrada, *Empresas y empresarios textiles de Puebla: análisis de dos casos*, Puebla, Universidad Autónoma de Puebla, 1986.

—— and Rosalina Estrada, *El patrimonio de la industria textil en Puebla*, Puebla, Universidad Autónoma de Puebla, 1994.

Gamboa Ramírez, Ricardo, 'Finanzas municipales y nacionales a mediados del siglo XIX: los casos de Saltillo y la Ciudad de México', in *Economía y sociedad en las regiones de México: siglo XIX*, ed. Jaime Olveda, Guadalajara, Colegio de Jalisco / Universidad de Guadalajara, 1996.

Gámez, Moisés, *Unidad de clase y estrategias de resistencia: los trabajadores en San Luis Potosí, 1890–1917*, San Luis Potosí, Editorial Ponciano Arriaga, 1997.

Garavaglia, Juan Carlos and Juan Carlos Grosso, *Puebla desde una perspectiva microhistórica: Tepeaca y su entorno agrario: población, producción e intercambio (1740–1870)*, Mexico, Claves Latinoamericanos / Universidad Autónoma de Puebla / Universidad del Centro de Buenos Aires, 1994.

García Avila, Sergio, 'Instituciones bancarias y agricultura: una perspectiva de desarrollo capitalista en Michoacán, 1820–1850', *Tzintzun* 8 (1987).

García Díaz, Bernardo, *Un pueblo fabril del Porfiriato: Santa Rosa, Veracruz*, México, SEP/80-Fondo de Cultura Económica, 1981.

——, 'Santa Rosa y Orizaba', in *Veracruz: imágenes de su historia*, Xalapa, Archivo General del Estado de Veracruz, 1989, 2.

—— and Laura Zevallos Ortiz, 'Orizaba', in *Veracruz: imágenes de su historia*, Xalapa, Archivo General del Estado de Veracruz, 1989, 1.

García Morales, Soledad, 'Análisis de la estadística de 1907: haciendas y hacendados', in *Veracruz, un tiempo para contar*, México, Universidad Veracruzana/Instituto Nacional de Antropología e Historia, 1989).

García Quintanilla, Alejandra, 'Producción de henequén, producción de hombres (Yucatán, 1850–1910)', in *El siglo XIX en México: cinco procesos regionales*, ed. Mario Cerutti, México, Claves Latinoamericanas, 1985.

——, *Los tiempos en Yucatán: los hombres, las mujeres y la naturaleza (siglo XIX)*, México, Claves Latinoamericanas, 1986.

—— and Raúl Murguía, 'El ejidatario henequenero, la tierra y sus dueños en Yucatán (1850–1910)', in *De los borbones a la revolución. Ocho estudios regionales*, ed. Mario Cerutti, México, GV Editores -Consejo Mexicano de Ciencias Sociales – Universidad Autónoma de Nuevo León, 1986.

García Ugarte, Marta Eugenia, 'Razones de la hegemonía social, política y económica de la hacienda queretana, y razones de su derrumbe (1880–1920)', *Historia y Grafía* 5 (1995).

Godoy D., Ernesto, 'Empresas y empresarios en la industria pública de Puebla: 1887–1913', in *Los empresarios mexicanos, ayer y hoy*, eds Cristina Puga and Ricardo Tirado, México, 1992.

——, 'El primer cuarto de siglo del sector eléctrico en Puebla', *Elementos* 3: 18 (1993).

Gómez Galvarriato, Aurora, and Bernardo García Díaz, 'La industria textil del valle de Orizaba y sus trabajadores: fuentes locales para su estudio', *América Latina en la Historia Económica: Boletín de Fuentes* 4 (1995).

Gómez Serrano, Jesús, *Aguascalientes: imperio de los Guggenheim*, México, SEP/80-Fondo de Cultura Económica, 1982.

——, 'El desarrollo industrial de Aguascalientes durante el Porfiriato', *Siglo XIX: Cuadernos de Historia* 11 (1995).

——, 'La inversión francesa en Aguascalientes: siglo XIX', in *Inversiones y empresarios extranjeros en el noroccidente de México: siglo XIX*, ed. Jaime Olveda, Zapopán, El Colegio de Jalisco, 1996.

González Cruz, Edith, 'La expansión territorial de El Boleo (1901–1913)', in *Sociedad y gobierno en el sur de la Baja California: cinco aproximaciones históricas*, eds Juan Preciado Llamas and María Eugenia Altable, La Paz, Universidad Autónoma de Baja California Sur, 1991.

——, 'El gobierno de Ortega: su relación con la Compañía El Boleo', *Memoria del V Congreso de Historia y Antropología Regionales*, La Paz, Universidad Autónoma de Baja California Sur, 1994.

González Gómez, Carmen Imelda and Ovidio González Gómez, *Transporte en Querétaro en el siglo XIX*, Querétaro, Instituto Mexicano del Transporte / Gobierno del Estado de Querétaro, 1990.

González Herrera, Carlos, 'La agricultura en el proyecto económico de Chihuahua en el porfiriato', *Siglo XIX: Cuadernos de Historia* 5 (1993).

——, Noé Palomares and Ricardo León G., 'Reflexiones en torno a la modernización porfiriana en Chihuahua', *Actas del Primer Congreso de Historia Regional Comparada, 1989*, Ciudad Juárez, Universidad Autónoma de Ciudad Juárez, 1990.

—— and Ricardo León, 'El nuevo rostro de la economía regional: Enrique C. Creel y el desarrollo de Chihuahua, 1880–1910', in *El poder y el dinero: grupos y regiones mexicanos en el siglo XIX*, ed. Beatriz Rojas, México, Instituto de Investigaciones Dr. Mora, 1994.

González Quiroga, Manuel, 'La puerta de México: los comerciantes texanos y el noreste mexicano', *Estudios Sociológicos* 11: 31 (1993).

——, 'Trabajadores mexicanos en Texas (1850–1865): los carreteros y el transporte de carga', *Siglo XIX:. Cuadernos de Historia* 9 (1994).

González Sierra, José, *Monopolio del humo (elementos para la historia del tabaco en México y algunos conflictos veracruzanos: 1915–1930)*, Xalapa, Universidad Veracruzana, 1987.

——, 'La rica hoja: San Andrés y el tabaco a fines del XIX', *La palabra y el hombre* 72 (1989).

Gracida, Juan José, 'Génesis y consolidación del porfiriato en Sonora (1883–1895)' and 'El Sonora moderno (1892–1910)', in *Historia general de Sonora*, Hermosillo, Gobierno del Estado de Sonora 1985, IV.

——, 'El problema de la harina y las relaciones comerciales entre Sonora y Sinaloa en 1881', *Boletín de la Sociedad Sonorense de Historia* 41 (1986).

——, 'El comercio del puerto de Guaymas al finalizar la década de los setentas del siglo XIX', *Boletín de la Sociedad Sonorense de Historia* 44 (1989).

——, 'Historia del Ferrocarril de Sonora bajo la propiedad del Atchison, Topeka and Santa Fe Railroad (1880–1897)', master's thesis, Universidad Nacional Autónoma de México, 1994.

——, 'Guaymas: notas para la historia comercial del puerto (1820–1910)', in *Los puertos noroccidentales de México*, eds Jaime Olveda and Juan Carlos Reyes G., Guadalajara, 1994.

——, 'La década de los 70 y la transición al capitalismo en Sonora', *Siglo XIX: Cuadernos de Historia* 11 (1995).

——, 'Notas sobre la inversión extranjera en Sonora, 1854–1910' in *Inversiones y empresarios extranjeros en el noroccidente de México: siglo XIX*, ed. Jaime Olveda, Zapopán, El Colegio de Jalisco, 1996.

Grosso, Juan Carlos, 'Estructura productiva y fuerza de trabajo en en el área del municipio de Puebla (siglo XIX)', in *El siglo XIX en México: cinco procesos regionales*, ed. Mario Cerutti, México, Claves Latinoamericanas, 1985.

Gutiérrez, Edgar, 'Comerciantes marítimos en el noroeste de México (1810–1835)', *Siglo XIX: Cuadernos de Historia* 13 (1995).

Gutiérrez Alvarez, Coralia, 'La reorganización institucional y la política industrial en Puebla, 1892–1911', in *Economía y sociedad en las regiones de México: siglo XIX*, ed. Jaime Olveda, Guadalajara, Colegio de Jalisco / Universidad de Guadalajara, 1996.

Guzmán Avila, José Napoleón, *Michoacán y la inversión extranjera. 1880–1917*, Morelia, Universidad Michoacana de San Nicolás Hidalgo, 1982.

—— 'Movimiento campesino y empresas extranjeras: la ciénega de Zacapú (1870–1910)', in *La cuestión agraria: revolución y contrarrevolución en Michoacán (tres ensayos)*, Morelia, Universidad Michoacana de San Nicolás Hidalgo, 1984.

——, 'La empresa agrícola Noriega y Cia. y la desecación de la ciénega de Zacapú', *Primer Coloquio de Historia Regional. Memorias*, Pachuca, Universidad Autónoma del Estado de Hidalgo, 1986.

——, 'Michoacán en vísperas de la revolución', in *La revolución en Michoacán. 1900–1920*, Morelia, Universidad Michoacana de San Nicolás Hidalgo, 1987.

Haber, Stephen H., *Industry and Underdevelopment: the Industrialization of Mexico, 1850–1940*, Stanford, Stanford University Press, 1989.

Hernández Elizondo, Roberto, 'Comercio e industria textil en Nuevo León, 1852–1890: un empresario: Valentín Rivero', in *Formación y desarrollo de la burguesía en México: siglo XIX*, ed. Ciro F. S. Cardoso, Mexico, Siglo XXI, 1978.

Herrera Canales, Inés, 'La circulación (comercio y transportes en México entre los años

1880 y 1910)', in *El siglo XIX en México: cinco procesos regionales*, ed. Mario Cerutti, México, Claves Latinoamericanas, 1985.

——, 'Comercio y comerciantes de la costa del Pacífico mexicano a mediados del siglo XIX', *Historias* (1988).

——, 'Empresa minera y región en México: la Compañía de Mina de Real del Monte y Pachuca (1824–1906)', *Siglo XIX: Revista de Historia* 8 (1990).

Herrera Canales, Inés and Rosa María Meyer, 'Comerciantes, comercio y estado en el siglo XIX', in *Espacios y perfiles: historia regional del siglo XIX*, ed. Carlos Contreras Cruz, Puebla, Universidad Autónoma de Puebla/Consejo Mexicano de Ciencias Sociales, 1989.

Herrera Pérez, Octavio, 'El ixtle en el Cuarto Distrito de Tamaulipas (1850–1913)', *Siglo XIX: Cuadernos de Historia* 10 (1994).

Hoffner Long, Margarita, 'la inversión extranjera en el siglo XIX zacatecano', in *Economía y sociedad en las regiones de México: siglo XIX*, ed. Jaime Olveda, Guadalajara, Colegio de Jalisco / Universidad de Guadalajara, 1996.

Huerta, María Teresa, 'Isidoro de la Torre: el caso de un empresario azucarero, 1844–1881', in *Formación y desarrollo de la burguesía en México: siglo XIX*, ed. Ciro F. S. Cardoso, Mexico, Siglo XXI, 1978.

——, 'Formación del grupo de hacendados morelenses', in *Morelos: cinco siglos de historia regional*, ed. Horacio Crespo, México, Centro de Estudios Históricos del Agrarismo-Universidad Autónoma de México, 1984.

——, 'Comportamiento político del grupo azucarero ante la creación del estado de Morelos: 1830–1870', *Primer Coloquio de Historia Regional. Memorias*, Pachuca, Universidad Autónoma del Estado de Hidalgo, 1986.

——, 'La influencia del parentesco en la integración del grupo azucarero morelense, 1780–1840', in *Espacios y perfiles: historia regional del siglo XIX*, ed. Carlos Contreras Cruz, Puebla, Universidad Autónoma de Puebla/Consejo Mexicano de Ciencias Sociales, 1989.

——, *Empresarios del azúcar en el siglo XIX*, México, Instituto Nacional de Antropología e Historia, 1993.

——, 'Los vascos en el sector azucarero morelense, 1780–1870' in *Los vascos en las regiones de México: siglos XIX al XX*, ed. Amalia Garritz, Mexico, UNAM / Ministerio de Cultura del Gobierno Vasco, 1996.

Huerta González, Rodolfo, 'Transformación del paisaje, recursos naturales e industrialización: el caso de la fábrica San Rafael, 1890–1934', in *Tierra, agua y bosques: historia y medio ambiente en el México central*, ed. Alejandro Tortolero Villaseñor, México, 1996.

Illades, Carlos, 'La empresa industrial de Estevan de Antuñano (1831–1847)', *Secuencia* 15 (1989).

——, *Presencia española en la revolución mexicana (1910–1915)*, México, Universidad Nacional Autónoma de México/Instituto de Investigaciones Dr. Mora, 1991.

——, 'Los propietarios españoles y la Revolución Mexicana', in *Una inmigración privilegiada: comerciantes, empresarios y profesionales españoles en México en los siglos XIX y XX*, ed. Clara Lida, Madrid, Alianza Editorial, 1994.

Jiménez Ornelas, Roberto, 'La tecnología en la modernización de Sonora', in *Historia general de Sonora*, Hermosillo, Gobierno del Estado de Sonora 1985, IV.

Lamas Lizárraga, Mario Alberto, 'Origen e influencia del Ferrocarril Sur Pacífico en Sinaloa, 1905–1917', master's thesis, Universidad Autónoma de Sinaloa, 1995.

Leal, Juan Felipe and Mario Huacuja Rountree, *Economía y sistemas de haciendas en México: la hacienda pulquera en el cambio: siglos XVIII, XIX y XX*, México, Ediciones Era, 1982.

Leal, Juan Felipe and Margarita Menegus, *Hacendados y campesinos. El caso de Tlaxcala, 1910–1920*, Mexico, UNAM / Eón, 1995.

Leon Fuentes, Nelly, 'Conformación de un capital en torno a la cafeticultura en la región de Xalapa-Coatepec: 1890–1940', master's thesis, Universidad Veracruzana, 1984.

León G., Ricardo (1991), 'Comerciantes extranjeros en Chihuahua: la casa Kettelsen y Degetau', *Chamizal* 10 (1991).

——, *Mariano Samaniego: medio siglo de vida fronteriza*, Ciudad Juárez, Gobierno del Estado de Chihuahua y Universidad Autónoma de Ciudad Juárez, 1991.

——, 'Comerciantes y mercado crediticio en el Chihuahua porfiriano: el caso del Banco Minero de Chihuahua', *Actas del Tercer Congreso Internacional de Historia Regional Comparada*, Ciudad Juárez, Universidad Autónoma de Ciudad Juárez, 1992.

——, 'La banca chihuahuense durante el porfiriato', *Siglo XIX: Cuadernos de Historia* 2 (1992).

Lida, Clara (ed.), *Una inmigración privilegiada: comerciantes, empresarios y profesionales españoles en México en los siglos XIX y XX*, Madrid, Alianza Editorial, 1994.

Lizama Silva, Gladys, 'Los capitales zamoranos a principios del siglo XX', *Historia Mexicana*, 34: 4 (1990).

——, '¿Burguesías o grandes fortunas? Zamora en el porfiriato', doctoral thesis, Universidad de Guadalajara, 1995.

Lloyd, Jane Dale, *El proceso de modernización capitalista en el noroeste de Chihuahua (1880–1910)*, México, Universidad Iberoamericana, 1987.

López González, Pedro, 'La Compañía Comercial Aguirre de Tepic', in *Los vascos en las regiones de México: siglos XIX al XX*, ed. Amalia Garritz, Mexico, UNAM / Ministerio de Cultura del Gobierno Vasco, 1996.

López Yesca, Ernesto, 'Fundador Cananea: William Cornell Green', *Memoria del XIV Simposio de Historia y Antropología de Sonora*, Hermosillo, Universidad de Sonora, 1990.

Ludlow, Leonor, 'La construcción de un banco: el Banco Nacional de México (1881–1884)', in *Banca y poder en México (1800–1925)*, eds Leonor Ludlow and Carlos Marichal, México, Enlace-Grijalbo, 1986.

——, 'El Banco Nacional Mexicano y el Banco Mercantil Mexicano: radiografía social de sus primeros accionistas, 1881–1882', *Historia Mexicana* 39: 4 (1990).

——, 'La primera etapa de formación bancaria (1864–1897)', in *Los negocios y las ganancias: de la Colonia al México moderno*, eds Leonor Ludlow and Jorge Silva Riquer, México, Instituto de Investigaciones Dr. Mora/Universidad Nacional Autónoma de México, 1993

——, 'Empresarios y banqueros: entre el Porfiriato y la Revolución', in *Una inmigración privilegiada: comerciantes, empresarios y profesionales españoles en México en los siglos XIX y XX*, ed. Clara Lida, Madrid, Alianza Editorial, 1994.

——, 'Las dinastías financieras en la ciudad de México: de la libertad comercial a la reforma liberal', doctoral thesis, El Colegio de Michoacán, 1995.

Luna, Patricia, 'Industria textil y clase obrera en Veracruz, 1920–1935', *Memoria del Primer Coloquio Regional de Historia Obrera*, México, Centro de Estudios Históricos sobre el Movimiento Obrero (CEHSMO), 1977.

Luna Jiménez, Pedro and Mario Contreras, 'Las inversiones extranjeras en Nayarit', in *Inversiones y empresarios extranjeros en el noroccidente de México: siglo XIX*, ed. Jaime Olveda, Zapopán, El Colegio de Jalisco, 1996.

Marroni de Velázquez, Maria da Gloria, *Los orígenes de la sociedad industrial en Coahuila, 1840–1920*, Saltillo, Archivo Municipal de Saltillo, 1992.

Martínez, Silvia, 'La minería del carbón en Coahuila: movimiento obrero (1920–1926)', master's thesis, Universidad Autónoma Metropolitana-Iztapalapa, 1992.

Martínez Alarcón, Juana, *San Cristóbal: un ingenio y sus trabajadores. 1896–1934*, Xalapa, Universidad Veracruzana, 1986.

Martínez García, Roberto, *Santa Anna de los Hornos y la Flor de Jimulco: dos haciendas laguneras*, Saltillo, Consejo Editorial del Gobierno de Coahuila, 1997.

Martínez Guzmán, Gabino, 'La minería en Durango en 1900', *Transición* 1 (1989).

——, 'Los orígenes de la industria en Durango', *Transición* 2 (1989).

——, 'Las compañías deslindadoras en Durango', *Transición* 11 (1992).

Martínez Moctezuma., Lucía, 'Un empresario en el valle de México: Iñigo Noriega Las, 1867–1913', in *Haciendas, pueblos y comunidades: los valles de México y Toluca entre 1530 y 1916*, ed. Manuel Miño Grijalva, México, Consejo Nacional para la Cultura y las Artes, 1991.

——, 'Españoles en Chalco: estrategias de empresarios frente a la fuerza de trabajo (1895–1913)', in *Entre lagos y volcanes: Chalco Amecameca, pasado y presente*, ed. Alejandro Tortolero Villaseñor, México, El Colegio Mexiquense, 1993, 1.

——, 'Máquinas, naturaleza y sociedad en el distrito de Chalco a fines del siglo XIX', in *Tierra, agua y bosques: historia y medio ambiente en el México central*, ed. Alejandro Tortolero Villaseñor, México, 1996.

Martínez Peña, Luis Antonio, 'Mazatlán: historia de su vocación comercial (1823–1910)', in *Los puertos noroccidentales de México*, eds Jaime Olveda and Juan Carlos Reyes G., Guadalajara, 1994.

——, 'Las casas comerciales alemanas en Mazatlán', in *Inversiones y empresarios extranjeros en el noroccidente de México: siglo XIX*, ed. Jaime Olveda, Zapopán, El Colegio de Jalisco, 1996.

Martínez Zepeda, Jorge, 'Las inversiones extranjeras en Baja California, 1821–1910', in *Inversiones y empresarios extranjeros en el noroccidente de México: siglo XIX*, ed. Jaime Olveda, Zapopán, El Colegio de Jalisco, 1996.

Menéndez Rodríguez, Hernán, *Iglesia y poder. Proyectos sociales, alianzas políticas y económicas en Yucatán (1857–1917)*, Mexico, Consejo Nacional para la Cultura y las Artes, 1995.

Meyer Cosío, Rosa María, 'Los Béistegui: especuladores y mineros. 1830–1869', in *Formación y desarrollo de la burguesía en México: siglo XIX*, ed. Ciro F. S. Cardoso, Mexico, Siglo XXI, 1978.

——, 'Empresarios, crédito y especulación (1820–1850)', in *Banca y poder en México (1800–1925)*, eds Leonor Ludlow and Carlos Marichal, México, Enlace-Grijalbo, 1986.

——, 'Empresarios españoles después de la independencia', in *El poder y el dinero: grupos y regiones mexicanos en el siglo XIX*, ed. Beatriz Rojas, México, Instituto de Investigaciones Dr. Mora, 1994.

—— and Eduardo Flores Clair, 'Empresarios y vida cotidiana (1820–1879)', in *Los empresarios mexicanos, ayer y hoy*, eds Cristina Puga and Ricardo Tirado, México, 1992.

Morales, María Dolores, 'Francisco Somera y el primer fraccionamiento de la ciudad de México. 1840–1889', in *Formación y desarrollo de la burguesía en México: siglo XIX*, ed. Ciro F. S. Cardoso, Mexico, Siglo XXI, 1978.

Morado Macías, César, *Minería e industria pesada: capitalismo regional y mercado norteamericano, 1885–1910*, Monterrey, Archivo General del Estado de Nuevo León, 1991.

Morales Pardo, Luz Marina, 'Oligarquía y burguesía en Puebla: los hermanos Furlong, 1880–1856', in *Espacios y perfiles: historia regional del siglo XIX*, ed. Carlos Contreras

Cruz, Puebla, Universidad Autónoma de Puebla/ Consejo Mexicano de Ciencias Sociales, 1989.

——, *La familia Furlong en el siglo XIX,* Puebla, Lecturas Históricas, 1992.

Moreno García, Heriberto, 'Los beneficiarios del crédito agrario en Puruándiro, Michoacán', in *Los negocios y las ganancias: de la Colonia al México moderno,* eds Leonor Ludlow and Jorge Silva Riquer, México, Instituto de Investigaciones Dr. Mora / Universidad Nacional Autónoma de México, 1993.

——, 'Compradores y vendedores de tierras, ranchos y haciendas en el Bajío michoacano guanajuatense', in *El poder y el dinero: grupos y regiones mexicanos en el siglo XIX,* ed. Beatriz Rojas, México, Instituto de Investigaciones Dr. Mora, 1994.

Navarro Gallegos, César, 'La economía duranguese al mediar el siglo XIX', *Actas del Tercer Congreso Internacional de Historia Regional Comparada,* Ciudad Juárez, Universidad Autónoma de Ciudad Juárez, 1992.

——, Guadalupe Villa and Graziella Altamirano, 'Capitalistas y grupos de poder en Durango, 1840–1910', *Transición* 8 (1991).

Nuñez de la Peña, Francisco, 'Un banco que vino del centro: una crónica (1884–1914)', in *Banca y poder en México (1800–1925),* eds Leonor Ludlow and Carlos Marichal, México, Enlace-Grijalbo, 1986.

Olveda, Jaime, 'El proceso formativo de la oligarquía en Guadalajara', in *De los borbones a la revolución: ocho estudios regionales,* ed. Mario Cerutti, México, GV Editores – Consejo Mexicano de Ciencias Sociales (COMECSO) – Universidad Autónoma de Nuevo León, 1986.

——, *La oligarquía de Guadalajara: de las reformas borbónicas a la reforma liberal,* México, Consejo Nacional para la Cultura y las Artes, 1991.

——, Empresarios e inversiones extranjeras en Jalisco, siglo XIX' in *Inversiones y empresarios extranjeros en el noroccidente de México: siglo XIX,* ed. Jaime Olveda, Zapopán, El Colegio de Jalisco, 1996.

Olvera, José Antonio, 'El Valle del Pilón: riego, producción e impactos socioeconómicos, 1880–1910', in *Agua, tierra y capital en el noreste de México. La región citrícola de Nuevo León (1850–1940),* ed. Mario Cerutti, Monterrey, Universidad Autónoma de Nuevo León, 1991.

——, 'Agricultura, riego y conflicto social en la región citrícola de Nuevo León (1880–1914)', *Siglo XIX: Cuadernos de Historia* 5 (1993).

——, 'Propiedad, riego y conflictos sociales en el noreste de México: Linares durante la primera mitad del siglo XIX', in *Producción, ejidos y agua en el noreste de México: la región citrícola de Nuevo León,* ed. Mario Cerutti, Monterrey, Universidad Autónoma de Nuevo León, 1994.

Ortiz Hernández, María de los Angeles, 'Consecuencias del porfiriato en el Soconusco, Chiapas: aspectos económicos, sociales y políticos', in *Economía y sociedad en las regiones de México: siglo XIX,* ed. Jaime Olveda, Guadalajara, Colegio de Jalisco / Universidad de Guadalajara, 1996.

Ortiz Peralta, Rina, 'El abasto de la sal para la minería: las salinas de Tepopoxtla, 1849–1900', *Historia Mexicana* 41: 1 (1992).

Oyarzábal Salcedo, Shanti, 'Gregorio Mier y Terán en el país de los especuladores, 1830–1869', in *Formación y desarrollo de la burguesía en México: siglo XIX,* ed. Ciro F. S. Cardoso, Mexico, Siglo XXI, 1978.

Pacheco Rojas, José de la Cruz, 'La inversión extranjera en la minería de Durango, 1821–1910', in *Inversiones y empresarios extranjeros en el noroccidente de México: siglo XIX*, ed. Jaime Olveda, Zapopán, El Colegio de Jalisco, 1996.

Pacheco Zamudio, María del Pilar, 'Un empresario porfirista del centro del país: el caso de Iñigo Noriega Lasso (1897–1899)' in *Espacios y perfiles: historia regional del siglo XIX*, ed. Carlos Contreras Cruz, Puebla, Universidad Autónoma de Puebla/Consejo Mexicano de Ciencias Sociales, 1989.

——, 'Los recursos financieros de la compañía de Remigio Noriega', in *Los negocios y las ganancias: de la Colonia al México moderno*, eds Leonor Ludlow and Jorge Silva Riquer, México, Instituto de Investigaciones Dr. Mora/Universidad Nacional Autónoma de México, 1993

—— and Humberto Morales Moreno, 'Subvenciones ferroviarias y expansión del mercado interno: el ferrocarril de San Rafael a Atlixco (1880–1927)', *Deslinde* 22 (1988).

Palomares Peña, Noé, *Propietarios norteamericanos y reforma agraria en Chihuahua, 1912–1942*, Ciudad Juárez, Universidad Autónoma de Ciudad Juárez, 1991.

——, 'Minería y metalurgia chihuahuense: Batopilas y Santa Eulalia entre 1880 y 1920', *Actas del Tercer Congreso Internacional de Historia Regional Comparada*, Ciudad Juárez, Universidad Autónoma de Ciudad Juárez, 1992.

Pedrero Nieto, Gloria, 'San Cristóbal y Tuxtla: capitales de Chiapas en el siglo XIX', *Deslinde* 10–11 (1985).

——, 'Los productores de alimento en el districto de Toluca: siglo XIX', in *Economía y sociedad en las regiones de México: siglo XIX*, ed. Jaime Olveda, Guadalajara, Colegio de Jalisco / Universidad de Guadalajara, 1996.

Pérez Acevedo, Martín, 'Sistema de alumbrado y compañías eléctricas en Morelia durante el porfiriato', *Tzintzún* 13 (1991).

——, *Empresarios y empresas en Morelia, 1860–1910*, Morelia, Universidad Michoacana de San Nicolás Hidalgo, 1994.

Pérez-Rayon Elizundia, Nora, *Entre la tradición señorial y la modernidad: la familia Escandón Barrón y Escandón Arango*, México, Universidad Autónoma Metropolitana-Azcapotzalco, 1995.

Pi-Suñer Llorens, Antonia, 'Negocios y política a mediados del siglo XIX', in *Una inmigración privilegiada: comerciantes, empresarios y profesionales españoles en México en los siglos XIX y XX*, ed. Clara Lida, Madrid, Alianza Editorial, 1994.

Piña Gritssman, Jorge, 'El comercio en el desarrollo económico de Durango durante el siglo XIX. 1930–1867', *Transición* 2 (1989).

Plana, Manuel, *El reino del algodón en México: la estructura agraria de La Laguna*, Torreón, 1991.

Radding, Cynthia, 'Las estructuras formativas del capitalismo en Sonora (1900–1930)', in *De los borbones a la revolución. Ocho estudios regionales*, ed. Mario Cerutti, México, GV Editores -Consejo Mexicano de Ciencias Sociales – Universidad Autónoma de Nuevo León, 1986.

Ramirez Rancaño, Mario, 'Haciendas y hacendados en Tlaxlaca durante el Porfiriato', *Deslinde* 14 (1986).

——, 'Los hacendados y el huertismo', *Revista Mexicana de Sociología* 48: 1 (1986).

——, 'Los empresarios textiles y la política a principios del siglo XX', in *De los borbones a la revolución: ocho estudios regionales*, ed. Mario Cerutti, México, GV Editores -Consejo Mexicano de Ciencias Sociales – Universidad Autónoma de Nuevo León, 1986.

——, 'El primer congreso de industriales y la constitución política', in *Grupos económicos y organizaciones empresariales en México*, ed. Julio Labastida, México, Alianza Editorial/Universidad Nacional Autónoma de México, 1986.

——, *Burguesía textil y política en la revolución mexicana*, México, Universidad Nacional Autónoma de México, 1987.

——, *El sistema de haciendas en Tlaxcala*, México, Consejo Nacional para la Cultura y las Artes, 1990.

——, 'Ignacio Torres Adalid: un hacendado pulquero', in *Los empresarios mexicanos, ayer y hoy*, eds Cristina Puga and Ricardo Tirado, México, 1992.

——, 'La aristocracia pulquera', *Siglo XIX: Cuadernos de Historia* 10 (1994).

Rendón Garcini, Ricardo, 'Aportación al estudio de las relaciones económico-morales entre hacendados y trabajadores: el caso de dos haciendas pulqueras en Tlaxcala', in *Paternalismo y economía en las haciendas mexicanas del porfiriato*, ed. Herbert J. Nickel, Mexico, Universidad Iberoamericano, 1989.

——, *Dos haciendas pulqueras en Tlaxcala, 1857–1884*, Tlaxcala, Gobierno del Estado de Tlaxcala / Universidad Iberoamericana, 1990.

Reyna, Carmen (with Ciro F. S. Cardoso), 'Las industrias de transformación (1880–1910)', in *México en el siglo XIX (1821–1910): historia económica y de la estructura social*, ed. Ciro Cardoso, México, Nueva Imagen, 1980.

Rivas Hernández, Ignacio, 'El Proceso Mining: su impacto social en El Triunfo (Baja California Sur)', in *Sociedad y gobierno en el sur de la Baja California: cinco aproximaciones históricas*, eds Juan Preciado Llamas and María Eugenia Altable, La Paz, Universidad Autónoma de Baja California Sur, 1991.

Rivera Castro, José, 'Notas acerca de la cuestión agraria en Chihuahua, 1917–1940', *Estudios Históricos* 1 (1993).

Rodríguez, María Guadalupe, 'Financistas en el XIX durangueño', *Transición* 1 (1989).

——, 'De usureros a banqueros', *Transición* 2 (1989).

——, 'Durango y La Laguna: desarrollos porfirianos', *Transición* 11 (1992).

——, 'La banca porfiriana en Durango', in *Durango (1840–1915): banca, transportes, tierra e industria*, Monterrey, Universidad Autónoma de Nuevo León / Universidad Juárez del Estado de Durango, 1995.

Rodríguez Piña, Javier, *Guerra de castas: la venta de indios mayas a Cuba, 1848–1861*, México, Consejo Nacional para la Cultura y las Artes, 1990.

Rojas Sandoval, Javier, 'Poder político, cerveza y legislación laboral en Monterrey (1917–1922)', in *México en los años 20: procesos políticos y reconstrucción económica*, ed. Mario Cerutti, México, Claves Latinoamericanas / Universidad Autónoma de Nuevo León, 1993.

Romero Gil, Juan Manuel (1988), 'El mineral El Boleo: los años de la revolución y la primera guerra', in *Memoria del XII Simposio de Historia y Antropología de Sonora*, Hermosillo, Universidad de Sonora, 1988, II.

——, 'Evolución de la minería sonorense (1860–1930)', in *Memoria del XIII Simposio de Historia y Antropología de Sonora*, Hermosillo, Universidad de Sonora, 1989, II.

——, 'Minería y sociedad en el noroeste porfiriano', *Siglo XIX: Cuadernos de Historia* 1 (1991).

——, *El Boleo: un pueblo que se negó a morir. 1855–1954*, Hermosillo, 1991.

Romero Ibarra, María Eugenia, 'Un empresario rural de Zinacantepec, estado de México', in *Economía y sociedad en las regiones de México: siglo XIX*, ed. Jaime Olveda, Guadalajara, Colegio de Jalisco / Universidad de Guadalajara, 1996.

Rosenzweig, Fernando, 'La formación y el desarrollo del estado de México, in *Breve historia del estado de México*, Toluca, El Colegio Mexiquense / Gobierno del Estado de México, 1987.

Ruiz, Ramón Eduardo, 'El surgimiento de una burguesía dependiente', in *Memoria del XI Simposio de Historia y Antropología de Sonora*, Hermosillo, Universidad de Sonora, 1987.

Salmerón, Rubén, *La formación regional, el mercado local y el poder de la oligarquía en Sonora: 1740–1840*, Hermosillo, Universidad de Sonora, 1990.

Sánchez, Gerardo D., *El suroeste de Michoacán: economía y sociedad, 1852–1910*, Morelia, Universidad Michoacana de San Nicolás Hidalgo, 1988.

Santibañez Tijerina, Blanca Esthela, 'La Trinidad: albores de una empresa textil del porfiriato, 1888–1910', *Boletín de Investigación del Movimiento Obrero* 11 (1988).

——, 'Aproximación al estudio de los empresarios textiles de la región de Puebla-Tlaxcala, 1888–1920', in *Espacios y perfiles: historia regional del siglo XIX*, ed. Carlos Contreras Cruz, Puebla, Universidad Autónoma de Puebla/ Consejo Mexicano de Ciencias Sociales, 1989.

Saragoza, Alex, *The Monterrey Elite and the Mexican State*, Austin, University of Texas Press, 1988.

Sariego, José Luis, 'La reconversión industrial en la minería cananense: historia de un viejo problema', *Memoria del XII Simposio de Historia y Antropología de Sonora*, Hermosillo, Universidad de Sonora, 1987, I.

——, *Enclaves y minerales en el norte de México: historia social de los mineros de Cananea y Nueva Rosita, 1900–1970*, México, Ediciones de la Casa Chata, 1988.

——, 'Historia minera de Chihuahua. Interpretaciones', *Siglo XIX: Cuadernos de Historia*, 13 (1995).

Serrano Alvarez, Pablo, 'La inversión extranjera en Colima, 1870–1911', in *Inversiones y empresarios extranjeros en el noroccidente de México: siglo XIX*, ed. Jaime Olveda, Zapopán, El Colegio de Jalisco, 1996.

Sieglin, Veronika, 'Agua, acumulación de capital y burguesía en la región citrícola de Nuevo León, 1900–1934', in *Agua, tierra y capital en el noreste de México. La región citrícola de Nuevo León (1850–1940)*, ed. Mario Cerutti, Monterrey, Universidad Autónoma de Nuevo León, 1991.

——, 'Reestructuración productiva y cambios sociales en el agro nuevoleonés. El área citrícola: de la revolución a Cárdenas', in *México en los años 20: procesos políticos y reconstrucción económica*, ed. Mario Cerutti, México, Claves Latinoamericanas/Universidad Autónoma de Nuevo León, 1993.

——, 'La disputa por el agua en el noreste de México (1820–1970)', in *Historia económica del norte de México (siglos XIX y XX)*, ed. Mario Cerutti, México, Universidad Autónoma de Nuevo León/Claves Latinoamericanas, 1995, I.

Sindico, Domenico, 'Inmigración europea y desarrollo industrial: el caso de los Ferrara en Monterrey', in *Capitales, empresarios y obreros europeos en América Latina, Actas del VI Congreso de AHILA*, Stockholm, University of Stockholm, 1983.

——, 'Azúcar y burguesía. Morelos en el siglo XIX', in *El siglo XIX en México: cinco procesos regionales*, ed. Mario Cerutti, México, Claves Latinoamericanas, 1985.

Skerrit, David, *Rancheros sobre tierra fértil*, Xalapa, Universidad Veracruzana, 1993.

Souto Mantecón, Matilde, 'Los comerciantes españoles en Vercaruz: del Imperio Colonial a la República', in *Una inmigración privilegiada: comerciantes, empresarios y profesionales españoles en México en los siglos XIX y XX*, ed. Clara Lida, Madrid, Alianza Editorial, 1994.

Suárez, Ana Rosa, 'Los intereses de Jecker en Sonora', *Memoria del XV Simposio de Historia y Antropología de Sonora*, Hermosillo, Universidad de Sonora, 1991, I.

Tenenbaum, Barbara, *The Politics of Penury: Debts and Taxes in Mexico, 1821–1856*, Albuquerque, University of New Mexico Press, 1986.

Tinker y Salas, Miguel, 'Sociedad y comercio en Sonora (1850–1879)', in *Memoria del XII Simposio de Historia y Antropología de Sonora*, Hermosillo, Universidad de Sonora, 1988.

Tirado Villegas, Gloria, 'La Compañía de Tranvías, Luz y Fuerza de Puebla, S. A., 1890–1906', in *Espacios y perfiles: historia regional del siglo XIX*, ed. Carlos Contreras Cruz, Puebla, Universidad Autónoma de Puebla/ Consejo Mexicano de Ciencias Sociales, 1989.

——, 'Puebla en el porfiriato: tranvías, el transporte moderno', *Enlaces* 1 (1994).

Torres Bautista, Mariano, 'En torno a los orígenes de la industrialización mexicana, 1830–1867', *Estudios Sociales* (1994).

——, *La familia Maurer de Atlixco, Puebla: entre el porfiriato y la Revolución*, México, Consejo Nacional para la Cultura y las Artes, 1994.

——, *El origen de la industrialización de Puebla*, México, Claves Latinoamericanos / Universidad Autónoma de Puebla, 1995.

Tortolero Villaseñor, Alejandro, 'Haciendas, pueblo y gobierno porfirista: los conflictos por el agua en la región de Chalco', in *Entre lagos y volcanes: Chalco Amecameca, pasado y presente*, ed. Alejandro Tortolero Villaseñor, México, El Colegio Mexiquense, 1993, 1.

——, 'Morelos durante el porfiriato: espacio y producción en una región cañera', *Estudios Históricos* 1993.

——, 'Espacio, población y tecnología: la modernización en las haciendas de Chalco durante el siglo XIX', *Historia Mexicana* 43: 4 (1994).

——, *De la coa a la máquina de vapor: actividad agrícola e innovación tecnológica en las haciendas mexicanas, 1880–1914*, México, Siglo XXI Editores/El Colegio Mexiquense, 1995.

——, 'Los usos del agua en la región de Chalco, 1893–1913: del Antiguo Régimen a la gran hidráulica', in *Tierra, agua y bosques: historia y medio ambiente en el México central*, ed. Alejandro Tortolero Villaseñor, México, 1996.

Trejo Barajas, Dení, 'La secularización de las misiones y la colonización civil en el sur de la Baja California, 1768–1842', in *Sociedad y gobierno en el sur de la Baja California: cinco aproximaciones históricas*, eds Juan Preciado Llamas and María Eugenia Altable, La Paz, Universidad Autónoma de Baja California Sur, 1991.

——, 'Propiedades y propietarios en la Baja California a mediados del siglo XIX', *Siglo XIX: Cuadernos de Historia* 12 (1995).

Trujillo Bolio, Mario, 'Producción fabril y medio ambiente en las inmediaciones del Valle de México, 1850–1880', in *Tierra, agua y bosques: historia y medio ambiente en el México central*, ed. Alejandro Tortolero Villaseñor, México, 1996.

Urías Hermosillo, Margarita, 'Manuel Escandón: de las diligencias al ferrocarril, 1833–1862', in *Formación y desarrollo de la burguesía en México: siglo XIX*, ed. Ciro F. S. Cardoso, Mexico, Siglo XXI, 1978.

Uribe Salas, José Alfredo, 'Un enclave minero en Michoacán: la formación de una empresa, 1898–1912', *Tzintzun* 8 (1987).

——, 'La industrialización de la seda en Michoacán: un proyecto nacional', *Tzintzún* 9 (1988).

——, 'Empresas y empresarios en la minería michoacana de la segunda mitad del siglo XIX', *Tzintzun* 10 (1989).

——, *Morelia: los pasos a la modernidad*, Morelia, Universidad Michoacana de San Nicolás de Hidalgo, 1993.

Valencia Ortega, Ismael (1988), 'La formación de los empresarios regionales: el caso de la familia Camou', in *Memoria del XII Simposio de Historia y Antropología de Sonora*, Hermosillo, Universidad de Sonora, 1988.

——, *'La minería sonorense en el siglo XIX: un proceso de transición'*, in *Memoria del XII Simposio de Historia y Antropología de Sonora*, Hermosillo, Universidad de Sonora, 1989, II.

Vallebueno, Miguel, 'Algodón y ferrocarriles: el desarrollo de la comarca lagunera', *Transición* 12 (1992).

Vargas-Lobsinger, María, *La hacienda de 'La Concha': una empresa algodonera de La Laguna, 1883–1917*, México, Universidad Nacional Autónoma de México, 1984.

Vázquez, Miguel Angel, 'Origen y evolución de los grupos de poder económico en Sonora', in *Memoria del XI Simposio de Historia y Antropología de Sonora*, Hermosillo, Universidad de Sonora, 1987.

——, 'Notas para una historia industrial de Sonora', in *Memoria del XII Simposio de Historia y Antropología de Sonora*, Hermosillo, Universidad de Sonora, 1988, I.

Vázquez Juárez, Juan Antonio, and Miguel González Quiroga, 'Capitalistas norteamericanos en Monterrey: Joseph A. Robertson', in *Monterrey, Nuevo León, el Noreste: siete estudios históricos*, ed. Mario Cerutti, Monterrey, Universidad Autónoma de Nuevo León, 1987.

Velasco Avila, Cuauhtémoc *et al.*, *Estado y minería en México (1767–1910)*, México, Fondo de Cultura Económica-SEMIP, 1988.

Velázquez A., Marco Antonio *et al.*, 'Revisión histórica de la producción de hule de guayule en México de 1903 a 1951', in *Guayule: reencuentro en el desierto*, Mexico, Consejo Nacional de Ciencia y Tecnología, 1978.

Villa Guerrero, Guadalupe, 'Durango y Chihuahua: los lazos financieros de una élite', in *Actas del Tercer Congreso Internacional de Historia Regional Comparada*, Ciudad Juárez, Universidad Autónoma de Ciudad Juárez, 1992.

——, 'La industria algodonera no textil: el caso de la Compañía Industrial Jabonera de La Laguna', in *El poder y el dinero: grupos y regiones mexicanos en el siglo XIX*, ed. Beatriz Rojas, México, Instituto de Investigaciones Dr. Mora, 1994.

——, 'La Compañía Agrícola del Tlahualilo: una mina de oro blanco', in *Durango (1840–1915): banca, transportes, tierra e industria*, Monterrey, Universidad Autónoma de Nuevo León/ Universidad Juárez del Estado de Durango, 1995.

Villanueva Mukul, Eric (ed.), *El henequen en Yucatán: industria, mercados y campesinos* Mérida, 1990.

Vos, Jan de, *Oro verde: la conquista de la selva lacandona pos los madereros tabasqueños, 1822–1949*, México, Fondo de Cultura Económica / Instituto de Cultura de Tabasco, 1988.

Walker, David W., *Kinship, Business and Politics: the Martínez del Río Family Group in Mexico, 1821–1867*, Austin, University of Texas Press, 1986.

Wasserman, Mark, *Capitalists, Caciques, and Revolution: the Native Elite and Foreign Enterprise in Chihuahua, Mexico, 1853–1911*, Chapel Hill, University of North Carolina Press, 1984.

——, *Persistent Oligarchs: Elites and Politics in Chihuahua, Mexico, 1910–1940*, Durham, NC, Duke University Press, 1993.

Wells, Allan, *Yucatán's Gilded Age: Haciendas, Henequen, and International Harvester, 1860–1915*, Albuquerque, University of New Mexico Press, 1985.

——, 'All in the Family: Railroads and Henequen Monoculture in Porfirian Yucatán', *Hispanic American Historical Review* 72 (1992), pp. 159–209.

Wells, Allan, and Gilbert M. Joseph, *Summer of Discontent, Season of Upheaval: Elite Politics and Rural Insurgency in Yucatán, 1876–1915*, Stanford, Stanford University Press, 1996.

Yen Fernández, Mauricio, 'Algunas notas sobre la industria textil en Durango, 1830–1910', *Transición* 1 (1989).

——, 'Panorama económico de Durango en el siglo XIX', *Transición* 3 (1989).

——, 'Los giros industriales en Durango (1848–1910): persistencia de la industria artesanal', *Transición* 4 (1990).

——, 'Modernos empresarios de ayer: los primeros industriales textiles en Durango', *Transición* 7 (1991).

——, 'La industria textil', in *Durango (1840–1915): banca, transportes, tierra e industria*, Monterrey, Universidad Autónoma de Nuevo León/ Universidad Juárez del Estado de Durango, 1995.

PERU

Rory Miller

Background and Bibliography

Basadre, Jorge, *Introducción a las bases documentales para la historia de la República del Perú con algunas reflexiones*, Lima, Eds. PLV, 1971.

Cotler, Julio, *Clases, estado y nación en el Perú*, Lima, Instituto de Estudios Peruanos, 1977.

—— ed., *Perú, 1964–1994: economía, sociedad y política*, Lima, Instituto de Estudios Peruanos, 1995.

Durand, Francisco, 'La industrialización en el Perú: bibliografía', *Estudios Andinos*, 17–18, 1981, pp. 195–246

Gootenberg, Paul, *Between Silver and Guano: Commercial Policy and the State in Post- Independence Peru*, Princeton, Princeton University Press, 1989.

Macera, Pablo, 'Los archivos de la Casa Dreyffus [sic] y la historia del Perú republicano', in *Trabajos de Historia*, 4 vols, Lima, Instituto Nacional de Cultura, 1977, I, pp. 271–81.

—— and Shane J. Hunt, 'Peru', in *Latin America: a guide to the economic history*, eds Roberto Cortés Conde and Stanley J. Stein, Berkeley, University of California Press, 1977, pp. 547–649

Nelles, H. V., 'Latin American Business History since 1965: a View from North of the Border', *Business History Review* 59 (1985), pp. 544–62.

Platt, D. C. M., 'Business Archives', in *A Guide to Manuscript Sources for the History of Latin America and the Caribbean in the British Isles*, ed. Peter Walne, London, Oxford University Press, 1973, pp. 442–513

Reber, Vera Blinn, 'Archival Sources for Latin American Business History', *Business History Review* 59, 1985, pp. 670–679.

Rodríguez Pastor, Humberto, 'El Archivo del Fuero Agrario, Lima, Perú', *Latin American Research Review* 14: 3 (1979), pp. 202–6.

TePaske, John J. (ed.), *Research Guide to Andean History: Bolivia, Chile, Ecuador, and Peru*, Durham, Duke University Press, 1981.

Thorp, Rosemary, and Geoffrey Bertram, *Peru, 1890–1977: Growth and Policy in an Open Economy*, London, Macmillan, 1978.

Yepes del Castillo, Ernesto, *Peru, 1820–1920: un siglo del desarrollo capitalista*, Lima, Instituto de Estudios Peruanos, 1972.

Individual Firms and Entrepreneurs

Albert, William, *An Essay on the Peruvian Sugar Industry, 1880–1920, and the Letters of Ronald Gordon, Administrator of the British Sugar Company in Cañete, 1914–1920*, Norwich, School of Social Studies, 1976.

Bardella, Gianfranco, *Setenta y cinco años de vida económica del Perú, 1889–1964*, Lima, Banco del Crédito, 1964.

——, *Un siglo en la vida económica del Perú: Banco del Crédito del Perú, 1889–1989*, Lima, Banco del Crédito, 1989.

Blanchard, Peter, 'The "Transitional Man" in Nineteenth-Century Latin America: the Case of Domingo Elías of Peru', *Bulletin of Latin American Research* 15 (1996), pp. 157–76.

Bonilla, Heraclio, *Guano y burguesía en el Perú*, Lima, IEP, 1974 [on Dreyfus Frères].

——, 'El impacto de los ferrocarriles: algunas proposiciones', *Historia y Cultura*, 1 (1972), pp. 93–120 [on the early years of the Peruvian Corporation].

—— and Alejandro Rabanal, 'La Hacienda San Nicolás (Supe) y la Primera Guerra Mundial', *Economía* 2: 3 (1979), pp. 3–48.

Burga, Manuel and Wilson Reátegui, *Lanas y capital mercantil en el sur: la casa Ricketts, 1895–1935*, Lima, Instituto de Estudios Peruanos, 1981.

Burgess, E. W. and F. H. Harbison, *Casa Grace en el Perú*, Washington, 1954.

Camprubí Alcazar, Carlos, *José Payán y de Reyna, 1844–1919: su trayectoria peruana*, Lima, 1967 [on a leading financier of the early twentieth century].

——, *Un siglo al servicio del ahorro, 1868–1968*, Lima, 1968 [history of the Caja de Ahorros de Lima].

Clayton, Lawrence A., *Grace: W. R. Grace & Co.: the Formative Years, 1850–1930*, Ottawa, IL, Jameson, 1985.

Empresas Eléctricas Asociadas, *Sesenta Años de Empresas Eléctricas Asociadas*, Lima, 1966.

Flores Galindo, Alberto, *Los mineros de la Cerro de Pasco, 1900–1930*, Lima, Pontificia Universidad Católica del Perú, 1974.

Freyre, Iris, *Exportaciones e industria en el Perú: el caso de Grace y Paramonga*, Lima, Universidad Católica / CISEPA, 1976.

Glave, Luis Miguel, 'Agricultura y capitalismo en la sierra sur del Perú (fines del siglo XIX y comienzos del siglo XX)', in *Estados y naciones en los Andes: hacia una historia comparativa*, eds Jean-Paul Deler and Yves Saint-Geours, 2 vols, Lima, Instituto de Estudios Peruanos / Institut Français des Etudes Andines, 1986, I, pp. 213–43.

Gonzales, Michael J., *Plantation Agriculture and Social Control in Northern Peru, 1875–1933*, Austin, University of Texas Press, 1985) [heavily based on papers from the Cayaltí estate].

Jacobsen, Nils, 'Comercio de lanas, estructura agraria y oligarquía en el sur del Perú', *Allpanchis* 19 (1982), pp. 255–66.

James, Marquis, *Merchant Adventurer: the Story of W. R. Grace*, Wilmington, Scholarly Resources, 1993.

Kapsoli, Wilfredo, 'Movimientos sociales en Cayaltí, 1915–1919', *Allpanchis* 11 (1978), pp. 103–22.

Kruijt, Dirk and Menno Vellinga, *Estado, clase obrera y empresa transnacional: el caso de la minería peruana, 1900–1980*, México, Siglo XXI, 1983 [on the Cerro de Pasco Corporation].

Laite, Julian, *Industrial Development and Migrant Labour*, Manchester, Manchester University Press, 1981 [on the Cerro de Pasco Corporation].

Macera, Pablo, 'El guano y la agricultura peruana de exportación, 1909–1945', in *Trabajos de historia*, Lima, Instituto Nacional de Cultura, 1977, IV, pp. 309–499 [on the Compañía Exportadora del Guano].

Mathew, W. M., *The House of Gibbs and the Peruvian Guano Monopoly*, London, Royal Historical Society, 1981.

Miller, Rory, 'Railways and Economic Development in Central Peru, 1890–1930', in *Social and Economic Change in Modern Peru*, eds Rory Miller et al, Liverpool, Centre for Latin American Studies, 1976, pp. 27–52.

——, 'Small Business in the Peruvian Oil Industry: Lobitos Oilfields Limited before 1934', *Business History Review* 56 (1982), pp. 400–23.

——, 'The Grace Contract, the Peruvian Corporation, and Peruvian History', *Ibero-Amerikanisches Archiv* 9 (1983), pp. 319–48.

Pinelo, Adalberto J., *The Multinational Corporation as a Force in Latin American Politics: a Case Study of the International Petroleum Company in Peru*, New York, Praeger, 1973.

Portocarrero, Felipe, 'El imperio Prado, 1890–1970: ¿oligarquía o burguesía nacional?', *Apuntes* 19 (1986), pp. 121–46.

Quiroz, Alfonso W., 'Las actividades comerciales y financieras de la casa Grace y la Guerra del Pacífico, 1879–1890', *Histórica* 7: 2 (1983), pp. 214–54.

——, *Banqueros en conflicto: estructura financiera y economía peruana, 1884–1930*, Lima, Universidad del Pacífico, 1989 [heavily based on the papers of the Banco del Perú y Londres].

Reaño, Germán and Enrique Vásquez, *El Grupo Romero: del algodón a la banca*, Lima, Universidad del Pacífico, 1988.

Renique, Gerardo, 'Movimientos campesinos en la Sociedad Ganadera del Centro, 1910–1950', *Allpanchis* 11 (1978), pp. 129–50.

Sánchez, Luis Alberto, *Historia de una industria peruana: cervecería Backus y Johnston S. A.*, Lima, Backus y Johnston, 1978.

Saulniers, Alfred W, 'ENCI: Peru's Bandied Monopolist', *Journal of Inter-American Studies and World Affairs*, 22 (1980), pp. 451–62.

Secada, C. G. Alexander de, 'Peru, Guano, and Shipping: the W. R. Grace Interests in Peru, 1865–1885', *Business History Review* 59 (1985), pp. 597–621.

Sectoral and Comparative History

The Business Elite

Bollinger, William, 'The Bourgeois Revolution in Peru: a Conception of Peruvian History', *Latin American Perspectives* 4: 3 (1977), pp. 18–56.

Burga, Manuel, and Alberto Flores Galindo, *Apogeo y crisis de la República Aristocrática*, Lima, Ed. Rikchay, 1979.

Gilbert, Dennis L., *The Oligarchy and the Old Regime in Peru*, PhD thesis, Cornell University, 1977; published in Spanish as *La oligarquía peruana: historia de tres familias*, Lima, Editorial Horizonte, 1982.

Gonzales, Michael J., 'Planters and Politics in Peru, 1895–1919', *Journal of Latin American Studies* 23 (1991), pp. 515–42.

Miller, Rory, 'The Coastal Elite and Peruvian Politics, 1895–1919', *Journal of Latin American Studies* 14 (1982), pp. 97–120.

Portocarrero, Felipe, 'Religión, familia, riqueza, y muerte en la élite económica peruana, 1900–1930', mimeo, 1990.

Quiroz, Alfonso W., 'Financial Leadership and the Formation of Peruvian Elite Groups, 1884–1930', *Journal of Latin American Studies* 20 (1988), pp. 49–81.

Foreign Investment

Becker, David G., *The New Bourgeoisie and the Limits of Dependency: Mining, Class and Power in 'Revolutionary' Peru*, Princeton, Princeton University Press., 1983.

Goodsell, Charles T., *American Corporations and Peruvian Politics*, Cambridge, Harvard University Press, 1974.

Hunt, Shane, 'Direct Foreign Investment in Peru: New Rules for an Old Game', in *The Peruvian Experiment: Continuity and Change under Military Rule* ed. Abraham F. Lowenthal, Princeton, Princeton University Press, 1975, pp. 302–49.

Miller, Rory, 'British Firms and the Peruvian Government, 1885–1930', in *Business Imperialism, 1840–1930: an Inquiry based on British Experience in Latin America* ed. D. C. M. Platt, Oxford, Clarendon Press, 1977, pp. 371–94.

——, 'Transferring Techniques: Railway Building and Management on the West Coast of South America', in Rory Miller and Henry Finch, *Technology Transfer and Economic Development in Latin America. 1850–1930*, Liverpool, Institute of Latin American Studies, 1986.

——, 'Enterprise and Inertia: British Business in Peru, 1850–1950', mimeo, 1988.

Philip, George, *Bonanza Development? The Selva Oil Industry in Peru, 1968–1982*, London, Institute of Latin American Studies, n.d.

Coastal Agriculture

Albert, Bill, 'External Forces and the Transformation of Peruvian Coastal Agriculture', in *Latin America, Economic Imperialism and the State: the Political Economy of the External Connection from Independence to the Present*, eds Christopher Abel and Colin M. Lewis, London, Athlone Press, 1985, pp. 231–49.

Bell, William, *An Essay on the Peruvian Cotton Industry, 1825–1920*, Liverpool, Centre for Latin American Studies, 1985.

Burga, Manuel, *De la encomienda a la hacienda capitalista: el valle del Jequetepeque del siglo XVI al XX*, Lima, Instituto de Estudios Peruanos, 1977.

Engelson, John R., 'Social Aspects of Agricultural Expansion in Coastal Peru, 1821–1878', PhD thesis, University of California at Los Angeles, 1977.

Gonzales, Michael J., 'The Rise of Cotton Tenant Farming in Peru, 1890–1920: the Condor Valley', *Agricultural History* 65 (1991), pp. 51–71.

Klarén, Peter, 'The Social and Economic Consequences of Modernisation in the Peruvian Sugar Industry, 1870–1930', in *Land and Labour in Latin America: Essays on the Development of Agrarian Capitalism in the Nineteenth and Twentieth Centuries*, eds Kenneth Duncan and Ian Rutledge, Cambridge, Cambridge University Press, 1977, pp. 229–52.

Low, Alaine M., 'Agro-Exporters as Entrepreneurs: Peruvian Sugar and Cotton Producers, 1880–1945', DPhil thesis, Oxford, 1979.

Macera, Pablo, 'Las plantaciones azucareras andinas (1821–1875), in *Trabajos de Historia*, 4 vols, Lima, Instituto Nacional de Cultura, 1997, IV, pp. 9–307.

Peloso, Vincent C., 'Cotton Planters, the State, and Rural Labour Policy: Ideological Origins of the Peruvian República Aristocrática, 1895–1908', *The Americas* 40: 2 (1983), pp. 209–28.

Portocarrero, Felipe, and L. Torrejón, *Modernizacón y atraso en las haciendas de la élite económica: Perú, 1916–1932*, Lima, Universidad del Pacífico, 1992.

Quiroz, Alfonso W., 'Desarrollo financiero y economía agraria de exportación en el Perú, 1884–1950', *Revista de Historia Económica* (Madrid) 10: 2 (1992), pp. 263–94.

The Central Sierra

Contreras, Carlos, *Mineros y campesinos en los Andes*, Lima, Instituto de Estudios Peruanos, 1988.

Deustua, José, *La minería peruana y la iniciación de la república, 1820–1840*, Lima, Instituto de Estudios Peruanos, 1986.

——, 'Mining Markets, Peasants, and Power in Nineteenth-Century Peru', *Latin American Research Review* 29: 1 (1994), 29–54.

——, 'Routes, Roads, and Silver Trade in Cerro de Pasco, 1820–1860: the Internal Market in Nineteenth-Century Peru', *Hispanic American Historical Review* 74 (1994), pp. 1–32.

Dore, Elizabeth, *The Peruvian Mining Industry: Growth, Stagnation, and Crisis*, Boulder, CO., Westview Press, 1988.

Long, Norman and Bryan Roberts, *Miners, Peasants, and Entrepreneurs: Regional Development in the Central Highlands of Peru*, Cambridge, Cambridge University Press, 1984.

Mallon, Florencia E., *The Defense of Community in Peru's Central Highlands: Peasant Struggle and Capitalist Transition, 1860–1940*, Princeton, Princeton University Press, 1983.

Manrique, Nelson, *Mercado interno y región: la sierra central, 1820–1930*, Lima, DESCO, 1987.

Roberts, Bryan R., 'The Social History of a Provincial Town: Huancayo, 1890–1972', in *Social and Economic Change in Modern Peru*, eds Rory Miller *et al.*, Liverpool, Centre for Latin American Studies, 1976, pp. 136–97.

Wilson, Fiona, 'The Conflict between Indigenous and Immigrant Commercial Systems in the Peruvian Central Sierra, 1900–1940', in *Region and Class in Modern Peruvian History*, ed. Rory Miller, Liverpool, Institute of Latin American Studies, 1987, pp. 125–61

The South

Bermúdez, Oscar, *Historia del salitre desde sus orígenes hasta la Guerra del Pacífico*, Santiago, Universidad de Chile, 1963.

Bustamante, Francisco, 'Dinámica y acumulación de dos grupos económicos regionales: el caso del mercado de fibra de alpaca en el sur andino, 1970–1987', *Apuntes* 25 (1989), pp. 61–79.

Caravedo Molinari, Baltazar, *Desarrollo desigual y lucha política en el Perú, 1948–1956: la burguesía arequipeña y el estado peruano*, Lima, Instituto de Estudios Peruanos, 1978.

Flores Galindo, Alberto, *Arequipa y el Sur Andino, siglos XVIII-XX*, Lima, Ed. Horizonte, 1977.

——, Orlando Plaza, and Teresa Oré, 'Oligarquía y capital comercial en el sur peruano (1870–1930), *Debates en Sociología* 3 (1978), 53–75.

Jacobsen, Nils, 'Cycles and Booms in Latin American Export Agriculture: the Example of Southern Peru's Liverstock Economy, 1855–1920', *Review* 7 (1984), pp. 443–507.

——, 'Auslandische Wirtschaftsinteressen und der Konflikt zwischen Zentralismus und Regionalismus in Peru, 1850–1930', *Geschichte und Gesellschaft* 14 (1988), pp. 178–192.

——, 'Libre comercio, élites regionales, y mercado interno en el sur del Perú, 1895–1932', *Revista Andina* 7 (1989), pp. 409–50.

——, *Mirages of Transition: the Peruvian Altiplano, 1780–1930*, Berkeley, University of California Press, 1993.

Krüggeler, Thomas, 'El doble desafío: los artesanos del Cusco ante la crisis regional y la constitución del régimen republicano, 1824–1869', *Allpanchis* 23: 38 (1991), pp. 13–66.

Finance

Camprubí Alcazar, Carlos, *Historia de los bancos en el Perú, 1860–1879*, Lima, Ed. Lumen, 1957.

Quiroz, Alfonso W., *Domestic and Foreign Finance in Modern Peru, 1850–1950: Financing Visions of Development*, London, Macmillan, 1993.

Fishing

Caravedo Molinari, Baltázar, *Estado, pesca, y burguesía, 1939–1973*, Lima, Teoría y Realidad, 1979.

Oroza, Jorge, 'Resurgimiento industrial y harina del pescado en el Perú, 1945–1960', *Estudios Andinos* 17–18 (1981), pp. 139–74.

Roemer, Michael, *Fishing for Growth: Export-Led Development in Peru*, Cambridge, MA., Harvard University Press, 1970.

Industry

Caravedo Molinari, Baltazar, *Burguesía e industria en el Perú, 1933–1945*, Lima, Instituto de Estudios Peruanos, 1976.

Durand, Francisco, 'Los primeros industriales y la inmigración extranjera en el Perú', *Estudios Migratorios Latinoamericanos* (Argentina), 3: 9 (1988), pp. 199–216.

Wils, Frits, *Industrialization, Industrialists, and the Nation-State in Peru: a Comparative Sociological Analysis*, Berkeley, Institute of International Studies, 1980.

Interest Groups

Basadre, Jorge and Rómulo A. Ferrero, *Historia de la Cámara de Comercio de Lima, 1888–1963* (Lima, Valverde, 1963).

VENEZUELA

Ruth Capriles and Marisol Rodríguez de Gonzalo

General economic histories of Venezuela

Acedo Mendoza, Carlos, *Venezuela: Ruta y Destino: estudios sobre el desarrollo integral de Venezuela enmarcado en el desarrollo continental de América Latina*, 2 vols, Barcelona, Ariel, 1966.

Aranda, Sergio, *La economía venezolana: una interpretación de su modo de funcionamiento, con un resúmen del período 1975–1984*, Caracas, Editorial Pomaire, 1984.

Arcila Farías, Eduardo, *La economía colonial de Venezuela*, Mexico, Fondo de Cultura Económica, 1946.

——, 'Evolución de la economía en Venezuela', in *Venezuela Independiente, 1810–1960*, Caracas, Fundación Eugenio Mendoza, 1962.

Arellano Moreno, Antonio, *Orígenes de la economía venezolana*, Caracas, Edine, 1960.

Banco Central de Venezuela, *La economía venezolana en los últimos veinticinco años*, Caracas, Banco Central de Venezuela, 1966.

——, *La economía venezolana en los últimos treinta años*, Caracas, Banco Central de Venezuela, 1971.

——, *La economía venezolana en los últimos 35 años*, Caracas, Banco Central de Venezuela, 1978.

——, *La economía contemporánea de Venezuela*, 4 vols, Caracas, Banco Central de Venezuela, 1990.

Brito Figueroa, Federico, *La estructura económica y social de Venezuela: una estructura para su estudio*, 2 vols, Caracas, Universidad Central de Venezuela, 1966.

——, *Venezuela contemporánea, ¿país colonial?*, Caracas, Ediciones Teoría y Praxis, 1972.

Carrillo Batalla, Tomás Enrique, *Desarrollo económico de Venezuela*, Caracas, 1963.

——, *Población y desarrollo económico*, Caracas, Banco Central de Venezuela, 1967.

Chen, J. Chi-yi, *Estrategia del desarrollo regional: caso de Venezuela*, Caracas, Ed. Arte, 1967.

Córdova, Armando, 'La estructura económica tradicional y el impacto petrolero en Venezuela', *Economía y ciencias sociales* 5: 1, pp. 7–28.

D'Ascoli, Carlos A., *Esquema histórico-económico de Venezuela (del mito del dorado a la economía del café)*, Caracas, Banco Central de Venezuela, 1970.

De la Plaza, Salvador, *Desarrollo económico e industrias básicas*, Caracas, Universidad Central de Venezuela, 1962.

Furtado, Celso, 'El desarrollo reciente de la economía venezolana' (1957), in Banco Central de Venezuela, *La economía cntemporánea de Venezuela*, 4 vols, Caracas, 1990, pp. 163–205.

Instituto de Investigaciones Económicas y Sociales, Universidad Central de Venezuela, *La dependencia de Venezuela: bases teóricas y metodológicas*, Caracas, Universidad Central de Venezuela, 1975.

International Bank for Reconstruction and Development (IBRD), *The Economic Development of Venezuela*, Baltimore, John Hopkins Press, 1961.

Márquez, Guillermo, *La economía venezolana en la década del 70: algunas reflexiones*, Caracas, Monte Avila Editores, 1976.

Mayobre, José Antonio, 'Desde 1936 hasta nuestros días', in *Política y economía en Venezuela, 1810–1976*, Caracas, Fundación John Boulton, 1976.

Maza Zavala, Domingo Felipe, *Hacia la independencia económica*, Caracas, 1960.

——, *Venezuela, una economía dependiente*, Caracas, Universidad Central de Venezuela, 1962.

Ortiz Ramírez, Eduardo (ed.), *Venezuela y la economía internacional*, Caracas, Universidad Central de Venezuela, 1992.

Pérez Dupuy, Henrique, *Algunas orientaciones sobre problemas económicos venezolanos*, Caracas, Lit. y Tip. del Comercio, 1939.

Pernaut, Manuel S. J., *Diez años de desarrollo económico y social de Venezuela*, Caracas. Edic. del Cuatricentenario de Caracas, 1966.

Polanco Martínez, Tomás, *Historia económica de Venezuela*, Caracas, 1968.

Rodríguez, Gumersindo, 'Una visión optimista del futuro económico y social de Venezuela', in Banco Central de Venezuela, *La economía contemporánea de Venezuela*, 4 vols, Caracas, Banco Central de Venezuela, 1990, I.

Toro Hardy, José, *Venezuela, 55 años de política económica, 1936–1991: una utopía keynesiana*, Caracas, Editorial Panapo, 1992.

Weil, Thomas E. *et al.*, *Area Handbook for Venezuela*, Washington D. C., Government Printing Office, 1971.

Sectoral Histories

Industry

Aguerrevere, P. I., 'Industrial Development in Venezuela', *Proceedings of the United Nations Scientific Conference on the Conservation and Utilization of Resources*, New York, 1949.

Alvarez, Ruben, *Pequeña y mediana industria en Venezuela*, Caracas, Paral, 1983.

Araujo, Orlando, *Situación industrial de Venezuela*, Caracas, Universidad Central de Venezuela, 1969.

Aristiguieta, Raimundo, *Venezuela y su industrialización*, Caracas, Ed. Egry, 1942.

Banko, Catalina, *Contribución a la historia de la manufactura en Venezuela*, Caracas, Universidad Santa María, 1983.

Bitar, Sergio and Eduardo Troncoso, *El desafío industrial de Venezuela*, Buenos Aires, Ed. Pomaire, 1983.

—— and Tulio Mejías, 'Más industrialización: alternativa para Venezuela', in *El caso Venezuela: una ilusión de armonía*, ed. Moisés Naím and Ramón Piñango, Caracas, Ediciones IESA, 1984, pp. 102–21.

Carrillo Batalla, T. E., *El desarrollo del sector manufacturero industrial de la economía venezolana*, Caracas, Universidad Central de Venezuela, 1962.

Estaba, Rosa M. and Ivonne Alvarado, *Geografía de los paisajes urbanos e industriales de Venezuela*, Caracas, Ariel-Seix Barral Venezolana, 1985.

Falcón Urbano, Miguel A., *Desarrollo e industrialización de Venezuela: un enfoque metodológico*, Caracas, Universidad Central de Venezuela, 1969.

Gonzalo, Marisol, 'Consideraciones generales sobre la historia de la industria en Venezuela', *Diccionario de historia de Venezuela*, Caracas, Fundación Polar, 1988, II, pp. 540–47.

Jongkind, Fred, 'Informe sobre investigación de la gran y mediana industria manufacturera en Venezuela: la participación nacional y extranjera en la industria', Caracas, mimeo IESA, 1977.

Karlsson, Weine, *Evolución y localización de la industria manufacturera en Venezuela*, Stockholm, Institute of Latin American Studies, 1979.

——, *Manufacturing in Venezuela: studies on development and location*, Stockholm, Aluqvist and Wiskell International, 1975.

Lollet Calderón, Carlos Miguel, 'El desarrollo regional de la industria en Venezuela', *Cuadernos de la Corporación Venezolana de Fomento*, I: 2 (1964), pp. 23–28.

Merhav, Meir, *Posibilidades de exportación de la industria venezolana*, Caracas, Cordiplan, 1974.

Montiel Ortega, Leonardo, *Nacionalismo e industrialización: programa para el rescate del petróleo y para el desarrollo de las industrias básicas en Venezuela*, Caracas, Pensamineto Vivo, 1962.

Nolff, M, 'La industrialización venezolana en la década de los ochenta', *Nueva Sociedad* (1981).

Rangel, Domingo Alberto, *La industrialización de Venezuela*, Caracas, Pensamiento Vivo, 1958.

SELA, *Desafío de la política industrial latinoamericana hacia fin de siglo*, Buenos Aires, 1988.

Commerce

Arenas, Nelly, *La denuncia del Tratado de Reciprocidad Comercial entre Venezuela y los Estados Unidos*, Caracas, Centro Venezolano Americano, 1990.

Banko, Catalina, *El capital comercial en La Guaira y Caracas (1821–1848)*, Caracas, Academia Nacional de la Historia, 1990.

Dupouy, Walter, 'Las Casas Blohm de Venezuela', *Boletín de la Asociación Cultural Humboldt* 11–12 (1974–75), pp. 113–31.

Garaicoechea, Manuel Felipe, *El comercio exterior y la estrategia del desarrollo económico venezolano*, Caracas, Universidad Central de Venezuela, 1969.

Gerstl, Otto, *Memorias e historias*, Caracas, Fundación John Boulton, 1977.

González Deluca, María Elena, *Los comerciantes de Caracas: cien años de acción y testimonio de la Cámara de Comercio de Caracas*, Caracas, Cámara de Comercio, 1994.

Lucena Salmoral, Manuel, *El comercio caraqueño a fines del período español: mercados, comerciantes e instrumentos de cambio*, Caracas, Universidad Santa María, 1984.

——, *Los mercados exteriores de Caracas a comienzos de la independencia*, Caracas, Academia Nacional de la Historia, 1992.

Machado de Acedo, Clemy and Marisela Padrón Quero, *La diplomacia de López Contreras y el Tratado de Reciprocidad Comercial con Estados Unidos*, Caracas, Instituto de Asuntos Internacionales, Ministerio de Relaciones Exteriores, 1987.

Banking, Finance, and Investment

Banco Central de Venezuela, *Historia de las finanzas públicas de Venezuela (1830–1899)*, Caracas, Banco Central de Venezuela.

Banco Industrial de Venezuela, *Veinticinco años del Banco Industrial de Venezuela*, Caracas, Gráfica Americana, 1962.

Banco de Venezuela, *Los cien millones de bólivares del Banco de Venezuela: una historia 1870–1956*, Caracas, Banco de Venezuela, 1957.

Banko, Catalina, 'Contribución a la historia del Banco de Maracaibo'. *Revista Universitaria de Historia* 2 (1982), pp. 79–123.

Baptista, Asdrúbal, *El capital fijo en la economía venezolana*, Caracas, IESA, 1990.

Belloso Rosell, David, *Historia del Banco de Maracaibo*, Madrid, Isla, 1974.

Berglund, Susan, 'La Casa Boulton y el Crédito Mercantil', *Tierra Firme* (1986), pp. 559–76.

——, 'Mercantile Credit and Financing in Venezuela, 1830–1870', *Journal of Latin American Studies* 17 (1985), pp. 371–96.

Capriles Mendez, Ruth, *Los negocios de Román Delgado Chalbaud*, Caracas, Academia Nacional de la Historia, 1991.

Carrillo Batalla, Tomás E., *Moneda, crédito y banca en Venezuela*, 2 vols, Caracas, Banco Central de Venezuela, 1964.

Castillo, Domingo, *La cuestión monetaria en Venezuela*, Amsterdam, B. Van Rompaey & Co., 1912.

Crazut, Rafael, *El Banco Central de Venezuela: notas sobre su historia y evolución, 1940–1980*, Caracas, ANH, 1986.

Egaña, Manuel R., *Obras y ensayos seleccionados*, 3 vols, Caracas, Banco Central de Venezuela, 1990.

Esteves Llamozas, Héctor (ed.), *Compilación de leyes del Banco Central de Venezuela*, Caracas, Banco Central de Venezuela, 1990.

Harwich Vallenilla, Nikita, *La crisis de 1929 en América Latina: el caso de Venezuela*, Caracas, Universidad Santa María, 1984.

——, *Formación y crisis de un sistema financiero nacional: banca y estado en Venezuela (1830–1940)*, Caracas, Fondo Editorial Buría, 1986

——, *Inversiones extranjeros en Venezuela, siglo XIX*, 2 vols, Caracas, Academia Nacional de Historia, 1992 and 1995.

Landaeta Rosales, Manuel, *Riqueza circulante de Venezuela*, Caracas, Imp. Bolívar, 1903.

Lecuna, Vicente and Leopoldo Landaeta, *El Banco de Venezuela*, Caracas, 'El Cojo', 1924.

Ministerio de Hacienda, 'Moneda y Banca en Venezuela', *Revista de Hacienda* 37 (1959).

Pacanins, Feliciano, *Evolución bancaria de Venezuela*, Caracas, Bolsa de Valores, 1962.

——, *Evolución bancaria en Venezuela*, Caracas, Empresa 'El Cojo', 1971.

Peláez, Luis A. (ed.), *Compilación de leyes de bancos y otros institutos de crédito*, 2 vols, Caracas, Banco Central de Venezuela, 1991.

Rangel, Domingo Alberto, *Capital y desarrollo. Tomo III: La oligarquía del dinero*, Caracas, Fuentes, 1972.

Rico López, Darío, *Banca comercial venezolana: una metodología para su análisis*, Caracas, Universidad Central de Venezuela, 1986.

Rodríguez Rosas, Victoriano José, *Sistema y ordenamiento bancario en Venezuela*, Caracas, Colegio Universitario de Caracas, n.d.

Silva, Carlos Rafael, 'Esbozo al desenvolvimiento institucional del sistema financiero venezolano, 1940–1965' in *Economía venezolana en los últimos 25 años*, Caracas, Banco Central de Venezuela, 1966.

Taborda, Luis, *Apuntes históricos relacionados con la fundación y la vida de los bancos en Valencia, 1883–1965*, Valencia, Banco de Venezuela, 1966.

Tejero, José M. and Henry Gómez, *La banca comercial en Venezuela*, Caracas, Universidad Católica Andrés Bello, 1967.

Thurber, O. E., *Origen del capital norteamericano en Venezuela: la época del asfalto, 1884–1907*, Caracas, Fondo Editorial Lola de Fuenmayor / Universidad Santa María, 1984.

Petroleum and Hydrocarbons

Arnold, Ralph, George A. Macready, and Thomas Barrington, *The First Big Oil Hunt: Venezuela, 1911–1916*, New York, 1960.

Balestrini, César, *Economía minera y petrolera*, Caracas, Universidad Central de Venezuela, 1959.

Baloyra, Enrique, A., 'Oil Policies and Budgets in Venezuela, 1938–1968', *Latin American Research Review* 9: 2 (1974), pp. 28–72.

Baptista, Federico G., *Historia de la industria petrolera en Venezuela*, Caracas, Creole Petroleum Corporation, 1961.

Betancourt, Rómulo, *Venezuela: política y petróleo*, Barcelona, Seix-Barral, 1979.

Boué, Juan C., *Venezuela: the political economy of oil*, Oxford, Oxford University Press, 1993.

Brown, Jonathan C., 'Why Foreign Oil Companies Shifted their Production from Mexico to Venezuela in the 1920s', *American Historical Review* 90 (1985), 262–85

Calderón Berti, Humberto, *Venezuela y su política petrolera 1979–1983*, Caracas, Ed. Centauro, 1986.

——, *Oposición y petróleo en Venezuela: cronología de una gestión errática, 1984–1988*, Caracas, Ed. Centauro, 1988.

De la Plaza, Salvador, *El petroleo en la vida venezolana*, Caracas, FACES-UCV, 1974.

Edwards, Gertrud G., 'Foreign Petroleum Companies and the State in Venezuela', in *Foreign Investment in the Petroleum and Mineral Industries*, ed. Raymond F. Mikesell, Baltimore, Johns Hopkins University Press, 1971, pp. 101–28.

Estaba, Rosa M., *Geografía de los paisajes urbanos e industriales de Venezuela*, Caracas, Ariel-Seix Barral Venezolana, 1985.

González G., Godofredo, *La revolución de los Barrosos*, Caracas, Centauro, 1987.

Harwich Valenilla, Nikita, *Asfalto y revolución: La New York and Bermúdez Company*, Caracas, Monte Avila – Funres, 1992.

Lieuwen, Edwin, *Petroleum in Venezuela: a History*, Berkeley, University of California Press, 1955.

——, 'The Politics of Energy in Venezuela', in *Latin American Oil Companies and the Politics of Energy*, ed. John D. Wirth, Lincoln, University of Nebraska Press, 1985, pp. 189–225.

Lucena R., Héctor, *Las relaciones laborales en Venezuela: el movimiento obrero petrolero, proceso de formación y desarrollo*, Caracas, Centauro, 1982.

McBeth, B. S., *Juan Vicente Gómez and the Oil Companies in Venezuela, 1908–1935*, Cambridge, Cambridge University Press, 1983.

Machado de Acedo, Clemy, *La Reforma de la Ley de Hidrocarburos de 1943: un impulso hacia la modernización*, Caracas, Oficina de Estudios Socioeconómicos, 1990.

Malavé Mata, Hector, *Petróleo y desarrollo económico en Venezuela*, Caracas, Universidad Central de Venezuela, 1962.

Martínez, Aníbal R., *The Journey from Petrolia*, Caracas, Petroleos de Venezuela, 1986.

——, *Venezuelan Oil: Development and Chronology*, London, Elsevier, 1989.

——, *El servicio técnico de hidrocarburos*, Caracas, Cepet, 1990.

Mommer, Bernard, *Petróleo, renta del suelo e historia*, Mérida, Corpoandes / Universidad de Los Andes, 1983.

Montiel Camacho, H. D., *La explotación del petróleo en Venezuela y la capitalización nacional*, México D. F., 1967.

Papail, Jean, *Des villes et du petrole. Aspects historiques et prospectives des populations urbaines au Venezuela*, Paris, Orstom, 1987.

Pérez Alfonso, Juan Pablo, *Venezuela y su petróleo: lineamientos de una política*, Caracas, Imprenta Nacional, 1960.

——, *Petróleo y dependencia*, Caracas, Síntesis Dos Mil, 1971.

Rabe, Stephen G., *The Road to OPEC: United States Relations with Venezuela*, Austin, University of Texas Press, 1982.

Randall, Laura, *The Political Economy of Venezuelan Oil*, New York, Preager, 1987.

Ríos de Hernández, Josefina, *Análisis histórico de la organización del espacio en Venezuela*, Caracas, Universidad Central de Venezuela, 1990.

Rodríguez, L. C., *Gómez, agricultura, petróleo y dependencia*, Caracas, Tropykos, 1983.

Rosales, Rafael M. (ed.), *El mensaje de La Petrolia*, Caracas, Presidencia de la República, 1976.

Salazar Carrillo, Jorge, *Oil and Development in Venezuela during the Twentieth Century*, Westport, Conn., Praeger, 1994.

Singh, Kelvin, 'Oil Politics in Venezuela during the López Contreras Administration, 1936–1941', *Journal of Latin American Studies* 21 (1989), 385–410.

Sociedad Venezolana de Ingenieros Petroleros, *Aspectos de la industria petrolera en Venezuela*, Caracas, 1963.

Sullivan, W. and Brian McBeth, *Petroleum in Venezuela: a bibliography*, Boston, Mass., G. K. Hall, 1985.

Taylor, Wayne C. and John Lindeman, *The Creole Petroleum Corporation in Venezuela*, Washington DC, National Planning Association, 1955.

Uslar Pietri, Arturo, *Venezuela en el petróleo*, Caracas, Urbina y Fuentes, 1984.

Valenilla, Luis, *Oil: the making of a new economic order*, New York, McGraw-Hill, 1975.

Venezuela, Ministerio de Minas e Hidrocarburos, *Cronología de la industria petrolera en Venezuela*, Caracas, MMH., 1976.

Agriculture

Ardao, Alicia, *El café y las ciudades en los Andes venezolanos (1870–1930)*, Caracas, Academia Nacional de la Historia, 1984.

Carvallo, Gastón, *El hato venezolano, 1900–1980*, Caracas, Tropykos, 1985.

Carvallo, Gastón and Josefina Ríos de Hernández, *Temas de la Venezuela agroexportadora*, Caracas, Trópykos, 1984.

Carvallo, Gastón and Josefina Ríos de Hernández, *La hacienda venezolana*, Caracas, Tropykos, 1988.

Hunziker, O. S. and R. E. Hodgson, 'The Dairy Industry in Venezuela', (U. S. Department of Agriculture, Washington, D. C., mimeo, 1942).

Hurtado, Héctor, 'Análisis de la política de desarrollo de la industria láctea en Venezuela', in *Política de ajustes al desarrollo industrial venezolano*, ed. Leonardo Montiel Ortega, Caracas, Ministerio de Fomento, 1967.

Lucena R., Héctor, *Las relaciones laborales en Venezuela: el movimiento obrero petrolero, proceso de formación y desarrollo*, Caracas, Centauro, 1982.

Luzardo, Rodolfo, *Business and Finances*, Englewood Cliffs, N. J., Prentice-Hall, 1957.

Llambi Insúa, Luis: *La moderna finca familiar*, Caracas, Fondo Editorial Acta Científica Venezolana, 1988.

Orta, Celio S., 'La agricultura y el desarrollo económico del país', in *Perfiles de la economía venezolana*, Caracas, U.C.V., 1964.

Roseberry, William, *Coffee and Capitalism in the Venezuelan Andes*, Austin, University of Texas Press, 1983.

Sanoja, Mario and Iraida Vargas, *Antiguas formaciones y modos de produccion venezolanos*, Caracas, Monte Avila, 1974.

Communications

Capriles Méndez, Ruth, *Los negocios de Román Delgado Chalbaud*, Caracas, Academia Nacional de la Historia, 1991.

Hurtado, Samuel, *Los ferrocarriles en Venezuela*, Caracas, Universidad Central de Venezuela, 1990.

Economic Policies and Private Business

Farías de Urbaneja, Haydee, *La autoridad de la Sociedad Económica de Amigos del País en la política gubernamental*, Caracas, Universidad Central de Venezuela, 1991.

Floyd, Mary B., 'Política y economía en tiempos de Guzmán Blanco: centralización y desarrollo, 1870–1888', in *Política y economía en Venezuela, 1810–1976*, Caracas, Fundación John Boulton, 1976.

Frankel, A., 'La Guerra Federal y sus secuelas, 1859–1869' in *Política y economía en Venezuela, 1810–1976*, Caracas, Fundación John Boulton, 1976.

Friedman, John, *Regional Development Policy: a Case Study of Venezuela*, Cambridge, MIT Press, 1966.

Fundación John Boulton, *Política y economía en Venezuela. 1810–1976*, Caracas, 1976.

Giordiani, Jorge A., 'Cuatro décadas de planificaión nacional', *Cuadernos del CENDES* 13: 31 (1993).

González Deluca, María Elena, 'Los intereses británicos y la política en Venezuela en las últimas décadas del siglo XIX', *Boletín Americanista* 30 (1980).

——, 'Conflictos politicos y negocios en la mineria venezolana en tiempos de Guzmán Blanco (1870–1888)', *Siglo XIX: Revista de Historia* 8 (1989).

——, *Negocios y política en tiempos de Guzmán Blanco*, Caracas, Universidad Central de Venezuela, 1991.

Harwich Vallenilla, Nikita, 'El modelo económico del Liberalismo Amarillo: historia de un fracaso, 1888–1908', in *Política y economía en Venezuela, 1810–1976*, Caracas, Fundación John Boulton, 1976.

——, *Banca y estado en Venezuela (1830–1940)*, Caracas, Fondo Editorial Buría, 1986.

——, 'Del estado centralizador al estado emprendador: el petroleo y la organización financiera de Venezuela, 190–1935', *Jahrbuch für Geschichte von Lateinamerika* 26 (1989), 261–94.

Hernández Ron, Ramón, *La política económica venezolana: bases, nuevos instrumentos*, Caracas, Imp. Nacional, 1940.

Kornblith, Miriam, 'Estado y política del Gasto Público' in *Apreciación del proceso histórico venezolano*, Caracas, Fundación Universidad Metropolitana, 1985, pp. 139–68.

Machado de Acedo, Clemy *et al.*, *Estado y grupos económicos en Venezuela*, Caracas, El Ateneo de Caracas, 1981.

——, Elena Plaza and Emilio Pacheco, *Estado y grupos económicos en Venezuela: análisis a través de la tierra, construcción y banca*, Caracas, Ateneo de Caracas, 1991.

Matthews, Robert P., 'La turbulenta década de los Monagas, 1847–1858', in *Política y economía en Venezuela, 1810–1976*, Caracas, Fundación John Boulton, 1976.

Montiel Ortega, Leonardo, *Política de ajustes al desarrollo industrial venezolano*, Caracas, Ministerio de Fomento, 1967.

Pérez Vila, Manuel, 'El gobierno deliberativo: hacendados, comerciantes y artesanos frente a la crisis, 1830–1848', in *Política y economía en Venezuela, 1810–1976*, Caracas, Fundación John Boulton, 1976.

——, *La hacienda pública de Venezuela, 1828–1830*, Caracas, Banco Central de Venezuela, 1964.

Shoup, Carl S. *et al.*, *The Fiscal System of Venezuela: a Report*, Baltimore, Johns Hopkins University Press, 1959.

Silva, Carlos Rafael, 'Esbozo al desenvolvimiento institucional del sistema financiero venezolano, 1940–1965', in *Economía venezolana en los últimos 25 años*, Caracas, Banco Central de Venezuela, 1966.

Sullivan, William M., 'Situación económica y política durante el período de Juan Vicente Gómez, 1908–1935', in *Política y economía en Venezuela, 1810–1976*, Caracas, Fundación John Boulton, 1976.

Toro Hardy, José, *Venezuela, 55 años de política ecónomica 1936–1991: una utopia keynesiana*, Caracas, Panapo, 1992.

Vaez-Zadan, 'Oil Wealth and Economic Behavior: the case of Venezuela, 1963–1984', *IMF Staff Papers* 36: 2 (1989), pp. 343–84.

Company History

Entrepreneurs and Businessmen

Jaén, Gustavo, *Eugenio Mendoza: apuntes para una interpretación*, Caracas, Centauro, 1987.

——, *Destino de pioneros (ejecutivos de Protinal)*, Caracas, Centauro, 1987.

Rodríguez, José Angel, *Alejandro Hernández: historias de una pasión*, Caracas, Centauro, 1988.

Private Enterprise

Center for Latin American Development Studies, *La ventaja comparativa de corto y mediano plazo en la producción manufacturera de Venezuela*, Boston University, 1986.

Chocron, Isaac, 'El cuarto mágico: cuarenta años de Corimon', *Revista M* 25: 92 (1989).

La Electricidad de Caracas, *Perspectivas de las empresas eléctricas en Venezuela*, Caracas, 1985.

Lansberg y Lansberg, *La empresa debe continuar: un caso de transición en un consorcio familiar*, Caracas, IESA, 1988.

Murguey Gutierrez, José, *La Explotación Aurífera de Guayana y la conformación de la compañía minera de 'El Callao' 1870–1900*, Caracas, Corporación Venezolana de Guayana – Minerven, 1989.

Naím, Moisés, 'El crecimiento de las empresas privadas en Venezuela: mucha diversificación, poca organización', in *Las empresas venezolanas: su gerencia*, ed. Moisés Naím *et al.*, Caracas, IESA, 1989, pp. 17–55.

——, 'Evolución y desarrollo de grandes empresas venezolanas', *I Congreso Venezolano de Ejecutivos de Finanzas*, 1982.

——, 'La empresa privada en Venezuela' ¿Qué pasa cuando se crece en medio de la riqueza y la confusión?' in *Las empresas venezolanas: su gerencia*, ed. Moisés Naím *et al.*, Caracas, IESA, 1989, pp. 152–82.

Padrón G., M. A., *Valencia: de agropecuaria a industrial*, Valencia, Historia de la Cámara de Industriales del Estado Carabobo, 1972.

Ramírez Bernal, Raquel, *Benedetti. 1889–1989: un siglo de historia*, Caracas, Poligráfica Industrial, 1989.

Rodríguez, José Angel, *Pampero, una tradición, una industria: medio siglo de Industrias Pampero, 1938–1988*, Caracas, Fundación Pampero, 1988.

Romero, Carlos, 'Los empresarios y el sistema político venezolano: las reglas de juego', *Politeia* 11 (1982), pp. 149–171.

Sánchez, Enrique, 'La empresa privada 1945–1989', *Gerente* (1989).

Sifontes Greco, Lourdes, *Nabisco: 50 años siendo La Favorita*, Caracas, Impresiones Refolit, 1988.

Ugalde, Luis, S. J., *Mentalidad económica y proyectos de colonización en Guayana en los siglos XVIII y XIX: el caso de la compañía Manoa en el Delta del Orinoco*, Caracas, Academia Nacional de Ciencias Económicas, 1994.

Public Enterprise

Azpúrua, Antonio J., *The Role of the Guayana Development Corporation in Venezuelan Industrialization: Diversification or Vertical Integration.*, master's thesis, MIT, 1987.

Boscán de Ruesta, Isabel, *El 'holding' en la organización del sector económico público*, Caracas, Procuraduría General de la República, 1975.

Brewer-Carías, Allan Randolph, *Régimen jurídico de las empresas públicas en Venezuela*, Caracas, CLAD, 1989.

Caballero Ortiz, Jesús, *Las empresas públicas en el derecho venezolano*, Caracas, Editorial Jurídica Venezolana, 1982.

Kelly de Escobar, Janet, *Empresas del estado en América Latina*, Caracas, IESA, 1985.

Ruocco, Saturno, Angel, *El impacto de las empresas eléctricas públicas sobre la economía nacional*, Caracas, Escuela Nacional de Administración y Hacienda Pública, 1979.

Index